Border Flows

Canadian History and Environment Series
Alan MacEachern, Series Editor
ISSN 1925-3702 (Print) ISSN 1925-3710 (Online)

The Canadian History & Environment series brings together scholars from across the academy and beyond to explore the relationships between people and nature in Canada's past.

ALAN MACEACHERN, FOUNDING DIRECTOR
NiCHE: Network in Canadian History & Environment
Nouvelle initiative canadienne en histoire de l'environnement
http://niche-canada.org

No. 1 · **A Century of Parks Canada, 1911–2011**
Edited by Claire Elizabeth Campbell

No. 2 · **Historical GIS Research in Canada**
Edited by Jennifer Bonnell and Marcel Fortin

No. 3 · **Mining and Communities in Northern Canada:
History, Politics, and Memory**
Edited by Arn Keeling and John Sandlos

No. 4 · **Canadian Countercultures and the Environment**
Edited by Colin M. Coates

No. 5 · **Moving Natures:
Mobility and the Environment in Canadian History**
Edited by Ben Bradley, Jay Young, and Colin M. Coates

No. 6 · **Border Flows:
A Century of the Canadian-American Water Relationship**
Edited by Lynne Heasley and Daniel Macfarlane

UNIVERSITY OF CALGARY
Press

Border Flows

A Century of the Canadian-American Water Relationship

Edited by
**LYNNE HEASLEY and
DANIEL MACFARLANE**

Canadian History and Environment Series
ISSN 1925-3702 (Print) ISSN 1925-3710 (Online)

© 2016 Lynne Heasley and Daniel Macfarlane

University of Calgary Press
2500 University Drive NW
Calgary, Alberta
Canada T2N 1N4

press.ucalgary.ca

This book is available as an ebook which is licensed under a Creative Commons license. The publisher should be contacted for any commercial use which falls outside the terms of that license.

LIBRARY AND ARCHIVES CANADA CATALOGUING IN PUBLICATION

Border flows : a century of the Canadian-American water relationship / edited by Lynne Heasley and Daniel Macfarlane.

(Canadian history and environment series ; no. 6)
Includes bibliographical references and index.
Issued in print and electronic formats.
ISBN 978-1-55238-895-2 (paperback).—ISBN 978-1-55238-896-9 (open access pdf).
—ISBN 978-1-55238-897-6 (pdf).—ISBN 978-1-55238-898-3 (epub).
—ISBN 978-1-55238-899-0 (mobi)

1. Water-supply—Canada—Management. 2. Water-supply—United States—Management. 3. Canadian-American Border Region. 4. Water—Government policy—Canada. 5. Water—Government policy—United States. 6. Water—Law and legislation—Canada. 7. Water—Law and legislation—United States. 8. Canada—Foreign relations—United States. 9. United States—Foreign relations—Canada. I. Heasley, Lynne, editor II. Macfarlane, Daniel, 1979-, editor III. Series: Canadian history and environment series ; 6

HD1694.A2B67 2016   333.91   C2016-907073-5
                                          C2016-907074-3

The University of Calgary Press acknowledges the support of the Government of Alberta through the Alberta Media Fund for our publications. We acknowledge the financial support of the Government of Canada through the Canada Book Fund for our publishing activities. We acknowledge the financial support of the Canada Council for the Arts for our publishing program.

  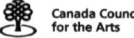 

Front cover: Blue Water Bridge over the St. Clair River. Photograph courtesy of Lynne Heasley.
Copyediting by Alison Jacques
Cover design, page design, and typesetting by Melina Cusano

Table of Contents

List of Figures — v
Acknowledgments — xiii

INTRODUCTION — 1

Negotiating Abundance and Scarcity: Introduction to a Fluid Border — 3
LYNNE HEASLEY AND DANIEL MACFARLANE

PART ONE — 27
Finding the Border: Political Ecologies of Water Governance and Tenure

Openings: Political Ecologies on the Border — 29
DAVE DEMPSEY

1. *A Citizen's Legal Primer on the Boundary Waters Treaty, International Joint Commission, and Great Lakes Water Management* — 39
   NOAH D. HALL AND PETER STARR

2. *Treaties, Wars, and Salish Sea Watersheds: The Constructed Boundaries of Water Governance* — 65
   EMMA S. NORMAN AND ALICE COHEN

3. *Contesting the Northwest Passage: Four Far-North Narratives* — 87
   ANDREA CHARRON

PART TWO
Constructing the Border: Hydropolitics, Nationalism, and Megaprojects

111

Openings: Transboundary Power Flows
MATTHEW EVENDEN

113

4. *Dam the Consequences: Hydropolitics, Nationalism, and the Niagara–St. Lawrence Projects*
DANIEL MACFARLANE

123

5. *Quebec's Water Export Schemes: The Rise and Fall of a Resource Development Idea*
FRÉDÉRIC LASSERRE

151

6. *Engineering a Treaty: The Negotiation of the Columbia River Treaty of 1961/1964*
JEREMY MOUAT

169

PART THREE
Challenging the Border: Ecological Agents of Change

205

Openings: Border Ecologies in Boundary Waters
JAMES W. FELDMAN

207

7. *Lines That Don't Divide: Telling Tales about Animals, Chemicals, and People in the Salish Sea*
JOSEPH E. TAYLOR III

215

8. *Resiliency and Collapse: Lake Trout, Sea Lamprey, and Fisheries Management in Lake Superior*
NANCY LANGSTON

239

PART FOUR   *263*
Reflections in the Water

Openings: The Lakes at Night   *265*
Jerry Dennis

9.   Finding Our Place   *271*

     ~ *Crossings*   *273*
     Jeremy Mouat

     ~ *Meditations on Ice*   *275*
     Colin A.M. Duncan and Andrew Marcille

     ~ *Bordering on Significance?*   *279*
     Daniel Macfarlane

     ~ *To Market, to Market*   *285*
     Joseph E. Taylor III

     ~ *Leading Waters*   *289*
     Noah D. Hall

     ~ *On Frames, Perspectives, and Vanishing Points*   *291*
     Lynne Heasley

     ~ *Headwaters of Hope*   *295*
     Dave Dempsey

AFTERWORD   *297*
Keeping Up the Flow   *299*
Graeme Wynn

Further Reading   *309*
Contributors   *327*
Index   *333*

List of Figures

0.1   Canada-U.S. border watersheds. Map by Jason Glatz, Western Michigan University.

0.2   Canada-U.S. precipitation. Map by Jason Glatz, Western Michigan University.

1.1   Great Lakes watershed. Map by Jason Glatz, Western Michigan University.

2.1   Constructing identity through maps: Canada. Wooden Canada map puzzle, Melissa & Doug, http://www.melissaanddoug.com.

2.2   Constructing identity through maps: The United States. Wooden USA map puzzle, Melissa & Doug, http://www.melissaanddoug.com.

2.3   Waterways of the Salish Sea and surrounding basin. Map by Stefan Freelan, Western Washington University.

2.4   Billy Frank Jr. (1931–2014). Photo by Mariah Dodd, Northwest Indian College.

2.5   Coast Salish Gatherings. Map by Eric Leinberger, University of British Columbia.

3.1 CCGS *John A. Macdonald*, 1969. "USCGC Staten Island WAGB-278: Historic Photo Gallery," U.S. Coast Guard Historian's Office, accessed August 19, 2016, http://www.uscg.mil/history/webcutters/img/statenisland_1969manhattan_1.jpg.

4.1 St. Lawrence Seaway. Map by Eric Leinberger, from *Negotiating a River* by Daniel Macfarlane (University of British Columbia Press, 2014). Reproduced with permission of the publisher.

4.2 Mosaic of Proposed Niagara Remedial Works, c. 1935. "Mosaic of Niagara Falls and Vicinity," plate 5, series A-3-b, vol. 2822, RG25, Library and Archives Canada, Ottawa.

4.3 Lake St. Lawrence and Lost Villages. Map by author.

4.4 Ingleside after inundation. Lost Villages Historical Society, Long Sault, Ontario.

4.5 Niagara waterscape. Map by Anders Sandberg and Rajiv Rawat, 2012, based on map by author.

4.6 Horseshoe Falls. Map by author.

4.7 Moses and Beck power stations. Photo by author.

4.8 Robert Moses generating station. Photo by author.

4.9 Lost Village remains. Photo by author.

5.1 GRAND Canal scheme. Map by author.

5.2 Quebec water diversions. Map by author.

6.1 Schematic of Columbia River development, 1948. U.S. Army Corps of Engineers. Elmer K. Nelson Papers, Water Resources Collections and Archives, University of California – Riverside.

6.2 The four treaty dams on the Columbia River. Map by Jason Glatz.

6.3 W.A.C. Bennett, Lester B. Pearson, and Lyndon Johnson. Cartoon by Stephen Norris, Vancouver Sun, September 16, 1964.

7.1 Salish Sea basin. Map by author.

7.2 PBDEs in salmon. Ronald A. Hites et al., "Global Assessment of Polybrominated Diphenyl Ethers in Farmed and Wild Salmon," *Environmental Science & Technology* 38, no. 19 (2004): 4947. © 2004, American Chemical Society.

7.3 Warning sign, 2015. Photo by Matthew W. Klingle.

8.1 Lean lake trout harvests, 1920–1980. Data from R.E. Hecky et al., Global Great Lakes, University of Minnesota Duluth, 2014, http://www.GlobalGreatLakes.org.

8.2 Lake Superior basin. Map by Jason Glatz, Western Michigan University.

9.1 Iceboating on the St. Lawrence River, 2014. Photo by John Curtis.

9.2 Old Highway 2. Photo by Daniel Macfarlane.

9.3 Terrapin Point. Photo by Daniel Macfarlane.

9.4 Edge of Horseshoe Falls. Photo by Daniel Macfarlane.

9.5 Maple leaf in water. Photo by Daniel Macfarlane.

9.6 "American Ruins 1." Photo by Lynne Heasley.

9.7 "American Ruins 2." Photo by Lynne Heasley.

List of Figures

Acknowledgments

Border Flows evolved from concept to volume because of the intellectual and financial support of NiCHE, the Network in Canadian History & Environment/Nouvelle initiative canadienne en histoire de l'environnement. NiCHE underwrote the pivotal 2012 workshop of *Border Flows* authors in Kingston, Ontario. Peer reviews and development of the volume extended from our Queen's University conference room to boating trips on Lake Ontario and the St. Lawrence River.

We want to thank the editors and staff with whom we worked at the University of Calgary Press: Brian Scrivener, Peter Enman, Helen Hajnoczky, and especially Canadian History and Environment series editor Alan MacEachern, on whose expert guidance we depended. Two external reviewers made the volume much better through their insights and comments.

We are indebted to our home institution, Western Michigan University, and especially to the Department of History, the Institute of the Environment and Sustainability, and the College of Arts and Sciences. The history department's Burnham Macmillan Fund and the Canadian government's Canadian Studies Faculty Research grant provided Lynne with research and travel support that led to the development of the volume.

In addition, the early stages of this manuscript progressed while Daniel held various positions predating WMU, and he would like to acknowledge the Fulbright Foundation, the Social Sciences and Humanities Research Council of Canada, the Department of History and School of

Canadian Studies at Carleton University, and the Canadian Studies Program at Michigan State University.

Jason Glatz of Western Michigan University's Map Library lent his superb mapmaking skills to the volume. Students in Lynne's course on Great Lakes history (HIST 4010) became our test audience and gave us terrific suggestions just in time for publication.

We are grateful for the generosity of many colleagues: our fellow *Border Flows* authors and collaborators, for their engagement, patience, and amazing work; Ruth Sandwell and Sarah Hill, who participated in the Kingston workshop and commented on the earliest drafts of our chapters; Colin A.M. Duncan and Andrew Marcille, who, in addition to participating in the Kingston workshop, provided an idyllic post-workshop Lake Ontario/ St. Lawrence River sailboat excursion with many of the authors; Jay Taylor, for his perceptive recommendations for our opening chapter; and Graeme Wynn, for his years-long mentorship, encouragement, and openness.

Finally, our deepest gratitude and appreciation go to our families: Philip and Jake; Jen, Elizabeth, and Lucas.

—Lynne Heasley and Daniel Macfarlane

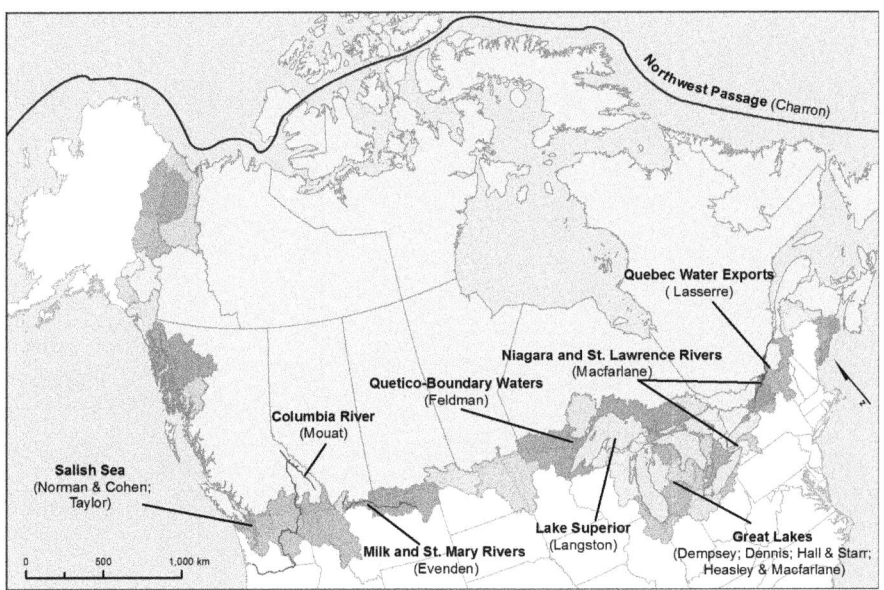

0.1 Canada-U.S. border watersheds. Map by Jason Glatz.

INTRODUCTION

Negotiating Abundance and Scarcity: Introduction to a Fluid Border

LYNNE HEASLEY AND DANIEL MACFARLANE

In 1982, a collective chill spread through the offices of two Canadian premiers and eight U.S. governors whose provinces and states encompassed the vast Great Lakes–St. Lawrence basin. In *Sporhase v. Nebraska*, the United States Supreme Court had just declared water an article of commerce subject to interstate trade under the commerce clause of the U.S. Constitution.[1] Henceforth states could not ban water diversions outside their borders, the question addressed in *Sporhase*. Imagine the implications from the perspective of policymakers and politicians in Great Lakes states. At six quadrillion gallons, 84 percent of North America's surface freshwater supply, the lakes were a kind of aquatic El Dorado, hypothetically open to those with the political or economic might to extract their water.

Such fears were not hyperbole to Great Lakes residents. The court decision came on the heels of a U.S. Army Corps of Engineers study on whether imported water, possibly from the Great Lakes, could restore a rapidly declining Ogallala Aquifer in the Great Plains. The corps provoked more paranoia by using uncharacteristically socialist language about fairness, or redistribution from "water rich" to "water poor" regions.[2] Proposing a national water policy became a kind of shorthand for water redistribution.[3]

The corps study followed the resurrection of an infamous proposal by Canadian engineer Tom Kierans. Kierans named his idea the Great Recycling and Northern Development Canal, or GRAND. GRAND would pump water to Lake Huron from James Bay, which lay far to the north on the southeast corner of Hudson Bay. According to the GRAND concept, Lake Superior would no longer be necessary to feed Huron. Therefore a channel could run Superior's "superfluous" water to the arid—i.e., water poor—American West. These and other epic ideas raised the hackles of whichever Great Lakes premiers or governors were in office.[4]

The *Sporhase* case galvanized an intense twenty-five-year saga of interstate, interprovincial, and binational negotiations with one goal: to find a constitutionally sound and mutually agreeable way to limit future diversions. Some of the twists and setbacks of this quest come later in the volume. Jumping ahead now, though: in December 2008, a binding Great Lakes–St. Lawrence River Basin Water Resources Compact took effect (hereafter the Great Lakes Compact). The compact and its companion Great Lakes–St. Lawrence River Basin Sustainable Water Resources Agreement with Ontario and Quebec put limits on water use and diversions from the basin. This was a stunning environmental landmark of the twenty-first century.

With the compact in hand, stakeholders from local to federal levels seemed to escape what Lynne Heasley has called "the paradox of abundance."[5] Many environmental histories share an abundance narrative—i.e., that the intense concentration of a valuable resource practically assured the decimation of that resource. The historical reasons vary, but for the nineteenth and twentieth centuries reasons often involved time lags between market-driven extraction, increased scales of production, catch-up policy responses, and true care for the natural world. Such boom-and-bust histories along today's Canada-U.S border include (1) near-extinction of the beaver in New France and bison on the nineteenth-century Great Plains, and the actual extinction of the passenger pigeon; (2) liquidation of old-growth white pine forests; (3) fishery crashes from the Grand Banks to the Great Lakes to the Pacific Northwest; (4) mineral mines, including gold strikes along the Alaska–British Columbia border; and (5) Canadian oil and especially the infamous Alberta tar sands crude, much of it sent south across the border.[6] Abundance stories are Sisyphean: our economic and cultural inability to prevent the next example, to push the proverbial rock over the crest, to *sustain* both the people and the nature of our homes.

In North American environmental history, abundance is a powerful narrative indeed.[7] But in North American *water* history, scarcity is the dominant narrative.[8] The western half of the continent—the American southwest especially—has had an understandable but nonetheless disproportionate influence on national narratives of water and debates over policy. Think of "the border" itself. For many Americans, and certainly the media, the first border that comes to mind is the U.S.-Mexico border and its borderline through the desert, the Rio Grande. Historically, think of American John Wesley Powell's explorations of the Colorado River in the nineteenth century and his unheeded recommendation that climate-appropriate property boundaries should restrain settlement in arid regions.[9] A decade before Powell, geographer John Palliser made nearly the same argument about semiarid dry prairies in southern Saskatchewan and Alberta. Much later, irrigation transformed "Palliser's Triangle" (the area's common name) into Canada's breadbasket of wheat production.[10] While scholars, policymakers, and environmentalists still look to Powell's journals for insight, a legal system of water rights at odds with his approach prevailed in the arid American West. The system's bulwarks were the Colorado Doctrine, governing individual user rights, and the Colorado River Compact of 1922, an agreement among the river basin's seven states to allocate water rights to the river and its tributaries.[11]

Better known as the prior appropriation doctrine, or "first in time, first in right," the Colorado Doctrine separated water rights from riparian land ownership.[12] In simpler terms, prior appropriation means the first user has the superior claim to a water source. This claim holds even if later users own land adjacent to the water and the first user owns no adjacent (i.e., riparian) land. The key is that the first user's purpose be "beneficial," which historically meant for agriculture or industry. For instance, if the first user was a mine operator who diverted water from a stream to run the mine, a second user could not interfere with that first use. After the first user, the second user had the next highest claim, and then the third user, until, theoretically, there was no water left to use. Prior appropriation made water a quantifiable and transferable commodity; therefore, a user could divert water to another location and sell his user rights and legal place in line to someone else.

Today, both prior appropriation and the Colorado Compact are broken. In an era of global warming and megadroughts, there is not enough water to share but still enough to fight over. "Colorado to California: Hands Off Our Water," shrills a Fox News headline.[13] "Rain Barrel Bill Dies on Calendar," runs a much blander headline in the *Colorado Statesman*, though this 2015 story is just as dramatic. "A bill that would have allowed Coloradans to collect rainwater died in the Senate late Tuesday night," begins the rain barrel story—and midway through is the crux:

> Opponents, including farmers and ranchers, believe that rainwater is covered under the state's prior appropriations law, since it runs off into groundwater and surface water, such as rivers. ... There's a reason why rain barrels have been illegal in Colorado for the past 160 years, according to Chris Kraft of Fort Morgan, who operates one of the largest dairies in the state. "We're short of water. People keep moving here. This is a worse idea today than it was a long time ago." Kraft explained that farmers have to get a water court decree to get water, and some of those decrees date back to Colorado's earliest days as a state. Kraft said his decree dates back to the 1890s, and he has to pay a lot of money for that decree and the ditch that supplies his farm with irrigation water. "This would allow people to steal water from my appropriation," he told the Ag Committee.[14]

To someone who lives east of the 100th meridian, "rain barrels" don't sound like fighting words. That collecting rain from one's roof is illegal anywhere might be a stunning idea for, say, a Michigander or an Ontarian. In more general terms, however, popular culture has made conflict over scarce water a Pan-American narrative. In the famous 1953 western film *Shane*, ranchers and homesteaders warred over land with access to water. As they fought, the story goes, a moral code and rule of law emerged to civilize the American West and point the country toward greatness. No matter that the 1950s parable about the 1880s frontier was belied, even then, by the 1930s Dust Bowl. With its prominence in American politics, literature, and film lore, scarcity dominates how many of us see water. Iconic images of Dust Bowl suffering and a new iconography of water scarcity are bookends to more than a century of dryland visuals.[15] From *National Geographic* to local newspapers, twenty-first-century photos of cracked landscapes make water the focal point by its absence. Often a dark line leads the eye through the parched scene—the S-curve of a bone-dry streambed.

All of this raises a question: If much of the history of the American and Canadian West is variations in the key of water, why is there no equivalent filmography or literature or iconography for the Great Lakes region?[16] Surely its history includes an awe-inspiring water narrative? Surely its immensity as the largest freshwater system in the world could rival the immensity of water scarcity out west? But we wager that the average Coloradan gets little exposure to the Great Lakes through education, political discourse, or the cultural imagination. Author Jerry Dennis once marvelled that the Great Lakes are so unknown beyond their shores that a funny online hoax about whale-watching in Lake Michigan made its way into a children's K–6 science magazine. A Michigan teacher had to alert the publisher's editorial staff in Utah that, no, whales and dolphins do not set forth each spring from Hudson Bay to breeding grounds in Lake Michigan.[17]

Dennis hypothesized that people do not "see" the Great Lakes because the lakes are too enormous and diverse to comprehend. Yet the West is enormous and diverse, too, on both sides of the border. So we'll add two other hypotheses. First, perhaps their low visibility in water discourse is because the Great Lakes make up the actual border between the United States and Canada. Their significance cannot wholly fit nationalist narratives of development and identity, and their governance is easily banished to the far-away realm of diplomatic niceties, rather than the knock-down, drag-out arena of the rain barrel. By contrast, the upper Colorado River is a wholly U.S. example. As such, even easterners might see a battle between rain barrel friend and foe in more familiar terms, as the latest local resource controversy to intersect with state or national politics.

For our second hypothesis, the Great Lakes might fade into another kind of distance—emotional and empathetic distance, or the degree to which people can imagine themselves in a distressing scene. A few ugly invasive species or an economic legacy of industrial water pollution in the Great Lakes might not trigger the same empathetic intensity or emotional visualization from outside the region as the apocalyptic specter of two countries' breadbaskets disintegrating into dust while scientists forecast the inexorable drain of ancient aquifers like the Ogallala. Perhaps water scarcity from arid conditions west of the continent's 100th meridian mapped a sharper, more dangerous geography in the public imagination than do water regimes east of the 100th meridian, even someplace as physically distinct as the Great Lakes. Nonetheless, we might have reached a turning point. A North American geography of water abundance—one in which Utah textbook writers could picture make-believe Lake Michigan whales—now includes its own all-too-real, fully imaginable site of empathetic horror: the water crisis in Flint, Michigan. A conspiracy of negligence that lead-poisoned an entire population became, if possible, more terrible because Flint residents once had, were recklessly deprived of, and yet remained painfully close to abundant safe water.[18] Flint has generated a new emotional Great Lakes geography that transcends politics, occupation, class, and color. How easy to imagine yourself in a Flint home whose water tap holds invisible terrors and irreversible harm for your family. On this mental map, the home is only inches from Lake Huron, the fourth largest freshwater lake on Earth.[19]

We propose scarcity *and* abundance as the two faces of U.S. and Canadian water history. Alongside scarcity, abundance has been a different but powerful driver of water law, policy, economics, and culture in both countries.[20] To give one abundance example from the same frontier period when western states and provinces were experimenting with laws on prior appropriation: far to the (humid) east, the state of Michigan, surrounded by four of the five Great Lakes, established a matrix of laws and property rights to *drain* water from as much land as possible.[21] "Don't go to Michigan, that land of ills, the word means ague, fever, and chills," warned a nineteenth-century chant about the state's reputation as a swampy, disease-ridden hellscape for settler farmers.[22] The culmination of Michigan's exertions to deal with surfeit or "too much" water was the Michigan Office of Drain Commissioner, a county-level elected position that some political scientists uphold as a candidate for the most powerful local elected office in the United States or Canada—or, "the state's most powerful man," according to a belligerent Shiawassee County drain commissioner in 1979.[23]

We would encourage water scholars to shout across the great arid-humid divide of the 100th meridian whenever possible, or even to "[erase] the 100th meridian as a scholarly demarcation," as historian Donald Pisani advocated.[24] To the famous 100th meridian we add the less-examined 49th parallel between Canada and the United States as an important locus for a more unified water studies. North America's largest waterway (the Great Lakes–St. Lawrence system) makes up such a long stretch of this border

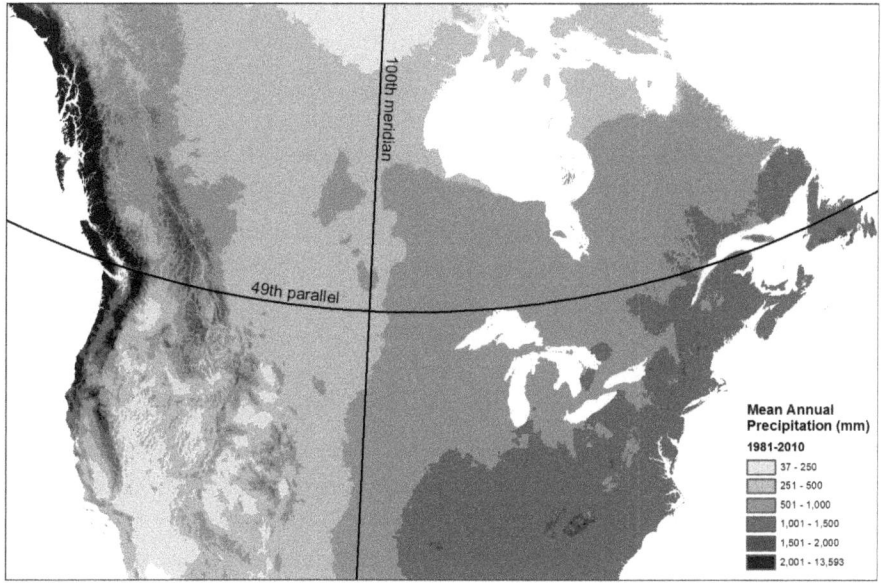

0.2 Canada-U.S. precipitation including 49th parallel and 100th meridian. Map by Jason Glatz.

that water history in either country would be incomplete without it. But the 49th parallel has importance beyond the Great Lakes. Whether scarce or seemingly abundant, whether west, mid-continent, or east, relationships between communities and water play out differently on the border and create their own spillovers to the north and south.[25]

The 2008 Great Lakes interstate compact and its companion binational agreement raise an important question. The compact marked a partial reprieve from boom-and-bust water exploitation. So far, at least, the basin is not on track to slake an insatiable dryland thirst, or become a liquid mine for twenty-first-century robber barons, or, scariest of all abundance nightmares, shrink into a poisonous salt barrens from economic hubris, like Russia's Aral Sea.[26] Why did the Great Lakes escape this paradox of abundance? With an international maritime corridor, with a withering industrial base (steel, chemical, paper, automotive), and with aquatic ecosystems compromised by toxic pollution, invasive species, shoreline development, and climate change, it seems remarkable that eight American states, two Canadian provinces, and two nations could come to an agreement on a legal, economic, and environmental matter as contentious as controlling water.[27] Yet they did.

Note that the question is not *how* the region escaped the paradox of abundance. The how is part of a recent history of negotiations. But *why*?

Was it because the basin's state and provincial governments were somehow more evolved than their brethren to the north or south? Were they more virtuous, more altruistic, and a heck of a lot smarter than their counterparts along the Colorado River? Hardly. (However, far be it for us to assume Mark Twain's mantle of political "moralist in disguise.")

Was it because water itself was such an exceptional resource, fundamentally different than trees, fish, or ore? No again—at least not legally. To the contrary, many warned, the compact enshrined water as a commodity and carried unfortunate echoes of the prior appropriation model. Critics like Dave Dempsey argued that policymakers compromised away a strong constitutional case that Great Lakes water should be subject to a public trust doctrine instead.[28] The public trust doctrine traced its roots from ancient Roman civil law to English common law and ultimately to a robust body of law in the United States—both in the states and nationally with affirmative Supreme Court decisions.

Was it a higher moral imperative that outweighed other considerations? That water is so fundamental to human and nonhuman life in the region that their welfare demanded it be protected from outside claims? One might hope so, but again, no. In fact, the moral argument often went against protection. In a world where billions of people are without potable water, how can you win an argument against urgent care for your brothers and sisters? The short answer is, you cannot win that particular argument.

So, why the good outcome? Our explanation begins at the U.S.-Canada border.[29]

Borders embody dualisms: they divide yet potentially unify, they are barrier yet possible gateway, they are solid (on paper) yet porous, they can intensify competition or inspire cooperation, they can stir resentment or nurture understanding. Borders are complicated. International borders are even more complex. They are actual places, just as regions and provinces and states are places. International borders can loom large and brooding in a nation's political consciousness, as the Canada-U.S border does for

Canadians. Or, they can recede to the edge of a Rand McNally atlas, as the same U.S.-Canada border does for many Americans.

Border *waters* complicate things still more. For Canada and the United States, shared waters were more than a river delineating two countries, like the St. Lawrence River. They were more than a major river crossing two countries, like the Columbia. The 49th parallel between our two countries includes 2,200 miles (3,540 kilometres) of boundary waters, from the Bay of Fundy on the Atlantic to the Salish Sea on the Pacific, and to the north the border continues between Alaska and British Columbia.[30] List these border rivers and lakes, and you will find signposts to great swaths of North American history and geography: in the northern reaches, the Yukon, Chilkat, Stikine, Taku, Firth, Whiting, and Alsek Rivers; along the southern Canada-U.S. border, Columbia, Skagit, Kootenay, Pend D'Oreille, Flathead, St. Mary's-Milk, Souris, Red, Roseau, Rainy, St. Mary's, St. Clair, Detroit, Niagara, St. Lawrence, St. John, and St. Croix Rivers. Osoyoos Lake, Waterton Lakes, Lake of the Woods, Quetico-Boundary Waters, Lake St. Clair, Lake Champlain, and Lake Memphremagog. Plus, of course, four of the five Great Lakes—Superior, Huron, Erie, Ontario—that form North America's inland seas, the industrial epicentre of Canada and the United States from the mid-nineteenth to mid-twentieth centuries.[31] The Canada-U.S. border contains over 20 percent of the world's available fresh surface water. The longest border shared by any two countries in the world is also the most fluid.[32]

With water, Canada and the United States have long faced disputes and mutual interests on a scale far greater than most international waterways.[33] A century before the 2008 Great Lakes agreement, these border waters set in motion diplomatic processes that created a transnational tenure regime governing access to water and responses to shared problems at various levels of government and industry. The sheer abundance of water along the border catalyzed a legal framework that evolved differently than water law and policy in regions that lie entirely within Canada or the United States.

The heart of this framework was the Boundary Waters Treaty of 1909.[34] The Boundary Waters Treaty created the formal diplomatic relationship both countries needed to peacefully share their wealth in water. The treaty also established a binational International Joint Commission (IJC) to resolve conflicts and facilitate mutual interests.[35] Thus, the Boundary Waters Treaty symbolized a new era of peaceful coexistence, and a diplomatic coup for Canada. Under the treaty, the fledgling nation—still under Mother Britain's wing in many regards (indeed, it was Britain that actually signed the treaty on Canada's behalf)—gained parity with its more powerful neighbour.[36] Because of their economic and geographic importance, border waters not only drove binational environmental diplomacy, they defined the Canadian-American relationship.

The Boundary Waters Treaty of 1909 and the IJC figure prominently in *Border Flows*. Contemporary scholarship rightfully problematizes the long history of both. Up to the 1960s, the IJC, like North American society writ large, facilitated industrial development that exploited border watersheds, with all the destructive environmental and social consequences thereof. At times, Canadian and American governments ignored or marginalized the IJC altogether. Still, these complicated, problematized cases can obscure one of the most important reasons that the long history of the Boundary Waters Treaty and its agent, the IJC, are worth sustained study.

Article IV of the treaty states that "boundary waters and waters flowing across the boundary shall not be polluted on either side to the injury of health or property on the other." Beneath the assertive stance of "shall not" lay a remarkably ambitious principle to *anticipate* and resolve *future* environmental conflicts. Anticipation is the antithesis of the paradox of abundance, in which reacting after the fact is the norm. Along the Canada-U.S. border, from the western Fraser River to the eastern Maritimes and mid-continent at the Lake of the Woods and Great Lakes, the treaty provided a legal basis and the IJC provided a forum to anticipate, study, and negotiate alternative futures.[37] Preceding the environmental movement by fifty years, the IJC's pioneering efforts on water research and policy foreshadowed modern concepts like ecosystem management, anticipatory policy, and sustainability. A twenty-first-century world in water crisis has pitifully few enduring models at this scale with which to find successes and hope along with the undeniable failures. With close study, perhaps the treaty's many tests of time will illuminate avenues for better water governance elsewhere.

The 2008 Great Lakes–St. Lawrence compact and agreement built on a century-in-the-making legal framework. The Boundary Waters Treaty of 1909 was its scaffolding. From these heights of international diplomacy and shared governance we get a continental vantage of the border. At this scale, our conflicted relationship with water comes into focus. Abundance and scarcity were indeed its two faces. The legal framework was also under construction at the grassroots, and so we have to be explicit about issues of scale. At the grassroots, the International Joint Commission loses its centrality: federal, state, and provincial governments, First Nations and Native American tribes, agencies, municipalities, industries, universities, and nongovernmental organizations were all participants.[38] At this (general) scale, the border fragments into regions, watersheds, and geographically specific issues. At still other scales, the nonhuman world becomes visible. Invasive species, pollution, climate change—these transcended the border but still shaped it. Perturbations of aquatic ecosystems pushed water development in new directions.

One challenge for any burgeoning literature on border waters is to welcome works at different scales, even if thematically and methodologically they don't mesh perfectly. Take one example from this volume: the St. Lawrence River, North America's second largest river (and, bizarrely, a river often missing from maps of the rivers of America). International relations, grassroots dynamics, and ecological processes are all promising scales of analysis. From its first tiny canal in the eighteenth century, the river's hydrological regime underwent constant reengineering to an engineering apex in the 1950s. This was when Canada and the United States embarked on their largest joint project to date, the St. Lawrence Seaway and Power Project. One billion dollars spent, fifteen thousand workers deployed, 200 million cubic yards of earth excavated, many islands obliterated—at this scale, the seaway was an expression of twentieth-century hydro-nationalism. Hydropower and shipping were the seaway's economic goals, but Cold War defense and the discovery of huge iron ore deposits in Labrador were also part of a border story that was, intrinsically, about globalization.[39]

At the grassroots we gain different insight from the St. Lawrence saga. On the Canadian side alone, the seaway displaced nine communities, 225 farms, and 6,500 people.[40] From this vantage we get the lived experience of dislocation. As Joy Parr reveals in her intimate portraits, those who once knew the river lost everyday sights, sounds, and smells—all the "physical reference points for the selves they had been.... benchmarks for the spatial practices of daily life, for the habits through which residents had embodied the place."[41]

Finally, at an ecological scale, the nonhuman world comes into view as a powerful agent of change.[42] In 1829, Canada's Welland Canal opened the upper Great Lakes to maritime traffic from the Atlantic.[43] Since then, the St. Lawrence has been an international vector for over two hundred non-native species.[44] The parasitic sea lamprey arrived early via the Welland Canal. Zebra and quagga mussels arrived 150 years later as biological stowaways on oceanic ships in the seaway. Wherever they colonized, mussels and other less-famous species hurt and then transformed indigenous food webs.[45] These ecological disturbances triggered new water management debates. At ecological scales, we not only perceive the natural world's changeability, we get a close-up view of nature's relationships with humanity.

The St. Lawrence River illustrates both the difficulties and the possibilities of a volume on U.S.-Canada border waters. To examine "waters" in the plural is to examine multiple places at some scale or scales, making each place its own universe of possible events, perspectives, stories, and insights. By pursuing a collection on border waters, with a multidisciplinary authorship, this volume necessarily becomes exploratory, and we necessarily forfeit perfect thematic consistency or exhaustive examination of either "the border" or "water." Yet heterogeneity can create its own organizational logic and insights, as we outline below.

No matter the locations, academic disciplines, or specific themes of its individual chapters, *Border Flows* advances five core insights:

- Canada-U.S. border waters are historically instrumental yet permeable.
- Canada-U.S. border waters at every scale (transnational to local) embody transformative *relationships*—between humans and the natural world, between Canada and the United States, and among different groups of residents, economic stakeholders, and policymakers.

- Canada-U.S. border waters are agents in a continuous process of place-making and place-remaking.
- Canada-U.S. border waters reveal a more unified framework for tracing water policy and governance in North America because scarcity and abundance so visibly make up a larger conceptual whole.
- Canada-U.S. border waters offer an early model of anticipatory environmental policymaking with contemporary (often cautionary) implications for sustainable water management in other parts of the world.

These shared insights emerged when our contributors met for a writers workshop in Kingston, Ontario, sponsored by the Network in Canadian History and Environment (NiCHE). At the workshop, we reviewed draft articles, explored their interconnections, and considered the overall flow of the volume. We embraced the puzzle and opportunity of our internal diversity—by country (we hail from both the United States and Canada), region, discipline, research focus, even writing genre. Regionally, our work spans the Pacific Northwest, Quebec, the Arctic North, and the Great Lakes–St. Lawrence. (We had hoped to fill in the border with scholarship from the eastern Maritimes and coast and more from the prairies, but we did not find willing contributors for those places.) Our authors—who come from law, history, geography, political science, environmental humanities, and creative nonfiction—all contribute distinct understandings of border dynamics and water studies to this single volume.

Despite our multidisciplinarity, intersecting scales and themes formed natural groupings. An unusual transdisciplinary experiment began to take shape, which became the fourth part of the volume. For a general roadmap, the four parts of *Border Flows* traverse, respectively, (1) international scales and interactions involving nation-states; (2) federalist scales (nations in relation to provinces and states) and binational interactions of corporate and state actors and regional communities; (3) bioregional and ecological scales and how nonhuman organisms interact with the border; and (4) intimate phenomenological scales wherein individuals relate on a personal level to vaster, often impersonal, histories of borders and water.

In some ways, part 1 of *Border Flows*, "Finding the Border: Political Ecologies of Water Governance and Tenure," is the volume's most challenging section. This is not because the individual case studies are more complicated than those in later sections; rather, subsequent parts of the volume depend on all our readers, layperson and academic alike, being comfortable with the shifting scales, overlays, and relationships that clarify or hide border processes. The burden therefore rests on the authors in part 1 to make sense of the Canada-U.S. border as an idea and a process, not as an actual thing, and Canada-U.S. border waters as locales for relationships, not as large glasses of H_2O on a table called North America. This section explores the basic problem of "finding the border," with guides from the realms of environmental policymaking (Dave Dempsey), water law (Noah Hall and Peter Starr), cultural geography (Emma S. Norman and Alice Cohen), and political science (Andrea Charron).

Dempsey opens part 1 by outlining tensions inherent in transboundary agreements such as those for the Great Lakes. These include differences between environmental law and policy, incompatible management from international to local levels, inconsistent decision making, fluctuating priorities, public expectations, and, unsurprisingly, the "media-unworthy messy business of implementation." Dempsey uses fish to illustrate the normality of such tensions. Fish cannot respect the boundaries that international diplomacy is meant to establish. As live beings, fish are not static; they move around, and they respond to pollution, habitat changes, predation, and climate change, all of which will undermine the original assumptions that guided any bilateral negotiation over their management. Dempsey thereby offers a key theme for the next three chapters of the section: border waters diplomacy is neither end point nor outcome; it is a succession of ambiguous outcomes and changing facts on the ground that cumulatively make for an open-ended process of negotiation. From here, "Finding the Border" examines the particularities of three famous U.S.-Canada border waters. Hall and Starr build on Dempsey's introduction to Great Lakes–St. Lawrence governance with a "citizen's primer" on Great Lakes water law. Consider this a crash course on the legal waterscape and its historical progress from resolving international and interstate water allocation and nuisance disputes toward governance more explicitly focused on environmental protection and sustainable water use. Norman and Cohen take readers to the Salish Sea (once called Puget Sound) at the western end of the 49th parallel. They expose a problematic history—one in which the Canada-U.S. border was a moveable line of control, a form of nationalism that privileged some geographic and political boundaries while erasing others. Norman and Cohen also populate the border with actual people, Coast Salish indigenous communities, whose cultural identity proved as important as economics in new forms of water governance. Charron then moves north to the fabled Northwest Passage (NWP) of the Arctic North, which connects the Pacific Ocean to the northern Atlantic.[46] This is the contested water of sovereigns, whose definitional arguments—Is the NWP "internal (Canadian) waters" or an "international strait"?—entailed enormous transnational interests, defense and shipping issues, and also the environmental well-being of NWP waters.

On a surface level, part 2 of *Border Flows*, "Constructing the Border: Hydropolitics, Nationalism, and Megaprojects," makes Canada-U.S. border waters the aspirational domain and canvas of twentieth-century engineers—those state-sponsored "artists" of borderland waterscapes, commissioned to bring nationalistic imaginations to life in epic public works of the technological sublime. In other words, "Constructing the Border" addresses the subordination of natural waterways and watersheds to a large-scale border infrastructure of dams, locks, canals, harbors, and hydropower plants. Beneath the surface of audacious engineering blueprints for the Columbia River, the Chicago River, the St. Lawrence Seaway, Niagara Falls, and James Bay run confusing undercurrents of binational treaties, national or subnational identities, federalist systems of power, cultural ideas about nature, and competing questions about water itself—both its purposes and its distribution. Water historian Matthew Evenden helps readers navigate these currents. He opens with examples of the roles mega-water-projects have played in a fraught Canada-U.S. relationship. He surveys categories of water development along an east–west corridor: irrigation, urban water supplies, and hydropower. Most importantly, though, Evenden establishes a historical zeitgeist of technological optimism that denied natural and social limits and rationalized underperformance (economically speaking) or outright bad consequences. Subsequent case studies deconstruct historical border water projects so mega they still awe today: the bilateral St. Lawrence Seaway and Niagara Falls water control projects (Daniel Macfarlane), unfulfilled schemes for bulk water exports from Quebec to the United States (Frédéric Lasserre), and the Columbia River Treaty and consequent reengineering of the Canadian side of that river (Jeremy Mouat). Each of these projects is geographically distinct and important to water and borderlands studies in its own right. Lasserre's chapter, for example, offers an archetypal abundance mindset: Quebec's water export proponents focused obsessively on how to exploit the province's wealth in water, the principle value of which, in their view, derived from its commodification and sale to water-scarce regions. But readers should also come away seeing the larger context for mega-water-projects on the Canada-U.S. border. As Macfarlane theorizes, these were nationalistic showpieces in a global era of high modernism, an era defined in large part by hubris.

In part 3, "Challenging the Border: Ecological Agents of Change," three of environmental history's most innovative thinkers bring their intense transdisciplinary engagement with hybrid ecologies to U.S.-Canada border waters. Taking the ecologically twinned but border-divided Boundary Waters Canoe Area (United States) and Quetico Provincial Park (Canada) as an accessible entry, James W. Feldman shows readers how cumulative differences in management and tourism did indeed demarcate two parks that look and feel different north and south of the border. Then Feldman introduces the natural forces of wind and fire, thus opening the hard work of this section: How do we understand causality and outcomes when the border is both water and land, when border waters are natural and human, when the scales of explanation are as broad as wind, as cellular as fish fat, as global as climate? In *Nature's Metropolis* (1992), William Cronon explicated the overlay of "second nature" on "first nature" in nineteenth-century Chicago. In this part of *Border Flows*, our authors take a deep dive into first and second ecology. It requires a humanist scholar both at ease and expert with scientific literature to analyze the natural cycling of wholly unnatural chemicals and heavy metals, as Joseph Taylor III does when he returns readers to the Salish Sea. Taylor traces the paths of persistent organic pollutants from industry through the marine ecosystem and beyond, to birds, mammals, and humans, and how these problems challenged a region that tried, but failed, to draw a line between sovereigns. Likewise, Nancy Langston interrogates the easy explanation that invasive sea lampreys decimated lake trout populations in Lake Superior (not only a crucial border water but the world's largest freshwater lake by surface). For one thing, the historical chronology does not support a simple cause and effect. Superior's aquatic ecosystems—powerful agents in their own right—interacted with the multiple stressors of watershed change, industrial pollution, fisheries management, and, recently, climate change. In the past, binational policy did not adequately map and address these interrelationships. Lake Superior and the Salish Sea illustrate how historically grounded transdisciplinary analysis might help policymakers respond to complexity in time (the next time).

In part 4, "Reflections in the Water," acclaimed nature writer Jerry Dennis guides readers into the realm of environmental humanities and creative nonfiction. Here, several of our contributors offer more intimate takes on their scholarship and the places they study, to draw out the experiential aspects and to show how scholarly themes get traction in our daily lives. These short, reflective essays are also an experiment of sorts for translating academic scholarship into relatable scenes, where real people (not faceless researchers) participate in the cares and woes and flows of care-worthy places. The authors want readers to imagine themselves in such places and situations—or better yet, to draw parallels with their own experiences and perceptions. The personalization in the essays is contemporary in form and function. Consider TED Talks, for instance, those short public-scholarly hybrids whereby the presenter places himself or herself emotionally *within* the narrative trajectory of a complex subject. First-person narrative is entirely normal for nature writers like Dennis but less comfortable for many academics. And so, this part of *Border Flows* consciously stands apart from the first three sections and tries to welcome readers who might care more about their childhood on the lake than high modernism.

Finally, Graeme Wynn revisits our many border waters in his inimitable way, map-melding the case studies with metaphor and meaning in an afterword that is also a prologue and blessing for future travel along this and other important borders.

The impetus for the entire *Border Flows* project is water itself—water as a fundamental environmental and moral concern of the twenty-first century. More than half the planet's population confronts severe water shortages. The World Economic Forum warns that our world faces water bankruptcy.[47] We must put our insights about the past in service to the precarious future of Earth's fresh water. A century of water relations along the Canada-U.S. border—with the lessons and models therein—should be part of that urgent dialogue.

Notes

1. Sporhase v. Nebraska ex rel. Douglas, 458 U.S. 941 (1982).

2. U.S. Army Corps of Engineers, *Six-State High Plains Ogallala Aquifer Regional Resources Study: Summary Report* (Washington, DC: U.S. Army Corps of Engineers, Southwestern Division, 1982).

3. During his short-lived presidential campaign, New Mexico governor Bill Richardson (Democrat) proposed a national water policy and "dialogue between [western and eastern] states," asserting that "states like Wisconsin are awash in water." Dan Egan, "A Water Query from Out West: Hopeful's Interest in Great Lakes Renews Calls for Compact," *Milwaukee Wisconsin Journal Sentinel*, Oct. 6, 2007.

4. Peter Annin, *The Great Lakes Water Wars* (Washington, DC: Island, 2006); Dave Dempsey, *On the Brink: The Great Lakes in the 21st Century* (East Lansing: Michigan State University Press, 2004); Terence Kehoe, *Cleaning Up the Great Lakes: From Cooperation to Confrontation* (Dekalb: Northern Illinois University Press, 1997); Lee Botts and Paul Muldoon. *Evolution of the Great Lakes Water Quality Agreements* (East Lansing: Michigan State University Press, 2005).

5. Lynne Heasley, "Paradigms and Paradoxes of Abundance: The St. Lawrence River and the Great Lakes Basin" (paper presented at the First World Congress of Environmental History, Copenhagen, August 2009). Heasley's current book project—*The Paradox of Abundance: Essays on the Great Lakes*—grew out of this paper.

6. James W. Feldman and Lynne Heasley, "Re-centering North American Environmental History," *Environmental History* 10, no. 3 (2007): 951–58. These stories of abundance involve vast subgenres of popular literature and academic scholarship, each with its own landscape types, regional memories, and cultural touchstones. On fisheries alone, readers might begin with Stephen Bocking, "Fishing the Inland Seas: Great Lakes Research, Fisheries Management, and Environmental Policy in Ontario," *Environmental History* 2 (1997): 52–73; Joseph E. Taylor III, *Making Salmon: An Environmental History of the Northwest Fisheries Crisis* (Seattle: University of Washington Press, 1999); Margaret Beattie Bogue, *Fishing the Great Lakes: An Environmental History, 1783–1933* (Madison: University of Wisconsin Press, 2000); and Michael J. Chiarappa and Kristin M. Szylvian, *Fish for All: An Oral History of Multiple Claims and Divided Sentiment on Lake Michigan* (Lansing: Michigan State University Press, 2003).

7. See William Cronon, "Landscapes of Abundance and Scarcity," in *The Oxford History of the American West*, ed. Clyde A. Milner II, Carol A. O'Connor, and Martha A. Sandweiss (New York: Oxford University Press, 1994), 603–37; and Martin Melosi, *Coping with Abundance: Energy and Environment in Industrial America* (Philadelphia: Temple University Press, 1985).

8. The foundational work of North American water history on which historians and theorists continue

to build and elaborate is Donald Worster's *Rivers of Empire: Water, Aridity, and the Growth of the American West* (New York: Oxford University Press, 1992). For a contemporary theoretical overview of the social production of water scarcity and abundance in service to a modern hydraulic society, see Andrew Biro, "River-Adaptiveness in a Globalized World," in *Thinking with Water*, ed. Cecilia Chen, Janine MacLeod, and Astride Neimanis (Montreal: McGill-Queen's University Press, 2013), 166–84.

9   For a rich historiography of Powell in the arid American West, and especially his 1878 "Report on the Lands of the Arid Region of the United States," work backward from John Wesley Powell, *Seeing Things Whole: The Essential John Wesley Powell*, ed. William DeBuys (Washington, DC: Island, 2001); Donald Worster, *A River Running West: The Life of John Wesley Powell* (New York: Oxford University Press, 2000); and Wallace Stegner, *Beyond the Hundredth Meridian: John Wesley Powell and the Opening of the West* (New York: Penguin, 1992).

10 Of the arid Canadian prairies, legal scholar David Percy says that "in a pattern that was familiar in the American West, the role played by water law in creating shortages became the subject of examination only after all efforts at augmenting the natural supply of water had been exhausted. In Canada, it became apparent only in the last two decades that *the basic model of prairie water law had never been designed to deal with water scarcity.*" Percy, "Responding to Water Scarcity in Western Canada," *Texas Law Review* 83, no. 7 (2005): 2097; emphasis ours. See also Tristan M. Goodman, "The Development of Prairie Canada's Water Law, 1870–1940," in *Laws and Societies in the Canadian Prairie West, 1670–1940*, ed. Louis A. Knafla and Jonathan Swainger (Vancouver: UBC Press, 2005), 266–79. Jim Warren and Harry Diaz offer a sympathetic view of dryland farmers in *Defying Palliser: Stories of Resilience from the Driest Region of the Canadian Prairies* (Saskatchewan: University of Regina Press, 2012). Sterling Evans provides a terrific model for binational, transnational, and comparative scholarship on this border region in *Bound in Twine: The History and Ecology of the Henequen-Wheat Complex for Mexico and the American and Canadian Plains, 1880–1950* (College Station: Texas A&M Press, 2007). See also Christopher Armstrong, Matthew Evenden, and H.V. Nelles, *The River Returns: An Environmental History of the Bow* (Montreal: McGill-Queen's University Press, 2009); and Shannon Stunden Bower, *Wet Prairie: People, Land, and Water in Agricultural Manitoba* (Vancouver: UBC Press, 2011).

11 Norris Hundley, *Water in the West: The Colorado River Compact and the Politics of Water in the American West*, 2nd ed. (Berkeley: University of California Press, 2009).

12 Donald J. Pisani offers a sophisticated but manageable entry with *Water, Land, and Law in the West: The Limits of Public Policy, 1850–1920* (Lawrence: University Press of Kansas, 1996). Then, for an alternative economic and legal history of the prior appropriation

doctrine, tackle David Schorr, *The Colorado Doctrine: Water Rights, Corporations, and Distributive Justice on the American Frontier* (New Haven: Yale University Press, 2012). In Canada, the provinces of Alberta and British Columbia experimented with, but ultimately rejected, prior appropriation models.

13 Alicia Acuna and David Burke, "Colorado to California: Hands Off Our Water," *Fox News Politics*, January 28, 2015.

14 Marianne Goodland, "Rainbarrel Bill Dead for Session," *Colorado Statesman*, May 4, 2015.

15 A recent stunning example is Matt Black's portfolio in "The Dry Land," *New Yorker,* September 29, 2014, http://www.newyorker.com/project/portfolio/dry-land.

16 We use the Great Lakes as our juxtaposition with the Colorado River because it is the most physically prominent system of water east of the 100th meridian, even by comparison with the Mississippi River basin, and also because historically it is the most important diplomatic and economic boundary water system between the United States and Canada.

17 Jerry Dennis, *The Windward Shore: A Winter on the Great Lakes* (Ann Arbor: University of Michigan Press, 2012), 11–12.

18 Flint Water Advisory Task Force, *Final Report*, commissioned by the Office of Governor Rick Snyder, State of Michigan, March 21, 2016.

19 Or the third largest, if you exclude the Caspian Sea.

20 In a different region of the border itself, Paul Hirt explores the unequal social consequences and the unsustainable ecological consequences of a bilateral "politics of abundance" running through the history of the Columbia and Fraser Rivers of the Pacific Northwest. Hirt, "Developing a Plentiful Resource: Transboundary Rivers in the Pacific Northwest," in *Water, Place, and Equity: Tempering Efficiency with Justice*, ed. John M. Whiteley, Helen Ingram, and Richard Perry (Cambridge, MA: MIT Press, 2008), 147–88.

21 Donald J. Pisani, "Beyond the Hundredth Meridian: Nationalizing the History of Water in the United States," *Environmental History* 5, no. 4 (2000): 476. For a national environmental history of wetlands, and specifically wetland drainage, see Ann Vileisis, "Machines in the Wetland Gardens," in *Discovering the Unknown Landscape: A History of America's Wetlands* (Washington, DC: Island, 1997), 111–41. For an important water history of settlement and development forces and governmental policies that transformed water-abundant landscapes of the American South, see Craig Colten, *Southern Waters: The Limits to Abundance* (Baton Rouge: Louisiana State University Press, 2014), esp. 41–115.

22 Willis F. Dunbar and George S. May, *Michigan: A History of the Wolverine State* (Grand Rapids: Wm. B. Eerdmans, 1995), 157.

23 Quoted in "Tisch: 'Drain Commissioner State's Most Powerful Man,'" *Argus Press,* May 17, 1979. Drain commissioners had and have the authority to condemn property, contract, assess all costs for drain work and projects to landowners in a designated drain, issue bonds, sue, and be sued—all unchecked

by any other official or agency, accountable only to the laws of the Michigan Drain Code and the voters at election time. For a timeline of drain-related Michigan law, see Appendix 2-D in Michigan Department of Transportation and Tetra Tech MPS, *Drainage Manual*, January 2006, https://www.michigan.gov/stormwatermgt/0,1607,7-205--93193--,00.html (see also the Michigan Drain Code of 1956). For a midwestern context of state drainage district legislative history, see Mary R. McCorvie and Christopher L. Lant, "Drainage District Formation and the Loss of Midwestern Wetlands, 1850–1930," *Agricultural History* 67, no. 4 (1993): 13–39.

24 Pisani, "Beyond the Hundredth Meridian," 478.

25 The perception of abundance is key here, as opposed to the more objective reality of finite limits. Karen Bakker calls out Canadians' optimistic belief in their nation's (mythical) abundant supplies of water. Bakker, introduction to *Eau Canada: The Future of Canada's Water*, ed. Karen Bakker (Vancouver: UBC Press, 2006).

26 Philip Micklin, Nikolay Aladin, and Igor Plotnikov, eds., *The Aral Sea: The Devastation and Partial Rehabilitation of a Great Lake* (Berlin: Springer Earth System Sciences, 2013).

27 For an examination of the U.S. interstate framework during that intense period of negotiation, see Noah D. Hall, "Toward a New Horizontal Federalism: Interstate Water Management in the Great Lakes Basin," *University of Colorado Law Review* 77 (2006): 405–56.

28 Dave Dempsey, *Great Lakes for Sale: From Whitecaps to Bottlecaps* (Ann Arbor: University of Michigan Press, 2008).

29 In the past decade, an important literature has emerged to rethink and theorize North American borderlands, with an emphasis on transnational and comparative history. See Benjamin Johnson and Andrew Graybill, eds., *Bridging National Borders in North America: Transnational and Comparative Histories* (Durham: Duke University Press, 2010); Michael Behiels and Reginald Stuart, eds., *Transnationalism: Canada–United States History into the Twenty-First Century* (Montreal: McGill-Queen's University Press, 2010); Matthew Evenden and Graeme Wynn, "Fifty-Four, Forty, or Fight? Writing within and across Boundaries in North American Environmental History," in *Nature's End: History and the Environment*, ed. Sverker Sörlin and Paul Warde (New York: Palgrave Macmillan, 2009); and Victor Konrad and Heather Nicol, *Beyond Walls: Re-inventing the Canada–United States Borderlands* (New York: Ashgate, 2008). The scholarship also examines regionality at the border: Sterling Evans, *The Borderlands of the American and Canadian Wests: Essays on Regional History of the Forty-Ninth Parallel* (Lincoln: University of Nebraska Press, 2006); Kyle Conway and Timothy Pasch, eds., *Beyond the Border: Tensions Across the 49th Parallel in the Great Plains and Prairies* (Montreal: McGill-Queen's University Press, 2013); John J. Bukowczyk et al., *Permeable Border: The Great Lakes Basin as Transnational Region, 1650–1990* (Pittsburgh: University of Pittsburgh

Press, 2005); Ken Coates and John Findlay, eds., *Parallel Destinies: Canadian-American Relations West of the Rockies* (Seattle: University of Washington Press, 2002).

30   The Beaufort Sea is another binational marine zone in the Arctic North.

31   Feldman and Heasley, "Re-centering North American Environmental History." Steven C. High explores the economic decline of the region in *Industrial Sunset: The Making of the North American Rustbelt, 1969-1984* (Toronto: University of Toronto Press, 2003).

32   Note that the Uruguay River makes up the entire (though shorter) border between Argentina and Uruguay.

33   Emma S. Norman, Alice Cohen, and Karen Bakker, eds., *Water without Borders? Canada, the United States and Shared Waters* (Toronto: University of Toronto Press, 2013).

34   Boundary Waters Treaty, U.S.-Great Britain [for Canada], January 11, 1909, Temp. State Dept. No. 548, 36 Stat. 2448.

35   L.M. Bloomfield and Gerald F. Fitzgerald, *Boundary Waters Problems of Canada and the United States: The International Joint Commission, 1912-1958* (Toronto: Carswell, 1958); Murray Clamen and Daniel Macfarlane, "The International Joint Commission, Water Levels, and Transboundary Governance in the Great Lakes," *Review of Policy Research* 32, no. 1 (2015): 40-59.

36   Chirakaikaran Joseph Chacko, *The International Joint Commission between the United States of America and the Dominion of Canada* (New York: AMS Press, 1968); Robert Spencer, John Kirton, and Kim Richard Nossal, eds., *The International Joint Commission Seventy Years On* (Toronto: Centre for International Studies, University of Toronto, 1981).

37   On industrialized waters, the IJC offered seminal ideas on water policy, such as the "virtual elimination" of persistent toxic substances.

38   Bradley C. Karkkainen, "Post-Sovereign Environmental Governance," *Global Environmental Politics* 4, no. 4 (2004): 72-96.

39   Daniel Macfarlane, *Negotiating a River: Canada, the U.S., and the Creation of the St. Lawrence Seaway* (Vancouver: UBC Press, 2014); J.R. McNeill and Corinna R. Unger, *Environmental Histories of the Cold War* (New York: Cambridge University Press, 2010); Richard White, "The Nationalization of Nature," *Journal of American History* 86, no. 3 (1999): 976-86.

40   On the American side, dikes protected communities around Massena, while the town of Louisville lost about a third of its taxable land, including Louisville Landing, a historic port on the St. Lawrence. Work on the American side was not as dramatic as the displacement on the Canadian side, but with eighteen thousand acres flooded, it still displaced 225 farms, five hundred cottages, 12.5 miles of highway, and 1,100 people. Macfarlane, *Negotiating a River*.

41   Joy Parr, "Movement and Sound: A Walking Village Remade: Iroquois and the St. Lawrence Seaway," in *Sensing Changes: Technologies, Environments, and the Everyday, 1953-2003* (Vancouver: UBC Press,

2009). See also Tina Loo, "Disturbing the Peace: Environmental Change and the Scales of Justice on a Northern River," *Environmental History* 12, no. 4 (2007): 895–919; and Tina Loo with Meg Stanley, "An Environmental History of Progress: Damming the Peace and Columbia Rivers," *Canadian Historical Review* 92, no. 3 (2011): 399–427.

42 John Riley, *The Once and Future Great Lakes: An Ecological History* (Montreal: McGill-Queen's University Press, 2013).

43 John N. Jackson, with John Burtniak and Gregory P. Stein, *The Mighty Niagara: One River—Two Frontiers* (Amherst, NY: Prometheus, 2003); John N. Jackson, *The Welland Canals and Their Communities: Engineering, Industrial, and Urban Transformation* (Toronto: University of Toronto Press, 1997). The Welland Canal was a contemporary of and competitor to another invasion corridor, the Erie Canal. Carol Sheriff, *The Artificial River: The Erie Canal and the Paradox of Progress, 1817–1862* (New York: Hill & Wang, 1996).

44 Jeff Alexander, *Pandora's Locks: The Opening of the Great Lakes–St. Lawrence Seaway* (East Lansing: Michigan State University Press, 2009).

45 Invasive species became an overwhelming problem in all directions. From their deliberate introduction in southern U.S. fishponds, silver and bighead "Asian" carp have migrated up the Mississippi River and into the Chicago Ship and Sanitary Canal, the man-made water bridge linking the Mississippi and Great Lakes basins. On the prairies, invasive species travelled from the Missouri River basin to Hudson's Bay via the Devil's Lake diversion. Asian carp are travelling in the opposite direction along the same route. Pacific ports have struggled with non-native mollusks and crabs.

46 Graeme Wynn, *Canada and the Arctic North America: An Environmental History* (Santa Barbara, CA: ABC-CLIO, 2007).

47 World Economic Forum Water Initiative, "The Bubble Is Close to Bursting: A Forecast of the Main Economic and Geopolitical Water Issues Likely to Arise in the World during the Next Two Decades" (unpublished draft for discussion at the World Economic Forum Annual Meeting, Davos, Switzerland, 2009); Mesfin M. Mekonnen and Arjen Y. Hoekstra, "Four Billion People Facing Severe Water Scarcity," *Sciences Advances* 2, no. 2 (2016), doi:10.1126/sciadv.1500323.

PART ONE

*Finding the Border:
Political Ecologies of Water Governance and Tenure*

Openings

Political Ecologies on the Border

DAVE DEMPSEY

"Pollution doesn't respect political boundaries."

Anyone who has worked on water pollution issues in the last several decades has heard this refrain, or something like it, countless times. The repetition of words can rob them of meaning, so it is appropriate to stop and to look at and listen to this use of language more closely. Doing so can tell us a great deal about water diplomacy across borders—especially as seen through the lens of a political practitioner. For the fact is that governance systems still very much respect boundaries.

In actual governance, the ideal and the achievable always collide, with the latter holding the power. That pollution does not respect boundaries leads theoretically to an imperative to remove or transcend those boundaries, but the reality is that the centuries-old construct of national sovereignty continues to dominate societal attitudes and public policy. Still, there is some reason to believe in movement toward a sweeping change in transboundary water management. The recent historical record offers some support for this trend—but with limits. The trajectory of Great Lakes agreements among states and provinces over time is an example.

In the mid-1980s, as elected officials in the Great Lakes region found it in their political and in the public interest to cooperate and undertake joint initiatives to conserve the lakes, public health advocates observed that the Great Lakes states and Ontario had varying methodologies for determining fish-consumption health advisories in their respective Great Lakes waters for sport and subsistence anglers.[1] A lake trout contaminated with a certain level of PCBs, for example, might trigger an advisory recommending limited or no consumption in one of the Great Lakes states, while it might be deemed safe for more frequent eating if it swam into the waters of another state or Ontario. The health advocates argued that the jurisdictions should agree on a methodology that would result in similar if not identical advisories, reducing public confusion while providing health advice of comparable caution. The governors of the Great Lakes states agreed and in 1986 set their health experts to work devising a common methodology. Ontario also participated.

Toiling arduously and in good faith, the states and Ontario conferred for seven years before producing their agreement, *Protocol for a Uniform Great Lakes Sport Fish Consumption Advisory*.[2] The result was a narrowing, but not the elimination, of differences among the jurisdictions in determining contaminant thresholds for the issuance of fish-consumption advisories. Using their best professional judgment, the experts found validity in a common methodology with enough jurisdiction-specific twists to yield slightly different results. Sovereign insistence on those twists overrode the objective of strict uniformity. Today, the advisories continue to differ, although not as widely as before.[3]

This episode illustrates lessons about issues that arise from the shared waters of the Great Lakes but are often applicable to waters along the entire border. Namely, political jurisdictions sharing boundary waters can and will, when prodded at the right moment in history by the right people, quickly strive to communicate about their water-related management differences; less quickly, but still genuinely, attempt to coordinate and perhaps arrive at compatible management approaches; and most slowly, if at all, come to agreement on a single, codified, enforceable management approach in which all governmental jurisdictions subscribe to uniform standards and share decision making across boundaries. This last tends to happen only when a common threat is perceived and no significant constituency at home opposes such an approach. In the end, managing the public's expectations about what can realistically be accomplished—and allaying any public fears about surrendering sovereignty—is as important as managing the shared resources themselves.

These realities have characterized public policy and governance affecting more than the Great Lakes. While globally unique, the Great Lakes are just one part of a U.S.-Canada border that is approximately 40 percent water.[4] Fish and pollutants in all of these waters also fail to recognize political boundaries. And typically, sovereignty has trumped any notion of unified management all along this watery boundary. But as chapters in this section attest, the future of water governance affecting shared waters may be less fixed than the past. A changing physical and social climate and a changing vision of boundary waters themselves support a hypothesis of continued evolution.

Indeed, climate already appears to be fostering shared problem solving in two watersheds straddling the U.S.-Canada border. In both the Red River–Lake Winnipeg and Lake Champlain–Richilieu River basins, toxic organisms have added urgency to the problem of coordinated water governance. Cyanobacteria (popularly known as blue-green algae) are apparently on the increase in these watersheds because of the interaction of nutrient pollution and climate change. These microorganisms pose risks to human health[5] that are significant enough to warrant nonbinding transboundary action plans for cleanup in both basins.[6] If these plans fail, new legal instruments may follow.

This is the pattern of more than a half century of innovation in the Great Lakes Basin. In the last sixty years, Great Lakes states and provinces and the U.S. and Canadian federal governments have been relatively nimble in responding to common threats to the lakes with consultation and coordination mechanisms and institutions. They move especially fast when catastrophe appears imminent and the public clamours for government action—as when populations of lake trout crashed in the late 1940s and when transfers of water from the Great Lakes to the arid West seemed likely in the 1980s. This crisis-and-response pattern accounts for, among other things, the 1955 U.S.-Canada Convention on Great Lakes Fisheries and the 1985 Great Lakes Charter among the eight Great Lakes states, Ontario, and Quebec (the latter of which is discussed in chapter 1).

Although the convention has treaty status and the charter is a good-faith agreement, they are alike in that they emphasize consultation and common effort without committing the parties to hard-and-fast regulatory efforts, let alone even the mildest infringements of sovereignty, perceived or real. Thus, they reflect an acknowledgment of common interest and, to a lesser extent, the need for common stewardship while guarding sovereign freedom of action.

Established by the 1955 convention, the Great Lakes Fishery Commission has proven to be remarkably effective in meeting its primary charge: suppressing and controlling populations of the destructive, non-native sea lamprey. But it has provided other benefits. The commission has successfully brought together state and provincial fishery managers to agree on a compatible fishery management plan and fish community objectives for each lake.[7] With less success but equally genuine intentions, the commission has promoted interjurisdictional, binational consultation on aquatic habitat conservation. There has never been a credible call for a single Great Lakes fisheries management agency or policy; Ontario and the states retain control of their respective fisheries (although these are in fact a single resource). The commission goes as far as it needs or anyone in the field wants it to go.

The 1985 Great Lakes Charter was the product of its time—the dawn of modern concern about water diversions from the lakes, when fear of water claims by southwestern U.S. states—with their growing populations and political clout—began to mount. An interstate compact, while probably desirable, was not politically feasible in the context of the early and mid-1980s. That left no meaningful alternative to a common statement of purpose and principle and a resolve to coordinate across boundaries and improve in-state and in-province water management. Even that was dicey in Michigan, where a leading sportsman's organization attacked the charter for implying there might, someday, be a diversion that could pass muster and urged that the state not become party to the agreement. The charter went as far toward common management as politics would allow.

Transboundary water agreements—and many major governmental initiatives generally—face another political problem. Whether for a statute, a charter, or a compact, the signing ceremony gets fanfare but implementation suffers from neglect. Compatible, let alone uniform, water management flags. Sunshine is the best disinfectant, but the execution of transboundary water management agreements has often occurred in shadow. In addition to political pressures that may drive a jurisdiction not to impose or enforce a strict regulatory decision, there is a question of funding for water resource programs, especially for mundane data collection and monitoring—particularly vexatious in a time of scarce government dollars. But as Noah Hall and Peter Starr convincingly argue in chapter 1, there is reason to be cautiously optimistic that implementation of the 2008 water management compact among the Great Lakes states, and a parallel agreement involving the same states, Ontario, and Quebec, will be more transparent than its predecessors.

Some decisions that could affect boundary waters are, and are likely to remain, the prerogative of one nation. At this writing, controversy rages over the proposed siting of a deep geologic repository for the disposal of low- and medium-level radioactive waste from nuclear reactors close to the Lake Huron shoreline at Kincardine, Ontario.[8] The repository would be at least two thousand feet below the surface, lie within a mile of Lake Huron, and store up to 200,000 cubic metres of waste. Citing the risk of a release into the Great Lakes, opponents are especially outspoken on the U.S. side—but also belated, as their outcry arose well after the siting process began. The U.S. critics complain that the Canadian siting process was not well publicized in the United States.

The early lack of transboundary communication is striking. A step toward better communication is a new clause of the U.S.-Canada Great Lakes Water Quality Agreement as updated in 2012.[9] Article VI, Notification and Response, provides in subsection (c) that the governments "shall notify each other, through the Great Lakes Executive Committee, of planned activities that could lead to a pollution incident or that could have a significant cumulative impact on the Waters of the Great Lakes," specifically mentioning "the storage and transfer of nuclear waste or radioactive materials" as one such activity. Nothing beyond notification is required or provided for. Sovereignty tops shared decision making. This is reminiscent of the charter. Still, the possibilities of future innovation cannot be dismissed.

The chapters in this section, in different ways, underscore that human constructs affecting border flows evolve, generally for the benefit of both the waters and the people who enjoy and use them. But the chapters also sketch inherent tensions between even the "evolved" constructs and sustainable human and water regimes. The result is not a linear march forward toward an arbitrary notion of "progress," but zigzag routes that may or may not lead to a single destination.

As Hall and Starr observe in their chapter, titled "A Citizen's Legal Primer on the Boundary Waters Treaty, International Joint Commission, and Great Lakes Water Management," adoption of pioneering legal principles addressing binational water management between Canada and the United States reaches back over a century to Article IV of the 1909 Boundary Waters Treaty. But as they also note, those rudimentary principles could come to fruition only with the passage of time and increasing human sensitivity to the indivisibility of shared waters. What they describe as a survey of the legal waterscape of water management agreements between the United States and Canada is a necessary and engaging history, documenting an unfolding of law in tandem with an evolution of ecosystem science. The authors make a critical observation about the historic innovation of the 2008 Great Lakes Compact among the states and the parallel agreement also including Ontario and Quebec: that the two agreements take into account the entire Great Lakes hydrologic system in a way "that still respects state autonomy and sovereignty." The authors also strike a hopeful note regarding a growing accent on environmental protection and citizen participation in Great Lakes transboundary management.

First popularized in the 1970s, the concept and image of a single natural water system indifferent to human-made international boundaries has claimed a large beachhead. But in chapter 2, "Treaties, Wars, and Salish Sea Watersheds: The Constructed Boundaries of Water Governance," Emma S. Norman and Alice Cohen pose difficult questions that arise from this view. To what extent will the borders defined by European-derived constructs yield to governance that respectfully accommodates Indigenous lifeways and traditional knowledge? And is the superficially "natural" watershed governance model complicated by implicit human assumptions? These questions and their alternative answers are an antidote to rosy optimism.

In "Contesting the Northwest Passage: Four Far-North Narratives," Andrea Charron compellingly describes the unique history of the strait and the evolution of Canadian views and policies regarding its place within the national identity, as a military frontier, as a sensitive ecosystem, and as a resource to be managed for sustainable development. The historical contrast between Canadian and U.S. views of the passage's role as territorial versus international waters illustrates the ways such border differences are carefully expressed in legal terms. Rapid changes in the environmental conditions of the Northwest Passage associated with climate change appear to be fostering comparably rapid change in policy, and perhaps law, but Charron concludes that the narrative is still a work in progress.

The relatively new ecosystem approach fosters public and political support for binational governmental coordination and conservation. But the policies and institutions responsible for such governance are circumscribed, as in other areas of governance, by fluctuating priorities, budgets, and philosophies—and typically, but not always, by sovereignty concerns.

A perceived external common threat is often the most potent source of intergovernmental consensus on binding action. The 2008 Great Lakes Compact reflected a shared urgency among Great Lakes state and provincial governments. A legally enforceable pact superseded state sovereignty concerns also in part because no serious objection was raised by any constituency in the basin. The idea of losing Great Lakes water has few adherents in the Great Lakes states and provinces.

The history of U.S.-Canada approaches—and state-provincial approaches—toward management of boundary waters is instructive. Cooperation and coordination are feasible, even likely as public awareness grows. Clear political rewards exist for executing transboundary water agreements.

But so do clear limits. Even when the agreements commit their parties to mirroring actions, differences in implementation occur. To some extent this is a natural result of sovereignty, but it is also a result of political ecology. Each jurisdiction has its own political history and pressures. And it is a reality that the media-worthy announcement of agreements is followed by the distinctly media-unworthy messy business of implementation.

This does not mean that treaties and other U.S.-Canada transboundary water management agreements are likely to always be confined within the limits of the past. Rather, they are gradually moving, in fits and starts, toward a full recognition of the responsibility for joint, binding management across state, provincial, and national boundaries. It will be exciting to see what may come next.

Perhaps most interesting is the question of whether the common external threat of climate change will drive jurisdictions on both sides of the Canada-U.S. border toward binding agreements supporting mitigation, adaptation, and resiliency to protect shared waters. Will climate change become as potent a political symbol and policy rallying point as vessels slurping up Lake Superior water and exporting it to Asia?

Fish do not respect political boundaries. Pollution does not respect political boundaries. Neither groundwater nor surface water respect political boundaries. But human beings do. The task for Canadians and Americans in the twenty-first century is to respect the disrespect of mobile natural resources, especially water, for political boundaries: to envision the lake trout and walleye that cross the boundaries and imaginatively follow them. In doing so, *Homo sapiens* can thoughtfully fashion ever more realistic and enforceable mechanisms for bridging the divide.

Notes

1. Originally viewed as a temporary information service in the late 1960s and early 1970s, government-issued fish-consumption advisories are now institutionalized, but in most jurisdictions have not been codified in statute, giving public health agencies considerable flexibility in methods of deriving appropriate advice.

2. Great Lakes Sport Fish Advisory Task Force, *Protocol for a Uniform Great Lakes Sport Fish Consumption Advisory*, September 1993, http://www.fish.state.pa.us/images/fisheries/fcs/pcb_fishtech.pdf.

3. For example, the 2013/2014 Ontario fish-consumption advisory for Lake Superior coho salmon, zone 11, advises no more than eight meals per month for fish 45 inches in size, for the general population of fish consumers. The 2014/2015 Michigan advisory recommends no more than four meals per month for Lake Superior coho salmon of any size—but it then encourages anglers to double that if they choose, clean, and cook the fish carefully. Ontario, Ministry of the Environment, *Guide to Eating Ontario Sport Fish, 2013–2014*, 27th ed. (Toronto: Queen's Printer for Ontario, 2013), https://dr6j45jk9xcmk.cloudfront.net/documents/834/guide-eating-ontario-sport-fishen.pdf; Michigan, Dept. of Community Health, *Eat Safe Fish Guide: Upper Peninsula, 2014–2015* (Lansing: Government of Michigan, 2014).

4. Michael Laitta, "Canada-U.S. Transboundary Hydrographic Data Harmonization Efforts Gain Momentum," October 11, 2010, PDF, http://nhd.usgs.gov/Canada-US_Hydro_Harmonization.pdf.

5. Documented human health impacts from microcystin, a common toxic form of cyanobacteria found in these boundary waters, range from abdominal pain and nausea to pneumonia. U.S. Environmental Protection Agency, "Health and Ecological Effects," EPA website, accessed March 26, 2016, https://www.epa.gov/nutrient-policy-data/health-and-ecological-effects#what1.

6. Lake Winnipeg Foundation, "Harmful Algae Blooms on Lake Winnipeg," LWF website, accessed March 25, 2016, http://www.lakewinnipegfoundation.org/harmful-algae-blooms-lake-winnipeg; Lake Champlain Basin Program, "Cyanobacteria (Blue-Green Algae)," LCBP website, accessed March 25, 2016, http://www.lcbp.org/water-environment/human-health/cyanobacteria.

7. Great Lakes Fishery Commission, *A Joint Strategic Plan for*

8 *Management of Great Lakes Fisheries*, Miscellaneous Publication No. 2007-01, revised June 10, 1997 (Ann Arbor, MI: GLFC, 1997), http://www.glfc.org/fishmgmt/jsp97.pdf.

8 See, for example, the Stop the Great Lakes Nuclear Dump website, at http://www.stopthegreatlakesnucleardump.com; and Colin Sullivan, "Mich. Lawmakers Irate over Canada's Proposed Burial Site near Lake Huron," *Energy and Environment News*, June 1, 2015, http://www.eenews.net/stories/1060019398.

9 Great Lakes Water Quality Agreement of 2012, Protocol Amending the Agreement between Canada and the United States of America on Great Lakes Water Quality, 1978, as amended in 1983 and 1987, Canada–United States, signed September 7, 2012, http://www.ijc.org/en_/Great_Lakes_Water_Quality.

A Citizen's Legal Primer on the Boundary Waters Treaty, International Joint Commission, and Great Lakes Water Management

NOAH D. HALL AND PETER STARR

I. Introduction: The Origins of United States–Canada Water Management

To modern ears, the term "water management" most likely evokes environmental concerns. This is appropriate, for water policy in North America has centred on environmental issues in recent years. But this was not always the case. Over a century ago, Canadian-American water relations grew out of very different interests. In North America, formal binational management took shape in 1903, when the United States and Canada first established the International Waterways Commission to address potentially conflicting rights in the countries' shared waterways.[1] The commission soon recommended that the two countries adopt legal principles to govern uses of their shared waters and form an international body to further advance protection of boundary waters. In 1907, the International

Waterways Commission drafted a proposed treaty, which was modified through negotiations and eventually led to the Boundary Waters Treaty of 1909. The treaty primarily provided for joint management and cooperation between the United States and Canada for the two countries' shared boundary waters. The treaty defined "boundary waters" to include the lakes, rivers, and connecting waterways through which the U.S.-Canada border passes, but not the tributaries that flow into these bodies or the waterways that leave them.

These earliest efforts at cooperative, transboundary water management were motivated not by environmental concerns but by the desire to erect a framework to govern navigation and equitable sharing of boundary waters.[2] For instance, the Boundary Waters Treaty addressed the taking and diversion of boundary waters in Article III, whereby neither party could use or divert boundary waters "affecting the natural level or flow of boundary waters on the other side of the [border]line" without the authority of the International Joint Commission (a six-member investigative and adjudicative body in which the United States and Canada were equally represented by political appointees).

While environmental degradation was not the top priority historically, it was a concern. For instance, by the late 1800s, the Great Lakes and surrounding waterways had become severely polluted as a result of the region's rapid industrialization. As one commentator put it, "the filth and stench in the waters of Great Lakes towns could be seen, tasted, and smelled."[3] This pollution also contributed to public health problems like typhoid and cholera. As a result, the first draft of the treaty included a provision forbidding water pollution that had transboundary consequences. The drafters also vested the international commission that would administer the treaty with "police powers" to enforce this rule, but the U.S. secretary of state objected. He would only agree to an antipollution provision that was limited to the defined boundary waters and had no enforcement mechanism.[4] Thus, the next (and ultimately final) draft of Article IV of the Boundary Waters Treaty simply provided the following: "It is further agreed that the waters herein defined as boundary waters and waters flowing across the boundary shall not be polluted on either side to the injury of health or property on the other." During ratification debates, some U.S. senators opposed even this more limited provision, fearing the growth of an international police power. But Canada won over the reticent senators by assuring them that the provision would be enforced only in "more serious cases."[5]

Since its ratification, the Boundary Waters Treaty of 1909 has provided the foundation for transboundary Canadian-American water management. The legal principle underlying Article IV—that one country's pollution should not harm another country—eventually catalyzed a shift in policy and public focus from water apportionment and navigation to water quality and protection. Beyond North America, this principle is now a central tenet of customary international environmental law, reflected in the United Nations Conference on the Human Environment Stockholm Declaration of 1972 and United Nations Conference on Environment and Development Rio Declaration of 1992.[6]

The rest of this chapter is an admittedly long survey of the legal waterscape of international agreements between the United States and Canada to co-manage their most precious shared resource. Such a survey is necessary for scholars, policymakers, and public audiences. Many have deep concerns over the outcome of contemporary water disputes but might lack sufficient grounding in the legal history that shapes those outcomes. Subsequent chapters in *Border Flows* examine some of the same themes, agreements, and places from different angles. We wish, in effect, to lay the foundation for multiple approaches—a crash course for citizens as well as a current state of the field for policymakers and fellow scholars in other disciplines. We focus most specifically on the vast freshwater system that is the Great Lakes, as that region acted as both catalyst and test case for dramatic and internationally significant legal and diplomatic processes. One cannot make sense of contemporary water diplomacy without understanding the intricate legal history of the Boundary Waters Treaty of 1909 and its Article IV, and these arose in a Great Lakes context. Part 2 of the article provides an overview of the evolving case law of transboundary water management within the United States (again, with a focus on the Great Lakes). This sets up part 3, which surveys the international arena of Canadian-American agreements. A nested analysis is necessary because of the different scales at which water law and management have developed: state and provincial, national, and international.

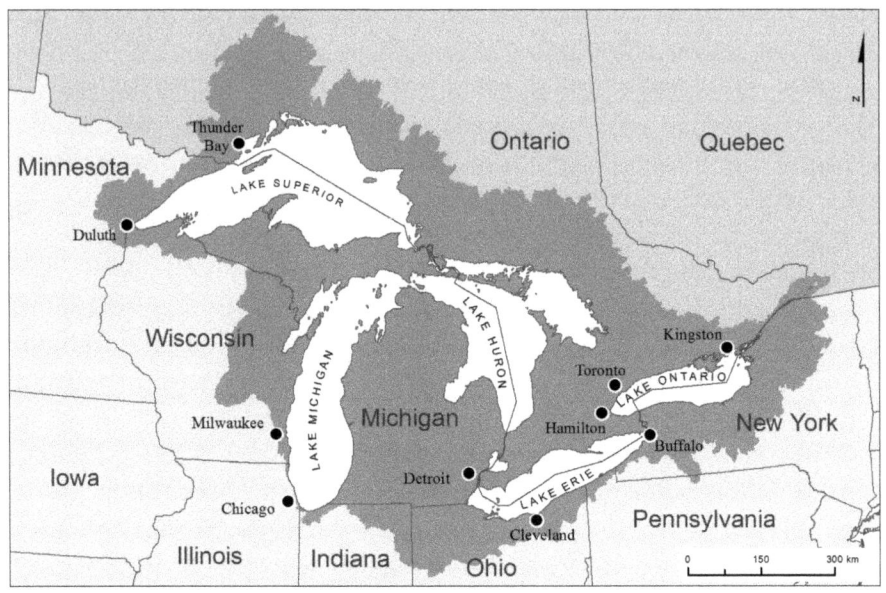

1.1 Great Lakes watershed. Map by Jason Glatz.

II. U.S. Context: Approaches to Transboundary (Interstate) Water Management

U.S.-Canada transboundary water management coevolved with interstate water management within the United States. During the twentieth century, the U.S. federal government—especially the judicial branch—resolved numerous water disputes between American states. The methods and principles that evolved in the United States to resolve interstate conflicts centred primarily on consumptive uses and diversion. The legal areas of equitable apportionment, interstate compacts, and interstate nuisance complaints all developed into major bodies of water case law that established precedents for future conflict resolution. These, in turn, would influence the development of U.S.-Canada water regimes and transboundary environmental law globally.

Interstate Water Allocation through Equitable Apportionment

In the federal system of the United States, states are coequal sovereigns. The U.S. Constitution vests the Supreme Court with jurisdiction over suits between states. The Supreme Court has allocated interstate waters pursuant to this authority with a doctrine it terms "equitable apportionment." Equitable apportionment relies heavily on the specific facts and circumstances of the interstate dispute before the court. It is premised on the states' status as sovereigns; thus, no single state can command an entire transboundary water body to the detriment of other neighbouring riparian states. The doctrine was explained succinctly in the Supreme Court's decision in *Kansas v. Colorado* (1907):

> One cardinal rule, underlying all the relations of the States to each other, is that of equality of right. Each State stands on the same level with all the rest. It can impose its own legislation on no one of the others, and is bound to yield its own views to none. Yet, whenever ... the action of one State reaches through the agency of natural laws into the territory of another State, the question of the extent and the limitations of the rights of the two States becomes a matter of justiciable dispute between them, and this Court is called upon to settle that dispute in such a way as will recognize the equal rights of both and at the same time establish justice between them.[7]

Despite its constitutional jurisdiction over these cases, the Supreme Court has been reluctant to exercise its authority. The court has made clear its desire that such disputes be resolved with the benefit of technical expertise, policy discussions, and cooperation through the interstate compact process, discussed below.

Interstate Water Allocation through Interstate Compacts

Interstate compacts are powerful tools for making law in the United States. A compact is essentially a contract between states entered into through state legislation. Because interstate compacts increase the power of the states at the expense of the federal government, they are subject to congressional approval. Once Congress grants its approval, the interstate compact has the full force and supremacy of federal law. This allows the terms of a compact to be enforced in federal court and prevents states from ignoring their compact duties.[8]

Historically, substantive interstate water compacts have followed one of two models: western and eastern. Western water compacts, such as the Colorado River Compact and the Rio Grande Compact, typically focused on allocating coveted water rights to a shared river among the party-states. Western compacts divided the proverbial pie into pieces, and what each state did (or does) with its piece is beyond the scope of the compact. In other words, these compacts restrict the total amount of water available to each state but do not provide any guidance for managing water withdrawals within the state's allocation.[9]

The two major eastern water compacts, the Delaware River Basin Compact and the Susquehanna River Basin Compact, use a very different approach.[10] They created centralized interstate management authorities comprised of the party-states and federal government. These authorities, termed compact commissions, assumed broad regulatory powers for permitting and managing individual withdrawals and diversions of all waters in the respective river basins. The commissions even set regional standards for discharges of water pollution.[11] This centralized approach had obvious benefits for uniform management of a single resource but required a significant loss of state autonomy.[12]

Regardless of the underlying approach employed by interstate water management compacts, the greatest challenge of allocating interstate waters through compacts has always been the political challenge of getting a compact enacted.[13] Enacting a compact requires uniform ratification by each party-state's legislature, the signature of each party-state's governor, approval by a simple majority in both houses of Congress (which can modify the terms of the compact to protect national interests), and presentment to the president. At any of those stages, the compact process can die. The process also requires all negotiation and compromise up front (before legislative deliberations), as no individual state can unilaterally modify the terms of the compact during ratification. The process for enacting a compact is thus a political obstacle course, and several recent efforts to allocate interstate waters through a compact have failed for political reasons.[14]

Another limitation inherent in the interstate compact approach is Congress's reluctance to include foreign governments in their compacts. In 1968, the Great Lakes states created an interstate compact (the Great Lakes Basin Compact) and attempted to include Canadian provinces as members. However, Congress explicitly refused to consent to the provision that would have allowed Ontario and Quebec to join as parties. Stymied by Congress, Ontario and Quebec eventually became "associate members" of the compact's governing commission, but they still do not enjoy full membership in the compact itself.[15]

The exclusion of Canadian provinces from the Great Lakes Basin Compact was not a major setback to transboundary water management efforts, for the compact did not substantively impact water law or rights in the basin.[16] The functions of the Great Lakes Basin Compact and its Great Lakes Commission were limited to gathering data and making nonbinding recommendations regarding research and cooperative programs. In fact, Joseph Dellapenna has characterized the Great Lakes Basin Compact as typical of the "let's keep in touch" approach used in many interstate water compacts in the eastern United States—and he notes that, "not surprisingly, such a 'let's keep in touch' approach failed to accomplish much toward protecting the biological, chemical, and physical integrity of the rivers and lakes addressed in the particular compacts."[17]

Historical Interstate Nuisance: Example of the Chicago Diversion Litigation

Despite the abundant supply of water in the Great Lakes, the region has not been immune to interstate disputes over water diversions and use. When one state's diversion results in a nuisance to another state, the states can resolve the dispute in the U.S. Supreme Court. A summary of the Chicago diversion litigation (the series of *Wisconsin v. Illinois* cases) provides an example of the role that this approach can play in transboundary water management.

In the early 1880s, Chicago was becoming one of the nation's largest cities when an outbreak of chronic water-borne illnesses threatened the health of residents. The problem, simply put, was that Chicago was disposing of its sewage into Lake Michigan (via the Chicago River), while taking its drinking water from the same source.[18] The solution was a bit more complicated: Chicago built a canal to reverse the flow of the Chicago River, changing its output from Lake Michigan to the Illinois River and ultimately to the Mississippi River. The project was bold, controversial, and successful in both protecting public health and linking the Great Lakes with the Mississippi River. Missouri, now downstream from Chicago's sewage, brought an interstate nuisance action in the Supreme Court, challenging Illinois's discharge of sewage into the Mississippi River system.

Missouri's challenge in the Supreme Court failed for lack of scientific proof of harm and causation, but this did not mark the end of litigation. Due to Chicago's growing population, the city increased its diversions from Lake Michigan by over 200 percent from 1900 to 1924.[19] That year, Wisconsin, Michigan, and New York brought suit in the Supreme Court against Illinois. The complaining states alleged that the Chicago diversion had lowered levels in Lake Michigan, as well as Lakes Huron, Erie, and Ontario, by more than six inches, harming navigation and causing serious injury to the complaining states' citizens and property. Illinois denied that the diversion had caused any such injuries and pointed out that the diversion was necessary.[20]

The Supreme Court appointed former Supreme Court justice and secretary of state Charles Evan Hughes to be special master. As special master, Hughes would review factual evidence and make a report with recommendations. His report found that Chicago's diversion had lowered the levels of Lakes Michigan and Huron by six inches and Lakes Erie and Ontario by five inches, which damaged numerous interests. The court adopted the special master's report, concluding that the reduced lake levels caused the complainant states and their citizens and property owners "great losses."[21]

While generally supporting the claims of the complaining states, the court recognized the public health implications and economic costs that would come from immediately halting the entire Chicago diversion. The court thus followed the special master's recommendation to allow Chicago to complete a phased reduction in the diversion, along with the construction of additional sewage treatment facilities. This did not, however, end the matter. Litigation in the Supreme Court continued over several decades regarding Illinois's compliance with the diversion reduction schedule and the amount of water allowed for domestic pumping.[22]

What is most notable about the case is the Supreme Court's recognition that Great Lakes water management was less an issue of apportionment of water rights and more an issue of defining the bounds of the states' shared reasonable-use duties. While the relatively short opinions do not advance this proposition directly, the leading Chicago diversion opinion was authored by Chief Justice William Howard Taft, the former U.S. president whose administration had negotiated the Boundary Waters Treaty of 1909 between the United States and Canada. Taft was an Ohioan, and he may have instinctively appreciated both the abundance of Great Lakes water that made allocation unnecessary and the shared importance of the resource between two countries and eight states that made protection of all of its values (including navigation, drinking supply, fishing, recreation, and property enhancement) critical.

Speculation about the court's motivations aside, the Chicago diversion litigation leaves two key legacies in shaping the law of the Great Lakes. First, the Chicago diversion, authorized at 3,200 cubic feet per second (90.6 cubic metres per second), remains the largest diversion of Great Lakes water out of the basin. Second, while the court's decisions stopped short of an absolute prohibition on diversions, they demonstrate a general preference for protecting the interests of other states and preserving the integrity of the Great Lakes system. Both of these legacies are an important part of the evolution of Great Lakes transboundary water management.

Contemporary Interstate Nuisance: Asian Carp and the Chicago Diversion Today

In light of the Chicago diversion's contentious past, it should come as little surprise that it is once again at the heart of a major legal dispute. This time, the issue is not what Chicago sends downstream but what might swim upstream through the diversion and into the Great Lakes: Asian carp. The term "Asian carp" refers to two non-native species of fish, Bighead and Silver carp. The carp were introduced into U.S. waters by the government and the private sector in hopes that the filter-feeding fish would prove useful for cleaning suspended particles and algae out of dirty ponds.[23] The carp were useful in this regard, but their efficient (and voracious) feeding habits also made them dangerous to native species. Thus, when these fish escaped their containment ponds in the southern United States, they began to wreak havoc in the Mississippi River. Due to their size (up to 100 pounds/45 kilograms), large appetites, and active spawning, Asian carp can outcompete native species. The preferred food of the carp is plankton—and since most native fish species also depend on this food source either directly or indirectly, the Asian carp's rapid consumption of it can truly decimate native species. As one journalist writes, the fish are "so thick in some stretches of [the Mississippi] River that they literally roil the water."[24]

The Asian carp's invasion of the Mississippi began in the South, and they have been steadily moving up the river. Thus, the Great Lakes states fear that the fish will enter the lakes through the Chicago diversion and do irreversible harm to the ecosystem. In 2009, Michigan, Wisconsin, Minnesota, Ohio, and Pennsylvania asked the Supreme Court to reopen its decree in *Wisconsin v. Illinois* in order to close the Chicago canal. Unfortunately, the court declined the states' request, leaving them to seek relief in the lower courts. The states then filed suit in federal district court, alleging that the U.S. Army Corps of Engineers and the City of Chicago had created a public nuisance by allowing the Asian carp to threaten the waters and fisheries of the Great Lakes. The litigation has worked its way through several rounds of court decisions, and while the presiding judges often recognize the potential catastrophic harm of an Asian carp invasion, the courts have consistently ruled against the plaintiff states.

With this lawsuit somewhat stalled in federal court, one might hope for Congress or the president to act, but that does not seem likely. Congressional proposals (the so-called CARP Act) have gone nowhere, and President Obama has declined to become directly involved. By failing to address this problem, the federal government has not only put the Great Lakes ecosystem at risk but, as we will see next, ignored the United States' obligations to Canada under the Boundary Waters Treaty and other international agreements.

III. Binational Context: International Agreements on Water Management

Ambitious but Unenforceable: International Agreements Prior to the Great Lakes–St. Lawrence River Basin Compact and Agreement

THE GREAT LAKES WATER QUALITY AGREEMENT

In the 1960s, citizens and scientists became increasingly alarmed about water pollution in the Great Lakes. In response to these concerns, the United States and Canada issued a joint reference to the International Joint Commission in 1964 regarding pollution in Lakes Erie and Ontario. It took the commission nearly seven years, but in 1970 it issued a report recommending new water quality control programs and the need for a new agreement for cooperative action on pollution. Two years of negotiations followed, and in 1972, Prime Minister Pierre Trudeau and President Richard Nixon signed the Great Lakes Water Quality Agreement.[25]

The 1972 signing of the Great Lakes Water Quality Agreement is emblematic of the historic shift in the countries' water relations. Long gone were the days when access and navigation were primary concerns; water quality had moved to the fore. However, the agreement also typifies the countries' practice of entering into ambitious but unenforceable agreements: implementation of the agreement was hobbled by its subtreaty status and lack of enforcement provisions.

As stated in the 1972 Great Lakes Water Quality Agreement, the two countries were "seriously concerned about the grave deterioration of water quality on each side of the boundary to an extent that is causing injury to health and property on the other side." The agreement set forth general and specific water quality objectives, provided for programs directed toward the achievement of the water quality objectives, and defined the powers, responsibilities, and functions of the International Joint Commission. However, the agreement gave primary responsibility for achieving its objectives to the two federal governments (specifically, the U.S. Environmental Protection Agency and Environment Canada), not the International Joint Commission.

Initially, the 1972 Great Lakes Water Quality Agreement focused on phosphorous pollution. As both countries were making progress on this front, however, new threats emerged. Scientists uncovered risks from previously unknown persistent organic chemicals that "were already affecting the health of wildlife and could be a threat to human health."[26] In response, the United States and Canada amended the agreement in 1978 with a new, more expansive purpose:

> to restore and maintain the chemical, physical, and biological integrity of the waters of the Great Lakes Basin Ecosystem. In order to achieve this purpose, the Parties agree to make a maximum effort to . . . eliminate or reduce to the maximum extent practicable the discharge of pollutants into the Great Lakes System. Consistent with the provisions of this Agreement, it is the policy of the Parties that [t]he discharge of toxic substances in toxic amounts be prohibited and the discharge of any or all persistent toxic substances be virtually eliminated.[27]

Nine years later, the parties again revised the agreement, signing the 1987 Protocol, which focused on critical pollutants and drew upon broad local community involvement. Canada and the United States expanded the Great Lakes Water Quality Agreement yet again in 2012, with another protocol, in order to address a number of new areas of concern such as increased phosphorous loadings, harmful vessel discharges, invasive species, habitat degradation, and climate change impacts.[28]

As previously mentioned, the effectiveness of the Great Lakes Water Quality Agreement was limited by its subtreaty status and its lack of enforcement provisions. Courts in the United States have refused to enforce the agreement domestically for these reasons.[29] However, this is not to say that the agreement did not effect real, positive change. One of the agreement's major achievements was to give citizens an increased role in shaping policy to address transboundary pollution in the Great Lakes. Prior to the agreement, the International Joint Commission had held public hearings on specific topics but essentially conducted its business in private. In the face of increased citizen pressure resulting from the growing environmental movement, the agreement opened the International Joint Commission up to the public. The increased public involvement in the implementation of the agreement became one of its most significant results. The International Joint Commission emphasized this point in its ninth biennial report:

> The public's right and ability to participate in governmental processes and environmental decisions that affect it must be sustained and nurtured. ... The Commission urges governments to continue to effectively communicate information that the public needs and has come to expect, and to provide opportunities to be held publicly accountable for their work under the Agreement.[30]

To some extent, the increased opportunity for public participation in decision making compensates for the failure of the Great Lakes Water Quality Agreement to contain specific enforcement provisions. With increased public participation comes increased accountability on the part of the two federal governments to comply with their joint responsibilities under the agreement. Equally important, the agreement has helped create an informed and engaged citizenry on both sides of the border, which has led to improved transnational protection of the Great Lakes.

THE GREAT LAKES CHARTER OF 1985

Like the Great Lakes Water Quality Agreement, the Great Lakes Charter is an international agreement with laudable but unenforceable goals. The charter was signed by all of the Great Lakes states and provinces, and while it is only a good-faith agreement, it contains individual commitments and a cooperative process for Great Lakes water management that would have been tremendously valuable if fully implemented. The problem with such "handshake agreements" is that they are not sanctioned by the U.S. Constitution and thus have limited legal value. The U.S. Constitution provides a mechanism for approved interstate compacts to have the full force of federal law, but no similar mechanism exists for informal agreements such as the Great Lakes Charter. Thus, the charter was an aspirational policy with no legal effect.

Within this informal framework, the Great Lakes Charter integrates three key components: (1) the commitment of the states and provinces to manage and regulate new consumptive uses or diversions of Great Lakes water greater than 2,000,000 gallons per day (7,570,000 litres per day); (2) the commitment of the states and provinces to gather and report comparable information on all new or increased withdrawals of Great Lakes water greater than 100,000 gallons per day (379,000 litres per day); and (3) the prior notice and consultation procedure with all of the states and provinces for new or increased consumptive uses or diversions of Great Lakes water greater than 5,000,000 gallons per day (18,900,000 litres per day).[31] If a state or province fails to meet its regulatory obligations—specifically, its commitment to regulate new uses of Great Lakes water exceeding 2,000,000 gallons per day—it will lose its right to participate in the prior notice and consultation process.

The charter's success is open to debate. On the one hand, the states and provinces largely met their information and reporting commitments. All of them enacted authority to gather and report comparable information on new or increased withdrawals of Great Lakes water over 100,000 gallons per day (379,000 litres per day). But on the other hand, not all states met the regulatory commitment contained in the charter, and some of their reporting programs failed to supply complete and reliable data on Great Lakes water withdrawals.

The weakness that permeates the charter's regime is encapsulated by its prior notice and consultation procedure. This procedure can be fairly characterized as a more specific version of "let's keep in touch."[32] It requires the state or province considering issuance of a permit for a new or increased consumptive use or diversion greater than 5,000,000 gallons per day (18,900,000 litres per day) to first notify the offices of the other governors and premiers, as well as the International Joint Commission. The issuing state or province will then "solicit and carefully consider the comments and concerns of the other Great Lakes States and Provinces"; if necessary, a "consultation process" is initiated to "seek and provide mutually agreeable recommendations to the permitting State or Province."[33] However, if this extensive consultation process proves fruitless, or if one state persists despite the objections of others, the Great Lakes Charter does not provide an enforcement mechanism or remedy. This shortcoming is due to the charter's nonlegal status. If the charter's terms had been incorporated into a binding and enforceable compact, it could have played a major role in achieving comprehensive water management of the Great Lakes. Instead, it has merely provided a framework for cooperation among the parties as a foundation for future efforts.

Annex 2001 to the Great Lakes Charter

In 2001, the Great Lakes governors and premiers signed an Annex to the Great Lakes Charter Agreement (commonly known as "Annex 2001"). While nonbinding—just like the Great Lakes Charter to which it was appended—the commitments and principles of Annex 2001 ultimately led to the creation of binding international authority: the Great Lakes–St. Lawrence River Basin Water Resources Compact and Agreement. Because the content of Annex 2001 helped to shape this seminal authority, it deserves some examination here.

Essentially, Annex 2001 reaffirmed the commitments in the Great Lakes Charter and contained a new commitment to develop an "enhanced water management system" that "protects, conserves, restores, and *improves* the Waters and Water-Dependent" resources of the Basin (emphasis mine). Annex 2001 also committed the governors and premiers to "develop[ing] and implement[ing] a new common, resource-based conservation standard" that would apply to new and increased water withdrawals from Great Lakes Basin waters.[34] To establish the new standard governing water withdrawals, Annex 2001 proposes four guiding principles:

- preventing or minimizing [Great Lakes] Basin water loss through return flow and implementation of environmentally sound water conservation measures;
- no significant adverse individual or cumulative impacts to the quantity or quality of the Waters and Water-Dependent Natural Resources of the Great Lakes Basin;
- an improvement to the Waters and Water-Dependent Natural Resources of the Great Lakes Basin; and
- compliance with the applicable local, federal, and international laws and treaties.[35]

These goals and principles created much excitement throughout the Great Lakes region. The concept of return flow—requiring diverted water to be returned to its source—could protect the lakes from being depleted by exports. Establishing water conservation ethics in a region accustomed to abundance would be a major step toward sustainable water use. The enlarged scope of the agreement also represents an important advancement. By encompassing *all* water withdrawals, not just diversions, Annex 2001 recognizes the effects of the basin's own water uses.

Yet the most interesting and promising principle was the improvement standard. Most environmental statutes are designed to protect the environment from increased harms, which often leads to a slow but steady loss of natural resources. The improvement principle would change the existing paradigm. It is premised on the notion that limiting harm to an already damaged system is insufficient. Users of Great Lakes water—the region's most valuable public resource—must leave the resource better than they found it. The principle even holds the potential to change public attitudes toward water withdrawal projects. As individual projects came to be seen for their environmental benefits and not simply their externalized costs, new projects would drive restoration of the Great Lakes ecosystem. However, as with any new policy proposal, the improvement concept raises thorny, practical questions: What exactly is an improvement? And how much improvement would be enough to satisfy regulators? The difficulty in answering these questions eventually undermined implementation of the improvement concept.

While the effectiveness of Annex 2001 was limited by the fact that it was a nonbinding agreement, it nevertheless resulted in vital water management dialogue. In fact, the importance of the Great Lakes Charter and of Annex 2001 lies not in the immediate effects they produced, but in what they eventually led to: the region's governors and premiers agreed in Annex 2001 to negotiate and draft a common decision-making standard. The product of this collective commitment was the Great Lakes–St. Lawrence River Basin Water Resources Compact and the companion Great Lakes–St. Lawrence River Basin Sustainable Water Resources Agreement, released in late 2005.

Creating Enforceable Authority: Domestic Legislation and the Run Up to the Great Lakes–St. Lawrence River Basin Water Resources Compact and Agreement

While the informal international agreements discussed above have limited practical impact in the United States, domestic legislation does have a tangible effect on Great Lakes water management. In 1986, Congress enacted section 1109 of the Water Resources Development Act (WRDA 1986), which provides that

> no water shall be diverted or exported from any portion of the Great Lakes within the United States, or from any tributary within the United States of any of the Great Lakes, for use outside the Great Lakes basin unless such diversion or export is approved by the Governor of each of the Great Lake [sic] States.[36]

Thus, the statute requires the unanimous approval of all governors for any diversion outside of the Great Lakes Basin.

While the 1986 act is remarkable as a clear statement of Congress's intent to leave Great Lakes water management to the states, it suffers from numerous limitations and flaws that have undermined its value in terms of both protection and process. For example, the statute contains no standards to guide the governors in deciding whether to approve or deny a proposed diversion. Nor does it provide any judicial remedy—even for another Great Lakes state—to challenge a governor's decision. From a citizens' perspective, the statute is fatally limited by its lack of a private right of action to enforce compliance. These omissions can be explained by understanding the threat that the statute was intended to address. When the law was passed, the Great Lakes states shared a common concern about the threat of water diversions to other parts of the country. The federal statute was thus meant to create a barrier to water diversions that would harm the region as a whole. In addition to these problems, WRDA 1986 is also limited by its narrow scope of coverage: it applies only to diversions out of the basin—not to in-basin consumptive uses—and it does not apply to ground water. This is a major gap, as ground water comprises over 15 percent of the total water supply in the Great Lakes Basin.[37]

Perhaps the most problematic aspect of the act is the power discrepancy it sets up. In every Great Lakes state except Michigan, a significant portion (usually a majority) of its land and population lies outside of the watershed line. Michigan, in contrast, sits entirely within the Great Lakes Basin; thus, Michigan's governor could unilaterally stop any other Great Lakes state from diverting water within its own borders—but outside the basin—without worrying about payback from that state in the form of a veto of its own. This exact scenario has already played out, when the town of Lowell, Indiana, sought a diversion from Lake Michigan to replace local water supplies and the governor of Michigan alone blocked the diversion.[38] Conflicts like these make the federal statute politically vulnerable to repeal by Congress.

In light of the shortcomings discussed above, Congress later encouraged the states to be more proactive and comprehensive in how they used their authority. Congress amended the 1986 version of WRDA in 2000 to urge the states, "in consultation with the Provinces of Ontario and Quebec," to develop a common standard for making decisions regarding "the withdrawal and use of water from the Great Lakes Basin."[39] Congress did not go so far as to condition the states' veto power on the success of implementing a standards-based management mechanism. Nor did it need to. The states' recognition of the flaws in the WRDA 1986 system was evidenced by their subsequent amendment to the Great Lakes Charter: the Great Lakes Charter Annex of 2001. As previously discussed, Annex 2001 was an intermediary step in the development of binding law (in the form of an interstate compact and analogous international agreement). It allowed state and provincial officials to articulate and enshrine common standards in a nonbinding context. And when the states and provinces were ready to formalize those standards, they made them binding in the Great Lakes–St. Lawrence River Basin Water Resources Compact and Agreement, discussed below.

The Great Lakes–St. Lawrence River Basin Sustainable Water Resources Agreement and Great Lakes–St. Lawrence River Basin Water Resources Compact

The Great Lakes–St. Lawrence River Basin Sustainable Water Resources Agreement (Great Lakes Agreement) and the Great Lakes–St. Lawrence

River Basin Water Resource Compact (Great Lakes Compact) represent a tremendous advancement in both the substantive legal rules for water use in the Great Lakes Basin and the cooperative management among the states and provinces that share this resource. The innovation of the Great Lakes Agreement and Compact was to cooperatively establish binding principles for sustainable water use and then leave administration of those principles to the individual states and provinces. Thus, the Great Lakes Agreement and Compact create an enforceable transboundary water management regime that still respects state autonomy and sovereignty.

Here we eschew the particulars in order to focus on the Great Lakes Compact as a new model for interstate water management and the Great Lakes Agreement as a new model for subtreaty international cooperation. However, to best understand the interstate and international management structures, it is important to first note the compact's common standards (referred to as the "decision-making standard") for new or increased water withdrawals of Great Lakes Basin water. The standard mandates that all withdrawals will

(1) return any leftover water to the source watershed;

(2) not cause any significant adverse impacts to the quantity or quality of the waters of the Great Lakes Basin;

(3) incorporate specific environmental and economic water conservation measures;

(4) comply with all applicable law and interstate and international agreements, including the Boundary Waters Treaty of 1909; and

(5) pass a reasonable-use balancing test.[40]

The fourth requirement, which requires compliance with all applicable laws, agreements, and treaties, has special significance. As discussed above, the key treaties and agreements between the United States and Canada regarding water management have suffered from a lack of enforceability and private causes of action. The Boundary Waters Treaty of 1909, expressly referenced in criterion 4, lacks any judicial review provisions or enforcement mechanisms short of Senate action. Similarly, the

Great Lakes Water Quality Agreement cannot be enforced in domestic court proceedings.[41] The Great Lakes Compact does much to remedy this problem. By requiring compliance with the Boundary Waters Treaty and the Great Lakes–St. Lawrence River Basin Sustainable Water Resources Agreement, the Great Lakes Compact elevates their terms to enforceable standards for new or increased water withdrawals. This feature of the Great Lakes Compact sets it apart from previous attempts to create international water management schemes.

It should also be noted that while the improvement concept did not become a requirement for new or increased water withdrawals, the concept was incorporated into the decision-making standard. One of the factors under criterion 5's reasonable-use balancing test allows consideration of proposals to restore "hydrologic conditions and functions" in the source watershed. Thus, improvements can be considered in the overall determination regarding the reasonableness of the proposed use. Water users can propose an improvement as a way of making their water use more compatible with the resources and limitations in the watershed.

State-Provincial Cooperation under the Great Lakes Agreement

State-provincial cooperation has been a regional goal for decades, but as the preceding sections note, drafting enforceable international agreements has proven difficult. For constitutional and political reasons, including the Canadian provinces in the Great Lakes Compact could have made the compact vulnerable to political and legal challenges. In order to steer clear of these problems while still achieving the goal of state-provincial cooperation, the Great Lakes governors and premiers developed the Great Lakes Agreement as a nonbinding, good-faith agreement that encompassed the provinces of Ontario and Quebec. This dual structure creates a legally and politically acceptable mechanism for cooperation with Canadian provinces.

The fundamental legal and political concerns raised by state cooperation with Canadian provinces are founded on the U.S. Constitution and on principles of federalism. The Compact Clause of the Constitution provides that "no State shall, without the Consent of Congress . . . enter into any Agreement or Compact with another State, or with a foreign Power." The same constitutional section also provides that "no State shall enter into any Treaty, Alliance, or Confederation."[42] Thus, the prohibition on states entering into a "Treaty, Alliance, or Confederation" is absolute, while the prohibition on states entering into an "Agreement or Compact," even with a foreign government, is limited only by the political decision of Congress to consent.

The question of what constitutes a "Treaty, Alliance, or Confederation" versus an "Agreement or Compact" raises constitutional questions of separation of powers and federalism. In the case of the Great Lakes, Congress has already exercised its treaty powers in this area through the Boundary Waters Treaty of 1909, and it could view any attempt by the states to enter into a binding management arrangement with the provinces on this subject as an impermissible treaty. Further, even if Congress viewed such an arrangement with the provinces as a compact rather than a treaty, it would likely reject either the entire compact or the inclusion of the provinces, as it did when the Great Lakes states proposed including Canadian provinces in the original Great Lakes Basin Compact over fifty years ago.

Despite these thorny legal issues, Congress has articulated its desire for the states to work "in consultation with" the provinces to develop a Great Lakes water management agreement.[43] Thus, the elegant solution developed by the Great Lakes states was to create a binding compact among themselves and a nonbinding agreement, consisting of the same terms, between them and the Canadian provinces. This arrangement apparently proved suitable to Congress; both the Senate and House of Representatives endorsed the compact in 2008, and President Bush signed it into law.

The Great Lakes Compact also incorporates the provinces through the Great Lakes Agreement's "Regional Body," comprised of representatives from each state and province. The Regional Body's authority could be fairly described as procedural rather than substantive and its determinations as advisory rather than final. The Regional Body's role includes notice, consultation, and public participation, but stops short of final decision making. The parties and Compact Council need only "consider" (but are not obliged to follow) the Regional Body's findings. The process thus avoids infringing on federal treaty powers while still giving the provinces an evaluative and procedural role that may prove useful for affecting major decisions.

Interstate Management under the Great Lakes Compact

As discussed above, the Great Lakes Compact includes only the American states, not the Canadian provinces. It creates two separate approaches to managing new or increased water withdrawals in the Great Lakes states. The differentiation is based almost entirely on whether the water is used inside or outside of the Great Lakes Basin surface watershed boundary. Water use inside of the Great Lakes Basin is managed by each state individually, with limited advisory input from other states for very large consumptive uses. Water uses outside of the basin (diversions) are subject to a spectrum of collective rules, including a general prohibition on most diversions.

The Great Lakes Compact requires the states to "create a program for the management and regulation of New or Increased Withdrawals [for use within the basin] . . . by adopting and implementing Measures consistent with the Decision-Making Standard" within five years. The states must make reports to the Compact Council, which is comprised of the governor of each party-state, regarding their implementation. The Compact Council then reviews the state programs and makes findings regarding their adequacy and compliance with the Great Lakes Compact. The states must further develop and promote water conservation programs and a water resources inventory.

While management of in-basin uses is left to the states, diversions of water outside the Great Lakes Basin are generally prohibited. Exceptions to this general ban are made for intrabasin diversions (lake-to-lake transfers within the entire Great Lakes Basin) and diversions to communities that straddle the basin divide, but these exceptions are not absolute. Even if a diversion qualifies under one of the exceptions, it is usually subject to the unanimous approval of all eight Great Lakes governors voting as the Compact Council.

The compact envisions a rather broad enforcement scheme. It gives the governors' Compact Council the ability to conduct special investigations and institute court actions, including enforcement. Crucially, ordinary citizens also have enforcement power. Citizens can bring legal actions in the relevant state court against any water user that has failed to obtain a required permit or is violating the prohibition on diversions. These broad enforcement provisions are complemented by similarly progressive public participation provisions. As with the minimum substantive decision-making standard, the compact provides minimum procedural public process requirements for the party-states and Compact Council. These include public notification of applications with a reasonable time for comments, public accessibility to all documents (including comments), standards for determining whether to hold a public meeting or hearing on an application, and open public inspection of all records relating to decisions.

The Great Lakes Compact has the potential to significantly reshape water management in the region. In large part, this potential for change derives from the compact's innovative design: it incorporates formerly unenforceable international agreements, provides for a common decision-making standard, and involves the Canadian provinces in regional water management. Furthermore, its broad enforcement provisions ensure that these promising reforms will have a real effect on the ways in which we use Great Lakes water.

IV. CONCLUSION

More fresh water is at stake in the management of the Great Lakes than of any other single freshwater resource in the world. As demand for fresh water grows worldwide, transboundary waters will be under increasing pressure. This pressure will lead to new disputes over water rights and usage. Protecting and managing the Great Lakes has been an ongoing exercise in cooperation among multiple jurisdictions and levels of government, with numerous and potentially overlapping legal regimes. During the past century, most transboundary water rights disputes were resolved by allocating access and use among competing parties. This approach did little to ensure protection of the transboundary freshwater ecosystem. It also did little to ensure that the water was used sustainably to avoid depleting our natural wealth for future generations. More recently, transboundary water management has focused on environmental protection and sustainable use. This shift in emphasis resulted in part from a growing role for a concerned public in managing transboundary waters. Examining agreements between the United States and Canada demonstrates the evolution of transboundary water management from simple allocation and dispute resolution to cooperative multilevel conservation of a shared resource. Transboundary water management also continues to evolve toward environmental protection and active citizen participation. These parallel developments provide reason for optimism as new threats such as climate change put further pressure on freshwater resources in the twenty-first century.

Notes

1. Jennifer Woodward, "International Pollution Control: The United States and Canada—The International Joint Commission," *New York Law School Journal of International and Comparative Law* 9 (1988): 326.
2. F.J.E. Jordan, "Great Lakes Pollution: A Framework for Action," *Ottawa Law Review* 5 (1971): 65–83.
3. Phil Weller, *Fresh Water Seas: Saving the Great Lakes* (Toronto: Between the Lines, 1990), 59.
4. Jordan, "Great Lakes Pollution," 67.
5. Ibid., 67–68.
6. Noah D. Hall, "Transboundary Pollution: Harmonizing International and Domestic Law," *University of Michigan Journal of Law Reform* 40 (2007): 699–700.
7. Kansas v. Colorado, 206 U.S. 46, 97–98 (1907).
8. Noah D. Hall, "Toward a New Horizontal Federalism: Interstate Water Management in the Great Lakes Region," *Colorado Law Review* 77 (2006): 410–11.
9. Ibid., 411.
10. Joseph W. Dellapenna, "Interstate Struggles over Rivers: The Southeastern States and the Struggle over the 'Hooch,'" *NYU Environmental Law Journal* 12 (2005): 831–32.
11. Ibid., 845.
12. Hall, "New Horizontal Federalism," 412.
13. Ibid., 454.
14. Ibid.
15. Ibid., 423n101.
16. Ibid., 423.
17. Dellapenna, "Interstate Struggles," 839.
18. Hall, "New Horizontal Federalism," 420.
19. Wisconsin v. Illinois, 278 U.S. 367, 417 (1929).
20. Ibid, 401.
21. Ibid., 409.
22. Wisconsin v. Illinois, 289 U.S. 395 (1933); Wisconsin v. Illinois, 388 U.S. 426 (1967); Wisconsin v. Illinois, 449 U.S. 48 (1980).
23. Dan Egan, "Chaos Uncorked," *Milwaukee Journal Sentinel*, October 15, 2006.
24. Ibid.
25. Great Lakes Water Quality Agreement, U.S.-Can., Apr. 15, 1972, 23 U.S.T. 301.
26. Lee Botts and Paul Muldoon, *Evolution of the Great Lakes Water Quality Agreement* (East Lansing: Michigan State University Press, 2005), 27.

27. Great Lakes Water Quality Agreement of 1978, 30 U.S.T. 1383 (Nov. 22, 1978).

28. Great Lakes Water Quality Agreement, 2012 Protocol, Great Lakes Water Quality Agreement of 1987, T.I.A.S. No. 11551 (Nov. 18, 1987).

29. Lake Erie Alliance for the Protection of Coastal Corridor v. U.S. Army Corps of Engineers, 526 F. Supp. 1063, 1077, W.D. PA (1981); American Iron and Steel Institute v. Environmental Protection Agency, 115 F.3d 979, 1001, D.C. Cir. (1996).

30. International Joint Commission, *Ninth Biennial Report on Great Lakes Water Quality: Perspective and Orientation*, July 1998, http://www.ijc.org/php/publications/html/9br/fs6.html.

31. Council of Great Lakes Governors (CGLG), *The Great Lakes Charter: Principles for the Management of Great Lakes Water Resources*, February 11, 1985, http://www.greatlakes.org/Document.Doc?id=148.

32. Dellapenna, "Interstate Struggles," 838.

33. CGLG, *Great Lakes Charter*, 4.

34. CGLG, *The Great Lakes Charter Annex: A Supplementary Agreement to the Great Lakes Charter*, June 18, 2001, p. 1, http://www.cglslgp.org/media/1369/greatlakescharterannex.pdf.

35. Ibid., 2.

36. Water Resources Development Act of 1986, 42 U.S.C. § 1962d-20 (amended 2000).

37. N.G. Grannemann et al., *The Importance of Ground Water in the Great Lakes Region*, Water-Resources Investigations Report No. 00-4008 (Lansing, MI: USGS, 2000), http://pubs.usgs.gov/wri/wri00-4008/pdf/WRIR_00-4008.pdf.

38. Peter Annin, *The Great Lakes Water Wars* (Washington, DC: Island, 2006), 139–53.

39. Water Resources Development Act of 1986 (amended 2000).

40. Great Lakes–St. Lawrence River Basin Water Resources Compact, Pub. L. No. 110-342, 122 Stat. 3739 (2005), http://www.greatlakeslaw.org/files/public_law_110_342.pdf.

41. *Lake Erie Alliance v. USACE*, 526 F. Supp. 1063, 1077 (1981); *Am. Iron & Steel Inst. v. EPA*, 115 F.3d 979, 1001 (1996).

42. U.S. Const. art. I, § 10, cl. 3.

43. Water Resources Development Act, Pub. L. No. 106-541, § 504, 114 Stat. 2572, 2644–45 (2000).

Treaties, Wars, and Salish Sea Watersheds: The Constructed Boundaries of Water Governance

EMMA S. NORMAN AND ALICE COHEN

I. Introduction

North America is a continent of meandering rivers, jagged coastlines, glaciated mountains, underground aquifers, and freshwater lakes. Water comes in different forms above and below ground, but the political systems that manage water are rarely hydrologically based. Rather, water management regimes emerge from societal administrative and jurisdictional units constructed unevenly over time. These socio-hydro "constructions" are nested in jurisdictional scale. Federal governments, provinces, states, municipalities, tribes, and bands—all may play a part in managing the water of a given place. These administrative authorities will have different roles and mandates, or different boundaries. Hence the water systems themselves may well be fragmented and contested, and their history will surely involve conflict and accommodation.

The international border between Canada and the United States provides a unique vantage point for analyzing water governance and especially for understanding complex, layered management systems. The international border affords the opportunity to investigate how nested scales of governance operate on the ground. In this chapter, we analyze the evolution of water governance along the Canada-U.S. border by overlaying two kinds of boundaries (our principle case studies) on top of the state-based political boundaries that conventionally define the international border. The first overlay is the traditional territory of Indigenous peoples (First Nations and tribes). We focus on the Coast Salish indigenous communities of the Pacific Northwest. The Coast Salish, who span and predate the Canada-U.S. border, have a long and sustained relationship to the Salish Sea ecosystem. As Coast Salish culture is grounded in this connection to place, the demarcation of a foreign, policed border has had tremendous impacts on its people. Overcoming the border has also been a source of cultural revitalization and unity between the Coast Salish tribes and First Nations. The second overlay consists of the physical hydrologic boundaries that characterize the flow of water. We focus on the "watershed" of contemporary environmental resource management, seemingly natural and apolitical, but with deeply political implications. Finally, we consider the politics of future decision making at "new" scales.[1]

We aim to make visible the social, ecological, and political consequences of bordering. In so doing, we argue that for successful shared water governance along the border, scholars, policymakers, and different public stakeholders must account for borders of all kinds—not simply the international boundary between nation-states.

II. Defining "The Border": A Process of Social Construction

For many people, where Canada begins or where the United States begins is unquestioned. People crossing through border patrols between the two countries might feel inconvenienced when contending with security, regulations, or long lines. But these are individual experiences rather than a collective national awareness of the border as its own space. Defining a border requires an inherent acceptance of a line drawn in time. Over time, this line becomes reified, entrenched, and defined into separate national identities, cultures, and political regimes. The line itself is a space. Policies and practices built around this linear space impact governance in every conceivable way: they form the boundary between domestic and foreign

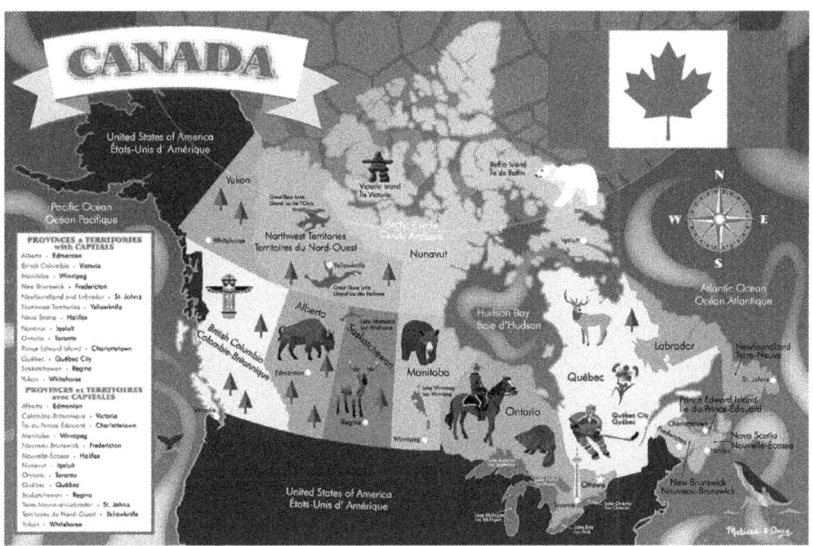

2.1 Constructing identity through maps: Canada as a separate place. Courtesy of Melissa & Doug.

2.2 Constructing identity through maps: The United States as a separate place. Courtesy of Melissa & Doug.

2.3 The waterways of the Salish Sea and surrounding basin. Courtesy of Stefan Freelan.

policy, between who is a citizen and who is not, between import and export. Most importantly, these lines deeply influence management of the natural resources that constitute a border—land, forests, water—or that move across it, as wildlife and water do. Yet those dimensions of a border are invisible on many maps.

In school, political maps emphasize national identities, depicting states or provinces in colorful detail, but fading "neighbouring countries" into a single neutral blank. Such cartographic constructions separating (and excluding) the neighbour country prevent, in effect, a public imagination. This default "discourse" (colorful detail/neutral blank) entrenches national identity at a young age. So it is no surprise that, for most Americans and Canadians, national boundaries—and the border itself—remain uncontested, unproblematized, and relatively unconsidered.

Cartographic constructions like maps 1 and 2 reinforce identities and shape allegiances. Therefore, they participate in the creation and privilege of some kinds of political boundaries and spatial relationships, while rendering others invisible. As David B. Knight so eloquently states, "Territory is not; it becomes, for territory itself is passive, and it is human belief and actions that give territory meaning."[2] This quote holds particular resonance for Indigenous communities in North America, who are invisible in maps 1 and 2. The quote also resonates for those concerned with still another kind of boundary: the watershed. Watersheds may seem like "natural" or "apolitical" boundaries on the land itself, but they too are social constructions (as we will soon demonstrate).

III. Sharing a Continent: Indigenous Space and Governing Water

Drawing Lines, Treaty by Treaty

Pinpointing the historical moment when territorial boundaries became conflated with citizenship and nationhood is a challenge. Scholars of international relations often point to the Peace of Westphalia (1648) as such a moment.[3] The "Westphalian system" marks a transition away from city-states and toward governments of larger territorial units—i.e., the nation compromises the territory and the people inhabit the land. The 1783 Treaty of Paris is one example of this transition. The treaty (which ended the war between Great Britain and the American colonies) defined much of today's Canada-U.S. international border. It made the 45th parallel the boundary between Lower Canada (Quebec) and New York State (including Vermont). The St. Lawrence River and the Great Lakes became the boundary between Upper Canada and the United States. For ten years the delineation was largely theoretical because the territory was rugged forest with no clear lines on the physical landscape. The subsequent Jay Treaty of 1794 established the International Boundary Commission to articulate the precise location of the border. The commission surveyed and demarcated the 45th parallel—a task that proved difficult given the terrain, the inclement weather, and the survey methods of the time.[4]

Westward settlement led to the Convention of 1818, which established the boundary along the 49th parallel between Lake of the Woods (in what is now Minnesota) and the Rocky Mountains (then known as the Stony Mountains). To the west of the Rocky Mountains the convention was more ambiguous, calling for "co-custody" of the territory that American settlers called Oregon Country and that the Hudson's Bay Company called the Columbia Department or Columbia District. During this period of co-custody, settlers could claim land on behalf of American or British interests.[5]

Not surprisingly, co-custody proved difficult in practice. Negotiations—and posturing—continued until U.S. President Polk and the British foreign secretary Lord Aberdeen finally agreed to demarcate British and American interests to the north and south of the 49th parallel, respectively.

During the years of co-custody, the United States made overtures of expanding its claim to the territory upwards to the 54th parallel (with President Polk running on the campaign promise "Fifty-four forty or fight!"). However, the Mexican-American War tempered the appetite for expansion and the two parties eventually settled their claims through the signing of the 1846 Oregon Treaty.[6]

Land south of the 49th parallel became the Oregon Territory, with a separate Washington Territory carved out in 1853. Land north of the 49th parallel remained unorganized until the new Colony of British Columbia was established in 1858, prompted by the Fraser Canyon Gold Rush and fears of American expansionism. In 1866, Vancouver Island and British Columbia amalgamated; in 1871, the Colony of British Columbia joined

2.4 Billy Frank Jr. (1931–2014). Photo by Mariah Dodd.

Canada. Thus, the 49th parallel and marine boundaries established by the Oregon Treaty became the Canadian-U.S. border (with negotiations over the northern boundary along Alaska, Yukon, and British Columbia temporarily tabled).

In theory, the Oregon Treaty provided a boundary along the 49th parallel (excluding Vancouver Island). On the ground, however, the line was ambiguous. No one could have identified *where* the line actually was. Eventually, the Northwest Boundary Survey (1857–1861) clarified this leg of the border. And finally, the two countries agreed to a water boundary between the Gulf Islands and the San Juan Islands in 1872.[7]

Through the 1850s, western North America began to feel the impacts of a "manifest destiny" approach to policy. This, in conjunction with the Donation Land Act of 1850, which led into the general homestead policy, facilitated an increased population seeking land in the Oregon Territory, including Washington.[8]

From a top-down perspective, this short chronology of events—of "how the international border came to be"—might sound like an inevitable progression of international diplomacy, almost "natural." On the ground, however, the simple chronology becomes a conflict-ridden, contingency-driven history of westward expansion, and one whose consequences for the region's original inhabitants were devastating.

Making Native Space: Water Is Life ... Billy's Story

We know today that the process of territorialization at work in boundary making was integral to the larger displacement of Indigenous communities. What happened along the emerging Canada-U.S. border was a version of colonialism in which colonial war-making and legal "innovations" disrupted Indigenous social structures, inhibited long-standing cultural exchanges (such as potlatch and other ceremonies), banned native languages (through boarding schools), and so on.[9] What's more, these colonial acts occurred in the context of a still longer, centuries-old history of European disease epidemics that decimated native populations: smallpox, measles, and tuberculosis. The Nisqually tribe, located near the base of Mount Rainier in what is now Washington State, experienced a population decline from two thousand in 1800 to seven hundred in 1880.[10] Population estimates for Indigenous communities throughout the Oregon Territory show a drop of more than 50 percent, with estimates as high as 80 percent in some communities.[11] For the Indigenous communities throughout North America—including the Coast Salish peoples—this history is far from academic or "past." The impacts of bordering continue to unfold in the present. Consider this reflection from Native American environmental leader and treaty rights activist Billy Frank Jr.:

> When our ancestors were fighting for our land—we were in a difficult position. ... Our camps were empty, our villages were underpopulated, we had shrunk in size through what we now consider "bio-terrorism"—yet this is the time where we had to stake our grounds and argue for what was rightfully ours. The settlers came in under the assumptions that the land was

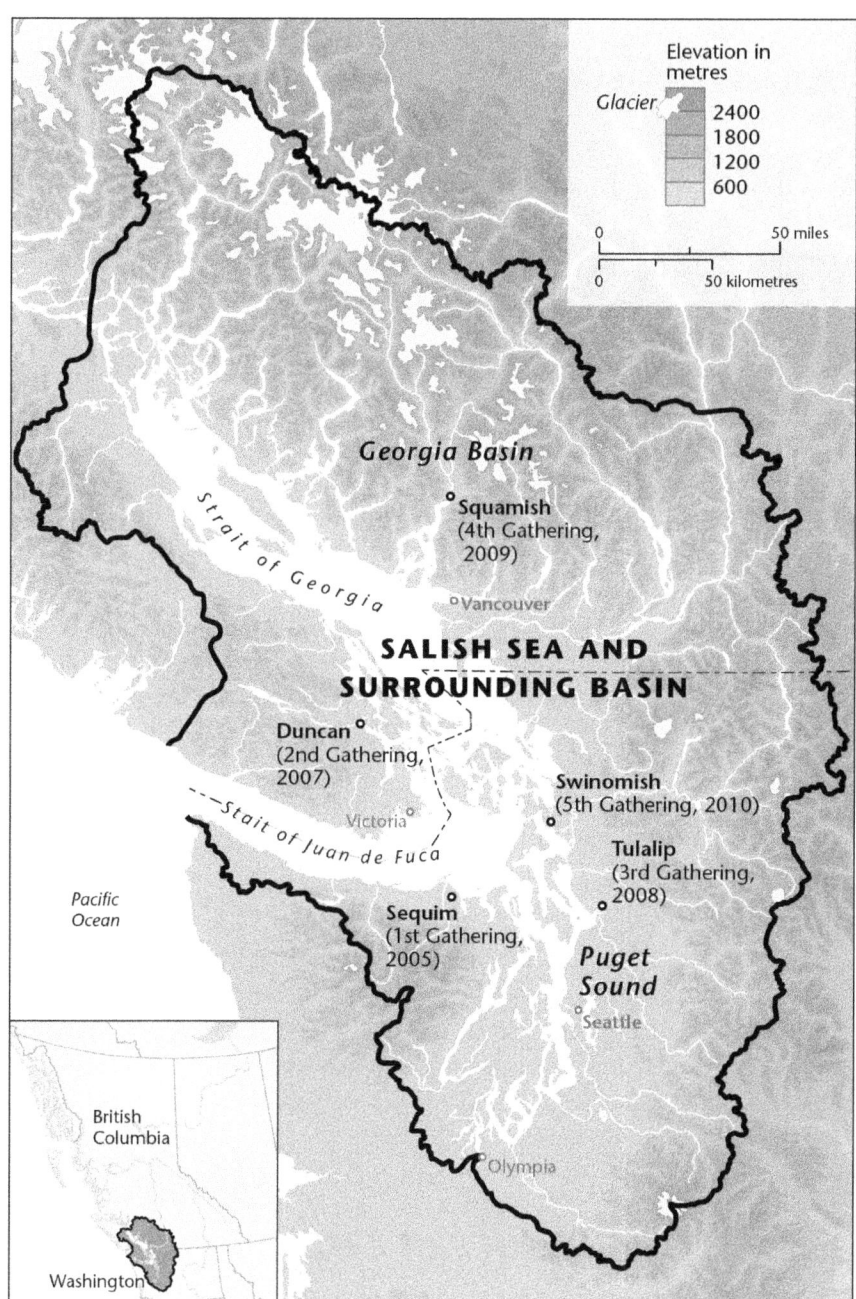

2.5 Coast Salish Gatherings. Map by Eric Leinberger.

empty; however, all of the islands, peninsulas, waterways were home to our ancestors.[12]

The Coast Salish peoples live day to day with a colonial history of borders and boundaries. And yet their more recent history is one of crossing or transcending and re-establishing traditional connections. To understand this overlay, we look to the life's work of Billy Frank Jr. and his sixty-year efforts on behalf of the Nisqually tribe of the wider Coast Salish. Billy Frank Jr.'s journey represents how twentieth-century Indigenous governance has been centrally concerned with navigating or renegotiating boundaries and borders.

A short character profile is in order. In the Pacific Northwest, Billy Frank Jr. was (and remains) a larger-than-life figure, and his legacy has continued since he passed into the spirit world in 2014. He was a gifted orator who speaks sagely about the twin needs to protect salmon and to protect Indigenous rights. He fought most passionately for the rights of his people to fish their traditional waters. Author Charles Wilkinson's biography of Billy paints a beautiful image of him at age fourteen, paddling in the middle of the night on the Nisqually River to pull up fishing nets. Billy had left his house under the moonlit sky, travelling swiftly through the forested trails from his family's home to the river. He had eased himself into the dugout canoe and paddled quietly out to the nets. Billy knew the route well. Although it was dark, he did not falter. It was "illegal" for his family to fish these traditional waters, which was why he went in darkness. As Billy was about to pull up his catch, two flashlights shone brightly on him. A man yelled "You're under arrest."[13] This would be the first of fifty arrests. Billy saw subsistence fishing as a fundamental right. Likewise, he saw the foreign laws and policies that denied those rights as illegitimate. During the 1960s and 1970s, Billy organized "fish-ins" to bring attention to Indigenous fishing claims. The movement was peaceful, but police nonetheless arrested hundreds of fish-in participants. The movement gained a binational platform when Hollywood superstar Marlon Brando joined the effort in 1964.

Billy's historical reference was a starkly different version of the chronology of treaties we laid out earlier. While British and American settlers staked claims in the Oregon Territory, American officials forced tribes into treaties of cession, under which they lost legal rights to land, including access to traditional fishing and hunting grounds. For its part, Canada created reserves without a formal treaty process. The Nisqually tribe—like other tribes in the Washington Territory—lost their land through an infamous series of treaties negotiated by Isaac Stevens, superintendent of Indian Affairs (and later, the first governor of Washington Territory). Stevens's first treaty, the disputed Treaty of Medicine Creek (1854), led to the "Leschi wars." Whether Chief Leschi's "X" on the treaty was genuine or a forgery remains unclear.

The Treaty of Medicine Creek created tremendous hardship for the Nisqually tribe. Under its terms, they relocated to a small stony outcrop at the base of Mount Rainier. Though the tribe lost access to sacred water sources, the treaty did allow them to fish from area rivers. British negotiators at the time, who saw no value in salmon, hoped this provision would encourage tribes to sign. A corollary was that the government would bear less responsibility to feed the tribes.[14]

During the twentieth century, the Medicine Creek Treaty came to be conveniently forgotten or ignored. Commercial and recreational interests in salmon became politically dominant, while the State of Washington took the position that the Nisqually were harvesting fish illegally. This was Billy Frank's fight. With each sit-in and arrest, Billy brought national attention to the importance of fish (especially salmon) among the Nisqually and larger Coast Salish peoples. The Indigenous activists ultimately prevailed when U.S. District Judge George Boldt ruled that native groups were entitled to 50 percent of the fish catch. More significant yet, the ruling provided for native-U.S. co-management of the fisheries.

As a youth, Billy had fought for fishing rights in the waters of his home. His vision grew to include the fish themselves. Overfishing, habitat destruction, and water pollution all came to threaten salmon populations. Billy Frank Jr. headed the Northwest Indian Fisheries Commission, a celebrated intertribal governance body, until the day he died, in May 2014 (a devastating loss for Indigenous communities and environmental and social justice activists alike). He was an internationally renowned cultural and environmental activist, having won the Albert Schweitzer Prize for Humanitarianism and the Presidential Medal of Freedom, the highest award that can be bestowed on a civilian. He was also a leader in the Coast Salish Gatherings, a cross-border governance body whose mission centres on salmon protection, environmental conservation, and tribal sovereignty.

Through the gatherings, we can consider once more the idea of territory and the acts of making and crossing borders.

The Coast Salish Gatherings Today: A Transboundary Success Story

In 2002, seventy tribes and bands across 72,000 kilometers of Coast Salish territory, cognizant of their need to provide for future generations, established the Coast Salish Gatherings (map 7). The Gatherings simultaneously pursue natural resource protection and community reunification. At annual gatherings, tribal leaders set collective priorities. Building on traditional leadership to tackle complex transboundary environmental and cultural issues, the Gatherings have emerged as an innovative model of governance.[15]

Border scholars have called for a more sophisticated treatment of the border.[16] The Coast Salish Gatherings are an important example of why we should heed this call. The Gatherings serve in part to address massive declines in traditional foods such as salmon and shellfish.[17] The governance structure also serves to reestablish a sense of unity between tribes and bands spanning the Canada-U.S. border. Far-reaching goals include revitalization of the language and, ultimately, self-determination. By situating their tribal nations within a wider Coast Salish Nation, Coast Salish communities collectively reclaim authority, legitimacy, and outside recognition as an Indigenous territory. Hence, this governance structure reinforces Coast Salish communities as a power base for managing and protecting the surrounding natural environment. In this way, the Coast Salish peoples have strengthened their own tenure claims and their control over a wider border space. Some important examples include

(1) successful efforts to restrict fish farms through Coast Salish territory;

(2) a renamed "Salish Sea," which acknowledges Coast Salish traditional waters, honors Coast Salish heritage, and brings public attention to a precolonial landscape; and

(3) coordination and co-management with governmental agencies such as the Environmental Protection Agency,

Environment Canada, and the U.S. Geological Survey for joint projects such as water quality testing (held in concert with traditional canoe journeys).

The Gatherings seek to disrupt and transcend what John Agnew refers to as the "territorial trap" to which many environmental organizations—and, we would argue, academic researchers—fall prey.[18] Here at the 49th parallel, the border itself cannot be understood (politically or materially) without accounting for the connection of Coast Salish history to a modern transboundary governance process. This section of the border—the now-Salish Sea region—is as much a construction of the Coast Salish as of the nation-state. Geographies and histories of water governance that exclude this overlay risk missing important policy implications and solutions.

IV. Sharing a Landscape: Watershed Boundaries as "New" Borderlands

Beyond the Westphalian Model

The Coast Salish territory represents one example of sub-state, decentralized, participatory arrangements for water governance. Since the 1990s, however, powerful new non-indigenous governance arrangements have emerged both within Canada and the United States and at the Canada-U.S. border. The most important example is integrated water resource management (IWRM), a process that takes watershed boundaries as the ideal management unit and a watershed board or council as the principle decision-making body. Like the Coast Salish Gatherings, watershed management via watershed councils is also decentralized. But because of hidden assumptions in the concept of "watershed," watershed management does not necessarily embody the same local empowerment or environmental protection that the Coast Salish case did. Watershed-scale management is a model that has not fully accounted for the assumptions and complexities within its own kind of boundary. Therefore, we wish to consider watershed management both as an important new overlay of boundaries on a larger pattern of water governance at the border and also as a (recent) conservation movement that might benefit from the Coast Salish experience.

As a management unit, the watershed was positioned to help address three centuries of problems with what legal historians and political scientists call the Westphalian model. The Westphalian model accepts the sovereignty of individual nation-states or subnational jurisdictions like provinces and states to manage territory within their borders. But the model has always posed problems for environmental governance. John Wesley Powell recognized this in 1890, when he argued unsuccessfully for water governance along hydrological rather than state boundaries in the American West. Powell saw the importance of an appropriate scale for the administration of water resources in water-scarce regions.[19]

It was not until the mid-1990s, during an international push for sustainable development, that hydrologic-based water management gained wide acceptance in North America. The approach involved a different scale of management—the watershed (a hydrological drainage basin)—and an alternative management regime: IWRM.[20] The 1992 Dublin Statement on Water and Sustainable Development, which came out of the International Conference on Water and the Environment, became a defining statement for this new paradigm of water management and governance. According to Collins and Ison, conducting science at an ecosystem scale was "intuitively attractive."[21] By the late 1990s, the World Bank and the Global Water Partnership were promoting watershed boundaries as the management unit for "best practices" worldwide. By the twenty-first century, acceptance was so complete that water scholars referred to IWRM as an "orthodoxy" enjoying "a 'near hegemony' as the language of international water policy."[22]

The first three of four core principles in the 1992 Dublin statement had some fascinating overlap with the Coast Salish's earlier vision: (1) fresh water is a finite and vulnerable resource, essential to sustain life, development, and the environment; (2) water development and management should be based on a participatory approach, involving users, planners, and policymakers at all levels; and (3) women play a central part in the provision, management, and safeguarding of water.[23] Participation, justice, decentralized decision making, and a more eco-centric approach were common threads between watershed management and the Coast Salish vision. At the same time, however, the watershed scale of IWRM contained hidden conflicts and contradictions that made this overlay different from that of the Coast Salish.[24] Watershed boundaries were, for example, often incongruent with other natural systems boundaries, including ecosystems, airsheds, and groundwater systems.[25]

The IJC Embraces Integrated Water Resource Management

Integrated water resource management came to have a profound influence on binational governance of U.S.-Canada border waters. Hall and Starr provide an important legal primer on the International Joint Commission (IJC) and its reference process (see chapter 1 of this volume). We want to focus on one specific reference to the IJC, whose outcome was a new overlay of boundaries on the border. Rather than a more typical reference to study a finite issue like boundary clarification, flood control, or water pollution in a particular place (like the Coast Salish territory), in 1997 the United States and Canada asked the IJC to broadly "examine its important mission . . . and to provide to the parties, within the next six months, proposals on how the Commission might best assist the parties to meet the environmental challenges of the 21st century." The IJC's draft response contained five recommendations, the first of which we abbreviate here:

> A reference from the parties to authorize the Commission to establish ecosystem-based international watershed boards from coast to coast to prevent and resolve transboundary environmental disputes. These boards would be available for monitoring, alerting, studying, advising, facilitating and reporting on a range of transboundary environmental and water-related issues . . . Anticipating and responding to the growing public demand for decision-making that begins in communities and builds upward, these watershed boards would also assure coordination with the increasing number of local and regional transboundary relationships and institutions.[26]

This recommendation marked a remarkable shift for the IJC, because it signalled a small but significant move away from a century-long nation-to-nation model.[27] The IJC's experimentation with watershed-scale governance was significant beyond North America, because the IJC is an internationally recognized transboundary organization. It piloted its new watershed-based approach by establishing five watershed boards: the Rainy Lake Board of Control, the Rainy River Water Pollution Board, the International Red River Board, the Souris River Board, and the International St. Croix River Watershed Board. Functionally, these boards operated much as their predecessors had, but tweaked the mandate, continuing to evolve toward more proactive forms of decision making and to develop ecologically based management plans (an important orientation that Heasley and Macfarlane discuss in their introduction to this volume).

It remains to be seen whether the IJC's move away from national capitals and toward watershed-scale organizations will strengthen its mission, improve long-term outcomes, or in fact be a real change to decentralized decision making (Jesse Ribot has cautioned about the potential "charade"[28]). The pilot projects are too recent for their community-level or binational impacts to be judged fully. But some cautions are in order.

The Hidden Complexity of Watershed Boundaries: Challenges and Uncertain Outcomes

Indeed, despite the apparent simplicity of watersheds, three important points have "muddied the waters" of this increasingly popular governance model. First, watersheds are not only about managing water. Because a watershed, in its basic definition, is a geographic area of *land* rather than a body of *water* (though that land area drains into a common body of water), watershed management is generally *"inclusive of land use,* so that all factors and events that impact on water resources are taken into consideration."[29] But including land in water management schemes is a knotty problem—one complex enough that, as Savenije and van de Zaag note in another case of international transboundary relations, the United Nations Convention on the Law of Non-Navigational Uses of International al Watercourses (1997) chose not to adopt the land-inclusive language of the Helsinki Rules (1966) because "most states prefer to use the term watercourse rather than river basin, since the latter concept comprises land areas which are also governed by administrative, land use and other laws. Letting land areas be governed by a water law might lead to legal complexities."[30] A number of cases along the 49th parallel highlight the complexities of integrating land use into water governance. The Flathead watershed is the most contentious example. There, cross-border tensions arose when Canadian officials (upstream) zoned land within the watershed for development, while American officials (downstream) zoned land within the same watershed for conservation.[31]

A second point is that a "natural" watershed may camouflage important socioeconomic and political dimensions of decision making. The 49th parallel originated from colonialism and was therefore a colonial social construction. We propose that contemporary choices about watershed boundaries (overlaid on the 49th parallel) involve another set of constructed boundaries, although watershed boundaries have not been subject to the same critiques because these boundaries are hidden under a more "natural" appearance.[32] For example, a large basin can have a number of watersheds, sub-watersheds, and tributaries, each of which constitute a mappable hydrologic boundary. Although each of these boundaries is "natural," decisions remain about *which* hydrologic boundary to use for data collection or decision making; each is as much a human decision as it is a "natural" landscape feature.[33] Nevertheless, watersheds are most often described in naturalizing language, with policy documents often referring to "nature's boundaries."[34]

The third point relates to a counterintuitive example of these hidden power relations involving the core watershed management principle of local participation. As Cohen and Davidson explain,

> There is nothing inherently participatory about the use of a hydrologic boundary instead of a municipal boundary: one can easily imagine a scenario in which autocratic decisions are made at the watershed scale, or one in which there is rich public discussion at the municipal scale. Yet stakeholder participation has become an axiomatic component of watershed-based governance frameworks, to the point where a watershed approach means participation, and the challenges associated with public participation in decision-making are seen as problems associated with a watershed itself.[35]

The type of participatory language described above can be seen in the IJC's watershed push, which emphasizes that "local people, given appropriate assistance, are those best positioned to resolve many local transboundary problems."[36] Yet some scholars are not convinced of the localness or usefulness of these decision-making arrangements.[37] This type of assertion reinforces what watershed researchers have identified as a conflation between "local," "watershed," and "participation."

V. Conclusion: Sharing a Landscape

That water knows no borders is a truism. Nonetheless, treaties, laws, policies, administrative hierarchies, even cultural and social constructs of boundaries—all shape environmental governance along the U.S.-Canada border. This governance, in turn, impacts the health of its border waters. We aimed in this chapter to expand on the truism by broadening the border to encompass other boundaries superimposed both on the international border itself and on waters shared by Canada and the United States. To that end, we overlaid two "alternative boundaries" on the conventional Canada-U.S. boundary: first, traditional territorial boundaries of First Nations and Indigenous peoples; and second, watershed boundaries that characterize hydrologic flows. In both cases, we emphasized the social construction of borders—historical and political processes that were in large part examples of colonial boundary drawing. We also examined the rise of hydrologic science, especially the discourses and policies around watersheds that naturalized hydro-political boundaries. Watershed boundaries, we suggest, provide a useful comparison to colonial boundaries because of the common assumption that watersheds are apolitical. In fact, the establishment of watershed boundaries, as well as the decision making about watersheds at these new management scales, has deeply political consequences. We underscore the importance of considering other boundary types—not only the international boundary—in contemporary understandings of governance of shared waters. Grappling with other boundary types forces scholars and policymakers alike to examine their own implicit assumptions about legal borders and water governance at these borders.

Most of all, we want to reinforce a basic premise of this volume: borders are complicated. This complexity is not simply the result of an academic exercise in which scholars complicate concepts for one another. Rather, we believe that policymakers, activists, and citizens must embrace more complex notions of boundaries and borders to accomplish more just social results and more effective environmental outcomes.

Notes

1. Alice Cohen and Karen Bakker, "The Eco-Scalar Fix: Rescaling Environmental Governance and the Politics of Ecological Boundaries in Alberta, Canada," *Environment and Planning D: Society and Space* 32, no. 1 (2014): 128–46.

2. D.B. Knight, "Identity and Territory: Geographical Perspectives on Nationalism and Regionalism," *Annals of the Association of American Geographers* 72, no. 4 (1982): 514–31.

3. Robert H. Jackson and Patricia Owens, "The Evolution of World Society," in *The Globalization of World Politics: An Introduction to International Relations*, ed. John Baylis, Steve Smith, and Patricia Owens (Oxford: Oxford University Press, 2005).

4. James G. Barber and Frederick S. Voss, *Blessed Are the Peace Makers: A Commemoration of the 200th Anniversary of the Treaty of Paris* (Washington: Smithsonian Institution Press, for the National Portrait Gallery, 1983); Max Savelle, *The Diplomatic History of the Canadian Boundary, 1759–1763* (New Haven: Yale University Press, 1940).

5. Savelle, *Diplomatic History*, 12.

6. Glenn W. Price, *Origins of the War with Mexico: The Polk-Stockton Intrigue* (Austin: University of Texas Press, 1967).

7. Rosemary Neering, *The Pig War: The Last Canada-U.S. Border Conflict* (Surrey, BC: Heritage House, 2011); Mike Vouri, *The Pig War* (Charleston, SC: Arcadia, 2008).

8. Leonard J. Evenden and Daniel E. Turberville, "The Pacific Coast Borderland and Frontier," in *The Borderlands and the American and Canadian Wests: Essays on Regional History of the Forty-Ninth Parallel*, ed. Sterling Evans (Lincoln: University of Nebraska Press, 2006).

9. Bruce Miller, "Defining the Region, Defining the Border" in *The Borderlands of the American and Canadian West*, ed. Sterling Evans (Lincoln: University of Nebraska Press, 2006); Cole Harris, *Making Native Space* (Vancouver: UBC Press, 2004).

10. Charles Wilkinson, *Messages from Frank's Landing: A Story of Salmon Treaties and the Indian Way* (Seattle: University of Washington Press, 2000), 9.

11. Richard White, *The Organic Machine: The Remaking of the Columbia River* (New York: Hill & Wang, 1995); Richard White, *Land Use, Environment, and Social Change: The Shaping of Island County, Washington* (Seattle: University of Washington Press, 1980); Joseph E. Taylor III, *Making Salmon: An Environmental History of the Northwest Fisheries Crisis* (Seattle: University of Washington Press, 1999).

12. Billy Frank Jr., "Staying the Course: Building the Next Generation of Native Leaders" (public lecture, Northwest Indian College, Bellingham, WA, May 15, 2010).

13. Wilkinson, *Messages*, 10.

14. Ibid.

15. Brian Thom, "The Anathema of Aggregation: Towards 21st-Century Self-Government in the Coast Salish World," *Anthropologica* 52,

no. 1 (2010): 33–48; Emma S. Norman, "Cultural Politics and Transboundary Resource Governance in the Salish Sea," *Water Alternatives* 5, no. 1 (2012): 138–60.

16   David Newman and Anssi Paasi, "Fences and Neighbours in the Postmodern World: Boundary Narratives in Political Geography," *Progress in Human Geography* 22, no. 2 (1998): 186–207; Anssi Paasi, "Region and Place: Regional Identity in Question," *Progress in Human Geography* 27, no. 4 (2003): 475–85; John Agnew, "No Borders, No Nations: Making Greece in Macedonia," *Annals of the Association of American Geographers* 97, no. 2 (2007): 398–422; Gabriel Popescu, *Bordering and Ordering the Twenty-First Century: Understanding Borders* (Lanham, MD: Rowman & Littlefield, 2012); Emma S. Norman, *Governing Transboundary Waters: Canada, the United States and Indigenous Communities* (London: Routledge, 2015).

17   Jamie Donatuto, "When Seafood Feeds the Spirit yet Poisons the Body: Developing Health Indicators for Risk Assessment in a Native American Fishing Community" (PhD diss., University of British Columbia, 2008).

18   John Agnew, "The Territorial Trap: The Geographical Assumptions of International Relations Theory," *Review of International Political Economy* 1, no. 1 (1994): 53–80; Matthew Sparke, "Excavating the Future in Cascadia: Geoeconomics and the Imagined Geographies of a Cross-Border Region," *BC Studies*, no. 127 (2000): 5–44.

19   Historians have identified governance along hydrologic boundaries as far back as the third century BCE in China. In the United States, the Tennessee Valley Authority is a twentieth-century example. François Molle, "River-Basin Planning and Management: The Social Life of a Concept," *Geoforum* 40, no. 3 (2009): 484–94.

20   Alice Cohen and Seanna Davidson, "The Watershed Approach: Challenges, Antecedents, and the Transition from Technical Tool to Governance Unit," *Water Alternatives* 4, no. 1 (2011): 521–34.

21   Kevin B. Collins and Ray L. Ison, "Trusting Emergence: Some Experiences of Learning about Integrated Catchment Science with the Environment Agency of England and Wales," *Water Resources Management* 24, no. 4 (2010): 671.

22   Paul Jeffrey and Mary Gearey, "Integrated Water Resources Management: Lost on the Road from Ambition to Realisation?" *Water Science and Technology* 53, no. 1 (2006): 1; K. Conca, *Governing Water: Contentious Transnational Politics and Global Institution Building* (Cambridge, MA: MIT Press, 2005), 161. J. Warner, P. Wester, and A. Bolding said IWRM was part of the "holy trinity of water governance," which also included river basin planning and multi-stakeholder platforms. Warner, Wester, and Bolding, "Going with the Flow: River Basins as the Natural Units for Water Management?" *Water Policy*, 2nd ser., 10 (2008): 121. For proponents of the watershed as an ideal scale, see Laura Cervoni, Andrew Biro, and Karen Beazley, "Implementing Integrated

Water Resources Management: The Importance of Cross-Scale Considerations and Local Conditions in Ontario and Nova Scotia," *Canadian Water Resources Journal* 33, no. 4 (2008): 333–50; Torkil Jønch-Clausen and Jens Fugl, "Firming Up the Conceptual Basis of Integrated Water Resources Management," *International Journal of Water Resources Development* 17, no. 4 (2001): 501–10; and Jeffrey and Gearey, "Integrated Water Resources Management," 1.

23 United Nations. "The Dublin Statement on Water and Sustainable Development" (International Conference on Water and the Environment, Dublin, Ireland, 1992), http://www.wmo.int/pages/prog/hwrp/documents/english/icwedece.html. The fourth principle states that water has an economic value in all its competing uses and should be recognized as an economic good.

24 For in-depth analysis of watersheds as governance scales, see William Blomquist and Edella Schlager, "Political Pitfalls of Integrated Watershed Management," *Society and Natural Resources* 18, no. 2 (2005): 101–17; Alice Cohen, "Rescaling Environmental Governance: Watersheds as Boundary Objects at the Intersection of Science, Neoliberalism, and Participation," *Environment and Planning A* 44, no. 9 (2012): 2207–24; Cohen and Davidson, "Watershed Approach"; C.B. Griffin, "Watershed Councils: An Emerging Form of Public Participation in Natural Resource Management," *Journal of the American Water Resources Association* 35, no. 3 (1999): 505–18; Paul A. Sabatier et al. (eds.), *Swimming Upstream: Collaborative Approaches to Watershed Management* (Cambridge, MA: MIT Press, 2005); Jeroen Warner, "The Beauty of the Beast: Multi-Stakeholder Participation for Integrated Catchment Management," in *Multi-Stakeholder Platforms for Integrated Water Management*, ed. Jeroen Warner (Cornwall, UK: Ashgate, 2007); and Warner et al., "Going with the Flow."

25 Respectively, Griffin, "Watershed Councils"; Peter P. Mollinga, Ruth S. Meinzen-Dick, and Douglas J. Merrey, "Politics, Plurality and Problemsheds: A Strategic Approach for Reform of Agricultural Water Resources Management," *Development Policy Review* 25, no. 6 (2007): 699–719; James M. Omernik and Robert G. Bailey, "Distinguishing between Watersheds and Ecoregions," *Journal of the American Water Resources Association* 33, no. 5 (1997): 935–49; N.A. Jaworski, R.W. Howarth, and L.J. Hetling, "Atmospheric Deposition of Nitrogen Oxides onto the Landscape Contributes to Coastal Eutrophication in the Northeast United States," *Environmental Science and Technology* 31, no. 7 (1997): 1995–2004; Hans W. Paerl, Robin L. Dennis, and David R. Whitall, "Atmospheric Deposition of Nitrogen: Implications for Nutrient Over-Enrichment of Coastal Waters," *Estuaries* 25, no. 4 (2002): 677–93.

26 International Joint Commission, 2000.

27 An interesting question is whether this undercuts what is arguably the central premise of the IJC. That is, the International Watershed Initiative model emphasizes the importance of hydrologic—rather than political—boundaries.

28 Jesse C. Ribot, *Waiting for Democracy: The Politics of Choice in Natural Resource Decentralization*, WRI Report (Washington, DC: World Resources Institute, 2004), http://pdf.wri.org/wait_for_democracy.pdf.

29 Sharon Pollard, "Operationalising the New Water Act: Contributions from the Save the Sand Project—An Integrated Catchment Management Initiative," *Physics and Chemistry of the Earth* 27 (2002): 943; emphasis in original.

30 Hubert H.G. Savenije and Pieter van der Zaag, "Conceptual Framework for the Management of Shared River Basins; with Special Reference to the SADC and EU," *Water Policy* 2, no. 1 (2000): 23.

31 Harvey Locke and Matthew McKinny, "The Transboundary Flathead Basin," in *Water without Borders? Canada, the United States and Shared Waters*, ed. Emma S. Norman, Alice Cohen, and Karen Bakker (Toronto: University of Toronto Press, 2013).

32 A. Cohen and L. Harris, "Performing Watersheds: Performativity and the Production of Scale," in *Performativity, Space, and Politics*, ed. R. Rose-Redwood and M. Glass (New York: Routledge, 2014).

33 Blomquist and Schlager, "Political Pitfalls"; Cohen and Davidson, "Watershed Approach."

34 Cohen and Harris, "Performing Watersheds," 201.

35 Cohen and Davidson, "Watershed Approach," 8.

36 International Joint Commission, *The IJC and the 21st Century* (Ottawa: IJC, 1997).

37 J. Christopher Brown and Mark Purcell, "There's Nothing Inherent about Scale: Political Ecology, the Local Trap, and the Politics of Development in the Brazilian Amazon," *Geoforum* 36, no. 5 (2005): 606–7.

Contesting the Northwest Passage: Four Far-North Narratives

ANDREA CHARRON

Is the Northwest Passage of the Arctic an international strait or historic internal waters? A transnational economic throughway or one country's sovereign territory? The diplomatic and environmental history of the Northwest Passage (NWP) is, in large part, a history of struggles over the answers to these questions. When and how Canadian and U.S. governments have clarified or obscured these questions provides an important window into different narratives about the passage.

While many modern narratives of territorial diplomacy begin with sovereignty over boundaries, transition through struggles to exploit resources, and culminate in environmental protection, the narrative trajectory of the NWP reverses the latter two: it begins with sovereignty over boundaries (a refrain that permeates discussions even today), continues through the Cold War with defence strategies, and eventually transitions to environmental concerns. However, the narrative does not end with environmental concerns; it culminates in the modern era with strategies to exploit natural resources (albeit an effort at responsible development in conjunction with Indigenous peoples).

Through these narratives of the Far North, and the Northwest Passage specifically, I will illustrate the fundamental rethinking of the NWP for Canada—from rugged Canadian periphery to a vulnerable, resource-rich site of potential for a modern, transnational economy. Changing conceptions of the passage, moreover, reveal both similarities and differences between northern and southern Canadian-American water borders. This chapter is divided into four parts representing the different historical time periods that correspond to different ideas about the NWP. In the nineteenth century until World War I, Canada focused on establishing its claim to the Arctic. World War II and the Cold War period saw a shift in focus to defence of the Arctic from Japanese and Soviet threats. The 1970s and 1980s to the end of Cold War witnessed perceived and new challenges for the NWP from the United States and from pollution. Finally, from the 1990s to the current day, the NWP is referenced in terms of resource development and exploitation. In turn, Canadian characterizations of the NWP have shifted from describing the passage as a frontier to a boundary to an asset that must be protected to one that is instrumental in achieving resource development. This does not represent an end point to discussions. Rather, it is another marker of continually changing ideas about the Arctic and the NWP.

I. A Nineteenth-Century Frontier: The Initial Claim

Canadians today assume that the NWP has always comprised the notorious Arctic channels linking the Davis Strait to the Beaufort Sea. Legendary stories of doomed missions headed by Munk[1] and Franklin[2] in search of a shorter route to the Far East continue to capture the imaginations of many armchair explorers and perpetuate the idea of the passage as an ice-infested labyrinth to be conquered. Most histories of the NWP begin with the fact that the Hudson's Bay Company owned Rupert's Land, a massive territory that included much of the Canadian prairies, northern Ontario and northern Quebec, as well as the Arctic, including the NWP.[3] Its 1670 charter made the Hudson's Bay Company the "true and absolute Lordes and Proprietors" of Rupert's Land, which was exploited for fur. HBC (or "Here before Christ," as it is vaingloriously referenced, negating the existence of Indigenous peoples who had lived and hunted the land for thousands of years) managed this territory. The potential to govern Rupert's Land in the cause of nation building was unrealized until its sale to Canada in 1869. Having acquired nearly four million square kilometres of land, the young country was more concerned with linking the East of Canada to the territories of the West than it was with exploring the frozen nether region of the Arctic. As a result, the Arctic NWP was largely ignored in favour of a more generalized "northwest passage" in the form of rail, river, and portage links that fulfilled the promise of westward exploration and travel to the Pacific Ocean, linking the new Dominion.[4]

When Britain transferred the remaining Arctic islands—those not captured under HBC's charter—to Canada in 1880, the Canadian government's chief concern was to establish ownership and control over the islands. Several states, including the United States, had designs on the islands and surrounding waters, and the fact that the precise boundaries of the territory were vague did not aid Canada's claim.[5] At this time, Canada had no navy or coastguard and little administrative presence in the Far North. The NWP continued to be neglected and ignored by Canadian writers and historians—indeed, by most of Canada, for whom the "passage" was still "the northwest passage by land."[6] Canada needed fertile grounds, not ice-infested waters.

Southern Canadians, therefore, did not actually "discover" the NWP; rather, it was the British and the Norwegians. Between 1576 and 1578, Martin Frobisher (an English privateer or pirate, depending on your point of view) made three voyages to the Canadian Arctic. With each trip he brought back ore and other samples to Britain, attracting the attention and assistance of Queen Elizabeth I and of the Royal Navy. With his 1903–1906 voyage, Roald Amundsen became the first European to traverse the NWP from the Atlantic to the Pacific. The Norwegian's success was largely due to his cerebral approach, which included studying past expeditions, especially Franklin's, and learning from their mistakes. Importantly, he was also receptive to learning from the Inuit, who taught him invaluable survival skills that would benefit him and future crews on other polar missions (both North and South).

These and other gripping stories of exploration brought northern adventure and tragedy into popular European culture of the era. For southern Canadians, however, the NWP remained primarily a source of fanciful stories. Meanwhile, the region's actual inhabitants—mainly Inuit but also Cree and Dene peoples—were badly misrepresented in the media. Robert J. Flaherty's 1922 black-and-white film about "Nanook of the North" and the 1940s Canadian comic book heroine "Nelvana of the Northern Lights" provided a glimpse of the Canadian Arctic, but it was a distinctly distorted version.[7] The Canadian Arctic was portrayed as an unspoiled frontier. The achievements of the Inuit as entrepreneurs, artists, and shrewd tacticians were downplayed. Instead, they were portrayed as primitive and simple-minded. Worse still, many Indigenous peoples faced persecution and displacement by the Canadian federal government.[8]

American ideas about the NWP were similar to those of Canadians. U.S. Secretary of State William H. Seward did not purchase his "folly" (Alaska) from the Russians until 1867. Therefore, early American Arctic naval explorations, like the 1850–1851 First Grinnell Expedition (a rescue mission in search of Franklin financed by Henry Grinnell, a wealthy U.S. businessman), were far from the consciousness of the American public, except for those wishing to learn more about the details of the Franklin crew's demise.[9] The territory mapped by these expeditions, for example, was largely ignored. Later U.S. expeditions by Kane, Hayes, Hall (all in search of Franklin), Peary, and MacMillan (explorers of the 1900s in search of the North Pole) fascinated the U.S. public, but also confirmed their suspicion that the Arctic was a desolate, inhospitable environment that made for incredible, if gruesome, adventures, but not much more.

Some of Canada's northern land boundaries were still not clearly defined by 1900, which had implications for Canadian Arctic maritime boundaries. Canada was slow to contest the Alaska boundary, for example, even though British Columbia maps of the border conflicted with American maps. The Yukon Gold Rush (1897 to 1900s) immediately awakened Canadians to the possible consequences of such territorial disputes. The two countries attempted to resolve the cartographic standoff through the Alaskan Boundary Tribunal of 1903, consisting of three American representatives, a British judge, and two Canadians. The name "Alaska boundary dispute" is somewhat misleading, as this disagreement involved only the panhandle—that is, the part of the boundary that does not follow the 141st meridian west. Both sides agreed that the 141st marked the land boundary north of the panhandle. Because neither Canada nor the United Kingdom had protested the 1825 Anglo-Russian Treaty that defined the boundaries between Russian, American, and British claims in the Pacific Northwest, the United States was on firm legal ground and could invoke the principle of uncontested occupation. Hence, Canadian demands that the boundaries be redrawn fell on deaf ears. The compromise boundary line was literally the middle ground between American and Canadian positions (at least in the estimation of the United States, since the Canadians were convinced that the boundary disadvantaged them). Significantly, Canada and the United States still disagree on whether or not the maritime boundary ought to extend out from the land into the sea. As a result, there remains, to this day, a fundamental disagreement between the United States and Canada over maritime boundaries in the Beaufort Sea.[10]

In the late nineteenth century, American whalers presented the main "challenge" to Canada's control of the NWP through their use of Canada's northern waterways to bring alcohol and other goods into the country without paying duty. This caused a public backlash, including a warning published in an 1891 issue of the *Canada Gazette* to foreign traders about their import responsibilities.[11] With no ports or customs houses in the Arctic in the late 1890s, however, Canadian law was not enforceable—an unacceptable situation for the Canadian government. To combat smuggling and reassert Canadian sovereignty in the North, Canada's Laurier government initiated a police presence (first the Northwest Mounted Police and later the Royal Canadian Mounted Police [RCMP]) followed by marine expeditions (for example, the *Neptune* [1903–1904] and later the *Arctic* [1904–1911]).[12] Although northern security was never a top concern, especially after the outbreak of World War I, the Canadian government now had a continuous program of patrolling the Arctic NWP by the RCMP by ship and later by the Canadian Forces via air patrols. Thus, in the early days of Canadian history, Prime Minister Louis St. Laurent's description of the governance of the North as having been performed in "a fit of absence of mind"[13] was probably accurate; the focus was on delineating the land boundaries, followed by establishing a presence in the region. Charting the NWP and solidifying maritime boundaries were still to come.

II. World War II and the Cold War: A Boundary to Control and Damn the Consequences

With new, bona fide military threats to both the United States and Canada, including World War II, the focus of the Canadian and U.S. governments vis-à-vis the Arctic shifted from establishing legal title to defending North America. Rather than discussing sovereignty, the United States and

Canada focused on defence strategies—the ice-infested Arctic and NWP were used as bulwarks. While letting lie discussions about the legal title of the islands of Canada's Arctic Archipelago, the Canadian government knew that the marine boundaries and the status of the NWP would need to be solidified someday. For the time being, however, there were far greater concerns.

Japan's 1941 attack on Pearl Harbor and 1942 occupation of the Alaskan Islands of Attu and Kiska demonstrated the need for stronger domestic defence systems for both the United States and Canada. The long, undefended North was the focus of much of this attention. Both countries operated critical facilities in the region throughout the war, including weather stations, airbases, and the famous Alaska Highway.[14] In the decade after World War II, a new "polar passion" gripped the Canadian and U.S. governments as a different threat emerged in the form of the Soviet Union. The two allies launched unprecedented military and civilian operations, cooperating to defend the North against threats from Soviet long-range bombers, paratroopers, even potential naval invasions via various polar routes—including the NWP.[15] Despite the working alliance, the Canadian ambassador to Washington (and, later, prime minister of Canada) Lester Bowles "Mike" Pearson, warned that Canada must enunciate its claim to the Arctic clearly and unequivocally as questions remained concerning the status of northern boundaries. In a 1946 *Foreign Affairs* article, Pearson noted that "a large part of the world's total Arctic area is Canadian. One should know exactly what this part comprises. It includes not only Canada's northern mainland but the islands and frozen sea north of the mainland between the meridians of its east and west boundaries, extending to the North Pole."[16] This was especially important given the number of U.S. personnel operating in the Canadian North.[17] Pearson's plea was noted but not acted upon; Canadian attention was elsewhere, fixed squarely on launching the new United Nations, rebuilding Europe, and keeping a wary eye on the Soviet Union.

For much of the Cold War, the Arctic remained a geographic barrier between the Soviet Union and the United States, which were separated by less than one hundred kilometres in the Arctic Ocean. This was a time of increased cooperation between Canada and the United States; the two countries worked to align their respective Arctic policies with their mutual defence interests. This cooperation took the form of projects such as the Joint Arctic Weather Stations (JAWS),[18] Distant Early Warning (DEW) Line (a series of radar sites), and the North American Air (later Aerospace) Defense Command (NORAD). The NWP was primarily a gateway to the strategically important North American Arctic. Over time, however, Canadians grew weary of the sovereignty threat posed by American involvement in the Canadian Arctic. Now, two threats loomed in the minds of Canadians: the Soviet Union and the United States.

The latter threat appeared in August 1960 with the Atlantic-to-Pacific transit of the U.S. nuclear submarine USS *Seadragon* through Canadian northern waterways. This underwater exploration via the NWP became the catalyst for renewed attention to the exact nature of Canada's maritime Arctic boundaries—especially the NWP. Months of planning went into the *Seadragon* operation. The U.S. military sought Canadian government approval of its plan to traverse the NWP en route from Baffin Bay through the Arctic Basin and Bering Strait to the Pacific Ocean. That the United States had notified Canadian authorities suggests it was keenly aware of Canadian sensitivity over the NWP. To further alleviate concerns, the United States invited the Canadian naval attaché, Commodore O.C.S. Robertson, on the *Seadragon* voyage because of his extensive polar experience.[19] The internal Canadian analysis below is telling, as it highlights the concern of the Canadian government vis-à-vis U.S. activities in Canada's Arctic and the impact of those activities on Canada's view on its legal position of its Arctic maritime boundaries. Every U.S. activity in Canada's North was analyzed through the lens of whether it was a boon or a bust to Canada's position:

> This [U.S.] request will greatly strengthen our claim to the waters of the Canadian Archipelago as Internal Waters. It is recommended, therefore, that advantage be taken of this development and that the request be granted in accordance with the Canada–United States agreed clearance procedure for visits by public vessels between Canada and the United States by a reply being sent on a service to service basis.[20]

During the Cold War, the Arctic and the NWP were regions to be protected against military threats and foreign invasions, but little thought was given to solidifying the exact maritime boundaries and/or the environmental damage caused by this "protection." For example, the DEW Line radar sites, the majority of which were located on Canadian soil, were notorious pollution dumps; empty oil drums, truck batteries, and chemicals like PCBs, lead, mercury, and antifreeze, not to mention spilled diesel fuel, littered the landscape. There was a decidedly cavalier attitude about the extent of the contamination, with no consideration of the environmental consequences to the land—that is, until the pollution threat seemed to originate from U.S. commercial interests.

III. 1970–1990: A Region to Protect Environmentally

With few Canadian regulations and/or government statements in place to govern the NWP, and given the heated background discussions that would lead to the UN Convention on the Law of the Sea (UNCLOS), the 1969 and 1970 transits of a modified U.S. supertanker—the *Manhattan*, owned by the American company Humble Oil (part of Exxon)—took on added significance, colouring both the Canadian and the American view of the NWP that persists today. At the heart of the binational imbroglio are different ideas about how to categorize the NWP: the United States thinks of it as Canadian but also as an international strait linking one body of high seas to another, to be used for international navigation. Canada, in contrast, views the NWP as representing "historic, internal waters" and therefore being under the complete control of Canada with no automatic right of navigation. Both arguments had received support in cases adjudicated by the International Court of Justice.[21] In the U.S. view, vessel passage cannot be unduly hindered by the adjacent coastal state. In Canada's view, the NWP is under the absolute jurisdiction of Canada due to the historic usage of the passage by the Inuit and the importance of the waters that serve to link the Arctic islands to Canada; therefore, vessels may be detained, seized, or inspected as required by it, the coastal state.[22] As a result, when Humble Oil approached the Canadian government with a plan to use the NWP and, specifically, to pilot the oil tanker *Manhattan* through it to test this shipping route, the governments had differing control expectations.

The truly gripping story of the *Manhattan* transits is often lost in the controversy that followed.[23] The largest vessel of its time, it was cut in two to be retrofitted with a new icebreaking bow, enormous propeller, and other modifications for its Arctic voyages. Scientists and engineers from around the world vied for an opportunity to be part of this historic undertaking. Humble Oil had discovered large oil reserves off the Alaskan North Slope and needed a fast and efficient transport system for shipping the oil to the southern U.S. market. Oil pipelines were a possibility, but an oil tanker had the advantage of variability of destination and economy not offered by a fixed pipeline. The voyages, from Chester, Pennsylvania, to the eastern coast of Greenland to Prudhoe Bay in Alaska via the NWP and then returning to New York Harbor, were billed as feasibility studies. Filled with ballast water (to simulate oil), and greeted by reporters, scientists, engineers, and well-wishers, the *Manhattan*'s maiden Arctic voyage was the media event of the day. Rather than asking the Canadian government for permission, which would add credibility to Canada's characterization of the NWP, Humble Oil sought the same sort of concurrence granted the USS *Seadragon* without formally asking permission to transit the NWP. The *Manhattan*'s route would stay outside of Canada's three nautical mile (nmi) territorial sea limit while transiting the NWP.[24] For the United States, therefore, the *Manhattan* and its American icebreaker chaperone would sail in the high seas corridor of the NWP, not, therefore, requiring authorization.[25] According to U. Alexis Johnson (then U.S. under secretary of state for political affairs), conceding to Canada's position by formally asking for permission to transit the NWP would give up "worldwide passage, the right of innocent passage, particularly through other archipelagos such as South East Asia, the Philippines [and others] all over the world."[26] Such concessions were unthinkable from a national-interest perspective. The Canadian government reiterated that it considered the waters of the NWP as Canadian internal waters, making a point of giving the United States express permission to transit the passage.[27] A U.S. Coast Guard vessel, the *Northwind*, and the Canadian Coast Guard icebreaker *John A. MacDonald* guided the *Manhattan* through the ice-infested NWP waters. Whereas entrepreneurs saw possibility, the Canadian government was decidedly cautious. Mitchell Sharp, then Canadian secretary of state for external affairs, commented:

> This is not a time for wide-ranging assertions of Canadian sovereignty in the Arctic made without regard to the international political and legal considerations [and] there is no necessity for

us to make sweeping assertions to reinforce our position. That might satisfy our ego but would not add a whit to the international acceptability of our position.[28]

Rather, a collaborative approach with the United States was thought to demonstrate that Canada did indeed have adequate control of the NWP—hence the decision to dispatch the CCGS *John A. MacDonald* to accompany the *Manhattan* on its voyage and provide ice services information. The more immediate concern for the Canadian government was protection of the pristine Arctic environment.[29] The Canadian public, however, took a much more hostile stance toward the transit of the *Manhattan*. Canadian newspapers portrayed the voyage as U.S. exploitation of the Canadian NWP, feeding the suspicions of Canadians who feared becoming too dependent on their superpower neighbour for defence and security.[30] Therefore, any possible suggestion or act that challenged Canadian control of the NWP (whether officially sanctioned or not) was now met with strong public reaction.[31]

The Canadian prime minister of the day, Pierre Trudeau, a lawyer by profession and an avid sportsman (canoeing and underwater diving, in particular), recognized that an oil spill in the Arctic would be a financial and environmental disaster for Canada. The grounding of the U.S. supertanker *Torrey Canyon* on Pollard's Rock, off the southwest coast of Great Britain, in 1967 was a vivid reminder of the dangers of tanker shipping. Her entire cargo of crude oil (more than thirty million gallons) washed up onto the shores of England and France.

To protect Canada's North and its NWP, Trudeau adopted the Arctic Waters Pollution Prevention Act (AWPPA) in 1970, five days after the second voyage of the *Manhattan* had commenced and four days after the United States had announced construction of the *Polar Sea* (which was at that time the most powerful nonnuclear icebreaker in the world).[32] What was unique about the AWPPA was that the standards it established for vessels operating in the Canadian Arctic went beyond those ordinarily permitted a coastal state. The AWPPA (Bill C-202) created a 100 nmi pollution-prevention zone in the Arctic—well beyond the 3 nmi territorial limit of the day. Canada exercised exclusive jurisdiction over this area, ensuring that economic development and, in particular, maritime shipping activities conformed to strict regulatory antipollution procedures. The

3.1 CCGS *John A. Macdonald* (right), 1969. Photo courtesy of U.S. Coast Guard Historian's Office.

accompanying regulations set standards for hull type and strength and for navigational and other safety equipment, not to mention standards for the pilot and crew.[33] Such boldness was just another in a series of controversial Canadian decisions that included extending its territorial sea limit to 12 nmi in 1970 and applying straight baselines in various parts of the Arctic in the late 1960s and 1970s until the archipelago was completely enclosed in 1985.[34] Waiting for the international community to negotiate, draft, and agree on international environmental regulations for Arctic waters (the position favoured by the United States) would take years and would not keep Canada's interests at the fore. However, recognizing the novel character of the AWPPA legislation, Canada preempted any court challenges by exempting the AWPPA from the compulsory jurisdiction of the International Court of Justice. The U.S. response was predictable:

> The United States does not recognize any exercise of coastal state jurisdiction over our vessels on the high seas and thus does

not recognize the right of any state unilaterally to establish a territorial sea of more than three (nautical) miles or exercise more limited jurisdiction in any area beyond 12 (nautical) miles. We, therefore, regret the introduction of this legislation by the Canadian government, which in our view, constitutes a unilateral approach to a problem we believe should be resolved by cooperative international action.[35]

At the time, four of the circumpolar states (Iceland, Sweden, Norway, and most importantly, the Soviet Union) accepted the Canadian legislation, much to the displeasure of the United States, which had hoped to convene an international conference to discuss the new legislation.[36] The AWPPA was eventually adopted by the international community as Article 234—"Ice-Covered Areas"—in the UNCLOS, but it remains controversial.[37] The decision by the Canadian government in 2009 to extend the reach of the AWPPA to 200 nmi (in keeping with the exclusive economic zone limits) has not helped to quiet detractors of this legislation. Moreover, Canada recently made mandatory its previously voluntary requirement that all vessels over 300 gross tonnage and/or vessels carrying pollutants or dangerous goods (1) report to the Canadian Coast Guard their intention to enter and (2) receive permission prior to navigating the waters covered by the AWPPA—a decision contested by the United States.[38]

Aware of Canada's sensitivities about its Arctic claims, the United States has let lie the dispute over the maritime boundary in the Beaufort Sea and does not actively fight against Canada's AWPPA or directly challenge Canada's categorization of the NWP. However, the United States was not prepared to ask permission for its Coast Guard vessel *Polar Sea* to navigate the NWP in 1985 to resupply the U.S. base in Thule, Greenland. To do so "would jeopardize the freedom of navigation essential for United States' naval activities worldwide."[39] Instead, the United States informed the Canadian Coast Guard of the planned voyage and received cooperation. Public sentiment and political capital, however, demanded a firm response from the Canadian government. Following the voyage of the *Polar Sea*, Secretary of State for External Affairs Joe Clark, in a stirring statement on Arctic sovereignty made in the House of Commons on September 10, 1985, announced six measures—including adoption of straight baselines around the Arctic archipelago, an increase of surveillance overflights of the Canadian Arctic waters, and construction of a polar (read nuclear) icebreaker—to preserve "Canada's sovereignty over land, sea, and ice."[40] The icebreaker, however, was never funded. Instead, and largely attributed to the close relationship between then Prime Minister Brian Mulroney and President Ronald Reagan, a newly signed 1988 Arctic Cooperation Agreement with Canada allowed U.S. Coast Guard vessels access to the NWP (for scientific purposes) without prejudice to the legal policies of either state.[41] This means that the United States notifies Canada and asks for consent when its vessels use the passage, but its actions in this regard cannot be interpreted to mean the United States has accepted Canada's broad legal position on the NWP.

Further, despite having contributed invaluable comments and scholarship to the meetings that led to the creation of the UNCLOS—the main body of law governing the Arctic Ocean (and all global oceans)—the United States failed to ratify it and Canada did so only in 2003. (Russia, in contrast, ratified UNCLOS in 1997.) By the end of the Cold War, therefore, Canada had enacted a series of regulations and acts to elaborate fully on and provide a precise definition of Canada's historic title to the waters of the NWP. The world recognized the importance of protecting polar regions from environmental marine damage (via the AWPPA and, later, Article 234 of UNCLOS). The United States continued to disagree with the characterization of the NWP, but more pressing matters (including the integration of the new Russian Federation into the world) took precedence.

IV. Present Day: Resources to Develop

Fast forward to 2016 and the situation remains unchanged: a political impasse exists based on principles and precedents. The United States maintains that the NWP represents an international strait (although it has not pressed its point by defiantly sending ships through) and Canada maintains that it is historic internal waters. In fact, a Canadian Conservative member of Parliament suggested renaming the NWP the "Canadian Northwest Passage" to reinforce its position.[42] Pressure is mounting to "solve" this impasse—especially from European and Asian commercial vessel operators interested in shaving off thousands of miles from their routes to destinations like Tokyo and Rotterdam by taking the increasingly ice-free NWP shortcut versus the usual and more reliable, but longer, Suez

Canal route.[43] The realization of the "shortcut" came at a time when the world was becoming alarmed at the dramatic impact of climate change on the world's environment and people. The poles suffer these effects most glaringly, and a clarion call by NGOs, world leaders, and citizens was made throughout the 1990s and 2000s to reverse the effects of climate change. Canada and the United States responded to such calls by joining the Arctic Environmental Protection Strategy (AEPS) in 1991—a declaration that sought to commit the eight Arctic states (the United States, Russia, Canada, Norway, Denmark, Iceland, Sweden, and Finland) to a joint action plan that would reverse pollution levels in the Arctic. The immediate concern was the damaged, fragile Arctic ecosystem that had been ravaged by decades of contamination and dumping of organic contaminants, oil, heavy metals, radioactive materials, and acidifying substances.[44]

The AEPS morphed into the Arctic Council in 1996 when Canada proposed that sustainable development be added to the agenda in addition to a focus on the environment. The creation of the Arctic Council has resulted in a marked, international shift away from the political and military categorization of the NWP to a focus on these twin goals: sustainable development and environmental protection. As a result of this shift in attention, the narrative of the NWP within Canada changed; the passage went from something to be claimed (early 1900s) to something to control and protect (Cold War) to something to develop responsibly (today). For Canada, this shift contributed to a subtle change from describing the NWP as integral to Canadian identity using emotional language (creating a rally-round-the-flag effect) to a more practical discussion, acknowledging that the NWP is geographically part of Canada and focusing on what is best for Canada and northern residents. What is helping to ensure the protection of the NWP and cement these shifts in describing it is the granting of Permanent Participant status to groups representing Indigenous peoples on the Arctic Council, as well soliciting input from northern residents and nongovernmental organizations in Arctic policy planning—a far cry from the days when only the Canadian federal government made the decisions.

Canada's four overriding priorities vis-à-vis the passage and the Arctic today are (1) environmental protection against pollutants and spills, (2) safe Arctic shipping, (3) increasing and coordinating search and rescue capabilities, and (4) responsible Arctic resource development. These priorities are echoed in Canada's Northern Strategy and Arctic Foreign

Policy[45]—although sovereignty is still one of the four "pillars"—and are also reflected in the U.S. Arctic Region Policy released in January 2009 as National Security Presidential Directive 66 (NSPD-66) and implemented in 2013 with a national strategy.[46] There is an air of optimism and anticipation concerning the possibilities that the NWP and the Arctic hold. The Arctic Council consults scientists, analysts, and Indigenous peoples from all eight Arctic states and decisions are made by consensus. The Arctic Council is responsible for drafting/negotiating a number of landmark documents including the Arctic Marine Shipping Assessment (2009), the Agreement on Cooperation in Aeronautical and Maritime Search and Rescue in the Arctic (2011), a new agreement on marine oil-pollution response (2013), and an Arctic Coast Guard Forum (2015).[47] These reports and agreements document the Arctic's shift from an area of "low" to "high" politics and from "high" to "low" military security in a short period of time.

The United States insists it is no longer a reluctant Arctic nation. Indeed, the secretary of state's participation at a number of Arctic Council meetings and the current U.S. chairmanship of the Arctic Council (2015–2017) represent the seriousness with which the United States and Canada view the Arctic, the NWP, and the potential of these areas.[48] Approximately 800,000 people live in Alaska and the Canadian Arctic. Both Canadian and American laws and policies require extensive consultation with the Aboriginal populations concerned before major projects can commence.[49] Increased activity on the NWP could potentially be a major boon for remote Indigenous communities which would benefit, financially, from these ventures. Northern Indigenous peoples are increasingly able to organize and articulate their demands, and Indigenous groups, like the Inuit Circumpolar Council, have created documents outlining their preferred terms of governance for the Arctic and NWP.[50] Furthermore, the Idle No More movement in Canada is helping to bring public attention to the rights of Indigenous peoples.[51] The fact remains, however, that no ports exist in Canada's Arctic (the port in Churchill, Manitoba—technically not in the Arctic—has been closed by its American owners).[52] All goods brought in by sea must be transferred to barges and unloaded by tractors on beaches—an unbelievably dangerous, slow, unpredictable, and archaic means of resupply management. Even in Iqaluit, Nunavut's capital, residents are dependent on a causeway built in the 1940s by the U.S. military. Vessels that run out of fuel need to be refuelled at sea given the absence of docking facilities. Meanwhile, many other Arctic towns across the circumpolar world, especially Nordic ones, are thriving because of sizeable population bases, decent infrastructure, and predictable resupply operations—all factors that Canada lacks in its Arctic.

How does the northern Canadian-American water border differ from its southern counterparts? Obviously, there are material differences. The North provides an interesting duality in terms of water scarcity and abundance; water is abundant, but often in the form of ice. Ice is essential for the Inuit and the ecosystem of the Arctic but a challenge for commercial interests. Still, there are conceptual similarities between northern and southern border waters. As is the case in other places examined in this volume, water diplomacy vis-à-vis the NWP revolves around fundamental questions about what a water resource is and to whom it belongs. Perhaps even more than the southern border, the northern water border is steeped in history, culture, and the identity of northerners—a fact often ignored or overlooked by decision makers in the South. Furthermore, like many other continental border flows, northern border waters can lead to both conflict and cooperation, but the latter requires compromise and a reevaluation of the role the NWP will play.

The fundamental disagreement between the United States and Canada over the categorization of the NWP has existed for decades and remains a point of contention. Old ideas about the NWP—namely, to protect it from foreign shipping, indeed, from any non-Arctic state involvement—are also slow to die.[53] Like most U.S.-Canada disagreements, bilateral negotiations are the usual modus operandi. Canada and the United States continue to work together, via survey work on the continental shelves in the Arctic and Atlantic, for instance, and extensive military cooperation via NORAD. The insistence of the Canadian government that the NWP is "not predicted to become a viable, large-scale transit route in the near term" is easing pressure to make a final determination of the status of the passage.[54] The search for energy sources and a number of other projects, like the open pit Mary River mine project in the North, will require the NWP as a transportation route.[55] Regardless of the classification of the NWP, issues of neglect abound: basic navigational and hydrographic services are still lagging, and regulations governing shipping in polar regions are insufficient generally.[56] The difference now is that Canada and the United States are recognizing these capability gaps openly and, through the Arctic Council, forging a more cooperative approach.

Canadian policy and the narrative of the NWP have shifted. Rather than focusing solely on staking a claim to the passage based on woolly adventure stories and ad hoc reactions to U.S. conduct there, the Canadian (and U.S.) emphasis is on responsible development—a phrase taken from one of three declarations issued by the Inuit Circumpolar Council.[57] This may mean that Canada has to consider the position of the United States and the European Union, which require the right of transit passage through international straits. Certain fundamental questions have yet to be asked: Does changing the categorization of the NWP affect its "Canadianness"? Or has Canada finally embraced the notion that it will best serve the NWP by protecting its marine species with the help of allies where it can, allowing commercial activity that benefits Indigenous and non- Indigenous Canadians, and making it the world standard in polar safety and navigability? If history is any guide, the collective narrative of the NWP remains a work in progress.

Notes

1   In 1619, Jens Munk (Norwegian), under the auspices of King Christian VI (King of Denmark-Norway), set out to transit the NWP. Only Munk and two of his sixty-four crew survived the cold, famine, and scurvy. The Canadian island off of Baffin Island is now called Jens Munk Island.

2   Sir John Franklin (UK) fared worse than Munk. Franklin's voyage began in 1845. All of his men died of similar causes when the expeditions of his two ships became ice-locked for multiple seasons. He is commemorated by several geographic features around the world, including Canada's Franklin Strait in the Arctic.

3   Rupert's Land was named for Prince Rupert, the cousin of the King of England, Charles I. Prince Rupert was granted the charter of the "Governor and Company of Adventurers of England trading into Hudson's Bay"—the full name of the HBC.

4   For an excellent discussion, see Janice Cavell, "The True Northwest Passage: Explorers in Anglo-Canadian Nationalist Narratives," *The Northern Review*, no. 32 (2010): 5–34.

5   Janice Cavell, "'A Little More Latitude': Explorers, Politicians, and Canadian Arctic Policy during the Laurier Era," *Polar Record* 47, no. 243 (2011): 289–309, esp. 292–93.

The concern was ownership and control of the islands more so than the waters, as they were considered unnavigable by all but a few, very hearty explorers.

6   See Cavell, "True Northwest Passage."

7   Robert Flaherty's films can be seen on YouTube. See Samantha Arnold, "Nelvana of the North, Traditional Knowledge, and the Northern Dimension of Canadian Foreign Policy," *Canadian Foreign Policy Journal* 14, no. 2 (2011): 95–107. The character of Nelvana is described as a superheroine based on a mythological Inuit woman. She was dressed in a miniskirt to give her mass appeal. Nelvana followed in the tradition of the white princess or goddess governing over "primitive" or "lost" peoples, specifically the "Eskimos"—a pejorative and southern term for Inuit. See *Truth and Reconciliation Commission of Canada: Calls for Action* (Winnipeg: TRC, 2015), http://www.trc.ca/websites/trcinstitution/File/2015/Findings/Calls_to_Action_English2.pdf.

8   Many Inuit children, beginning at the turn of the nineteenth century, were sent to day and residential schools and thus deprived of their family, language, and country food, and some were exposed to sexual and other forms of abuse. As well, eighty-seven Inuit from Inukjuak and Pond Inlet were "relocated" to Grise Fiord and Resolute Bay in the High Arctic in the 1950s. In March 1996, based on the recommendations of the Royal Commission on Aboriginal Peoples (1994) and other studies, the Canadian government paid a $10 million trust on behalf of the High Arctic relocatees and finally, on August 18, 2010, apologized formally. See "Apology for the Inuit High Arctic Relocation," Indigenous and Northern Affairs Canada, last modified September 15, 2010, http://www.aadnc-aandc.gc.ca/eng/1100100016115/1100100016116. In 2015, the TRC, chaired by the Honourable Justice Murray Sinclair, released its public report about what happened in Indian residential schools and provided recommendations for building a new relationship between Aboriginal peoples and Canadians; see *TRC: Calls to Action*.

9   On the Arctic in U.S. culture, see Michael F. Robinson, *The Coldest Crucible* (Chicago: University of Chicago Press, 2006).

10 Canada and the United States disagree on where the Beaufort Sea should be divided by the Alaska-Yukon border. Canada prefers that the boundary follow a straight line to the North Pole along 141st meridian west, while the United States would locate the boundary line perpendicular to the Alaskan coast, out to a distance of 200 nmi (370 km/230 mi), following a line of equidistance from the coast. This remains a managed dispute that will likely be solved via bilateral discussions.

11 Cavell, "'A Little More Latitude,'" 293.

12 Ibid., 296–99, 301–4.

13 Canada, Parliament, House of Commons, *Debates*, 22nd Parl., 1st sess., December 8, 1954, p. 698. St. Laurent, prime minister of Canada from 1948 to 1957, made the remark on the occasion of the creation of the Department

of Northern Affairs and Natural Resources.

14   Shelagh Grant, *Sovereignty or Security: Government Policy in the Canadian North (1936-1950)* (Vancouver: UBC Press, 1988).

15   Kenneth C. Eyre, "Forty Years of Military Activity in the Canadian North, 1947–1987," *Arctic* 40, no. 4 (1987): 294.

16   Lester B. Pearson, "Canada Looks Down North," *Foreign Affairs* 24 (July 1946): 638.

17   At the height of World War II, over 33,000 American military and civilian personnel operated in Canada's North. James Eayrs, *In Defence of Canada*, vol. 3, *Peacemaking and Deterrence* (Toronto: University of Toronto Press, 1972), 349.

18   JAWS comprised five stations located in the Arctic and staffed by U.S. and Canadian personnel between 1946 and 1972. On a related research project by Whitney Lackenbauer, Peter Kikkert, and Daniel Heidt, see the Joint Arctic Weather Stations (JAWS) Project website, accessed August 9, 2016, http://www.lackenbauer.ca/JAWS.

19   For a wonderful account of Commodore Robertson's career in the Arctic, see Jason M. Delaney and Michael Whitby, "'The Very Image of a Man of the Arctic': Commodore O.C.S. Robertson," *Canadian Naval Review* 4, no. 4 (2009): 25–29, http://naval.review.cfps.dal.ca/archive/1928859-6427241/vol4num4art6.pdf. Commodore Robertson was the former commanding officer of the HMSC *Labrador*—the Royal Canadian Navy's first icebreaker, which transited the NWP—and he joined the crews of several U.S. missions in the Arctic.

20   See Janice Cavell, ed., *Documents on Canadian External Relations, 1960*, vol. 27 (Ottawa: Foreign Affairs and International Trade Canada, 2007), documents 663–65.

21   For a summary, see Andrea Charron, "The True North Stronger and Freer with Help," in *Defence Requirements for Canada's Arctic*, ed. Brian MacDonald (Ottawa: Conference of Defence Associations Institute, 2007): 24–35, http://www.cdainstitute.ca/images/vimy_paper2.pdf.

22   Ted McDorman, *Salt Water Neighbors: International Ocean Law Relations between the United States and Canada* (New York: Oxford University Press, 2009); Ted McDorman, "Canada's Ocean Policy Framework: An Overview," *Coastal Management* 40 (2012): 133–44, esp. 136.

23   For a wonderful overview of the *Manhattan*'s voyage, see Ross Coen, *Breaking Ice for Arctic Oil: The Epic Voyage of the SS Manhattan through the Northwest Passage* (Fairbanks: University of Alaska Press, 2012).

24   *Canadian Territorial Sea and Fishing Zones Act*, S.C. 1964, c. 22. Section 3 provided for the 3 nmi territorial sea.

25   For a discussion of the various legal views of archipelagos and transit rights, see Sophia Kopela, *Dependent Archipelagos in the Law of the Sea* (Leiden: Martinus Nijhoff, 2013): 209–27.

26   Quoted in Christopher Kirkey, "The Arctic Waters Pollution Prevention Initiatives: Canada's

27 See Michael Byers and Suzanne Lalonde, "Who Controls the Northwest Passage?" *Vanderbilt Journal of Transnational Law* 42, no. 2 (2009): 1148–50.

28 Quoted in Coen, *Breaking Ice*, 66.

29 Although Gordon Robertson, then clerk of the Privy Council and secretary to the cabinet, was of a different opinion: "The ultimate objective was to establish and get international recognition for Canadian sovereignty over the waters of the Canadian Arctic archipelago. That was the overall objective.... There was also a legitimate concern about the consequences of oil spills or even just pollution from ships operating [in the area] and we did want to have some means for controlling those possibilities, but we also recognized that if we did something of that kind and if it was legitimate and if we carried out jurisdiction in a respectable and responsible way, that would over a period strengthen the claim that there was effective Canadian administration of these waters and therefore provide a better basis for an overall claim for sovereignty at some appropriate time." Quoted in Kirkey, "Arctic Waters Pollution Prevention," 43. After the decision of the International Court of Justice in the Anglo-Norwegian Fisheries case, plans had been developed for implementing straight baselines in the Arctic, but these were put on hold by the Pearson government. See U.S. Dept. of State, *Foreign Relations of the United States, 1964–1968*, vol. 12, *Western Europe*, ed. James E. Miller (Washington, DC: U.S. Government Printing Office, 2001), 678–714. The civil service wanted to go ahead with the baselines, but then Prime Minister Pierre Trudeau and his foreign policy advisor, Ivan Head, preferred the environmental stewardship approach, so the baseline approach was delayed until 1985.

30 This is often referred to in the literature as the "defence against help" security dilemma, first articulated by Nils Orvik. A weaker state, like Canada, often fears that its more powerful security assurer—in this case, the United States—will also become a threat. See Donald Barry and Duane Bratt, "Defense against Help: Explaining Canada-U.S. Security Relations," *American Review of Canadian Studies* 38, no. 1 (2008); published online November 11, 2009: 63–89.

31 Ivan Head and Pierre Trudeau, *The Canadian Way: Shaping Canada's Foreign Policy, 1968–1984* (Toronto: McClelland & Stewart, 1995): 25–64.

32 John Kirton and Don Munton, "The Manhattan Voyages and their Aftermath," in *Politics of the Northwest Passage*, ed. Franklyn Griffiths (Montreal: McGill-Queen's University Press, 1987), 93.

33 In addition, in March 2000, the Marine Liability Act (MLA) was introduced. The MLA places absolute responsibility and liability for safety, damages, and pollution on the owners and/or operators of vessels and on owners of docks, canals, and ports. Vessel owners and operators are responsible for such things as the safety of their crew and passengers, their cargo,

and any pollution created. The MLA, which applies to all incidents governed by Canadian maritime law, provides a uniform method for establishing liability that balances the interests of ship owners and passengers. The MLA extends north of latitude 60° north. In the event of an inconsistency between the MLA and the provisions of the *Arctic Waters Pollution Prevention Act*, or any regulation made under it, the MLA prevails to the extent of the inconsistency. See Transport Canada, "List of Marine Transportation Acts," accessed January 18, 2016, http://www.tc.gc.ca/eng/acts-regulations/acts-marine.htm.

34 Applying straight baselines is another method of calculating a coastal state's maritime boundaries. While used widely, it is not the method preferred by the United States, which has adopted the normal baseline method.

35 Kirkey, "Arctic Waters Pollution Prevention," 52.

36 Ibid., 55.

37 Article 234 reads, in full, that "Coastal States have the right to adopt and enforce non-discriminatory laws and regulations for the prevention, reduction and control of marine pollution from vessels in ice-covered areas within the limits of the exclusive economic zone, where particularly severe climatic conditions and the presence of ice covering such areas for most of the year create obstructions or exceptional hazards to navigation, and pollution of the marine environment could cause major harm to or irreversible disturbance of the ecological balance. Such laws and regulations shall have due regard to navigation and the protection and preservation of the marine environment based on the best available scientific evidence." UN Convention on the Law of the Sea, accessed August 11, 2016, http://www.un.org/depts/los/convention_agreements/texts/unclos/part12.htm.

38 The Northern Canada Vessel Traffic Services Zone (NORDREG) is the tracking system for certain vessels operating in Canadian Arctic waters. See "Vessel Traffic Reporting Arctic Canada Traffic Zone (NORDREG)," Canadian Coast Guard, last modified June 24, 2013, http://www.ccg-gcc.gc.ca/eng/MCTS/Vtr_Arctic_Canada.

39 U.S. Dept. of State, *Foreign Relations of the United States, 1969–1976*, vol. E-1, *Documents on Global Issues, 1969–1972*, ed. Susan K. Holly and William B. McAllister (Washington, DC: U.S. Government Printing Office, 2005).

40 Canada, Parliament, House of Commons, *Debates*, 33rd Parl., 1st Sess., September 10, 1985, pp. 6462–4.

41 Agreement on Arctic Cooperation, Can.-U.S., January 11, 1988, 1852 U.N.T.S. 31529.

42 MP Daryl Kramp (Prince Edward–Hastings) put forward a private member's bill (Motion No. 387) in 2009. The time provided for the consideration of business expired, and the order was dropped to the bottom of the order of precedence on the order paper. Canada, Parliament, House of Commons, *Debates*, 40th Parl., 2d sess., October 5, 2009.

43 The NWP is "ice-free" only in the summer months.

44 *Arctic Environmental Protection Strategy* (Rovaniemi, Finland, June 14, 1991), 20–23.

45 Both documents are available on the Global Affairs Canada website, accessed 11 August 2015, http://www.international.gc.ca/arctic-arctique/index.aspx?lang=eng.

46 The U.S. Senior Arctic Official, who represents the United States in most Arctic Council contexts, is based in the Office of Ocean and Polar Affairs within the Bureau of Oceans and International Environmental and Scientific Affairs, which falls under the State Department. See United States, *National Strategy for the Arctic Region*, May 2013, http://www.whitehouse.gov/sites/default/files/docs/nat_arctic_strategy.pdf.

47 All documents and updates can be found on the Arctic Council website, at http://www.arctic-council.org.

48 "U.S. Chairmanship of the Arctic Council," U.S. Dept. of State, October 29, 2015, http://www.state.gov/e/oes/ocns/opa/arc/uschair/index.htm. The theme of the U.S. term (2015–2017) is "One Arctic: Shared Opportunities, Challenges, and Responsibilities."

49 The need for this consultation was set out in two documents: President Bill Clinton's "Consultation and Coordination with Indian Tribal Governments" (Exec. Order No. 13175, November 6, 2000) and the Millennium Agreement (April 11, 2001). The Millennium Agreement recognizes tribes in Alaska and provides a framework for cooperation between federally recognized tribes and the State of Alaska. North Star Group, "Millennium Agreement Review," accessed August 11, 2016, http://www.ruralgov.org/wordpress/wp-content/uploads/2015/01/14-12-17-NSG-Millennium-Agreement-Review.pdf

50 A Circumpolar Inuit Declaration on Sovereignty in the Arctic (2009) and A Circumpolar Inuit Declaration on Resource Development Principles in Inuit Nunaat (2011) are both available at the Inuit Circumpolar Council Canada website, accessed August 18, 2016, http://www.inuitcircumpolar.com/declarations.html.

51 For example, many of the documents are available on the Idle No More website, accessed January 18, 2016, http://www.idlenomore.ca.

52 Bartley Kives, "Trudeau Government Still Mulling Port of Churchill Options," *CBC News*, August 4, 2016, http://www.cbc.ca/news/canada/manitoba/carr-churchill-port-1.3707953.

53 China, South Korea, Japan, India, Singapore, and Italy joined the UK, France, Germany, Poland, the Netherlands and Spain as non-Arctic state observers of the Arctic Council in 2015. This list represents major shipping and export states.

54 Government of Canada, *Statement on Canada's Arctic Foreign Policy: Exercising Sovereignty and Promoting Canada's Northern Strategy Abroad* (Ottawa: Government of Canada, 2010), 12.

55 See "Location and Project History," Baffinland Iron Mines Corporation website, accessed January 18, 2016, http://www.baffinland.com/the-project/location-and-project-history.

56 U.S. Coast Guard, *Report to Congress: U.S. Coast Guard Polar Operations* (Washington, DC: USCG, 2008).

57 See Leona Aglukkaq, "Canada's Second Chairmanship of the Arctic Council" (address, Arctic Frontiers Conference, Tromsø, Norway, January 21, 2013), http://www.arcticfrontiers.com/downloads/arctic-frontiers-2013/conference-presentations/monday-21-january-2013/62-03-leona-aglukkaq/file.

PART TWO

*Constructing the Border:
Hydropolitics, Nationalism, and Megaprojects*

Openings

Transboundary Power Flows

MATTHEW EVENDEN

Water and power have been central to the Canada-U.S. relationship. Before the twentieth century, the system of rivers, lakes, and canals that tied eastern ports to the interior of the continent structured the geography of North American political and economic development. While American settlement pressed westward along rivers like the Ohio, the Hudson, and the Potomac, Canadian westward development cleaved to the shores of boundary waters like the St. Lawrence and the Great Lakes. Canals built on either side of the border competed to improve rivers for navigation, overcoming cataracts and falls and, with them, the barriers to commerce and settlement. After Canadian Confederation (1867), as Canadians moved into the Northwest Territories to establish a settlement at Red River, they travelled to their destination by rail through the United States and then north by riverboat. At numerous points along the Canada-U.S. border, north–south trending rivers facilitated cross-border interaction, trade, and communications. The coming of the railroad began to diminish the importance of rivers as highways; yet, before the second industrial revolution, boundary waters provided some of the most crucial sites and spaces of interaction, where ships, goods, peoples, and ideas crossed and recrossed the line.[1]

Water began to take on a new significance after 1900 due to the expansion of irrigation agriculture in the West and water diversions and hydroelectricity in the East. Irrigation grew significantly in semiarid and arid sections of the western United States after 1840. Initially confined to valley bottoms and small projects, the scale of development expanded in the late nineteenth century. In 1902, the Reclamation Act transformed the U.S. federal government into a major developer of projects and water control infrastructure.[2] In Canada, the pace of development was much slower and less significant, confined primarily to fruit-farming regions of British Columbia's interior and mixed farming districts of southern Alberta.[3] Most of the early irrigation projects in Canada either were peopled by immigrant American farmers or deployed the expertise of American engineers.[4] Some exploited boundary waters. In the most southerly sections of Alberta in the late nineteenth century, for example, immigrant Mormon farmers originally from Utah took up land developed by the Alberta Irrigation Company and drew water off the St. Mary and Milk Rivers, both of which wended back and forth across the 49th parallel.[5] Across the border in Montana, American farmers irrigated crops with waters drawn from these same rivers. As the downstream users, however, Montana farmers stood at a disadvantage. They could use only what was left behind by irrigators upstream in Canada.[6] The resulting conflict modelled a larger problem: how to allocate shared waters for consumptive uses, where water taken out of a river or lake would not be replaced for uses on the other side of the border. In short, how could shared waters be developed, by whom, and for whom?

Irrigation agriculture raised one set of problems, urban water supply another. On the Great Lakes, the rapid rise of Chicago in the second half of the nineteenth century produced an intractable sanitation problem. The city dumped its wastes into the diminutive Chicago River, which faithfully carried the growing volume of sewage and industrial waste to Lake Michigan—from which the city also drew its water supply. To solve the problem, the State of Illinois empowered a newly formed Chicago Sanitary District to reverse engineer the problem. Because Chicago sat a mere sixteen kilometres from the watershed line between the Great Lakes and the Mississippi basin, engineers determined that it would be possible to divert water from Lake Michigan via a canal and control the outflow of the Chicago River, causing it to reverse its flow toward the west and south. These actions would effectively tip the polluted waters from Chicago into the upper Mississippi Basin and separate them from the city's water supply. Completed in 1900, the Chicago River diversion created controversy in the downstream Mississippi jurisdictions, because of the introduction of pollutants to the river, but also raised concerns in the Great Lakes because of the potential volume of flow that would now be withdrawn on an annual basis, in perpetuity, and with unknown but potential effects on navigation and water development downstream through the whole Great Lakes–St. Lawrence system.[7]

In the same period, the expansion of hydroelectric technology in the eastern United States and Canada suggested a new era of water relations on boundary rivers and lakes. Hydroelectricity operates by turning flowing water into controlled canals and penstocks that deliver the kinetic energy of falling water into powerhouses, to be converted by turbines into electrical energy. The infrastructure required for hydro developments involves the transformation and training of rivers with dams, the creation of reservoirs, and the regulation of flows. Given the abundant opportunities for hydro development in the Great Lakes–St. Lawrence basin and the undesirable effects of water diversion on downstream users, both Canada and the United States considered how best to manage this new technological complex with a view to existing uses—e.g., transportation, tourism at Niagara Falls—while also protecting national interests. To facilitate but also manage the new technology, some kind of framework was needed to structure the diversion and use of boundary waters and to accommodate binational concerns.[8]

With a border stretching from the Pacific to the Atlantic and cutting across a vast northern expanse, punctuated by some of the largest lakes in the world and major continental flows like the St. Lawrence, the Yukon, and the Columbia, the volume of potential areas of common interest or conflict was staggering. In its dealings with Mexico, the United States had been less troubled. As the upstream nation on north–south flowing rivers, the United States had pursued the Harmon doctrine, a simple and self-serving legal principle that asserted territorial sovereignty and allowed the upstream nation to divert and use waters as it saw fit.[9] Pressed into service on the Canada-U.S. border, such a doctrine would benefit Canada perhaps more than the United States. Rivers flow south as well as north. The Great Lakes presented more complex problems than rivers like the Rio Grande or the Colorado. At a time of limited continental diplomacy, when Britain retained its central role in negotiating Canadian foreign policy, an International Waterways Commission (IWC) was established in 1903, at the prompting of the United States, to investigate how best to manage boundary flows. Following several years of study and negotiation, which involved the IWC morphing into the International Joint Commission (IJC), a treaty was concluded in 1909 and subsequently ratified.[10]

The negotiators who framed the Boundary Waters Treaty of 1909 could not have envisioned the scale and complexity of problems that hydroelectric development would bring. As Canada and the United States began to transmit power across the border, most significantly from Canada to the United States, electrical systems grew in size and scale.[11] Dams were conceived as components of megaprojects—large-scale infrastructural investments that coordinated different water uses within the frame of river basins. When rivers crossed borders, so did the impacts of dams, as their reservoirs flooded valleys upstream and regulated water flows downstream.[12] Power plants located on boundary waters also contributed to vast and complex networks of power transmission, sometimes reaching far from the border. During World War II, for example, as both countries laboured to develop sufficient electrical power to drive wartime production, electricity transmission systems diverted power across the border and local projects were made to interconnect with more spatially extensive grids.[13] Thus, the particular and general contexts of boundary waters changed as flows came to be managed according to system demands over distance. By the mid-1960s, as Canadian provincial governments and power companies sought new opportunities for power sales in the United States, the links between Canadian hydro development and American markets grew more significant. Not only did American demands affect boundary waters, but, as U.S. utilities signed power contracts with Canadian utilities, they served to underwrite new development schemes as well, often located in the middle North at a vast distance from Canadian metropolitan centres and the U.S. border. North–south grids carried this power to market, while visions of a national, east–west grid in Canada foundered.[14]

The growth of irrigation agriculture across North America in the mid-twentieth century coincided with increased urban and industrial demands on water in the western states. Although some boundary waters were affected by this general trend, the more significant process was growing water consumption, marked by aquifer depletion and growing conflict over surface waters, sometimes at the local scale and sometimes across state boundaries, though rarely across the Canada-U.S. border. Periods of drought highlighted a looming problem, leading some to investigate new water conservation measures and others the promise of large water diversions, carrying surface flows from various northern Canadian rivers through elaborate canal and pipeline networks to dry regions of the western United States. With a breathtaking hubris about the capacity of modern technology to transcend environmental and social constraints, promoters conceived major manipulations of continental water systems.[15] Water, from this perspective, was a valuable and transportable resource. Where it flowed, and from whence, mattered only insofar as it affected costs. Any potential undesirable social and environmental consequences fell outside of the frame.

Promoters of water diversion did not anticipate the extent to which diverse interests, both American and Canadian, would come together to denounce their bold visions. Canadian and American politicians from the Great Lakes region pressed back against the easy assumptions of massive water diversions and sought to enhance safeguards against further withdrawals from the St. Lawrence–Great Lakes system. As Canadian and American relations entered a new period of economic continentalization after the signing of the Free Trade Agreement (1988) and, subsequently, the 1994 North American Free Trade Agreement (NAFTA), the linkages between trade and water came to be highly charged in Canadian politics. Canadian water advocates argued that *any* trade in bulk water exports to the United States from Canada would effectively open this resource to commercial trade under the terms of NAFTA. Although this claim has never been tested in practice or in the courts, the concern highlights both the new national and continental frames of water politics and the confluence of environmental and economic nationalist politics in Canada since the 1990s.[16]

As Canadians and Americans now face the challenges of climate change and ponder the links between global processes and regional climate systems, water and power take on renewed significance at the border. As glaciers recede in the Rockies and water levels decline in the Great Lakes, as the Ogallala Aquifer contracts with the years, how will the two countries respond to new challenges? What new political and technological pressures will be brought to bear on Canadian-American waters, at the boundary and beyond? What will the distribution be among different water uses both within national borders and across them?

The chapters that follow help us to consider the historical foundations of these problems. In "Dam the Consequences: Hydropolitics, Nationalism, and the Niagara–St. Lawrence projects," Daniel Macfarlane examines the shared development projects that transformed the St. Lawrence River and Niagara Falls in the mid-twentieth century, exploiting waters for hydroelectricity, building locks to assist navigation, and engineering Niagara Falls to preserve the appearance of a visually impressive cascade. While Macfarlane explains the political give-and-take that lay in the background of these megaprojects and outlines the cooperation required to execute them, he also notes how these binational endeavours bore different meanings north and south of the border. Despite the close relations that Canada and the United States struck in the context of these binational projects, Macfarlane underlines the different interests that both national parties understood to be in play and the different levels of significance that different national communities attached to them.

Nationalist politics also inflect Frédéric Lasserre's examination of the history of water export schemes and the particular position of Quebec politicians and companies in the debate. In chapter 5, "Quebec's Water Export Schemes: The Rise and Fall of a Resource Development Idea," he locates the origins of the water export idea in the mid-twentieth century, when massive schemes were envisioned to construct canals linking northern Canadian rivers to American markets. Considered alongside the St. Lawrence Seaway discussed by Macfarlane, it is not difficult to imagine how or why technological optimists and promoters conceived of such gargantuan schemes. In a period of surging postwar growth, megaprojects were viewed as achievable and desirable with a host of benefits. The sheer cost of continental diversion schemes, not to mention a rising chorus of nationalist criticism in Canada, headed off various incarnations of continental diversion, from the Great Recycling and Northern Development (GRAND) Canal in the late 1950s to the North American Water and Power Alliance (NAWAPA) in the 1960s. Nevertheless, Lasserre reminds us that this was not and may not be the end of the story. Quebec Premier Robert Bourassa, who famously and proudly described himself as a conqueror of the North with respect to the James Bay hydroelectric projects, eagerly explored the possibilities of bulk water export sales to the United States in the mid-1980s.[17] While Lasserre identifies some of the reasons why these efforts failed, and elaborates on the range of ways in which subsequent governments both in Quebec and elsewhere have sought to legislate against their possibility, he remains skeptical that renewed calls for water exports might not emerge again.

While the revisitation of the water export debate remains a possibility, the renewal of some dimensions of the Canadian-American water relationship is a certainty. The Columbia River Treaty, for example (struck in 1961 and amended with a protocol in 1964), lies today at the centre of a growing debate over how to adjust, modify, or eliminate some of its original terms—or, more seriously, how to cancel it. Created with a view to coordinating the flows of the Columbia River in order to manage the flood threat and optimize hydroelectricity at existing plants in the United States, the treaty contained a revision clause, Article XIX, allowing either signatory to exit the treaty after 2014, provided that ten years' notice is given. Jeremy Mouat's chapter, "Engineering a Treaty: The Negotiation of the Columbia River Treaty of 1961/1964," does not attempt to outline the likely outcome of this emerging negotiation, but rather provides the context to understand how the original treaty emerged and, by implication, how its terms structure the current moment of reconsideration. Mouat makes clear that the original negotiation was complicated first by binational disagreements over its terms and the identification and assignment of so-called downstream benefits to Canada because of the improvements to American flood protection and hydro generation downstream. He also explains, however, the significant role of the Province of British Columbia because of its constitutional authority over waters and resources, which were necessarily implicated by the international treaty, and BC Premier W.A.C. Bennett's ambition to harness the treaty to his own megaproject ambitions for the province's northern Peace River. While the current goals of Canadian and American negotiators and sub-national politicians differ dramatically from those of the formative days of the Columbia River Treaty, Mouat's analysis is nevertheless a timely reminder that cooperation on transboundary rivers has been hard-earned in the past and has both foreclosed other possibilities and come with costs as well as benefits.

Notes

1. A riverine perspective on North American development was most famously expounded by Donald Creighton in his classic study, *The Commercial Empire of the St. Lawrence, 1750–1850* (Toronto: Ryerson Press, 1937).

2. Donald Worster, *Rivers of Empire: Water, Aridity and the Growth of the American West* (New York: Pantheon, 1985); Donald Pisani, *To Reclaim a Divided West: Water, Law, and Public Policy, 1848–1902* (Albuquerque: University of New Mexico Press, 1992).

3. Matthew Evenden, "Precarious Foundations: Irrigation, Environment and Social Change in the Canadian Pacific Railway's Eastern Section, 1900–1930," *Journal of Historical Geography* 32, no. 1 (2006): 74–95; Christopher Armstrong, Matthew Evenden, and H.V. Nelles, *The River Returns: An Environmental History of the Bow* (Montreal: McGill-Queen's University Press, 2009).

4. Lawrence B. Lee, "The Canadian-American Irrigation Frontier, 1884–1914," *Agricultural History* 40, no. 4 (1966): 271–83.

5. Andy den Otter, "Irrigation in Southern Alberta 1882–1901," Occasional Paper No. 5, Whoop-up Country Chapter, Historical Society of Alberta, Lethbridge, AB, 1975.

6. N.A.F. Dreisziger, "Wrangling over the St. Mary and Milk," *Alberta History* 28, no. 2 (1980): 6–15.

7. Louis P. Cain, "Unfouling the Public's Nest: Chicago's Sanitary Diversion of Lake Michigan Water," *Technology and Culture* 15, no. 4 (1974): 594–613.

8. David Massell, "A Question of Power: A Brief History of Hydroelectricity in Quebec," in *Quebec Questions: Quebec Studies for the Twenty-First Century*, ed. Stéphan Gervais, Christopher Kirkey, and Jarrett Rudy (Oxford: Oxford University Press, 2011): 338–56; Daniel Macfarlane, *Negotiating a River: Canada, the United States and the Creation of the St. Lawrence Seaway* (Vancouver: UBC Press, 2014); Daniel Macfarlane, "'A Completely Man-Made and Artificial Cataract': The Transnational Manipulation of Niagara Falls," *Environmental History* 18, no. 4 (2013), 759–84; H.V. Nelles, *The Politics of Development: Forests, Mines, and Hydro-Electric Power in Ontario, 1849–1941* (Toronto: Macmillan, 1974).

9. Stephen C. McCaffrey, "The Harmon Doctrine One Hundred Years Later: Buried, Not Praised," *Natural Resources Journal* 36, no. 3 (1996): 549–90.

10. Robert Craig Brown and Ramsay Cook, *Canada: A Nation Transformed, 1896–1921* (Toronto: McClelland & Stewart, 1974), 174–77.

11. Janet Martin-Neilsen, "South over the Wires: Hydro-Electricity Exports from Canada," *Water History* 1 (2009): 109–29.

12. Phil Van Huizen, "Flooding the Border: Development, Politics and the Environmental Controversy in the Canada-U.S. Skagit Valley" (PhD diss., University of British Columbia, 2013).

13. Matthew Evenden, *Allied Power: Mobilizing Hydro-Electricity during*

Canada's Second World War (Toronto: University of Toronto Press, 2015); David Massell, "'As Though There Was No Boundary': The Shipshaw Project and Continental Integration," *American Review of Canadian Studies* 34, no. 2 (2004): 187–222; David Massell, *Quebec Hydropolitics: The Peribonka Concessions of the Second World War* (Montreal: McGill-Queen's University Press, 2011).

14   Karl Froschauer, *White Gold: Hydroelectric Power in Canada* (Vancouver: UBC Press, 1999); Alexander Netherton, "The Political Economy of Canadian Hydro-Electricity: Between Old 'Provincial Hydros' and Neoliberal Regional Energy Regimes," *Canadian Political Science Review* 1, no. 1 (2007): 107–24.

15   Benjamin Forest and Patrick Forest, "Engineering the North American Waterscape: The High Modernist Mapping of Continental Water Transfer Projects," *Political Geography* 31, no. 3 (2012): 167–83.

16   Frank Quinn, *Water Diversion, Export and Canada-U.S. Relations: A Brief History*, MCIS Briefings No. 8, Program on Water Issues, MCIS, University of Toronto, 2007, http://powi.ca/wp-content/uploads/2012/12/Water-Diversion-Export-and-Canada-US-Relations-A-Brief-History-2007.pdf.

17   Bourassa made this claim in an interview included in the film *Power*, VHS recording, directed by Magnus Isaacson (Toronto: Cineflix Productions / National Film Board of Canada, 1996).

Dam the Consequences: Hydropolitics, Nationalism, and the Niagara–St. Lawrence Projects

DANIEL MACFARLANE

Introduction

For first-time visitors to Niagara Falls, it can be difficult to find the actual waterfall, at least when approaching from the eponymous Ontario city. After running the gauntlet of Clifton Hill attractions, casinos, and souvenir stands, one of the few roads descending the Niagara gorge (or the incline railway tucked behind a hotel) still needs to be located. As the falls come into view, tourists assume they have exchanged the artificial and constructed for the natural and untouched; if only they knew that the great cataract has been built and shaped to no less a degree than the surrounding tourist traps. Then again, given the banality of the carnivalesque at this North American landmark—what with its tightrope walkers, erupting mini-golf volcanoes, barrels going over the falls, and so on—perhaps this should come as no surprise.

Indeed, the waterfalls at Niagara are themselves a type of infrastructure that was remade over the course of the twentieth century. The same is true of the St. Lawrence River farther downstream. In fact, much of the upper St. Lawrence is not even a river anymore, but a lake. The Niagara and

St. Lawrence Rivers are both key transportation links in the Great Lakes–St. Lawrence system, as well as the most prominent rivers that form—rather than cross—the border between Canada and the United States, and between Ontario and New York. Both river systems are iconic cultural waterscapes. The St. Lawrence River—which starts at Lake Ontario and carries the waters of all the Great Lakes before emptying into the Atlantic Ocean—was the historical water highway for the area that would become the Canadian state. Niagara Falls, which is made up of the larger Horseshoe Falls and the smaller American Falls, has in the past been held up as the North American epitome of the natural sublime. And, of course, both waterways were modern centres of industrial and hydroelectric development.

Niagara and the St. Lawrence are connected physically and conceptually. Measures to physically alter Niagara Falls were part of the diplomatic negotiations, stretched over the first half of the twentieth century, to build a St. Lawrence deep waterway. The 1950 Niagara Diversion Treaty authorized bilateral engineering works—the International Niagara Control Works—that enabled huge amounts of water to be diverted and used downstream at hydroelectric power stations, while also manipulating the river and waterfalls in order to maintain their scenic appeal. The St. Lawrence Seaway and Power Project, made legally possible by a 1954 diplomatic agreement, involved a deep-draft canal system stretching from Montreal to Lake Erie in conjunction with a massive hydroelectric project.

The power aspects of both of these megaprojects were built mostly by the same governments and planners in the 1950s (i.e., the Power Authority of the State of New York and the Hydro-Electric Power Commission of Ontario) utilizing many of the same engineers and workers. Moreover, both water systems were intimately tied to wider ideas about national development and the sublime, both natural and technological. Directly contrasting these two projects allows for unique insights about the North American manipulation of border waters in the early Cold War era. Niagara and the St. Lawrence developments up to the 1950s suggest shared approaches to water, nature, and technology; at the same time, these megaprojects simultaneously reveal important differences in Canadian and American conceptions of these borders waters and the links between national/regional identity and natural resources.[1]

Negotiations

Canadian-American negotiations for the eventual St. Lawrence undertaking began in the late nineteenth century and continued episodically until the project was built in the 1950s. A number of natural obstacles required many pre-twentieth-century "improvements" to the navigability of waters on, and connected to, the Great Lakes–St. Lawrence waterway, such as the Welland Canal, to avoid Niagara Falls, and the Soulanges/Beauharnois, Williamsburg, and Lachine Canals, to bypass rapids on the St. Lawrence River. Since the St. Lawrence forms the border between New York and Ontario, before running fully in Canadian territory through Quebec, as of 1909 (the year of the Boundary Waters Treaty, which created the International Joint Commission) bilateral cooperation was legally necessary if the St. Lawrence was to be turned into a deep-draft waterway. In the early twentieth century, Canada and the United States bandied back and forth proposals to further canalize the St. Lawrence. By the 1920s serious engineering studies were underway, and the idea of wedding a deep waterway to a hydro project had been cemented.

Transnational talks about improving the St. Lawrence tended to also include plans for comprehensive development of the connecting channels of the Great Lakes, such as the Niagara River. Large-scale hydroelectric production and distribution was born at Niagara Falls in the late 1800s. The many power stations and factories operating by the time of the Boundary Waters Treaty diverted water away from the Horseshoe and American Falls. The tailraces belched water down the sides of the gorge, and to those who equated industrial power with beauty, these channelled plumes were more attractive than the actual waterfall. At first, however, most of the power produced on the Canadian side was exported across the border, because the companies tended to be American-owned, despite their Canadian-sounding names.

Before the end of the nineteenth century, worries had already been raised about the aesthetic impact of the industry that crowded the shoreline to take advantage of the water power; of equal concern were the decreased water flows resulting from the diversions funnelled to the factories and power station. The reduced water volume detracted from the visual appeal, as did the natural process of erosion that had for eons steadily caused the falls to recede upstream. Both the American Burton Act (1906) and the

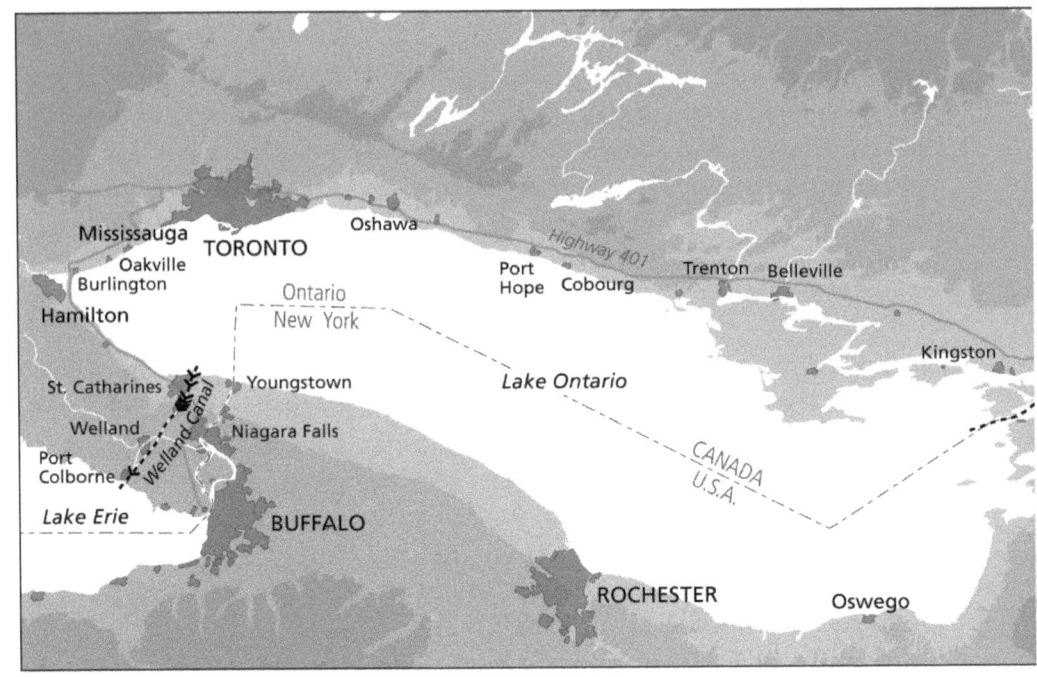

4.1 St. Lawrence Seaway. Map by Eric Leinberger. Reproduced with permission of University of British Columbia Press.

bilateral Boundary Waters Treaty put restrictions on the amount of water that could be diverted away from the falls. The latter limits were lifted during World War I, but then reinstituted afterward—though not always adhered to. In response to public worries about the scenic grandeur and diversions, Canada and the United States formed the International Niagara Board of Control in 1923, followed by a Special International Niagara Board in 1925. Based on the recommendations of the latter, the two countries signed the Niagara Convention and Protocol in 1929.[2] It called for remedial works that would disperse water to ensure an unbroken crest line in all seasons while reducing erosion rates, and it permitted each country experimental diversions of 10,000 cubic feet per second (cfs) from the Niagara River above the falls for seven years during the period from October 1 to March 31. However, the 1929 convention was not able to make it through the U.S. Senate, for it granted too much to private power interests;

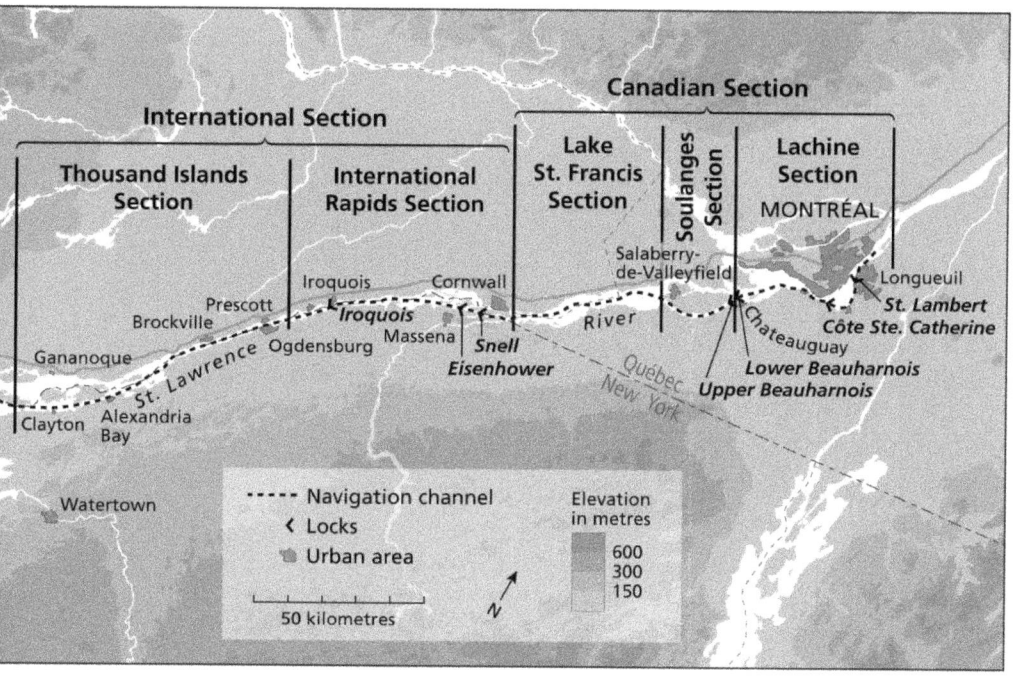

indeed, the scenic aspect of the agreement had been included largely to curry public favour for increasing diversions.

Was it the height, width, volume, colour, or lines that made Niagara Falls such a spectacle? In 1931 the Special Niagara Board released a report titled "Preservation and Improvement of the Scenic Beauty of the Niagara Falls and Rapids." The report's sections on colour were fascinating, and a special "telecolourimeter" was developed to test for the desired "greenish-blue" hue, which was considered superior to the whitish colour resulting from a thin flow over the precipice. The excessive mist and spray at the Horseshoe Falls was considered a turnoff because it obscured the view and, unsurprisingly, made people wet. The denuded bare rock at the flanks of the falls was labelled as one of the greatest detriments to the visual appeal, while erosion threatened to ruin the "symmetry" of the falls.

4.2 Mosaic of Proposed Niagara Remedial Works, c. 1935. Courtesy of Library and Archives Canada.

The report concluded that a sufficiently distributed volume of flow, or at least the "impression of volume," which would create an unbroken crest line, was most important. The board therefore recommended that the riverbed above the falls be manipulated in order to apportion the volume of water necessary to achieve the desired effect. Remedial works, in the form of submerged weirs and excavations, would achieve that while allowing for increased power diversions. This report, along with the 1929 convention, would serve as the conceptual basis for subsequent attempts in the following decades to deal with the tension between beauty and power at Niagara; the waterfalls were to be treated essentially as a tap, turned on and off according to aesthetic whims and power needs.

At the same time, St. Lawrence Seaway discussions were heating up, culminating in the Great Lakes Waterway Treaty. This treaty, signed in July 1932, authorized a deep waterway from the head of the Great Lakes to Montreal as well as hydro development in the St. Lawrence River. The treaty also dealt with a range of boundary water issues in the Great Lakes–St. Lawrence basin, including Niagara Falls and other Great Lakes diversions whose water could be utilized at Niagara, such as those at Chicago and Long Lac–Ogoki.[3] These were tit-for-tat; basically, Long Lac–Ogoki diversions into Lake Superior would make up for the water lost by the Chicago diversion. The 1932 treaty, however, failed to pass the U.S. Congress due to the range of interests opposed to the project. After all, why would railway magnates, and the votes they held in their pocket, want government-subsidized competition?

The Niagara landscape was nonetheless altered in other ways. For example, in 1921 the Hydro-Electric Power Commission of Ontario (HEPCO) brought online the first turbine of a new power plant, Sir Adam Beck No. 1 (the world's largest hydroelectric plant when it was completed in the 1930s). The plant diverted water via a canal starting above the falls that required the flow of the Welland River to be reversed. In addition to building a parkway and making other aesthetic improvements, Canada also reconfigured Table Rock in the 1930s by blasting off a large overhanging section. At about the same time, in the United States the Roosevelt administration decided to withdraw the still-unratified 1929 Niagara convention from Senate consideration and fold the Niagara issue into a new comprehensive agreement to deal with all Great Lakes–St. Lawrence basin navigation, power, and diversion issues.[4] But Ontario Premier Mitch Hepburn was obstreperously opposed, wanting Niagara development separate from the rest.

The onset of World War II changed the picture dramatically. Because of the need for power created by the conflict, Hepburn reversed his opposition to St. Lawrence development.[5] Roosevelt was now the more reluctant partner, because he would have to face the electorate in 1940. To help compensate for this delay, Roosevelt consented to Ontario undertaking the Long Lac–Ogoki diversions into the Great Lakes watershed and utilizing up to 5,000 cfs of the resulting extra water for hydro production downstream at Niagara Falls stations.

Canada and the United States decided to give a St. Lawrence agreement another try, covering the same ground as in the previous 1932 St. Lawrence treaty and 1929 Niagara treaty. On March 19, 1941, Canada and the United States entered into the Great Lakes–St. Lawrence Basin Agreement, an executive agreement rather than a treaty. This agreement created the Great Lakes–St. Lawrence Basin Commission to oversee construction of a twenty-seven-foot waterway in conjunction with a hydro dam in the International Rapids section of the St. Lawrence River. In addition to stipulating limits for the Chicago diversion and parameters for other diversions into the Great Lakes–St. Lawrence watershed, Article IX of the 1941 agreement provided for the construction of remedial works in the Niagara River, as well as means of testing their utility and authorization for immediate diversions of 5,000 cfs per side. But the Canadian-American St. Lawrence agreement also failed to receive the assent of Congress—a constant refrain in the St. Lawrence story—largely because of the entrance of the United States into World War II.

Nonetheless, the two countries agreed that the limits on the amount of water diverted at Niagara Falls could be temporarily increased for wartime needs: 5,000 cfs for the United States (to be followed by another 7,500 cfs) and 3,000 cfs for Canada. By June 1941, diversion of the extra water had begun, and subsequently, further withdrawals were allowed during the war, rising to a total diversion of 54,000 cfs for Canada and 32,500 cfs for the United States. In early January 1942, the two countries agreed to split the cost of constructing remedial works above the falls, with HEPCO as the responsible Canadian entity and the U.S. Army Corps of Engineers handling the American share. These works took the form of a stone-filled weir—a submerged dam—in the Chippawa–Grass Island Pool above the falls, which raised the water level about a foot in order to facilitate greater diversions while preventing an apparent loss of scenic beauty.[6]

Postwar Agreements

The wartime Niagara diversions continued indefinitely after the end of the war. In 1948, Canada and the United States exchanged notes endorsing a 4,000 cfs diversion at the falls, and another 2,500 cfs diversion from Queenston to DeCew Falls during the non-navigation winter season. The two countries continued to deal with Niagara diversion issues separate from the repeatedly stalled St. Lawrence issue, and a Niagara Diversion Treaty was signed in February 1950. This Canadian-American accord called for more comprehensive remedial works, to be approved by the International Joint Commission (IJC), and virtually equalized water diversions while restricting the flow of water over Niagara Falls to no less than 100,000 cfs during daylight hours (during what it deemed the tourist season: 8:00 a.m. to 10:00 p.m. from April to mid-September, and from 8:00 a.m. to 8:00 p.m. in the fall) and no less than 50,000 cfs during the remainder of the year. This worked out to Canada and the United States collectively taking, outside of tourist hours, three-quarters of the total 200,000 cfs flow of the Niagara River that would otherwise plummet over the falls, and approximately half of the total flow during tourist hours.[7]

In the immediate postwar years a variety of economic and defence factors brought further pressure to bear on a St. Lawrence Seaway and Power Project: the need for hydroelectricity for industrial and defence production, the ability of a deep waterway to transport the recently discovered iron ore deposits from the Ungava district in Labrador and northern Quebec, the possibility of protected inland shipbuilding on the Great Lakes, and the economic and trade stimulation that a seaway would bring. Additionally, the United States proposed that a seaway could pay for itself through tolls, which Canada eventually agreed to in 1947.

But the 1941 St. Lawrence agreement remained stalled in the U.S. Congress. In 1949, with Ontario experiencing major power shortages, the Liberal government of Louis St. Laurent realized that an "all-Canadian" waterway might be feasible and would not need the permission of the United States because it would not substantially change boundary water levels. But an all-Canadian seaway was viable only in conjunction with an Ontario–New York power dam. In 1948, both New York and Ontario had asked their respective federal governments for permission to forward to the IJC a "power priority plan" whereby the province and state would build a hydro dam separate from a deep waterway system. This scheme had initially been opposed by both President Harry Truman and Prime Minister St. Laurent. But, since this Ontario–New York plan would accommodate the all-Canadian waterway approach, the Canadians reversed their position.

Ottawa began taking steps to condition public opinion on both sides of the border for the possibility of an all-Canadian seaway coupled with an

Ontario–New York power project. A waterway entirely in Canadian territory quickly resonated with Canadians and the idea continued to build momentum throughout the 1950s; in fact, the government's campaign soon boomeranged, for the St. Laurent government then felt strong pressure to pursue a wholly Canadian waterway in order to satisfy popular opinion. An all-Canadian seaway, however, clearly threatened important American national security and economic interests. How could the leading country in the world let Canada control who came into the American backyard? Truman was opposed to the St. Lawrence project unless it proceeded as a joint Canada-U.S. endeavour. The president also favoured federal, rather than state (i.e., New York State), development of the hydro power.

The New York share of the hydro works, to be built by the Power Authority of the State of New York, needed a license from the U.S. Federal Power Commission (FPC). But the commission refused to grant a license. Although the FPC was supposedly free of partisan political influence, its commissioners were presidential appointees. It was clear that the White House was impacting the FPC's decision, and would continue to do so. To be fair, American interference was also partially the result of Washington's misreading of Canada's intentions to proceed alone with the waterway—a situation to which Ottawa had contributed by sending mixed messages about its commitment to proceed unilaterally. Since the hydroelectric works were needed to make a Canadian waterway a reality, Ottawa was essentially caught in a catch-22. The Canadian government tentatively left the door open to American participation in the hopes that doing so would allow the hydro aspect to commence. Dwight Eisenhower, who became president in January 1953, was noncommittal about the seaway until several months into his term. The Eisenhower cabinet finally came out in favour of American participation in May 1953, primarily for defence reasons. The FPC—surprise, surprise—quickly approved a license for New York. However, sectional and regional interests then conspired to exploit the appeals process so as to further hinder a start on the St. Lawrence project until 1954, when Congress finally approved American participation via the Wiley-Dondero Act.

In the end, Canada's prime minister consented to American involvement, chiefly because of the likely negative ramifications for the Canadian-American relationship if Canada resisted. Through a 1954 bilateral St. Lawrence agreement, Canada reluctantly acquiesced in the construction of a joint project—but not before it extracted certain concessions from the United States during the ensuing negotiations, such as the placement of the Iroquois lock and Ottawa's right to later build an all-Canadian seaway if it so desired.

Construction

The construction of the St. Lawrence Seaway and Power Project wrought huge changes in the St. Lawrence basin.[8] But that probably goes without saying, since an enormous river was being channelized and transformed into a reservoir-cum-lake. In excess of 210 million cubic yards of earth and rock—more than twice what was involved in building the Suez Canal—were moved through extensive digging, cutting, blasting, and drilling, using a plethora of specialized equipment and enormous machines. Approximately 110 kilometres of channels and locks were built and others rerouted, and even more kilometres of cofferdams and dikes were required. The entire project was completed on schedule, which, given its magnitude, was an amazing feat. Dubbed the "greatest construction show on earth,"[9] the St. Lawrence project required three new dams: the Moses-Saunders powerhouse, the Long Sault spillway dam, and the Iroquois control dam. The third regulated water levels on Lake Ontario and the portion of the St. Lawrence River to the west of Iroquois, while the Long Sault dam helped control water levels at the eastern end of the newly created Lake St. Lawrence. The Moses-Saunders powerhouse, a gravity power dam with thirty-two generator units that generated a combined 1.8 megawatts, was a bilateral project, with the Canadian and American halves bisected by the international border. The seaway cost $470.3 million (Canada paid $336.5 million; the United States, $133.8 million). Including the cost of the power phase, the bill for the entire project was over $1 billion.

In order to construct the new power dam, the International Rapids section of the river had been dried out through extensive cofferdamming. On July 1, 1958, some twenty thousand people gathered for "Inundation Day" to witness the creation of Lake St. Lawrence. Some twenty thousand acres of land on the Canadian side, along with another eighteen thousand acres on the American shore, were inundated. Because of differing population densities, relatively few Americans were directly affected compared

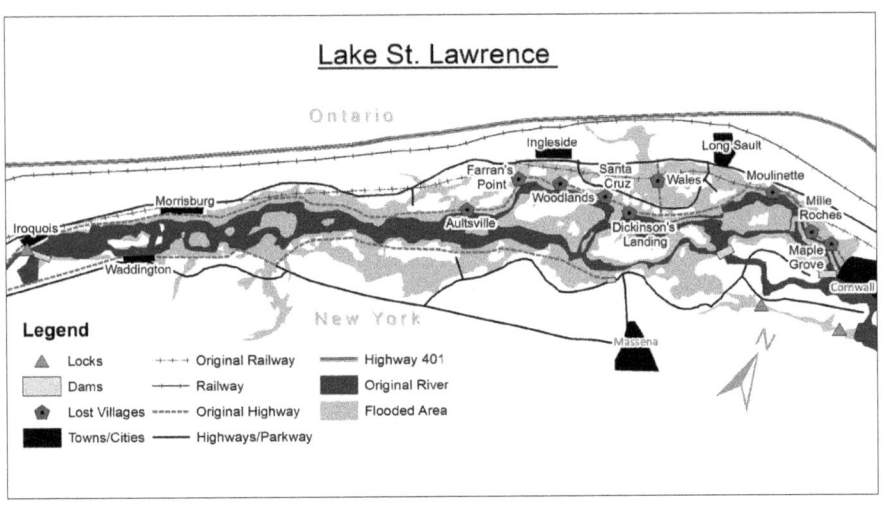

4.3 Lake St. Lawrence and Lost Villages. Map by author.

to the Canadian side. In addition to land in Ontario—where the seaway displaced 6,500 people in nine communities (often referred to as the Lost Villages) as well as farms and cottages—the seaway also submerged property in two Mohawk communities and southwestern Quebec.[10] Over one hundred kilometres of the main east–west highway and railway in Ontario had to be relocated, as did other infrastructure such as bridges and power lines, especially in the Montreal area. So as not to create navigation and other difficulties at the bottom of the new lake, *everything* had to be moved, razed, or flattened, including trees and cemeteries.[11] One would not want to run a boat onto a submerged chimney or tree—or gravestone. Since most of this rehabilitation work was in Ontario, HEPCO was responsible for compensating those who were relocated, which required an enormous logistical and public relations effort. A number of people chose to transport their houses via special vehicles to the new communities created to house the displaced residents, Ingleside and Long Sault, or the towns that were pushed north to accommodate the new shoreline, Iroquois and Morrisburg. While many relocatees bought into the idea that they were sacrificing for progress and benefitting in terms of material living conditions, for others the relocation took an enormous psychological and

4.4 Ingleside after inundation. Reproduced with permission of Lost Villages Historical Society, Long Sault, Ontario.

emotional toll.[12] Compensation for a sentimental attachment to a location, or the omnipresent sound of the rapids, was a tricky business.

After U.S. Senate approval, the Niagara treaty came into force in October 1950. It was then referred to the IJC, which subsequently created the International Niagara Falls Engineering Board. Studies by this board showed that, without remedial works, the diversions authorized in the 1950 treaty would have a very negative impact on the scenic beauty of the area: the Chippawa–Grass Island Pool level would drop by as much as four feet, exposing areas of the riverbed, turning the American Falls into an unsightly spectacle, and greatly marring the appearance of the flanks of the Horseshoe Falls.[13] In 1953 reports by the IJC and International Niagara Falls Engineering Board, the objectives remained basically the same as they had been in the 1920s: to ensure the appearance of an

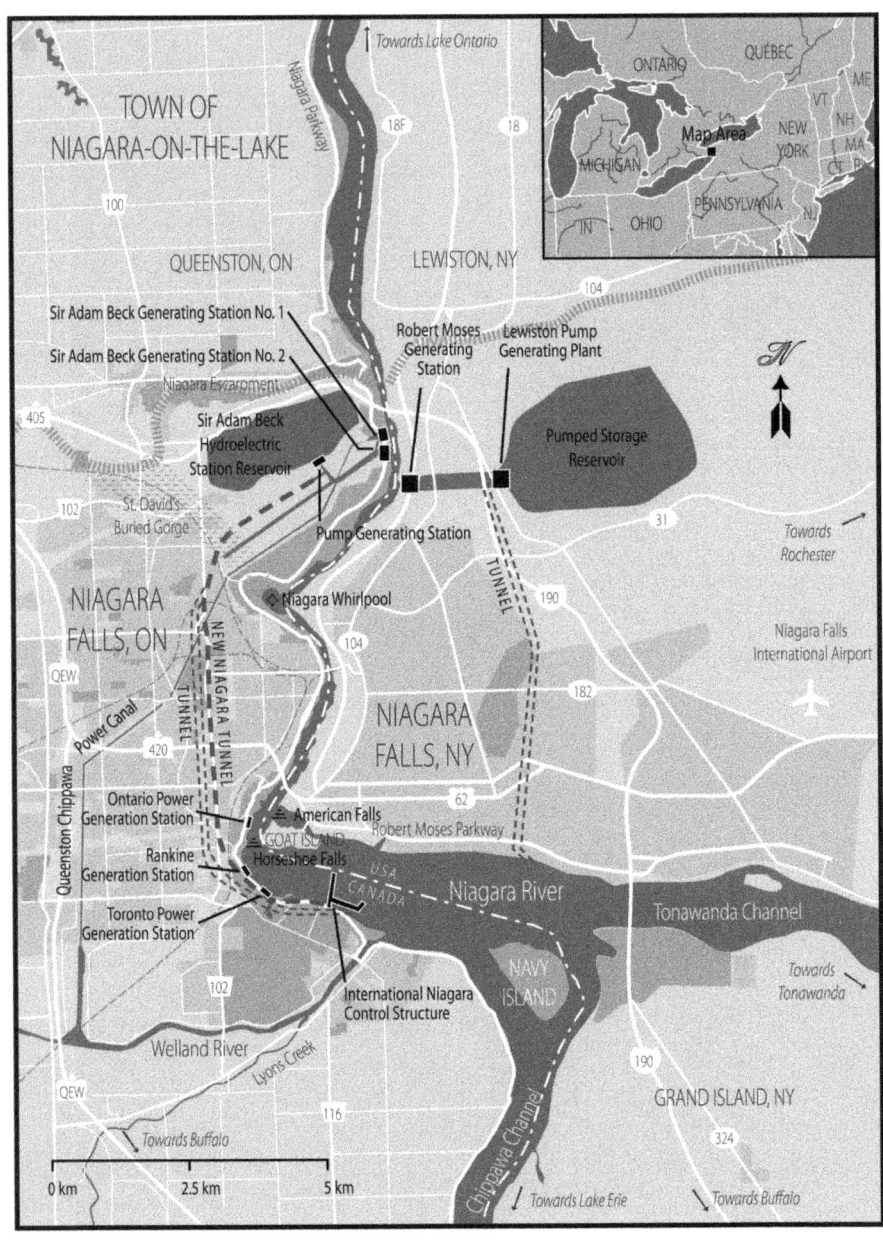

4.5 Niagara waterscape. Niagara Falls hydroelectric waterscape showing the various tunnels, conduits, reservoirs, and remedial works connected to hydroelectric production. Map by Anders Sandberg and Rajiv Rawat.

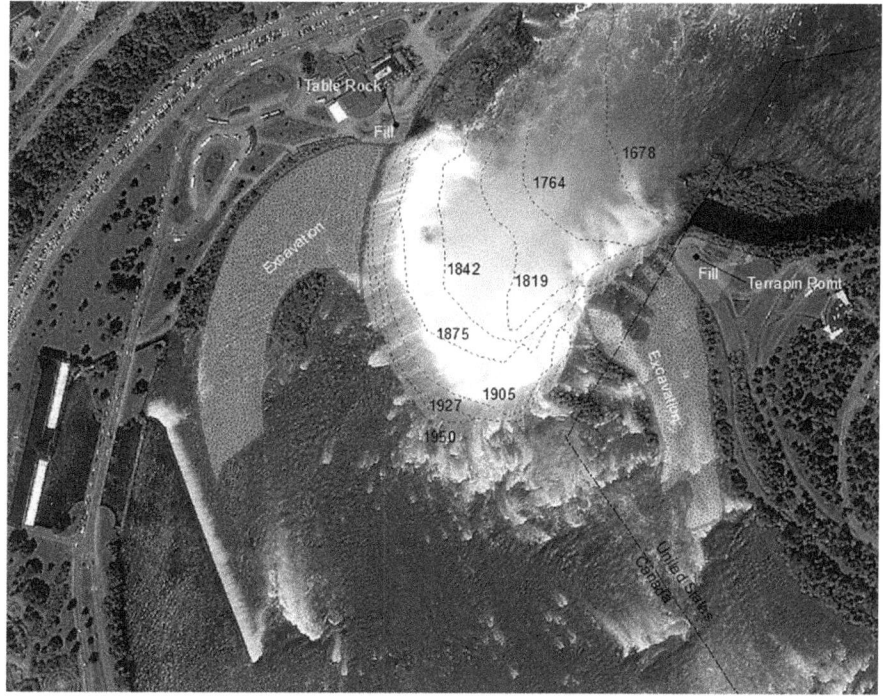

4.6 Horseshoe Falls showing rate of recession, crest fills, and flank excavation. Map by author.

unbroken and satisfactory crest line while allowing for the diversion of water for power production.[14]

The cost of the total Niagara remedial works was estimated at about $17.5 million, but it ending up totalling around $12.5 million when finished in 1957.[15] A 1,550-foot control structure extended in a straight line from the Canadian shore, parallel to and about 225 feet downstream from the weir built in the 1940s, eventually featuring eighteen sluices equipped with control gates. The purpose of this structure was to control water levels and spread out the water, for appearance and because flows concentrated in certain places caused more erosion damage. Excavation took place along the flanks of the Horseshoe Falls (64,000 cubic yards of rock on the Canadian flank; 24,000 cubic yards on the American flank) in order to create a better distribution of flow and an unbroken crest line at all times.

To compensate for erosion, crest fills (100 feet on the Canadian shore and 300 feet on the American side) were undertaken, parts of which would be fenced and landscaped in order to provide prime public vantage points.[16]

Water, Technology, and Nationalism

The history of developments on both the St. Lawrence and Niagara is indicative of a North American confidence in the ability of technology to control, tame, and exploit the natural environment, an impulse that took on even more urgency as the Cold War dawned after 1945. Because of the strategic security roles of the St. Lawrence and Niagara projects—both created necessary electricity, and the seaway added additional continental security value—they represented state-building enterprises that served as physical defences against the growing threat presented by the Soviet Union. Fascination with the "technological sublime" was intimately intertwined with Cold War symbolism in Canadian and American attempts to assert the nature of capitalist democracies as more progressive, modern, and powerful than that of communist nations.[17]

Both states—along with their respective bureaucracies and experts—displayed key characteristics of high modernism. High modernism is essentially the hubristic twentieth-century idea that governments and their experts and bureaucracies had the infallible knowledge, technology, and power necessary to control society and the environment and could do so with such expertise that they need not fear any repercussions.[18] As a state-building exercise controlled by centralized bureaucracies with the aim of reordering both the natural environment and society for the sake of progress, the St. Lawrence and Niagara schemes certainly fit key elements of high modernism. But the high modernist concept, generally applied to nonauthoritarian states, needs to be contextualized and modified when applied to historical Canadian and American subjects. A number of scholars have already done so in the Canadian context.[19] I suggest that we see in post–World War II North America what can be called *negotiated* high modernism: in order to dominate and control both nature and society, Canadian and American governments had to repeatedly adapt, negotiate, and legitimize themselves and their grand schemes to those they governed.[20]

4.7 Moses and Beck power stations. Photo by author.

4.8 Robert Moses generating station. Photo by author.

Niagara is a unique high modernist case because, rather than seeking to visually dominate the natural setting, as did the St. Lawrence project, the control works at and above the actual cataract were largely hidden (to be sure, the downstream power projects were designed to invoke awe from the general observer). Instead of making the technology obvious, they were designed to be unseen. This can be partially explained pragmatically—Niagara Falls had to continue to look like itself, or at least some idealized version of itself—and the states' interest in Niagara's beauty can be boiled down to tourism dollars. But it also speaks to a different variant of high modernism in which the desire to dominate was so pervasive that technology was not so much imposed on nature; rather, nature itself was controlled to become the technology and thus the beautiful and sublime. The overarching goal was to create an uninterrupted "curtain of water" over the precipice that displayed a pleasing consistency and colour. The remedial works were intended to reduce "spray problems," as excessive mist was scaring visitors away from the tunnels behind Table Rock. All of this speaks to the commodification of the Niagara experience, a process intertwined with the other tourist trappings prevalent at Niagara Falls: nature should be sanitized, made predictable and orderly, and packaged for easy consumption.

It was a manufactured landscape, a hybrid of the real and artificial. Ginger Strand calls Niagara an "in-between" landscape, which is compatible with other concepts that academics have provided for discussing hybrid environments that blended the organic and industrial.[21] The great cataract was reduced to cubic feet per second and linear feet of crest line, a schematic or blueprint where the beauty for the engineers lay in their precision and control over the waterfall. It was to be regulated and fine-tuned to produce maximum beauty and maximum power. The water still flowed over a rock cliff, and thus was natural, but it did not go over the precipice in a natural way. It had been radically altered and modified to suit humanity's tastes. The majority of the Niagara River's water was not even going over the lip of the falls, but passing around to form a different type of waterfall in the penstocks of the Niagara power plants farther down the gorge. There was a transnational willingness to sacrifice the epitome of the sublime for the sake of power and industry.

The creation of both the St. Lawrence and Niagara projects speaks to transborder ideas about technology and environment, but also to the ways

4.9 Partially submerged remains of a Lost Village in the St. Lawrence. Photo by author.

that national identities were bound up in such ideas. The St. Lawrence River was historically seen as a national, rather than a shared, river. This view of the St. Lawrence as a primarily "Canadian" river manifested itself in the attempts for an all-Canadian seaway. The St. Lawrence River holds an exalted and iconic place in the Canadian national imagination, as the river served as the crucible of Canadian settlement and development. The meaning of the river was extended to the seaway. Canadian historiography is replete with notions of the river narrative and aquatic symbolism—Canadians "consider water part of their natural identity," because "rivers are Canadian cultural icons; they have consistently communicated the idea of Canada, its meta-narrative of nation-building and collective identity."[22] This is exemplified by the Laurentian thesis, forwarded most prominently by Donald Creighton. In Creighton's words, "the dream of the commercial empire of the St. Lawrence runs like an obsession through the whole of Canadian history. ... The river was not only a great actuality; it was the central truth of a religion."[23] Put simply, the Laurentian thesis holds that the St. Lawrence River was the dominant element in shaping the territorial, political, economic, and cultural evolution of Canada.

A number of other prominent post–World War II historians, such as W.L. Morton and J.M.S. Careless, also pointed to the pivotal role of the St. Lawrence in Canada's historical development, and many popular histories from the era adopted similar themes and approaches.[24] Historian Janice Cavell argues that "no other interpretation of history has ever been so widely and whole-heartedly accepted [in Canada] as Laurentianism once was" at the height of its popularity, from the 1930s to the 1960s.[25] It is no coincidence that this was also the time period during which the seaway was completed. The Laurentian thesis helped sustain the conception of the St. Lawrence watershed as the defining and fundamental aspect of Canadian history and identity and, in turn, infused the notion of an all-Canadian seaway with the same nationalist importance and symbolism.

The St. Lawrence could serve as both a bridge and a barrier between, alternatively, English and French Canada, and Canada and the United States.[26] The sense of identity with, and ownership of, the St. Lawrence resulted in a fear of American encroachment on the river, particularly in connection with the reaction of Canadian nationalists against their nation's subservient role as a mere raw-material exporter to the United States. St. Lawrence nationalism had seized Canadians. The St. Lawrence project also fit neatly into the St. Laurent government's nation-building agenda. An all-Canadian project, along with other contemporary transportation projects such as the Trans-Canada Highway, had nation-building parallels with the transcontinental railways.[27] The seaway effectively served as a conduit for many different expressions of Canadian nationalism, which can be subsumed under the term "hydraulic nationalism."[28] Incidentally, the seaway never came close to paying for itself, and when we consider factors such as allowing invasive species into the Great Lakes, the seaway should perhaps be characterized as a mistake. Granted, such assessments are complicated, for the resulting hydroelectricity met expectations and the project would have proven very useful had the feared World War III actually occurred.

The desire to dominate the natural world has been well established in American historiography,[29] and various views of the link or dialectic between nationalism, identity, environment, and technology exist in modern

Canadian history.³⁰ Both Canadian and American identities have strong ties to their respective landscapes and have environmentally determinist forms of explanatory development paradigms: e.g., the frontier thesis in the United States; the metropolitan-hinterland, staples, and aforementioned Laurentian theses in Canada. Yet it has been suggested that Canadians tend to see nature in more antagonistic terms. Some commentators argue that this antagonism stems from the conception of Canada as a small population struggling against a vast, foreboding, cold, and hostile landscape,³¹ while other identifiable factors can also serve as partial explanations for differing Canadian and American views of nature.³²

The argument that "technological nationalism has characterized the Canadian state's rhetoric concerning identity" is extremely persuasive—from the early Canadian staples trade to railroad building to the St. Lawrence Seaway and Power Project.³³ Hydroelectricity in particular was seen as a means of delivering Canada from its "'hewer of wood' servitude to American industry and its bondage to American coal."³⁴ Technology was historically seen by Canadian nationalists as the means by which the United States could dominate and control Canada. However, technology was a "double-edged sword"; by the mid-twentieth century, Canadian access to modern technology—which could be used to conquer the hostile environment—held out the potential for the nation to evolve independently of the United States, rather than further integrating the two countries.³⁵

Hydraulic and technological nationalism were apparent in both the St. Lawrence and Niagara projects. Patrick McGreevy argues that Niagara resonated with Canadian nationalists for various reasons (many of which could equally apply to the St. Lawrence), including Niagara's proximity to the Canadian heartland, its connection to the St. Lawrence–Great Lakes system, its sites of Canadian resistance to American encroachment in the War of 1812, and uniquely Canadian views of the environment. Put another way, Niagara Falls was Canada's front door and America's back door; again, this metaphor could apply to the St. Lawrence.³⁶ However, Niagara Falls was more strongly linked to the United States during the nineteenth century, from the Grand Tour to Frederic Church's iconic painting. In the Canadian consciousness, Niagara Falls was traditionally conceived of as a border water, and though the "better" part of it was in Canada (i.e., Horseshoe Falls), the Niagara River and falls were not seen as "Canadian" to the same extent as the St. Lawrence.

Public pressure seemed stronger on the American side for work to retain the visual quality of the cataract. This can be attributed to Niagara's past association with the American natural sublime, though the American side had been degraded by industry and electrochemical production over the years to a greater extent than had the Canadian share. Granted, support for remedial works was in many ways and for many interests a convenient cover for supporting increased diversion for industrial development—the U.S. federal government and the State of New York were, like the Canadian and Ontario governments, attracted most by the power they could get from Niagara, though this tended to have nationalist motivations for Canada and imperialist motivations for the United States.

Niagara Falls was a Canadian nationalist expression for many of the reasons McGreevy suggests, and his back door/front door metaphor is quite apt for describing the Great Lakes–St. Lawrence border; however, it was the technological control of Niagara Falls for hydroelectric development that resonated most strongly with Canadian nationalists, at least during the early Cold War period. Just as was the case with the St. Lawrence, the hydro power of the Niagara River was a stronger nationalist expression than was its natural beauty, for it represented the full usage of the nation's natural birthright. Though the Niagara works were a joint undertaking with the United States, this partnership was as much a result of practical necessity as of a desire to cooperate. For some Canadians, such technological development and resource exploitation would allow for greater integration with the United States; for others, it was the means by which to distance Canada from reliance on the United States.

Conclusion

The Niagara and St. Lawrence rivers were replumbed to provide hydroelectricity, navigation, and scenic appeal. Both the federal and the state-provincial governments shared fundamental assumptions about the role of the state in developing and exploiting water resources for the national benefit. Waters running wasted to the sea were to be channelled and made productive, and the state possessed the means to manipulate the environment in many ways. Such ideas also permeated the general public in both countries, as few questioned the logic of the projects, even among those relocated by the St. Lawrence project.

Both of these projects required cooperation between the Canadian and American federal governments, the Ontario and New York governments, and the IJC. The Niagara and St. Lawrence projects are generally portrayed as a testament to bilateral cooperation, which is true, though we should not let the enormous level of integration that resulted from the planning and execution of these massive megaprojects obscure the fact that, during the first half of the twentieth century, their negotiations were defined more by conflict. Moreover, we should not automatically assume that national collaboration is a good thing; from a border river's point of view, whether or not cooperation is positive depends on the end goals. When it comes to pollution and water quality, joint national action—such as the Great Lakes Water Quality Agreements of the 1970s—appears to have been mostly beneficial. But if the purpose is industrial development and the manipulation of water quantity, which was the case with the St. Lawrence and Niagara Rivers, then governmental cooperation appears to be ecologically detrimental, since cross-border coordination leads to the construction of works with major environmental consequences. The St. Lawrence and Niagara Rivers eluded large-scale development and environmental degradation until the second half of the twentieth century precisely because they were border waters; if these rivers had been wholly within one country, they almost certainly would have been dammed and developed decades earlier. Perhaps it is fair to say that, in the Canadian-American context, border waters are more likely to escape—or at least forestall for a longer period—the most catastrophic consequences of industrial exploitation. Put another way, a lack of political cooperation across the border can lead to inadvertent environmental protection on the border.

Nonetheless, the completion of these power/navigation developments further merged Canada and the United States as economic, defence, and cultural allies. The building of both projects was intimately intertwined with Cold War symbolism in Canadian and American attempts to assert the superiority of the Western way of life. However, the historical development of these two megaprojects also reveals differing, even competing, national conceptions of border waters. In both cases, water was perceived as inherent to Canadian identity, and evolving technologies as the means by which Canada could fully embrace its hydrological birthright.

Notes

1. Thanks to the various participants in the 2012 Border Flows workshop for their feedback.

    The information and arguments presented here are drawn from larger studies by the author on both the St. Lawrence and Niagara projects. See Daniel Macfarlane, *Negotiating a River: Canada, the U.S., and the Creation of the St. Lawrence Seaway* (Vancouver: UBC Press, 2014); "Creating a Cataract: The Transnational Manipulation of Niagara Falls to the 1950s," in *Urban Explorations: Environmental Histories of the Toronto Region*, ed. Colin Coates, Stephen Bocking, Ken Cruikshank, and Anders Sandberg (Hamilton, ON: L.R. Wilson Institute for Canadian Studies / McMaster University, 2013); and "'A Completely Man-Made and Artificial Cataract': The Transnational Manipulation of Niagara Falls," *Environmental History* 18, no. 4 (2013): 759–84. The author is in the process of writing a book on the history of the Canadian-American engineering and hydroelectricity landscape of Niagara Falls.

2. Col. W.H. Potter (Office Chief of Engineers, U.S. Army), statement, June 27, 1950, file: St. Lawrence Seaway, Box 69, staff file: Records of John S. Bradgon, St. Lawrence Seaway – 1954, Dwight D. Eisenhower Presidential Library and Archives, Abilene, KS (hereafter, Eisenhower Archives); Special International Niagara Board, Preservation and Improvement of the Scenic Beauty of the Niagara Falls and Rapids, S. Doc. No. 128-71/2 (Washington, DC: Government Printing Office, 1931).

3. The Chicago diversion, which from the early twentieth century took water from Lake Michigan through the Chicago Sanitary and Ship Canal into the Mississippi River basin and eventually to the Gulf of Mexico, was a continual irritant in Canadian-American relations.

4. Franklin D. Roosevelt, memorandum to Secretary of State, December 23, 1935, 711.42157 SA 29/1375-½, Box 4048, RG59, Government of the United States, National Archives and Records Administration (NARA) II, College Park, MD.

5. On Canada's growing development of hydro power during World War II, see Matthew Evenden, *Allied Power: Mobilizing Hydro-Electricity during Canada's Second World War* (Toronto: University of Toronto Press, 2015).

6. Col. W.H. Potter statement, June 27, 1950, Eisenhower Archives.

7. The allowable diversion volume was split evenly between the two countries. As the United States was not able to utilize its full complement of the water, because it did not have enough hydroelectric generating facilities in place, Canada was allowed to use this extra water—until the United States was able to, which would prove to be later in the 1950s with the construction of the Moses plant. Proposed FPC Plan for Niagara Power Redevelopment, 1953, Eisenhower Archives.

8. For extended studies of the construction phase, see Macfarlane, *Negotiating a River*, as well as Robert W. Passfield, "The Construction of the St. Lawrence Seaway,"

Canal History and Technology Proceedings 22 (2003): 1–55; Claire Parham, *The St. Lawrence Seaway and Power Project: An Oral History of the Greatest Construction Show on Earth* (Syracuse, NY: Syracuse University Press, 2009); William H. Becker, *From the Atlantic to the Great Lakes: A History of the U.S. Army Corps of Engineers and the St. Lawrence Seaway* (Washington, DC: U.S. Army Corps of Engineers, 1984); and William R. Willoughby, *The St. Lawrence Waterway: A Study in Politics and Diplomacy* (Madison: University of Wisconsin Press, 1961). Passfield and Becker provide the best overview of the technical aspects, while Parham focuses on the social and cultural aspects.

9   The phrase, used in Parham's subtitle, is attributed to M.W. Oettershagen, deputy administrator of the Seaway Development Corporation in 1959. Parham, *St. Lawrence Seaway*, xxiii.

10   On the American side, approximately eighteen thousand acres were flooded, requiring the clearance of around 1,100 people, 225 farms, five hundred cottages, and 12.5 miles of highway. No entire communities were relocated, in part because of dikes that protected Massena, though the waterfront area of Waddington was affected and the town of Louisville lost about a third of its taxable land, including Louisville Landing, a historic port on the St. Lawrence.

11   While this razing was undoubtedly a pragmatic consideration, Tina Loo argues that a key aspect of modernity was a rejection of the past, symbolized by the removal of buildings and infrastructure in areas to be flooded as part of hydroelectric projects. The relocation of buildings and resettlement and consolidation of communities was also part of the Arrow Lakes project. Loo, "People in the Way: Modernity, Environment, and Society on the Arrow Lakes," *BC Studies*, no. 142–143 (Summer/Autumn 2004): 177–80.

12   Reginald Hardy, "Many Fine Homes Soon to Disappear—St. Lawrence Families' Plight," *Ottawa Evening Citizen*, August 11, 1954, copy, SPP Series, HEPCO Archives, Toronto.

13   IJC, Canadian Section, *Preservation and Enhancement of Niagara Falls: Report to the International Joint Commission by the International Falls Engineering Board* (Washington/Ottawa: IJC, 1953).

14   IJC, Canadian Section, *Report to the Governments of the United States of America and Canada on Remedial Works Necessary to Preserve and Enhance the Scenic Beauty of the Niagara Falls and River* (Washington/Ottawa: IJC, 1953).

15   Nuala Drescher, *Engineers for the Public Good: A History of the Buffalo District U.S. Army Corps of Engineers* (Washington, DC: U.S Army Corps of Engineers, 1982), 258.

16   "Niagara Falls Preservation Program Starts," press release, January 15, 1954, file 1268-D-40, vol. 6348, pt. 25.2, St. Lawrence General Correspondence (November 25, 1953–January 29, 1954), LAC.

17   David E. Nye, *American Technological Sublime* (Cambridge, MA: MIT Press, 1994).

18   James C. Scott, *Seeing Like a State: How Certain Schemes to Improve the Human Condition Have Failed*

(New Haven: Yale University Press, 1998), 4.

19 Tina Loo with Meg Stanley, "An Environmental History of Progress: Damming the Peace and Columbia Rivers," *Canadian Historical Review* 92, no. 3 (2011): 399–427; Tina Loo, "High Modernism, Conflict, and the Nature of Change in Canada: A Look at *Seeing like a State*," *Canadian Historical Review* 97, no. 1 (2016): 34–54; James Murton, "Creating Order: The Liberals, the Landowners, and the Draining of Sumas Lake, British Columbia," *Environmental History* 13, no. 1 (2008): 96, 104; Matthew Farish and P. Whitney Lackenbauer, "High Modernism in the Arctic: Planning Frobisher Bay and Inuvik," *Journal of Historical Geography* 35, no. 3 (2009): 519.

20 For a further elaboration of "negotiated high modernism," see Macfarlane, *Negotiating a River*, 228–29; and Daniel Macfarlane, "Negotiated High Modernism: Canada and the St. Lawrence Seaway and Power Project," in *Science, Technology, and the Modern in Canada: An Anthology in Honour of Richard Jarrell*, ed. Edward Jones-Imhotep and Tina Adcock (Vancouver: UBC Press, forthcoming).

21 Ginger Strand, *Inventing Niagara: Beauty, Power, and Lies* (Toronto: Simon & Schuster, 2008), 197; Richard White, *The Organic Machine: The Remaking of the Columbia River* (New York: Hill & Wang, 1995). See also Paul R. Josephson, *Industrialized Nature: Brute Force Technology and the Transformation of the Natural World* (Washington, DC: Island / Shearwater, 2002); David E. Nye, *American Technological Sublime* (Cambridge, MA: MIT Press, 1994); Erik Swyngedouw, "Modernity and Hybridity: Nature, *Regeneracionismo*, and the Production of the Spanish Waterscape, 1890–1930," *Annals of the Association of American Geographers* 29, no. 3 (1999): 443–65.

22 Carolyn Johns, introduction to *Canadian Water Politics: Conflicts and Institutions*, ed. Mark Sproule-Jones, Carolyn Johns, and B. Timothy Heinmiller (Montreal: McGill-Queen's University Press, 2008), 4; Jean Manore, "Rivers as Text: From Pre-Modern to Post-Modern Understandings of Development, Technology and the Environment in Canada and Abroad," in *A History of Water*, vol. 1, *Water Control and River Biographies*, ed. Terje Tvedt and Eva Jakobsson (London: I.B. Tauris, 2006), 229.

23 Donald Creighton, *The Commercial Empire of the St. Lawrence, 1750–1850* (Toronto: Ryerson Press, 1937), 6–7.

24 W.L. Morton, "Clio in Canada: The Interpretation of Canadian History," *University of Toronto Quarterly* 15, no. 3 (1946): 227–34; W.L. Morton, *The Kingdom of Canada: A General History from Earliest Times* (Toronto: McClelland & Stewart, 1963); J.M.S. Careless, *Canada: A Story of Challenge* (Toronto: Macmillan of Canada, 1963).

25 Janice Cavell, "The Second Frontier: The North in English-Canadian Historical Writing," *Canadian Historical Review* 83, no. 3 (2002): 4.

26 For examples of literature from Quebec that identify with the St. Lawrence, see Jean-Claude Lasserre, *Le Saint-Laurent, grande*

porte de l'Amérique (LaSalle, QC: Hurtubise, 1980); Jean Gagne, À la découverte du Saint-Laurent (Montreal: Éditions de l'Homme, 2005); Gilles Matte and Gilles Pellerin, Carnets du St-Laurent (Montreal: Heures Blues, 1999); Marie-Claude Ouellet, Le Saint-Laurent-Fleuve à découvrir (Montreal: Éditions de l'Homme, 1999); and Alain Franck, Naviguer sur le fleuve au temps passé 1860–1960 (Quebec: Publications du Québec, 2000).

27 See A.A. den Otter, The Philosophy of Railways: The Transcontinental Railway Idea in British North America (Toronto: University of Toronto Press, 1997).

28 Andrew Biro uses the term "hydrological nationalism," but since St. Lawrence nationalism is tied up in both the waters of the St. Lawrence and the manipulation of these waters, it is both hydrological and hydraulic—the former is generally accepted as referring to the water itself and the latter to the ways it is manipulated and modified. Andrew Biro, "Half-Empty or Half-Full? Water Politics and the Canadian National Imaginary," in Eau Canada: The Future of Canada's Water, ed. Karen Bakker (Vancouver: UBC Press, 2007), 323.

29 Prominent examples include Josephson, Industrialized Nature; Nye, American Technological Sublime; and Leo Marx, The Machine in the Garden: Technology and the Pastoral Idea in America (New York: Oxford University Press, 1964).

30 These links are discussed by prominent intellectuals such as Harold Innis, George Grant, Marshall McLuhan, and Ramsay Cook. See Marco Adria, Technology and Nationalism (Montreal: McGill-Queen's University Press, 2010); R. Douglas Francis, The Technological Imperative in Canada: An Intellectual History (Vancouver: UBC Press, 2009); Cole Harris, "The Myth of the Land in Canadian Nationalism," in Nationalism in Canada, ed. Peter Russell (Toronto: McGraw-Hill, 1966); and Damien-Claude Bélanger, Prejudice and Pride: Canadian Intellectuals Confront the United States, 1891–1945 (Toronto: University of Toronto Press, 2011).

31 In Donald Worster's chapter on Canadian-American differences, he cites Marilyn Dubasak, Margaret Atwood, and Northrop Frye in support of this hostility argument. Worster, "Wild, Tame, and Free: Comparing Canadian and U.S. Views of Nature," in Parallel Destinies: Canadian-American Relations West of the Rockies, ed. John M. Findlay and Kenneth S. Coates (Montreal: McGill-Queen's University Press, 2002).

32 These include cultural differences (e.g., fusion between freedom/liberty and wilderness in American thinking), the greater Canadian reliance on resource extraction industries, a relatively greater abundance of wilderness, and the lack of federal control over land in Canada. Worster, "Wild, Tame, and Free," 257–60. See also George Altmeyer, "Three Ideas of Nature in Canada, 1893–1914," in Consuming Canada: Readings in Environmental History, ed. Chad Gaffield and Pam Gaffield (Toronto: Copp Clark, 1995).

33 Adria, Technology and Nationalism, 45.

34 H.V. Nelles, *The Politics of Development: Forests, Mines, and Hydro-Electric Power in Ontario, 1849–1941*, 2nd ed. (Montreal: McGill-Queen's University Press, 2005), 216.

35 Francis, *Technological Imperative*, 2. This view of the impact of technology on North American integration was forwarded by philosopher George Grant; see his *Lament for a Nation: The Defeat of Canadian Nationalism* (Toronto: McClelland & Stewart, 1965) and *Technology and Empire: Perspectives on North American* (Toronto: House of Anansi, 1969).

36 Patrick McGreevy, *The Wall of Mirrors: Nationalism and Perceptions of the Border at Niagara Falls* (Orono: Canadian-American Centre, University of Maine, 1991), 1–3.

Quebec's Water Export Schemes: The Rise and Fall of a Resource Development Idea

Frédéric Lasserre

For more than a century, Quebec has relied heavily on its freshwater resources for water-based transportation, pulp and paper production, and hydropower. The second-largest Canadian province by area—and unique in the Canadian confederation because of its French-speaking majority—Quebec is bisected by the St. Lawrence River in the south and abuts James Bay (the southern part of Hudson Bay) in the northwest. As a result of its abundant water resources, Quebec leads all other provinces in hydroelectric power exports, including Newfoundland and Labrador with its massive Churchill Falls power project.[1] Perhaps the most famous hydroelectric developments in Quebec are those on the waters flowing to James Bay (the so-called Project of the Century, in the 1970s), which have secured large hydropower exports for the province. Former premier Robert Bourassa authored a book, *L'énergie du Nord: La force du Québec* (1985), in which he looked back with pride at the completion of the first phase of his government's James Bay hydro project.[2] This project paved the way for additional hydro developments in the North. But most significantly, Bourassa turned his attention beyond power, including a chapter that anticipated the export of water itself. Bourassa was influenced by the GRAND Canal model first developed by Thomas Kierans in 1959.[3] GRAND was one of several

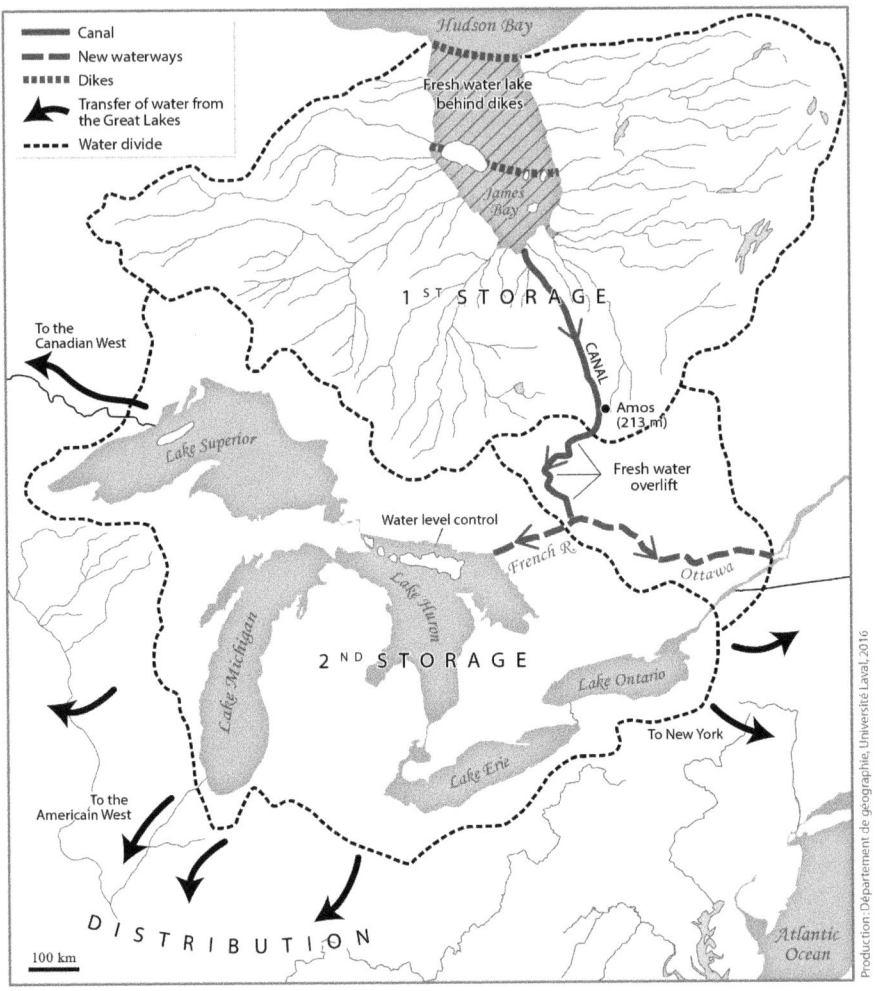

5.1 The GRAND Canal scheme. Map by author.

large-scale, long-distance Canadian water diversion schemes promoted by the private sector and, at times, by provincial governments. Kierans expected that the United States would want to purchase this resource. Such schemes have invariably been dismissed because of intense public opposition. More recently, however, Quebec has emerged as the centre of renewed plans to divert fresh water into the heart of the continent. Advocates hope to create a profitable market for this plentiful Quebec resource.[4]

The idea of exporting water from Canada dates back to the late 1950s, a period that saw a rise in intercontinental projects (such as the St. Lawrence, Niagara, and Columbia projects discussed in chapters 4 and 6 of this volume).[5] It stems from the engineer-bred reasoning that technology is available to move water from where it flows to where it is needed to sustain economic growth, at a time when environmental impacts were not considered a priority and when public money was considered abundant. Canada and the United States were not alone in considering such schemes; similar projects were being considered in the Soviet Union, China, and the Middle East. The GRAND project was one among several that blossomed during the 1960s. The North American Water and Power Alliance—which proposed flooding most major valleys in the Rockies to build reservoirs for water from northwestern Canada and then transferring the water via canals to most regions of the western United States and northern Mexico—and the Alaska-California Subsea pipeline project were also proposed. None of these megaprojects was ever built.

Abundant scholarly and popular literatures depict both the history of water export ideas and the political debate these ideas generated, especially when they concerned the waters of the Great Lakes.[6] A few analysts and advocacy groups remain anxious that American interests could someday force Canada to sell its waters.[7] The debate has subsided somewhat since the enactment of a number of controls: ratification of the Great Lakes–St. Lawrence River Basin Water Resources Compact in September 2008 (discussed in chapter 1 of this volume; new legislation controlling water exports in all provinces except New Brunswick; and the May 2010 introduction (though not the passage) of Bill C-26 in the House of Commons.[8]

However, the debate over water exports is far from over. Contrary to the view of doomsday prophets, the main proponent of water diversions is no longer the United States with its potential appetite for water. Rather, the locus is now Canada itself, and particularly Quebec. Though the provincial government long championed water diversions for hydropower production (as had British Columbia, Manitoba, and Newfoundland), it did not endeavour to export water, despite Premier Robert Bourassa's advocacy of the idea in 1985.[9] But today Quebec's business community and symbiotic economic think-tanks are providing the main impetus for water export proposals. Let us consider the history of these proposals to the present day, and specifically how they evolved in the province.

Power from the North: Quebec experimenting with the water export idea

Quebec's power is generated and distributed by a government-owned corporation, Hydro-Québec, which was founded in 1944. At first it competed with private companies, but the provincial government used Hydro-Québec as a tool to foster electricity production so as to attract industries and drive energy prices down. In 1963, the government decided to nationalize the eleven remaining private companies that still controlled a substantial share of the electricity generation and distribution business in Quebec, creating a single Crown corporation that could enable the government to wholly control its energy policy. After briefly considering the nuclear option, the government—headed by Bourassa, a young and ambitious economist—decided in 1971 to dam the La Grande River and divert three northern rivers (Caniapiscau, Rupert, and Eastmain) so as to develop ten thousand megawatts of power. This was the James Bay Project; it was fully completed only in 2007.

Bourassa, leader of the provincial Liberal Party and premier of Quebec from 1970 to 1976 and then again from 1985 to 1994, was proud that his James Bay project could provide Quebec with energy autonomy. If opposed to the independence stance put forth by the Parti Québécois, Bourassa was nevertheless determined to increase Quebec's autonomy in every way, voting for Bill 22 in 1974 to increase the prominence of the French language, pleading for the (failed) Meech Lake Accord (1987–1990) that would have granted greater autonomy to Quebec, and fostering economic tools that could enhance Quebec's economic independence. Seduced by Kierans's GRAND Canal proposal to divert water from James Bay to the American Southwest through a Great Lakes route (an idea first floated in 1959), Bourassa, along with several major engineering companies, enthusiastically endorsed damming James Bay so as to turn it into a freshwater reservoir, pumping the water over the Canadian shelf, and ultimately exporting it to multiple destinations. The premise of the GRAND project is that freshwater runoff from natural precipitation would be collected in a dammed James Bay by means of a series of outflow-only sea-level dikes constructed across the northern end of the bay, cutting it off from the rest of Hudson Bay. The stored fresh water would be pumped from the new freshwater reservoir in James Bay via a series of canals and pumping stations south to the

Great Lakes and then to the U.S. Southwest. Several nuclear plants would be needed to generate the power to haul the water above the Canadian Shield to the Great Lakes and then to the Southwest.

This project was a natural extension of Bourassa's economic approach to divert Quebec's northern rivers for hydropower production. His reasoning was that if fresh water could be exploited for power exported to the United States and Ontario, why not export water, too—a natural resource with which the province was richly endowed?[10] What's more, previous large diversions in Quebec on the Eastmain and Caniapiscau Rivers had met with little opposition.[11] Enthusiasm for the project waned, however. Its costs were astronomical in a time of rising public deficits and debt, while the business community was suffering the financial shock of 1987.

In 1998, the Nova Group water export project from Sault Ste. Marie, Ontario, had been granted a license to export 600,000 cubic metres per year of Lake Superior water to Asian markets. Confronted with a public outcry, the federal government revoked the license. In 1999, the Quebec government under the Parti Québécois enacted a two-year ban on water export projects.[12] Over the next two years, an extended cabinet debate over water exports oscillated between a temporary moratorium and a permanent ban. The Quebec Ministry of International Relations studied scenarios in which the province might become a major binational water player. Likewise, public researchers partnered with private industry to study the economic viability of water exports.[13] The Ministry of Trade and Industry also left open the door to water exports.[14] But in the wake of the Nova Group controversy, Ottawa lobbied the provinces to pass water export bans as part of a federal framework to manage and regulate water. The Quebec government initially rebuffed what it considered a blatant infringement on its constitutional rights over natural resources within Quebec's borders.[15] But advocates of the ban prevailed, with a permanent ban on water exports. In 1999, the province enforced a temporary moratorium on the exportation of water, the Water Resources Preservation Act; then in December 2001, Environment Minister André Boisclair's Bill 58 entrenched the ban on large-scale diversion of water out of the province.[16] Boisclair also elaborated Quebec's policy on water in 2002, which formalized for the first time a comprehensive resource management policy for water that integrated environmental and social dimensions and departed from the previous view that water was basically an economic natural resource to be exploited.[17]

The saga over water exports continued in new forms, raising questions about behind-closed-doors political struggles to revise this new ban on water exports. In 2004, Quebec's environment minister, Thomas Mulcair, renewed the debate by publicly advocating for water export projects.[18] Liberal Premier Jean Charest quickly disavowed Mulcair's position, committing to Bill 58. This time, the business community showed little enthusiasm for the project.[19] Note how the controversy transcended party politics and loyalties: the Parti Québécois was in power in 1999, while the Liberals ruled in 2004. Both periods resulted in deep divides within the ruling parties. Promoters of water exports were present in both major political parties and in both periods, but the issue was contentious throughout. As for Mulcair, one may wonder why he endorsed the idea of water exports in the first place: Was it his personal opinion? Or a trial balloon that his governing cabinet had asked him to float? His past position proved controversial during the 2015 federal election when opponents, notably Justin Trudeau, challenged him to clarify his present point of view.

The Liberal government never renewed the idea that water exports could be beneficial for Quebec. To the contrary, on June 11, 2009, the National Assembly unanimously passed Bill 27—*Loi affirmant le caractère collectif des ressources en eau et visant à renforcer leur protection* (An act to affirm the collective nature of water resources and provide for increased water resource protection)—a permanent ban on water exports.[20] As of 2016, among the parties represented in the National Assembly, three major political parties (the Liberal Party, the Parti Québécois, and Québec Solidaire) oppose water export schemes officially; the Coalition Avenir Québec, while not advocating water exports, stresses instead the need to protect the resource. Of the political parties in Quebec, only the Quebec Conservative Party (zero MPs and 0.39 percent of the vote in the 2014 provincial general election) advocates water exports. In the short term, a revival and political endorsement of such schemes thus seems unlikely. In the long term, though, one might expect the business community—which supported Bourassa's export ideas in 1985 and renewed its interest later—to continue evaluating both the economic and political possibilities.

Strong Lobbying by the Business Community

Water Tanker Exports: Saving the Water-Poor Is Not Profitable

To backtrack from the previous section, let us return to 1996 and a different angle on water exports: this was a time when government and industry were strategizing to revive a weak economy. As a result, Quebec business projects engaged with water exports received a big boost. In October 1996, the provincial government, led by Lucien Bouchard, held the Summit on the Economy and Employment in an effort to develop new economic options for growth. The summit included representatives from the social, NGO, and business communities. Proponents of water exports at the summit reasoned as follows: water is an increasingly scarce resource globally but abundant in Quebec; water is one of the natural resources—and provincial assets—the government should develop, just like forest resources and hydropower; and the sale of water could quickly be taken advantage of and developed. Several businesspeople—including Jean Coutu, the founder of a very successful drugstore distribution empire, the oil company Ultramar, and engineering firm Navtech—envisioned a future in which Quebeckers would be "the Arabs of water."[21] This group based its plans on estimates that the global population will reach ten billion by 2020, the fact that 15 percent of the world's countries already lacked water, and Quebec's boast that it contains 16 percent of the planet's freshwater resources (a major error: in fact it has no more than 3 percent).

Coutu was the most active booster of the economic promise in exporting water. Using the summit's framework, Coutu strategized with several firms about how, exactly, to capitalize on the province's abundant water resources, focusing primarily on export revenues and job creation. The oil company Ultramar envisioned increased revenues for its outgoing oil tankers if the ships could carry large quantities of water. Ship design firm Navtech and shipbuilding firm Davie also proposed designing a removable coating that could prevent oil from contaminating fresh water, or a specialized polyvalent ship designed to carry bulk water.[22] Optimism ran high, and these stakeholders considered shipments to be possible as early as December 1997 or January 1998. Coutu asserted that

> Time has come to take advantage of Quebec's immense freshwater resources by exporting it to countries that face scarcity. ... The next century will be that of water, which will be worth as much as oil. Quebec holds more potable water than Saudi Arabia holds oil, and could develop ways to organize its export on a large scale, by tanker ships or another way.[23]

Coutu's message was twofold: first, Quebec was richly endowed with a precious natural resource that was at least the economic equal of hydropower; and second, sharing this resource with the world would be a moral act of compassion (by contrast, locking it up was utterly selfish).

The project faced a number of obstacles. One was a reluctance to invest in costly public projects at a time when proponents of government austerity and privatization were ascendant. The public debate emerged first in the Symposium on Water Management in Quebec, organized by the INRS-Eau and held in Montreal in December 1997.[24] Then, concern ran high among opinions on water issues. Reportedly, major cities, including Montreal, were planning to privatize municipal water services, and much ado was made about water issues at public hearings during the Beauchamp Commission (1998–2000)[25] that would eventually lead to the National Policy on Water written by Boisclair. The commission's final report lambasted the idea of massive water exports.

However, and this point is often overlooked by water export advocates, it was not so much public resistance that led to the project's demise. To the contrary, public opinion was rather favourable in 1996: the idea of exporting another abundant natural resource was considered at first by the public—just as it had been by Premier Bourassa in the past—a good thing inasmuch as it could foster Quebec's economic autonomy and strengthen its relative economic and political status within Canada. A strong connection between nationalism, identity, water, and hydroelectricity emerged in Quebec, something not witnessed in other parts of Canada where hydropower was not seen by the public as a way to transcend the potential for cultural endangerment. Hydropower was a political tool with which to assert Quebec's financial, economic, and political status; water exports could be considered just another way of taking advantage of the province's natural resources.

What caused the demise of the water export idea was the advent of environmental concerns, as illustrated in the forestry policy scandals triggered by the film *L'Erreur boréale* (1999), which denounced clearcutting practices, and the poor economics of the project. When the working group on water exports first convened around Coutu in mid-December 1996, there were no completed market studies. As such studies unfolded, difficult questions soon emerged. Would there be buyers? Would exported water be cheaper than water produced from desalination plants? Would potential buyers be eager to buy water over a long period so as to turn investments into a profit?[26] The Coutu working group predicted revenues of about $2.6 billion annually and claimed that Quebec indeed had a firm order.[27] The claim about an order was never verified and was probably wrong.[28] Straightforward cost-benefit analyses were negative as well. It turned out that water shipped by tankers from Sept-Îles would be more expensive than water produced from desalting plants at the destination.[29] While visiting Montreal in September 1997, Egypt's minister of water resources, Mahmud Abu-Zeid, commented on water export schemes from Quebec:

> Ever since I arrived in Montreal, I have been asked if we are going to import water from here. But Egypt has many other opportunities, all much cheaper than importing water from as far away as Canada. Transportation costs would prove prohibitive. I have no idea where this idea could have come from.[30]

The Egyptian minister emphasized that a cubic metre of water cost about $0.70 in Egypt, whereas the most optimistic forecast for Quebec's water exports was $3.25 per cubic metre—a highly unfavourable comparison. A few days before the Symposium on Water, the daily *La Presse* published the opinions of several foreign water experts on Quebec's project. Jean Margat in particular asserted, regarding drinking water, that

> For many countries, . . . the problem is not a scarcity issue, but a financial problem to purify and distribute this potable water. Where would these countries find money to buy imported water? It would thus first be necessary to assess they have the means to pay. Otherwise, exports will be gifts.[31]

Unable to prove that tankers could export water at an affordable cost, and unable to find customers willing and able to pay such premiums, export advocates lost public and private support. In the end, it was economics rather than conservation that killed these projects.

Renewal of the Export Scheme to the United States

For advocates of water exports, the United States was the only remaining potential customer. In the late 1990s, public fear of water exports to the U.S. had abated, but from 1998 to 2004, the economic think tank Institut Économique de Montreal (IEM) floated a debate over the opportunities in water exports from Quebec.[32] The federal government's efforts to ban water exports were pointless, explained Marcel Boyer, as the resource was provincially managed.[33] The argument in favour of water exports revolved around three main points:

(1) Water was abundant in Quebec, so export could be very profitable when water scarcity was increasing elsewhere; exporting just 10 percent of Quebec's water would generate $65 billion in revenue.

(2) Quebec was richly endowed and, therefore, had a duty to share a vital resource.

(3) Several water export schemes were working well around the world, a trend Quebec should follow.[34]

Boyer did not detail specific plans but suggested, as an example, intercepting flood water from rivers flowing toward James Bay—an idea reminiscent of the GRAND project—and turning them south above the Canadian Shield. Boyer estimated that exporting that water to the United States, at about 800 m³/sec, could generate $0.65 per cubic metre and $16 billion in revenue. In general, Quebec could dedicate 10 percent of its renewed water to export.[35] The paper made no mention of a cost-benefit analysis or market study. Nor did it mention that extracting 10 percent of the renewed water would require construction of a grid of aqueducts and pipes. The paper also did not indicate that local impacts could be much greater than

10 percent of the flowing water. What's more, Boyer was unable to quote any international example to support his proposal. For example, of existing water export schemes from Lesotho to South Africa, France to Spain, and Turkey to Israel, the Lesotho–South Africa water diversion is the only demonstrable success. By contrast, desalination projects have proven economically viable. France's export project from the Rhone to Spain finally collapsed in 2009 after facing intense opposition both in France and in Spain,[36] while the 2004 Memorandum of Understanding for the export of water from Turkey to Israel was first put on ice by Israel in 2006, before being cancelled by Turkey in 2010.[37] In 2008, at the time the IEM published its report, sufficient information existed to suggest that chances of success were low for both the Turkish and the French water projects. There is definitely no trend toward development of commercial water export schemes in the world; however, there definitely is a trend toward building desalting plants, hundreds of them.[38] Most recent or future projects for water diversions are still domestic, as in Quebec, China, and India, for instance.[39]

And yet water export hopes live in the present. In 2009, Pierre Gingras, an engineer retired from Hydro-Québec, again advocated harnessing the three rivers flowing northwest into James Bay, then diverting them into the Ottawa River and indirectly to the United States; he argued that added flow through the Ottawa River could compensate for diversions from the Great Lakes (Figure 2).[40] His diversion scheme thus does not include a direct pipeline between western Quebec and the American Midwest, but rather works as a water swap between the Great Lakes and the Ottawa River. Gingras estimated the project would cost $15 billion but would generate $2 billion in power and $7.5 billion in revenues from the selling of the water itself. While Gingras demonstrated the technical feasibility of the concept, he included no credible cost-benefit analysis or market study.

Odette Nadon, a lawyer for the law consulting group BCF, also advocated in 2010 for the right to export water on a commercial basis. She mentioned that she already represented business customers exporting water from Quebec for irrigation purposes, but did not disclose which firms these were. Doubts were raised as to the credibility of her assertions, since water for irrigation implies very large volumes, which could not easily leave Quebec unnoticed.[41]

These three proposals contend that enough demand exists in the United States to recover costs and offer a profitable investment. But the

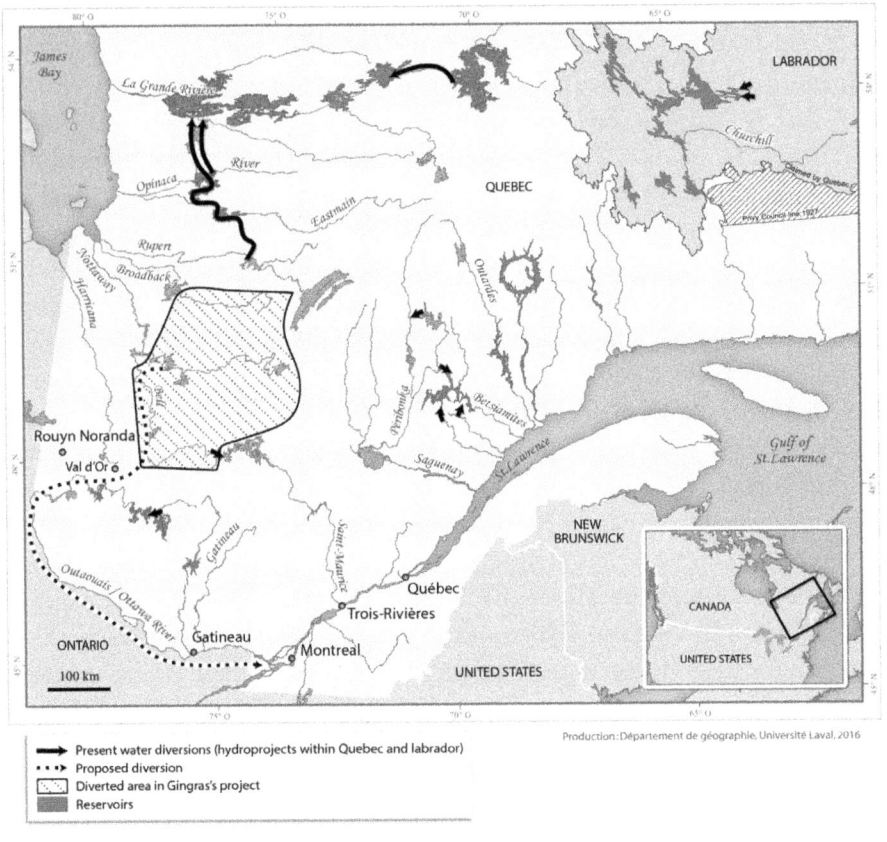

5.2 Quebec water diversions. Map by author.

proposals never prove this hypothesis, instead simply asserting as a matter of fact that there is substantial U.S. interest. If cities and industries in the West are indeed eager to pay such sums for a cubic metre, their actual share of Western water consumption is meager. Agriculture absorbs about 80 percent of the region's water—water that is heavily subsidized for farmers (who pay a few cents per cubic metre). So how can export proponents assume that U.S. farmers—the major consumers of water—would buy Canadian water priced at, say, eighty-five cents per cubic metre? This lack of a credible analysis for the marketing of bulk water helps explain why the Quebec government paid little attention to the proposal. The National Assembly unanimously voted in favour of Bill 27 in 2009. The new law, titled

An Act to affirm the collective nature of water resources and provide for increased water resource protection, provides for both surface and groundwater withdrawal projects being subject to conditional authorization by the government. Water cannot be appropriated and thus exported or pumped without the government's approval.

For Quebec, the economics of water export do not justify large public or private investments. Apart from their severe environmental impacts and public disapproval, water is simply too heavy and not valuable enough to profitably export. Debt-battling governments are no longer willing to invest in such unpopular and costly projects, even when important constituencies might profit in the interim (for example, through construction contracts). Even in the United States, the Western States Water Council (WSWC) reckons that the era of large-scale water diversions is over, even from its neighbour Canada, because they are too expensive to build and operate.[42]

Conclusion

In Canada, the public continues to worry about water diversions to the United States. But such diversions already exist in Canada, and in Quebec. The extent of negative impacts on the environment is disputed. Even among biologists, the conservation concept of minimum ecological flow is controversial.[43] Water does remain in Canada for each of these diversions, but this is not the point; Canadians collectively forget that their daily comfort and economic activity depend on major river diversions. For a long time, Quebeckers thought water exports could be beneficial, though that view has waned over the last fifteen years, bringing Quebeckers closer to other Canadians on the issue of water export schemes. It is therefore a contradiction to protest water transfers to the United States on environmental grounds while refusing to assess—and possibly to consider phasing out—transfers within Canada.[44] In the end, however, environmental reasons were not the only barrier to water export projects from Canada. Economic barriers loomed just as large. Hence, the water export projects never materialized. In the short term, at least, water exports from Quebec will not be the solution to water scarcity problems in other parts of North America.

Notes

1 Patrick Forest and Frank Quinn, "Quebec's Northern Waters: Export Opportunity or Illusion?" (Munk School Briefings No. 16, Munk School of Global Affairs, University of Toronto, 2011).

2 The James Bay Project refers to the construction by state-owned utility Hydro-Québec of a series of hydroelectric power stations on the La Grande River in northwestern Quebec and the diversion of neighbouring rivers into the La Grande watershed.

3 The Great Recycling and Northern Development (GRAND) Canal of North America is a water management proposal that was designed to alleviate North American freshwater shortage problems. It stems from the idea that James Bay can be diked and transformed into a freshwater reservoir; its water, which would be pumped back across the Canadian Shield, would then be available for reuse in North America. In 1985, the GRAND Canal received an enthusiastic response from Quebec Premier Robert Bourassa and from within Quebec business circles. However, feasibility studies never materialized and governmental support for this project no longer exists.

4 Canada's renewable freshwater resources are estimated at about 7 percent of the world's total, and Quebec's at about 3 percent. Given the small population size of both Canada and Quebec, this large water resource nurtured the idea that Canada could share part of its resources so as to alleviate the water stress elsewhere.

5 J.C. Day and Frank Quinn, "Water Diversion and Export: Learning from the Canadian Experience" (Dept. of Geography Publ. Series No. 36, University of Waterloo, 1992); Frédéric Lasserre, "Les projets de transferts massifs continentaux en Amérique du Nord: La fin de l'ère des dinosaures?," in *Transferts massifs d'eau: Outils de développement ou instrument de pouvoir?*, ed. Frédéric Lasserre (Quebec City: Presses de l'Université du Québec, 2005); Frank Quinn, "Canada's Water in a Continental Context," Paper No. 76 (paper presented at Universities Council on Water Resources conference, Santa Fe, July 2006), http://opensiuc.lib.siu.edu/ucowrconfs_2006/76; Frank Quinn, "Water Diversion, Export, and Canada-U.S. Relations: A Brief History" (Munk Centre for International Studies Briefings No. 8, Program on Water Issues, MCIS, University of Toronto, 2007).

6 Wendy Holm, ed., *Water and Free Trade: The Mulroney Government's Agenda for Canada's Most Precious Resource* (Toronto, James Lorimer & Company, 1988); Peter Annin, *The Great Lakes Water Wars* (Washington, DC: Island, 2006); Dave Dempsey, *Great Lakes for Sale* (Ann Arbor: University of Michigan Press, 2008).

7 If Bill C-26 would indeed regulate diversions from transboundary waters, it includes nothing about watersheds farther north, which therefore—in theory—can be diverted.

8 David Johansen, *Bulk Water Removals: Canadian Legislation*, Background Publication No. 02-13-E (Ottawa: Library of Parliament,

rev. July 7, 2010), 6, http://www.parl.gc.ca/content/LOP/Research-Publications/prb0213-e.pdf.

9   Robert Bourassa, *Power from the North* (Toronto: Prentice-Hall, 1985).

10 Ibid.

11 The diversion of the Eastmain and Caniapiscau Rivers was part of the hydropower development of the La Grande River, and at the time these diversion projects met with little opposition. The diversion of the Rupert River, decided in 2002, completed the diversion schemes aimed to increase the flow of the La Grande River. See Day and Quinn, "Water Diversion and Export"; and Lasserre, "Les projets de transferts," 490–91.

12 *Loi visant la préservation des ressources en eau* [Water Resources Preservation Act], National Assembly, Quebec, 36th Leg., 1st Sess. (1999); Louis-Gilles Francoeur, "Québec prolonge le moratoire sur l'exportation de l'eau," *Le Devoir*, December 22, 2000.

13 Researchers from INRS-Eau partnered with Crown corporations Société Générale de Financement and Investissement-Québec. Frédéric Lasserre, "L'eau, la forêt, les barrages du Nord du Québec: Un territoire instrumentalisé," in *Le territoire pensé: Géographie des représentations territoriales*, ed. Frédéric Lasserre and Aline Lechaume (Quebec City: Presses de l'Université du Québec, 2002), 19.

14 Louis-Gilles Francoeur, "Québec songe à exporter son eau, malgré l'avis des autres provinces," *Le Devoir*, March 19, 1999.

15 Louis-Gilles Francoeur, "Gestion des eaux: Bégin rabroue Ottawa; "La stratégie fédérale fait fi des compétences que le Québec exerce pleinement," *Le Devoir*, February 12, 1999.

16 *Loi modifiant la Loi visant la préservation des ressources en eau* [An Act to amend the Water Resources Preservation Act] (Bill 58), National Assembly, Quebec, 36th Leg., 2d Sess. (2001).

17 Quebec, *Water. Our Life. Our Future: Quebec Water Policy* (Quebec City: Environnement Québec, 2002), http://www.mddelcc.gouv.qc.ca/eau/politique/policy.pdf.

18 Louis-Gilles Francoeur, "Mulcair rouvre la porte aux exportations d'eau," *Le Devoir*, June 15, 2004.

19 Louis-Gilles Francoeur, "Exportation d'eau potable: Les industriels de l'eau trouvent l'idée inopportune," *Le Devoir*, June 19, 2004.

20 *Loi affirmant le caractère collectif des ressources en eau et visant à renforcer leur protection* (Bill 27), National Assembly, Quebec, 39th Leg., 1st Sess. (2009) chap. 21, s. 31.105.

21 Luc Chartrand, "Le mirage de l'or bleu," *L'Actualité* (Montreal), November 1, 1997, 23.

22 Daniel Allard, "Exportation d'eau en vrac: Québec en tête de pont," *Commerce Monde*, November 1997, http://www.commercemonde.com/archives/nov97/sommaire/sphoto.html; Dany Fougères, "Des projets qui tombent à l'eau: Transferts, dérivations et exportation de l'eau du Canada et du Québec depuis les années 1960" (working paper, INRS, Montreal, n.d. [2003?]), 21–22, accessed June 25, 2012, http://www.hydrologie.org/hydrodinosaures/usa.htm.

23 Hélène Baril, "Eau potable exportable," *Le Soleil*, October 30, 1996; translation mine.

24 The INRS-Eau is the branch of the Quebec Institut national de la recherche scientifique (INRS) dedicated to research on water.

25 Quebec, Bureau d'audiences publiques sur l'environnement, *Rapport de la Commission sur la Gestion de l'eau au Québec: L'eau, ressource à protéger, à partager et à mettre en valeur* (Quebec City: BAPE, 2000).

26 Fougères, "Des projets qui tombent à l'eau," 24.

27 Kathleen Lévesque, "L'exportation d'eau rapporterait 2,6 milliards aux promoteurs québécois," *Le Devoir*, April 16, 1997.

28 Fougères, "Des projets qui tombent à l'eau," 24.

29 "Les projets d'exportation d'eau douce laissent Québec plutôt froid," *Le Devoir*, August 30, 1997.

30 Denis Arcand, "Douche froide sur l'exportation d'eau en Égypte," *La Presse*, September 3, 1997; translation mine.

31 André Pratte, "Rêver en bleu," *La Presse*, November 27, 1997; translation mine.

32 Marcel Boyer, *L'exportation d'eau douce pour le développement de l'or bleu québécois* (Montreal: Les Cahiers de recherche de l'Institut économique de Montréal, 2008), http://www.iedm.org/files/cahier0808_fr.pdf; Forest and Quinn, *Quebec's Northern Waters*.

33 Boyer, *L'exportation d'eau douce*, 19.

34 Ibid., 6, 24, 20–22.

35 Ibid., 6.

36 Marc Laimé, "L'inquiétante 'croisade espagnole' des barons de l'eau français," *Carnets d'Eau* (blog), March 25, 2009, http://blog.mondediplo.net/2009-03-25-L-inquietante-croisade-espagnole-des-barons-de-l. See Jean-Paul Bravard, "Barcelone et le projet de transfert de l'eau du Rhône," and Michel Drain, "Les transferts d'eau en Espagne," both in *Transferts massifs d'eau: Outils de développement ou instrument de pouvoir?*, ed. Frédéric Lasserre (Quebec City: Presses de l'Université du Québec, 2005).

37 Israel/Palestine Center for Research and Information, "Water Imports: An Alternative Solution to Water Scarcity in Israel, Palestine, and Jordan?" IPCRI Fact Sheet No. 2, January 15, 2010, p. 3, http://www.ipcri.org/index.php/publications/research-and-information/152-water-imports-an-alternative-solution-to-water-scarcity-in-israel-palestine-and-jordan; United Press International, "Turks Cancel Project to Sell Israel Water," *UPI.com*, June 18, 2010, http://www.upi.com/Business_News/Energy-Resources/2010/06/18/Turks-cancel-project-to-sell-Israel-water/UPI-50501276883374.

38 Frédéric Lasserre, "Gestion de l'eau dans la péninsule arabique: Le dessalement est-il une solution durable?" *Maghreb-Machrek* 197, no. 3 (2008): 69–86.

39 There are, however, preliminary talks on a water export project from Turkey to Lybia. Amiram Cohen, "Turkey: Water Deal with Libya Would Preclude Future Exports to Israel," *Haaretz*, July 3, 2012, http://www.haaretz.com/print-edition/news/

turkey-water-deal-with-libya-would-preclude-future-exports-to-israel-1.14183.

40 F. Pierre Gingras, *L'eau du Nord: Un projet réaliste, durable et rentable pour exploiter l'or bleu québécois*, Les notes économiques series (Montreal: Institut économique de Montréal, July 2009), http://www.iedm.org/files/juillet09_fr.pdf; F. Pierre Gingras, *L'eau du Nord* (Montreal: Marcel Broquet, 2010).

41 Hugo Joncas, "'Mes clients exportent de l'eau en vrac,' dit une avocate de BCF," *Les Affaires* (Montreal), October 27, 2010.

42 Tony Willardson (deputy director, WSWC), personal communication, February 22, 2005.

43 It proves very difficult to set harmonized thresholds of water withdrawal impacts given the diverse environmental conditions of every river. The matter of which indicators should be used to track impacts is also debated among the scientific community.

44 Frédéric Lasserre, "La Continentalisation des Ressources en Amérique du Nord: L'ALENA oblige-t-elle le Canada à céder son eau aux États-Unis?," in *Transferts massifs d'eau. Outils de développement ou instrument de pouvoir?*, ed. Frédéric Lasserre (Quebec City: Presses de l'Université du Québec, 2005), 463–88; Frédéric Lasserre, "Drawers of Water: Water Diversions in Canada and Beyond," in *Eau Canada: The Future of Canada's Water*, ed. Karen Bakker (Vancouver: UBC Press, 2007).

Engineering a Treaty: The Negotiation of the Columbia River Treaty of 1961/1964

Jeremy Mouat

The Columbia River Treaty first came to my attention in the mid-1990s.[1] A regional power utility in British Columbia, West Kootenay Power, had commissioned me to write its centennial history. As I did the research for that book I came to appreciate the treaty's significance. The creation of the Columbia Basin Trust in 1995, with its mandate to return some of the treaty's financial benefits to that part of the province it had affected most, underlined the treaty's continuing relevance in southeastern British Columbia. However, the orthodox view of the treaty—dominated by Neil Swainson's *Conflict over the Columbia*[2]—seemed unsatisfactory because it appeared to give the treaty an inexorable logic. Swainson's book failed to take seriously other possible outcomes or to do justice to the raucous debate that accompanied the treaty's negotiation and signing. Contemporary accounts of the treaty in newspapers and journal articles contrasted sharply with Swainson's reasoned prose. All of this piqued my interest, but I was working to a deadline and scrambled to finish the "treaty chapter."

Some years later an American colleague encouraged me to give a paper on the treaty, and I began to reexamine the agreement more systematically. I was struck by the fact that the Columbia River had attracted a great deal of attention from American scholars, whose work offered much detail on the river's history as well as suggesting its important role in the American imagination.³ This led me to question why Canadian scholars were less interested in the river than their American counterparts. I also came to appreciate that this greater American interest had had a very real impact on the Columbia's history. Long before Canadians imagined harnessing the Columbia River's hydroelectric potential, American engineers had devoted thousands of pages to that project—attention that led to a series of dams on the river. Canadian disinterest in the potential benefits of hydroelectricity, as Matthew Evenden has pointed out, reflected an unwillingness on the part of both governments and private industry to take decisive action: "Whereas large U.S. federal projects rose on the Columbia and Tennessee Rivers in the late 1930s with importance for American wartime production, in Canada public and private utilities sought to follow rather than promote demand." This timidity would have important consequences when war came: "Canada's major power systems were in a poor position to meet surges in wartime demand."⁴

Such a perspective sees the Columbia River receiving the same neglect as other rivers in Canada. However, I want to argue that the Columbia River Treaty's convoluted negotiation and the manner in which the treaty came to define the river made the Columbia unique, or, at least in some important respects, unlike many other rivers in Canada and shared transborder water basins. For example, Canadian interest in developing the Columbia River came long after American facilities had been planned and built along its length south of the border. This meant that any Canadian project would have to accommodate existing American installations on the Columbia. In addition to this constraint, the Canadian position in the treaty negotiations was weakened by significant political differences. As will be seen, the federal government of Prime Minister Louis St. Laurent disagreed with BC Premier W.A.C. Bennett's plans for the Columbia River and prevented him from realizing them. When the Progressive Conservatives assumed power in Ottawa under John Diefenbaker, a very different set of actors assumed key roles, although relations with Premier Bennett did not improve. Personal animosity also affected the work of the International Joint Commission (IJC). The head of the Canadian section of the IJC from 1950 to 1962, General A.G.L. McNaughton, argued powerfully in defence of Canadian interests—a position that was not well received by his American counterpart, Len Jordan.

One consequence of these circumstances was that the "Treaty between Canada and the United States of America relating to Cooperative Development of the Water Resources of the Columbia River Basin"—the treaty's formal title—was negotiated and signed not once but twice, first in early 1961 and then again in 1964. Much controversy and political squabbling accompanied the treaty's negotiation, which was why a second signing was necessary. While both the United States and Canada appeared satisfied with the original treaty that President Eisenhower and Prime Minister Diefenbaker signed at the White House in January 1961, British Columbia's premier made it clear that he found aspects of the treaty objectionable. Without his acquiescence the projects envisioned by the treaty could not proceed. The 1964 revision to the treaty accommodated Bennett's objections and enabled the construction of the four treaty dams, three in BC and one in Washington State.⁵

The treaty has assumed a new significance as its renegotiation or termination becomes possible. (Article XIX gives either signatory the right to terminate the treaty with ten years' notice, as of 2014.) The signatories to the treaty showed little concern for the Indigenous peoples of the Columbia Basin or for the environmental impacts of ongoing dam construction and flow regulation. The political landscape has changed fundamentally since then, which will loom large in any substantive renegotiation of the treaty.⁶ This chapter will look backward rather than forward, however, exploring two related questions: Why was the Columbia River Treaty necessary? And why was the negotiation of the treaty and the treaty itself so controversial?

To begin by stating the obvious: the border between Canada and the United States meant that a treaty was necessary. The Columbia River flows from British Columbia through Washington and Oregon before entering the Pacific Ocean. Because the river crosses the border between Canada and the United States, efforts to manage the river required a degree of consensus between the two countries. A legal structure was already in place for achieving this: early in the twentieth century the Boundary Waters Treaty established an institutional framework for managing bodies of water that defined or crossed the border between the two countries, although the plans to "develop" the Columbia came after that treaty was signed, in 1909.

That is not the whole story, of course. The Columbia River Treaty is part of the much larger narrative of global electrification as well as widespread acceptance of the idea that hydroelectric development was a public good. If dams were to be built on the Columbia River to enable such development, engineers, utilities, and governments had to conceive of the river as an organic machine, to use Richard White's memorable phrase.[7]

The controversy surrounding the treaty arose in part from the changing relationship between the United States and Canada through the 1940s, '50s, and '60s. The two nations had drawn closer during World War II, but the postwar boom led to some tensions—tensions heightened by the 1957 federal election that brought John Diefenbaker and the Progressive Conservatives to power in Ottawa.[8] By the early 1960s the growing American presence in the country created unease among a significant proportion of the Canadian public. This mood coloured attitudes toward both the treaty negotiations and the treaty itself. In addition, tensions between the provincial and federal governments led to considerable acrimony between members of Diefenbaker's cabinet and BC's Social Credit government.

As these comments suggest, the Columbia River Treaty was a product of its time. It did more than implement a rational development scheme, as its formal title suggested. The "Cooperative Development of the Water Resources of the Columbia River Basin" initiated by the treaty was the culmination of longstanding American plans for the Columbia. Canadians had shown little to no interest in the river, at least in the river conceived as a whole.[9]

Since the 1920s, American engineers had been studying the Columbia River closely. This interest reflected the river's obvious power potential as well as the possibility of irrigation, inherent in a vast river system like the Columbia's. It was also part of a larger strategy initiated by the federal government in the mid-1920s. The American government directed the Army Corps of Engineers (USACE) in 1926 to estimate the cost of surveying the country's navigable rivers "with a view to the formulation of general plans for the most effective improvement of such streams for the purposes of navigation and the prosecution of such improvement in combination with the most efficient development of the potential water power, the control of floods, and the needs of irrigation."[10] These instructions were contained in House Document Number 308; consequently, the reports on the various rivers were known as 308 reports.

The 308 report on the Columbia River appeared in 1934.[11] In its nearly two thousand pages, the two-volume study outlined, as its subtitle indicated, "A General Plan for the Improvement of the Columbia River and Minor Tributaries for the Purposes of Navigation and Efficient Development of Its Water Power, the Control of Floods, and the Needs of Irrigation." Another investigation soon followed, commissioned by the National Resources Committee and undertaken by the Pacific Northwest Regional Planning Commission. This second study dealt "with immediate and urgent problems in the Columbia Basin and particularly with the policies and organization which should be provided for planning, construction, and operation of certain public works in that area."[12]

These immediate and urgent problems had arisen because the federal government was building major dams on the main stem of the Columbia—the Bonneville and the Grand Coulee—and the former project was nearing completion. After considerable debate, the plans for the Columbia River articulated in the 308 report and specified by the Pacific Northwest Regional Planning Commission culminated in the Bonneville Project Act of 1937. This federal legislation in turn led to the creation of the Bonneville Power Administration (BPA).[13] (It is worth noting that a quarter century would elapse before a Canadian entity with similar jurisdiction to the BPA emerged to deal with power development on the Canadian section of the Columbia River. By then the Columbia River Treaty had already been signed.)[14] Then in 1943, Congress directed the USACE to review "the 308 Report submitted in 1932 and assess it in the light of the completed dams and the newly formed Bonneville Power Administration."[15]

That report—filling an impressive eight volumes—took five years to prepare. It included a series of appendices, the first of which, Appendix A, bore the title "Columbia River Basin in Canada." It concluded that coordinated development of the river had to extend to the whole basin; it could not just happen on the American side:

> Substantial storage ultimately must be developed in Canada if economic utilization of the Columbia River water resource is to be accomplished. Therefore, provision must be made in the projects now planned so that they may be able to use the added dependable flow from such storage when it becomes available.[16]

One final document that should be added to this list of American studies of the Columbia River is a reminder of the larger context in which these documents were undertaken. Not only was this period, from the mid-1940s through to the mid-1960s, one of incredible growth but also one of considerable tension. The long shadow of the Cold War—as well as the conflict that had preceded it—was directly tied to developments along the Columbia.

The ample hydroelectric power produced by dams such as Grand Coulee had enabled remarkable industrial growth in the Pacific Northwest during World War II. Quite apart from the wartime production of ships and aircraft, an energy-intensive aluminum industry had developed. This rapid industrialization did not simply come to a halt with the end of the war. One can argue that a kind of path dependency dictated that growth must follow growth, a trajectory encouraged by Cold War anxieties.[17] Such anxieties underlay the 1952 report of the President's Materials Policy Commission, published with the ringing title "Resources for Freedom," although usually known simply as the Paley report, after the commission's chair. The Paley report included a brief but telling reference to the Columbia River Basin. Under the heading "Untapped Hydro Potential in Canada," the report's authors noted that

> A significant part of the potential hydroelectric power development in Canada is on the Columbia River and its tributaries in British Columbia. This can best be developed in cooperation with the United States. . . . Only by coordinating the operations of storage reservoirs with the operations of downstream plants can maximum power production be realized."[18]

The official river studies undertaken by the American government demonstrate its ongoing interest in the Columbia over a number of years. A clear sense of what was needed for optimum use of the Columbia River system emerged from these studies. And in this conception of the river-as-system, the underdevelopment on the Canadian side was a problem, because it prevented maximum efficient use of the river's potential hydroelectric generation.[19]

Dams on the Canadian section of the Columbia would solve this "problem." The huge reservoirs created by these dams could hold vast quantities

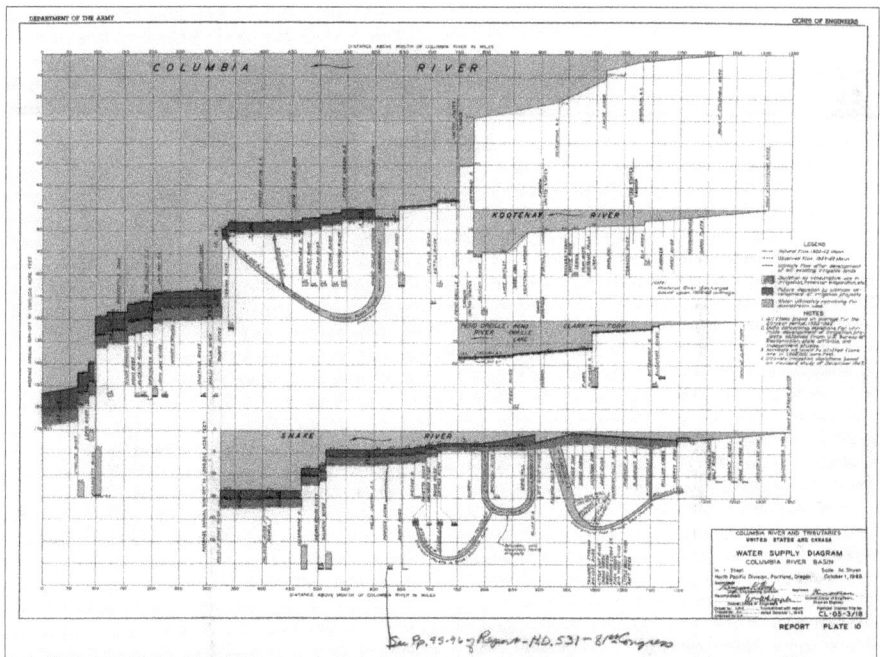

6.1 The U.S. Army Corps of Engineers prepared this graphic representation of the rivers of the Columbia Basin in March 1948 for the revised 308 report, submitted to Congress in 1950. The diagram reflects the care and detail with which the American side were studying the Columbia River. A copy survives in the the Elmer K. Nelson Papers, held in the Water Resources Collections and Archives at the University of California – Riverside, in Riverside, California.

of water and consequently make the downstream American dams much more efficient and thus more profitable. The river's natural flow resembled a roller coaster ride, peaking in the summer with the snow melt and with much-reduced flow during the rest of the year. Existing American dams on the river's main stem could not stabilize this flow effectively; during the peak summer period, vast amounts of water spilled over the dams without generating power. In 1966, two senior BPA officials described the financial impact, pointing out that the administration had lost $47.5 million dollars between 1958 and 1962. During the same period, the amount of water that spilled over the dams would have earned close to $150 million dollars in power sales, had that water spun turbines and the electricity been sold.[20] This meant a loss of close to $50 million versus a potential revenue of $150 million: that was the difference Canadian water storage could make. In addition, further advantages could be achieved in terms of the seasonal rhythms of energy consumption. The BPA came to appreciate that its abundant summer energy—when snow melt typically caused the highest flows in the Columbia and when domestic energy use was relatively modest—could be wheeled south to urban centres in California to meet the soaring consumption of air conditioning there.[21]

Events during World War II encouraged a much closer alliance between Canada and the United States, in terms of both a common defence strategy and coordinated war economies. As part of the discussions to achieve the latter, government officials in both countries undertook an inventory of strategic materials, a decade before the Paley report.[22] Canadian officials were now well aware of the significance of the American studies of the Columbia. For example, when civil servants in Ottawa compiled a chronology of events relevant to the Columbia River Treaty, the first significant event they listed was the U.S. Congress committee's 1943 resolution asking the USACE to undertake a comprehensive survey of the Columbia.[23] Nor can it have been a coincidence that within a year of that resolution, the American and Canadian governments asked the IJC "to determine whether a greater use than is now being made of the waters of the Columbia River system would be feasible and advantageous. . . . It is desired that the [International Joint] Commission shall determine whether in its judgment further development of the water resources of the river basin would be practicable and in the public interest."[24] Given the exhaustive American studies of the Columbia, this exercise had a foregone conclusion. If one looked at American development on the main stem of the Columbia and studied the data from power generation, it was plain that greater use of the waters was feasible. In the first instance, however, the major benefit of this "greater use" would be more efficient generation of power in the American facilities along the main stem of the Columbia.

The IJC responded to the joint American-Canadian request to study the Columbia's further development by establishing the International Columbia River Engineering Board. The board's study of the river turned into a fifteen-year project, with its final report presented to the IJC in 1959.[25] In the intervening years, another proposal to develop the Columbia was referred to the IJC. After a devastating Columbia River flood in 1948, the American government proposed an upstream dam on the Kootenay

River, in Libby, Montana, which would help to avert similar flooding in the future. This proposal went to the IJC in early 1951, but the dam—which would flood parts of both Montana and British Columbia—raised some difficult issues. No one questioned the potential benefits of the Libby Dam, but the very prospect of these benefits raised the thorny question of fair compensation. For example, if flooding land in British Columbia gave certain advantages to American residents living downstream, in terms of flood protection and/or energy supply, what formula could be used to determine these downstream benefits? What could be considered reasonable compensation for those who would have lost their homes and even their livelihoods? The issue of downstream benefits would cause much heated discussion during the lengthy negotiations surrounding the development of the Columbia River. In the short term, however, difficulties in resolving the issue led to the shelving of the Libby proposal in 1953.[26]

The 1909 Boundary Waters Treaty did more than create the IJC as a body to adjudicate issues relating to those waters. It also specified the right of the upstream riparian (literally, the occupant of the riverside) to control the waters of rivers, a clause inserted into the treaty at the insistence of the American negotiators and over the objections of Canada.[27] This became significant when General McNaughton, the chair of the Canadian section of the IJC, proposed diverting rivers in the Columbia River Basin before they crossed into the United States.

A number of Americans viewed this possibility with alarm, as such diversions would undermine the American plans for the Columbia, predicated on maximizing upstream storage in Canada and then coordinating that storage with electrical generation in the U.S. system.[28] McNaughton's proposal and the American reaction stimulated a flurry of legal papers, debating the finer points of international river law, in particular the meaning of that clause in the Boundary Waters Treaty.[29] Part of the problem, however, was not matters of principle but ill will between McNaughton and his counterpart, Len Jordan, chair of the American section of the IJC. Two things smoothed the way through the subsequent impasse: Jordan's departure as American section head and the American side's willingness to accept the principle of downstream benefits.[30]

The tensions were not restricted to the IJC negotiations, however. The relationship between the provincial government in British Columbia and Canada's federal government in Ottawa was also strained. As with the tensions at the IJC, those between levels of government reflected matters of principle as well as the politics of personality. The principle was jurisdictional: water resources were (mostly) within provincial jurisdiction. The personality was the larger-than-life W.A.C. Bennett, who with his Social Credit party ruled British Columbia from 1952. Such was the force of Bennett's personality that his views tended to be indistinguishable from those of the provincial government. Bennett's plans and strategies arguably had the greatest impact on the precise terms of the Columbia River Treaty in its final (1964) version. Given the significance of his role, some discussion of his actions is warranted.[31]

Prior to entering politics, Bennett had been a hardware merchant in the BC interior—a background that influenced his politics in several important ways. He was dedicated to the province's growth and worked assiduously to expand the province's infrastructure, notably its roads, railways, and electrical supply. He was particularly anxious to bring the putative benefits of development to the province's interior.[32] Bennett was suspicious of the motives and actions of BC's urban business elite and, in keeping with Social Credit ideology, opposed too heavy a reliance on debt financing. Although he declared the province debt-free in the summer of 1959, Bennett (his own minister of finance) had simply changed financing techniques, turning from direct to indirect debt financing. Nonetheless, the move underscored the Bennett government's fundamental aversion to debt.[33]

Bennett was keen to see dams on the Canadian portion of the Columbia River. For example, he had welcomed a proposal made in 1954 by the Kaiser Aluminum Corporation, under which the company would build a dam on the Arrow Lakes on the Columbia River, just north of the 49th parallel. This would provide power for Kaiser's operations south of the border, although the company would also return 20 percent of the power generated to the province. Although Bennett enthusiastically supported the scheme, others argued that

> it would be economic folly for Canada to accept [the proffered Kaiser deal], since the very cheap power generated downstream in the United States as a result of the Canadian storage would be used by the corporation to manufacture aluminum which, being produced within the protective tariff walls of

the United States, would therefore be highly competitive with the Canadian aluminum manufactured at Kitimat, British Columbia. ... In the broader context of the economy of British Columbia and of Canada as a whole. ... [the Kaiser plan] would expose British Columbia's aluminum industry to damaging competition and would affect Canada's export trade. In this light the price offered by the Kaiser Corporation for the benefits that would be conferred downstream by Canadian storage seemed less than adequate.[34]

Despite Bennett's enthusiasm, the federal government effectively killed the project when it enacted the International River Improvements Act in the summer of 1955. Under its terms, dams on international rivers—rivers over which the federal government had constitutional authority—required federal approval. However, the failure of the Kaiser proposal did not dampen American interest in development on the Canadian section of the Columbia River.[35]

The Columbia was not the only river in which Bennett was interested. He was also anxious to see projects go ahead along the Peace River. In 1956 a Swedish industrialist, Axel Wenner-Gren, became interested in the possibilities of northern British Columbia and was assured of provincial government support. Two years later, Wenner-Gren formed the Peace River Power Development Company to inaugurate a large hydroelectric development in northeastern BC.[36] However, the company soon encountered a major stumbling block. The vast hydroelectric potential of the northern river system could only be realized if the company could find a guaranteed market for the considerable energy that it hoped to generate. Long-term energy contracts had to be in place—tangible evidence for would-be investors of the plan's financial feasibility—if the company hoped to raise the capital necessary for construction. The private utility, BC Electric, along with its parent company, the BC Power Corporation, was the province's leading energy company and thus the obvious customer for Peace River power. Although quite interested in the Peace River project (and represented on the board of the Peace River Power Development Company), BC Electric had plans in place for the future. When pushed by Bennett, the company flatly refused to sign any long-term contract to purchase Peace River power. But the premier was not easily dissuaded from his plans for northern development. Increasingly he had come to see the Peace River power project as key to his government's development strategy. The project dovetailed perfectly with his vision of the province's future as well as providing a lever with which to apply pressure on the federal and U.S. governments as the Columbia River talks continued.[37] Bennett invented what he would call his "two river policy," that is, a commitment to develop both the Columbia and the Peace.

As Bennett pursued his plans for Peace River development, the federal government became more interested in pushing ahead with Columbia River development. Part of the reason was the election of a new government in Ottawa. The federal Liberals—who had been in power for over twenty years—were defeated and the federal Conservatives under John Diefenbaker came to power. The Conservatives were keen to push ahead with Columbia River development, and Diefenbaker's first Throne Speech, in October 1957, underlined the new government's commitment to the project. Although the pace of discussions on the Columbia accelerated, this does not appear to have been a direct consequence of increased political pressure but rather to have been due to the fact that the American section finally accepted the principle of downstream benefits. When this concession was made in late January 1959, the American and Canadian governments asked the IJC to determine how to apportion those benefits.[38] In March of the same year the International Columbia River Engineering Board produced its long-awaited report, *Water Resources of the Columbia River Basin: Report to the International Joint Commission*, and at the end of the year the IJC submitted its report, *Principles for Determining and Apportioning Benefits from Cooperative Use of Storage of Waters and Electrical Interconnection within the Columbia River System*, to the Canadian and American governments. The stage was set for the formal negotiation of the Columbia River Treaty.

On January 25, 1960, Prime Minister Diefenbaker announced in the House of Commons that "negotiations between Canada and the United States for the co-operative development of the Columbia River system are to commence in Ottawa on Thursday, 11 February."[39] In just under a year, on January 17, 1961, Diefenbaker and Eisenhower formally signed the treaty. Never one for understatement, Diefenbaker proclaimed his hope that "in the years ahead this day will be looked back on as one that represents the greatest advance that has ever been made in international relations

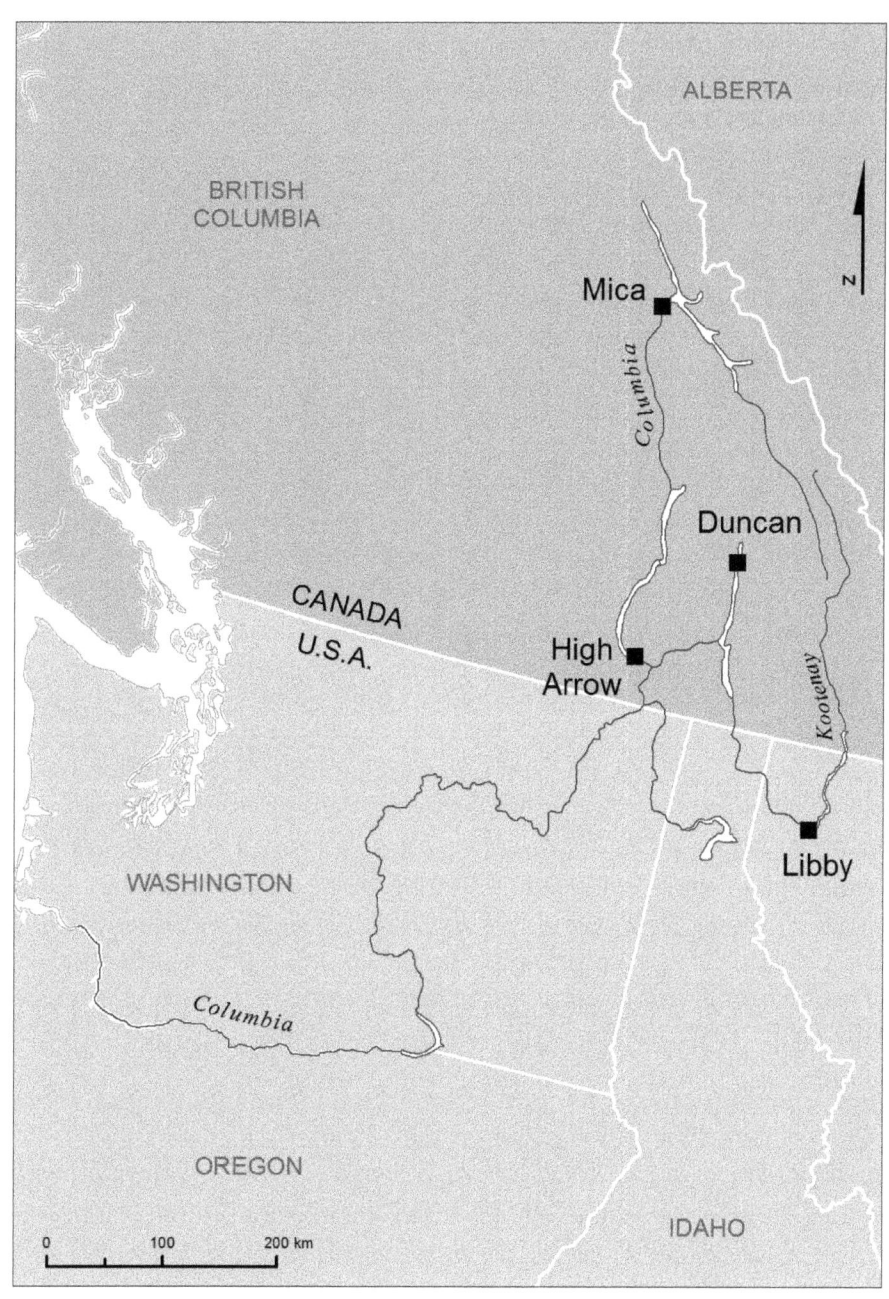

6.2: The four treaty dams on the Columbia River. Map by Jason Glatz.

between countries."[40] This turned out to be wishful thinking. For the next three years, the treaty—and indeed the larger issue of Canadian-American relations—provoked bitter public controversy in Canada.

The negotiators of the Columbia River Treaty had the International Columbia River Engineering Board's *Water Resources of the Columbia River Basin* report to assist them in their discussions. This very extensive report outlined three possible development schemes, two of which proposed diverting the headwaters of the Kootenay River north into the Columbia (the Copper Creek diversion and the Dorr diversion), and a third that instead proposed constructing the Libby Dam farther south on the Kootenay River, with no diversion of its waters into the Columbia. The negotiators ultimately settled on a scheme that would involve no diversion of the Kootenay, but included construction of the Libby Dam as well as three dams in Canada. These were to be built at Mica, Duncan Lake, and—most controversially—a High Dam for the Arrow lakes. The provisions in the treaty signed on January 17, 1961, were criticized for several reasons. The treaty's fundamental flaw was Premier Bennett's refusal to accept its terms.

Diefenbaker signed the Columbia River Treaty in the final days of the Eisenhower administration, likely to avoid having to deal with the newly elected president, John F. Kennedy.[41] Premier Bennett had conveyed his misgivings about the treaty to Ottawa prior to this staged event, yet the federal government assumed that it had the province's support. Cabinet ministers and senior civil servants from British Columbia who had participated in the Canada-BC Policy Liaison Committee had not objected to the terms of the treaty.[42] Bennett, however, was concerned about the financing of the treaty dams and just days before the formal treaty signing he conveyed these concerns to Donald Fleming, the federal minister of finance. Fleming's reply to Bennett suggests his consternation:

> The Treaty with the United States, as you are aware, has now been signed by the Prime Minister of Canada and the President of the United States of America. The negotiations and the signing of the Treaty were both carried through with the full knowledge and approval of your Government at every stage. The only occasion on which doubt ever arose as to the readiness of British Columbia to carry out the Columbia River Treaty as negotiated was on the occasion of the reference made by you

last December to the British Columbia Energy Board of certain questions involving a comparison of engineering and economic aspects of the Columbia and Peace River projects. At the meeting of the Policy Liaison Committee early in January our representatives expressed their concern that this might involve doubt and delay on the part of British Columbia in proceeding with the Columbia River development. Your representatives on the Committee assured us that this was not the case, and that on the contrary the reference was designed to hasten the taking of effective action by British Columbia under the proposed Treaty. On the basis of these assurances, the Treaty negotiations were concluded and the Treaty was signed, as above stated, with the full knowledge and approval of your Government.

In the light of these circumstances, for you to write as you now have, expressing doubts as to the feasibility of the Columbia River development "from engineering and financial standpoints," is a most extraordinary development, and must necessarily raise again our doubts as to British Columbia's intentions which we had thought were set at rest by the assurances of the British Columbia members of the Policy Liaison Committee. I do hope that we will not now be met by delaying action on the part of British Columbia.[43]

A shrewd political strategist, Bennett had won a significant advantage in the ongoing debate over the Columbia. He knew that the signatures of the Canadian prime minister and the U.S. president on the treaty would amount to very little if his government refused to accept its conditions. The federal government could negotiate any treaty it liked, but no dams could be built on BC's rivers without the approval of the provincial government. Following the treaty's signing, the U.S. Senate quickly ratified the treaty, with only one vote opposing it.[44] Approval of the treaty in Canada would take far longer and prove much more contentious.

Bennett's next move caught everyone by surprise (including members of his cabinet). In one of his most controversial and unexpected acts, the premier announced in the provincial legislature on August 1, 1961, that he intended to take over both BC Electric and Wenner-Gren's Peace River Power Development Company and to subsequently create the provincially owned electrical utility BC Hydro. This move meant that he could control the long-term energy contracts in the province. Thus, Bennett could ensure that both the Columbia and the Peace developments could proceed simultaneously—his own "two river policy."

Controversy raged over the government takeover of BC Electric, but Bennett continued to participate in the Columbia River negotiations. He had no objections to a Columbia River treaty; in fact, it was essential to his two river policy. His concern was with the treaty's bearing on his overall energy strategy: he wanted to ensure that it did not hinder the development of the Peace. In particular, Bennett was anxious that any power entitlements to emerge from the treaty's downstream benefits would be sold south of the border. This was essential if Peace River power was to have a market in the province, although it ran counter to the federal government's view, which was that it made more sense to receive power rather than money for the downstream benefits.[45] Bennett was also concerned with the treaty's financial arrangements, that is, how much money was to flow into his government's purse. As far as Bennett was concerned, any money earned by BC's rivers belonged to the province. Not only did he expect the money from the sale of the Columbia's downstream benefits, he also had definite ideas about the price. The instability of the federal government helped Bennett to achieve most of what he was after.

Bennett's relationship with the federal government became quite stormy in the wake of his refusal to accept the treaty. The two cabinet ministers in the federal government who were considered BC representatives—Davie Fulton and Howard Green—became particularly hostile toward Bennett.[46] When Bennett gave a widely publicized speech in Prince George in September 1961, which was highly critical of the treaty, Davie Fulton replied in a speech of his own a week later.[47] Two months later, Fulton was in Prince George himself and gave an equally controversial speech, linking Bennett's actions to comments reportedly made by the U.S. secretary of state, Stewart Udall. These speeches were becoming major news stories. For example, the *New York Times* carried a story on Fulton's speech, reprinting his allegations.[48]

A federal election in June 1962 ended Diefenbaker's majority in the House of Commons, putting the federal government in a much weaker position in its dispute with British Columbia. Diefenbaker decided to reverse the longstanding federal prohibition on the export of electrical power, a key BC demand in its argument with Ottawa. Diefenbaker also demoted Davie Fulton, removing him from the justice portfolio. In response, Fulton decided to quit federal politics and return to British Columbia, where he took charge of the provincial Conservative party and led it in an electoral battle against Bennett's Social Credit government.[49] The federal Liberals seized on the growing weakness of the Diefenbaker government, pressing it on the Columbia River Treaty. When Fulton announced he was leaving federal politics in late 1962, for example, Liberal leader Lester B. Pearson tried unsuccessfully to force a special debate on the treaty in the House of Commons.[50]

In late December 1962, American officials made another offer to Canada, intended to move the treaty process forward. Several weeks later, in a report entitled "Memorandum on Implications of Treaty Delay," senior federal civil servants in Ottawa urged the government to act, warning that, in their view, "failure to ratify the Columbia River Treaty in the near future would not only involve the loss of the downstream benefits, which are a major and very economic resource in themselves, but could also mean the loss of the immense renewable resource that the Treaty makes economically feasible on the Columbia River in Canada."[51] At precisely the same time, a widely circulated report appeared in a Vancouver newspaper, arguing in favour of the treaty.[52] Momentum seemed to be building behind the treaty talks. The federal minister of justice, Donald Fleming, continued to work with Premier Bennett in hopes of resolving the latter's misgivings but the Diefenbaker cabinet could not come to any agreement on the issue.[53]

A second federal election, in the spring of 1963, saw the end of Diefenbaker's Conservative government. Pearson and the Liberals formed a minority government, one that was to prove a good deal more durable than Diefenbaker's. Unlike their predecessors, the Liberals had little interest in continuing what they regarded as a pointless fight with the BC government, and Pearson was committed to improving relations with the United States. Shortly after taking office, Pearson and key federal officials met with President Kennedy and others in Hyannis Port, with Canada's ratification of the Columbia River Treaty assuming a prominent role in their discussions.[54] Two months later, in July 1963, the public announcement came that Ottawa had come to terms with British Columbia. Bennett had got what he wanted.[55]

6.3 Cartoon of Lyndon Johnson, W.A.C. Bennett, and Lester B. Pearson, published in the *Vancouver Sun* on September 16, 1964. Reproduced with permission of Stephen Norris.

In September 1963, Bennett and his Social Credit government were reelected in British Columbia. Bennett confidently began serious discussions with the new federal government in Ottawa over possible changes to the Columbia River Treaty. Soon talks were underway with the Americans as well. The Canadian side was led by Paul Martin, Pearson's minister of external affairs and a skilled negotiator, who worked closely with several senior BC cabinet ministers.[56] The result of these discussions was a protocol—in effect, a revised treaty—signed early in 1964 by Prime Minister Pearson and President Lyndon Johnson, with the enthusiastic support of Bennett and his government.

The treaty's signing meant that the province would receive cash for the downstream benefits—at least, the first thirty years' worth of those benefits. This amounted to nearly $255 million, money that would be used to pay for the construction of the three treaty dams in British Columbia. It was good news for the American side as well: not only could the river now be managed as a unit, as the several studies had suggested, but also the treaty dams meant an impressive increase in potential water storage and, with that increase, a more efficient use of the main stem's many turbines. Additionally, the long sought after Libby Dam would be built in Montana and the Pacific Intertie would be built down to Los Angeles, carrying much of the power that would have gone north to Canada had the downstream benefit not been sold.[57]

With an election a couple of months away, President Johnson was happy to travel north in September 1964 for a ceremonial event at the Peace Arch, on the border between Seattle and Vancouver, where he handed over a replica cheque to the Canadian side. In an ensuing newspaper cartoon (Figure 6.3) a limousine is being driven at speed by Phil Gaglardi, Bennett's minister of highways and a man famous for the number of speeding tickets that he accumulated while in office (hence his nickname, "Flying Phil"). The signatories to the treaty—the U.S. president and the Canadian prime minister—sit on either side of Premier Bennett in the back of the limousine. LBJ and Pearson hang on for dear life while Bennett expansively outlines his future plans. The view of the treaty implicit in the cartoon—that is, Bennett in charge and expansively waxing on about future plans—is deeply flawed. Bennett was far more a political opportunist than he was a dynamic visionary. His willingness to cut a deal with the Kaiser company for a dam on the Columbia in 1954 indicates just how limited his vision of development was, to say nothing of his encouragement of Wenner-Gren's plans in the North; his refusal to agree to the original terms of the 1961 treaty was duplicitous; and as Charles Luce recalled, Bennett tried to cut a deal with the BPA without the knowledge or consent of the federal government.[58]

Not everyone was pleased with the treaty's ratification. Popular media—newspapers, magazines, radio, and TV—had followed the story from the mid-1950s, with much of the coverage questioning the benefits that the treaty would bring to Canada. Many came to regard the treaty as a sellout to American interests, a view reflecting the growing public concern over the American presence in Canada. The report of the 1957 Royal Commission on Canada's Economic Prospects catalogued the growing dominance of the Canadian economy by the United States, adding considerable weight to such attitudes.[59] Four years later—in 1961, the year that the Columbia River Treaty was signed—anti-Americanism was palpable in Canada. For example, when Harvard University Press published Hugh Aitken's *American Capital and Canadian Resources* that year, it was noted on the book's dust jacket that "many Canadian industries are virtually controlled by the United States. This fact . . . has led to considerable resentment in Canada."[60] A report commissioned by the Canadian and American governments, detailing "Principles for Partnership" between them, was greeted with outrage in Canada when it appeared in 1965.[61] This was the context in which Canadians examined the Columbia River Treaty.

Opposition to the treaty came from many quarters, although it was nearly unanimous in the Kootenays. That region would feel its impact most heavily, in the short as well as the long term, with the most obvious—and controversial—result being the plan to flood the Arrow Valley. Richie Deane, an electrical engineer first with West Kootenay Power and then with Cominco, led a spirited attack against what would be the cause of this flooding: the High Arrow dam. Deane presented a thoughtful critique to the House of Commons's External Affairs Committee when it considered the final version of the treaty in the spring of 1964. Deane was only one of the indignant witnesses who spoke at these perfunctory hearings, where various concerned citizens registered their opposition to the treaty.[62] By that time, however, the negotiations were effectively over; the federal government was unwilling to alter the terms of a document that had been so long in the making. Kootenay residents were left with no choice but to live with the treaty's consequences, even though their views had rarely been taken into account during the lengthy process that culminated in the final agreement of 1964.[63] Only the lone voice of Bert Herridge, the region's member of Parliament in the House of Commons, reminded the federal government of the extent of local opposition to the treaty. Since the creation of the Columbia Basin Trust, some of the financial benefits that the province derived from the treaty are now being returned to the people living in the region.[64]

In 1974, various participants in the negotiation of the Columbia River Treaty spoke publicly about that experience at Simon Fraser University, as part of an interdisciplinary course in Canadian-American relations. Their presentations, noted the course's coordinator, "were greeted [by students] with a very mixed reception ranging from howls of derision to lavish praise."[65] The following year, CBC Television broadcast a documentary on the treaty, "The Reckoning." Its partisan nationalist account also provoked a passionate response, particularly from Hugh Keenleyside and Ray Williston, who threatened the CBC with legal proceedings.[66] Since then, tensions have subsided and few remain interested in the treaty itself.[67]

Fifty years after the event, a triumphalist narrative has come to describe the treaty, seeing it as the best possible outcome and as benefitting both countries—a moment when self-interest was set aside in the interest of mutual benefit. In a similar vein, commemorative events held in 2009 around the centenary of the Boundary Waters Treaty characterized that treaty and the work of the IJC as examples of the amicable relations and effective dispute resolutions that two good neighbours had developed.[68] Science too has been coopted, reflected in the ongoing work of the IJC-sponsored Transboundary Hydrographic Data Harmonization Task Force.[69] While the amicable relationship between Canada and the United States is unquestionably a positive development, airbrushing some difficult questions from the historical account serves no useful purpose.

The signing of the treaty meant that other options were no longer possible. Arguably the most significant such option was the creation of a national electric grid within Canada, a key feature of the national development program articulated by the Diefenbaker government.[70] As its advocates noted, sound reasons existed for establishing such a grid, although the more limited goals of some provincial governments—notably British Columbia—raised obstacles that ultimately ended any hope for such a national project.[71] Indeed one could argue that the Columbia River Treaty contributed to the erosion of the idea of a centralized state structure in Canada. Ironically, the BC government began to advocate for a national grid in February 2016, in part to justify its commitment to further hydroelectric development on the Peace River.

The treaty undermined the pursuit of economic development tied to cheap power, such as that pursued in Quebec and Ontario with their public utilities. It was also at odds with the more general assumptions that informed the postwar province-building projects in Alberta and Saskatchewan.[72] Such strategies took a more rational approach to the provincial state and how best to promote its growth. Bennett's plan of development, by contrast, was simply to encourage dam construction. Apart from the considerable environmental damage done to the Athabasca-Peace watershed and the impact of the Bennett Dam on First Nations in British Columbia and Alberta, Bennett's two river policy achieved very little beyond stimulating pulp mill construction in northeastern British Columbia.[73] This was a far more modest achievement than the benefits Bennett had claimed for the policy. By contrast, the treaty ensured that American industry in the Pacific Northwest would continue to receive cheap Columbia River power.[74]

Notes

1 I'd like to thank several people and organizations for their help with this chapter. I am grateful to Bill Lang at Portland State University for encouraging me to revisit the history of the Columbia River Treaty; to Heather Marshall for the editorial scrutiny; to Stephen Norris for permission to reproduce the cartoon of W.A.C. Bennett; to the U.S. Army Corps of Engineers for the schematic diagram of the Columbia River; and finally to the Canada-U.S. Fulbright Program for my appointment as a Visiting Research Chair at Arizona State University, where much of the work for this paper was undertaken. My thanks also to Dan and Lynne for inviting me to participate in this project.

This chapter is a substantially revised version of an earlier study of the treaty: Jeremy Mouat, "The Columbia Exchange: A Canadian Perspective on the Negotiation of the Columbia River Treaty, 1944–1964," in *The Columbia River Treaty Revisited: Transboundary River Governance in the Face of Uncertainty*, ed. Barbara Cosens (Corvallis: Oregon State University Press, 2012), 14–42.

2 Neil A. Swainson, *Conflict over the Columbia: The Canadian Background to an Historic Treaty* (Montreal: McGill-Queen's University Press, 1979).

3 For a few representative works of American scholarship on the Columbia, see Gus Norwood, *Columbia River Power for the People: A History of the Policies of the Bonneville Power Administration* (Portland, OR: Bonneville Power Administration, 1980); Paul C. Pitzer, *Grand Coulee: Harnessing a Dream* (Pullman: Washington State University Press, 1994); Robert E. Ficken, *Rufus Woods, the Columbia River, and the Building of Modern Washington* (Pullman: Washington State University Press, 1995); Richard White, *The Organic Machine: The Remaking of the Columbia River* (New York: Hill & Wang, 1995); David P. Billington

and Donald C. Jackson, *Big Dams of the New Deal Era: A Confluence of Engineering and Politics* (Norman: University of Oklahoma Press, 2006), esp. "The Columbia River Control Plan," 152–99; and William L. Lang and Robert C. Carriker, eds., *Great River of the West: Essays on the Columbia River* (Seattle: University of Washington Press, 1999).

4   Matthew Evenden, "Mobilizing Rivers: Hydro-Electricity, the State, and World War II in Canada," *Annals of the Association of American Geographers* 99, no. 5 (2009): 847.

5   The earlier agreement of July 1963 between the federal and BC governments effectively resolved their differences, paving the way for the signing of the 1964 protocol with the United States.

6   For a sense of the changes in the political climate, see Barbara Cosens, ed., *The Columbia River Treaty Revisited: Transboundary River Governance in the Face of Uncertainty* (Corvallis: Oregon State University Press, 2012).

7   White, *The Organic Machine*. Electricity's impact on Western culture and society is examined in William J. Hausman, Peter Hertner, and Mira Wilkins, *Global Electrification: Multinational Enterprise and International Finance in the History of Light and Power, 1878–2007* (New York: Cambridge University Press, 2008); Thomas P. Hughes, *Networks of Power: Electrification in Western Society, 1880–1930* (Baltimore: Johns Hopkins University Press, 1983); and David E. Nye, *Electrifying America: Social Meanings of a New Technology, 1880–1940* (Cambridge, MA: MIT Press, 1990).

8   For example, a memo prepared January 2, 1959, by an American official referred to "the present atmosphere of radical nationalism in Canada as championed by the Conservative Government." Reprinted in U.S. Dept. of State, *Foreign Relations of the United States, 1958–1960, Canada*, vol. 7, part 1, ed. Ronald D. Landa et al. (Washington, DC: Government Printing Office, 1993), 746.

9   A conspicuous exception was a CPR subsidiary, the Trail-based Consolidated Mining and Company (Cominco), which had built a series of dams in the area around its operations. Most of these were operated by West Kootenay Power and Light. For a description of West Kootenay's evolution and operations, see Jeremy Mouat, *The Business of Power: Hydro-Electricity in South Eastern British Columbia 1897–1997* (Victoria: Sono Nis, 1997).

10 Dwight F. Davis (secretary of war and Federal Power Commission chairman) to the Speaker of the House of Representatives, April 12, 1926, in *Estimate of Cost of Examinations, Etc., of Streams Where Power Development Appears Feasible*, 69th Cong., 1st Sess., House Document 308 (Washington, DC: Government Printing Office, 1926), 1.

11 *Columbia River and Minor Tributaries*, 73rd Cong., 1st Sess., House Document 103, vols. 1–2 (Washington, DC: Government Printing Office, 1934). Note the comments on this report in Billington and Jackson, *Big Dams*, 155–56; and Norwood, *Columbia River Power*, 44–45.

12 These comments are from the cover letter by Harold L. Ickes, secretary of the interior and chair of the National Resources Committee, April 21, 1936, in *Regional Planning, Part I—Pacific Northwest* (Washington, DC: Government Printing Office, 1936), iii. On the genesis and significance of this report, see Charles McKinley, *Uncle Sam in the Pacific Northwest: Federal Management of Natural Resources in the Columbia River Valley* (Berkeley: University of California Press, 1952): 158–60, although it is worth noting that McKinley himself played a significant role in the drafting of the report. See Paul C. Pitzer, *Grand Coulee: Harnessing a Dream* (Pullman: Washington State University Press, 1994), 441n14.

13 See the discussion of this legislation in Herman C. Voeltz, "Genesis and Development of a Regional Power Agency in the Pacific Northwest, 1933–43," *Pacific Northwest Quarterly* 53, no. 2 (1962): 65–76; McKinley, *Uncle Sam*, 157–228; and Norwood, *Columbia River Power*, 61–72. Pitzer provides the best summary account of the BPA's formation in his magisterial book, *Grand Coulee*, 233–45.

14 The Canadian entity I am referring to is the provincial Crown corporation, BC Hydro and Power Authority, created in March 1962 when the recently nationalized BC Electric was merged with the BC Power Commission. President Eisenhower and Prime Minister Diefenbaker had signed the Columbia River Treaty in January 1961, one of the last acts of the American president before leaving office.

15 Billington and Jackson, *Big Dams*, 192. The USACE duly produced an eight-volume report (known as the 308 Review Report): *Columbia River and Tributaries, Northwestern United States*, 81st Cong., 2nd Sess., House Document 53 (Washington, DC: Government Printing Office, 1952).

16 USACE, Seattle District, "Columbia River Basin in Canada," Appendix A, *Columbia River and Tributaries, Northwestern United States* (Washington, DC: Government Printing Office, 1948), 403, sec. 164.

17 This point is made by Matthew Evenden in "Mobilizing Rivers," 847. On the role of the aluminum industry, see Marc Reisner, *Cadillac Desert: The American West and Its Disappearing Water*, rev. ed. (New York: Penguin, 1993), esp. 161–62; David Massell, "'As Though There Was No Boundary': The Shipshaw Project and Continental Integration," *American Review of Canadian Studies* 34, no. 2 (2004): 187–222; and Matthew Evenden, *Allied Power: Mobilizing Hydro-Electricity during Canada's Second World War* (Toronto: University of Toronto Press, 2015).

18 United States, President's Materials Policy Commission, *Resources for Freedom: A Report to the President*, vol. 3, *The Outlook for Energy Sources* (Washington DC: Government Printing Office, 1952), 39–40. Note also the comments on this report in Melissa Clark-Jones, *A Staple State: Canadian Industrial Resources in Cold War* (Toronto: University of Toronto Press, 1987); and Hugh G.J. Aitken, *American Capital and Canadian Resources* (Cambridge, MA: Harvard University Press, 1961).

19 A study undertaken by Ebasco Services—"Preliminary Report on Effect of Mica Creek and Arrow Lakes Storage on Columbia River Power Supply in the United States"—noted that "the possibility of constructing large storage reservoirs in the Canadian portion of the Columbia Basin has received extensive publicity [in the United States]." The study was reprinted in *Upper Columbia River Development: Joint Hearings Before the Comm. on Interior & Insular Affairs and a Special Subcomm. of the Comm. on Foreign Relations*, 84th Cong., 2nd Sess. 354 (1956).

20 Charles F. Luce and J. Kenneth Kaseberg, "Bonneville Power Marketing Area Legislation: Is Regionalism in Electric Power Planning Old Fashioned?," *Oregon Law Review* 45, no. 4 (1966): 255.

21 See Joshua D. Binus, "Bonneville Power Administration and the Creation of the Pacific Intertie, 1958–1964" (MA thesis, Portland State University, 2008), 17–24. As Binus notes, there was a further advantage to sending electricity south to California. BPA's hydro was well suited to meeting peak power demands because its generation could easily be adjusted. Much of the power generated in California was thermal power, well suited to constant demand but much less adaptable to sudden spikes or falls.

22 The Ogdensburg agreement between Prime Minister Mackenzie King and President Roosevelt established a system of continental defence overseen by the Permanent Joint Board on Defence. On the context in which this agreement was signed, see J.L. Granatstein, "Mackenzie King and Canada at Ogdensburg, August 1940," in *Fifty Years of Canada–United States Defense Cooperation: The Road from Ogdensburg*, ed. Joel L. Sokolsky and Joseph T. Jockel (Lewiston, NY: Edwin Mellen Press, 1992), 9–29. The mood of wartime cooperation lent considerable weight to strategic discussions of mutual benefit; see, for example, Lawrence R. Aronsen, "From World War to Limited War: Canadian-American Industrial Mobilization for Defence, 1939–1954," *Revue Internationale d'Histoire Militaire* 51 (1982): 208–45.

23 See Canada, Dept. of External Affairs, *The Columbia River Treaty and Protocol: A Presentation* (Ottawa: Queen's Printer, 1964), 21.

24 Reference from the Canadian and United States Governments to the International Joint Commission (Canadian Note), March 9, 1944, in Canada, Dept. of External Affairs, *The Columbia River Treaty: Protocol and Related Documents* (Ottawa: R. Duhamel, Queen's Printer, 1964), 17.

25 International Columbia River Engineering Board, *Water Resources of the Columbia River Basin: Report to the International Joint Commission*, 7 vols. (Ottawa: ICREB, 1959). Note the comments on the genesis of this report in Neil A. Swainson, "The Columbia River Treaty—Where Do We Go From Here?" *Natural Resources Journal* 26, no. 2 (1986): 243–46.

26 For a recent description of the controversy surrounding the construction of the Libby Dam, see Philip Van Huizen, "Building a Green Dam: Environmental Modernism and the Canadian-American Libby

Dam Project," *Pacific Historical Review* 79, no. 3 (2010): 418–53. Cf. Swainson, *Conflict over the Columbia*, 45–51; and L.M. Bloomfield and Gerald F. Fitzgerald, *Boundary Waters Problems of Canada and the United States: The International Joint Commission 1912-1958* (Toronto: Carswell, 1958), 190–95. Contemporary American views of the Libby project were discussed at length in *Upper Columbia River Development*, 84th Cong., 2nd Sess. (1956).

27 Canada's right to divert under the Boundary Waters Treaty was contested by some American legal scholars in the late 1950s, but their arguments were tenuous. For a persuasive rationale for the right to divert, see the discussion in C.B. Bourne, "The Columbia River Controversy," *Canadian Bar Review* 37, no. 3 (1959): esp. 450–55.

28 In 1955, for example, anxiety over the possibility of Canadian diversion led the chair of the Senate Committee on Interior and Insular Affairs to send Senator Richard L. Neuberger on a fact-finding mission to British Columbia. See the telegram and letter appended to Neuberger's subsequent report, *Study of Development of Upper Columbia River Basin, Canada and United States: Report to the Chairman of the Senate Comm. on Interior & Insular Affairs* (Washington, DC: Government Printer, 1955), Appendix 1, 36–37. Neuberger would go on to play a significant public role in the treaty negotiations. For an account of his actions, see J. Richard Wagner, "Congress and United States–Canada Water Problems: Senator Neuberger and the Columbia River Treaty," *Rocky Mountain Social Science Journal* 11, no. 3 (1974): 51–60, as well as Neuberger, "Power Struggle on the Canadian Border," *Harper's Magazine*, December 1957, 42–49, and Neuberger, "Sternest Crisis in 111 Years," *Toronto Star Weekly Magazine*, March 29, 1958, 2–4.

29 Note, for example, the published proceedings of the 1956 regional meeting of the American Society of International Law, held at the University of Washington, *The Diversion of Columbia River Waters: Proceedings, Regional Meeting, American Society of International Law* (Seattle: Institute of International Affairs, 1956); Ernest Watkins, "The Columbia River: A Gordian Knot," *International Journal* 12, no. 4 (1957): 250–61; Gilbert F. White, "A Perspective of River Basin Development," *Law and Contemporary Problems* 22 (1957): 157–87; Charles E. Martin, "The Diversion of Columbia River Waters," *Proceedings of the American Society of International Law* 51 (1957): 2–8; Maxwell Cohen, "Some Legal and Policy Aspects of the Columbia River Dispute," *Canadian Bar Review* 36, no. 1 (1958): 25–41; C.B. Bourne, "Diversion: An International Problem," *Pacific Northwest Quarterly* 49, no. 3 (1958): 106–9; Charles B. Bourne, "The Columbia River Diversion: The Law Determining Rights of Injured Parties," *UBC Legal Notes* 2 (1958): 610–22; Bourne, "Columbia River Controversy"; and Jacob Austin, "Canadian–United States Practice and Theory Respecting the International Law of International Rivers: A Study of the History and Influence of the Harmon Doctrine," *Canadian Bar Review* 37, no. 3 (1959): 393–443.

30 For a critique of Jordan's views, see *Upper Columbia River Development*, 84th Cong., 2nd Sess., March 22, 26, 28, and May 23 (1956), esp. 7 & 21–23 (comments of Richard Neuberger). According to the IJC website, Jordan chaired the American section from January 7, 1955, to July 18, 1957; by contrast, his predecessor had held the post for twenty-one years. McNaughton chaired the Canadian section from March 1950 until April 1962. As Daniel Macfarlane notes, McNaughton's experiences dealing with the Americans about the St. Lawrence Seaway and Power Project influenced his approach to the Columbia. Macfarlane, *Negotiating a River: Canada, the U.S., and the Creation of the St. Lawrence Seaway* (Vancouver: UBC Press, 2014), 215.

31 This analysis of BC politics draws on several excellent contemporary accounts, notably, Paddy Sherman, *Bennett* (Toronto: McClelland & Stewart, 1966); Pat McGeer, *Politics in Paradise* (Toronto: Peter Martin, 1972); and Maurice Hodgson, *The Squire of Kootenay West: A Biography of Bert Herridge* (Saanichton, BC: Hancock House, 1976). Two unpublished studies are also useful: H. William Tieleman, "The Political Economy of Nationalization: Social Credit and the Takeover of the British Columbia Electric Company" (MA thesis, University of British Columbia, 1984); and John R. Wedley, "Infrastructure and Resources: Governments and their Promotion of Northern Development in British Columbia, 1945–1975" (PhD diss., University of Western Ontario, 1986). As John English noted, David Mitchell's biography of Bennett—*W.A.C. Bennett and the Rise of British Columbia* (Vancouver: Douglas & McIntyre, 1983)—should be read with caution, although it does provide an excellent account of how Bennett himself felt his actions ought to be interpreted. English, review, *BC Studies*, no. 63 (1984): 73–74.

32 See Stephen G. Tomblin, "W.A.C. Bennett and Province-Building in British Columbia," *BC Studies*, no. 85 (1990): esp. 47–51.

33 See Alfred Edgar Carlsen, "Major Developments in Public Finance in British Columbia, 1920 to 1960" (PhD diss., University of Toronto, 1961), esp. chapter on debt policy, 162–82. As Mitchell notes in his biography of Bennett, "Debt reduction was the prime economic objective of the Social Credit government during this period [the 1950s]; it was a virtual obsession of the premier" (p. 277). Mitchell is one of the few writers to take seriously Bennett's views on this issue; see, for example, *W.A.C. Bennett*, 272–84.

34 Charles B. Bourne, "The Development of the International Water Resources: The 'Drainage Basin Approach,'" *Canadian Bar Review* 47, no. 1 (1969): 82.

35 This ongoing American interest is clear from the (U.S.) Senate hearings held during the spring of 1956. The four-hundred-plus pages of *Upper Columbia River Development* (84th Cong., 2nd Sess.) also suggest the depth of American concern over the possibility of the Columbia's diversion.

36 On Wenner-Gren, see Wedley, "Infrastructure and Resources," esp. 247–310.

37 In 1961, for example, one well-informed observer suggested that "it is quite conceivable that the [BC government's] negotiations with the Wenner-Gren interests in connection with the Peace were, in part at least, motivated by a desire to accelerate Canada-U.S. agreement re the Columbia" (Carlsen, "Major Developments," 146). Cf. the comments of Ray Williston, quoted in "Hailed as First Step," *Globe and Mail* (hereafter, *Globe*), January 30, 1959, 2. In addition, as Tomblin points out, the provincial government saw developing the Peace as a way to curtail Alberta's growing influence in the region.

38 Specifically the IJC was asked for "its recommendations concerning the principles to be applied in determining: (a) the benefits which will result from the cooperative use of storage of waters and electrical interconnection with the Columbia River System; and (b) the apportionment between the two countries of such benefits more particularly in regard to electrical generation and flood control." Sidney Smith (Canada's secretary of state for external affairs) to the secretary of the IJC, Canadian Section, January 29, 1959. The same day, Smith announced in the House of Commons that the American side now recognized the principle of downstream benefits. (See "Columbia Agreement Indicated," *Globe*, January 30, 1959, 1–2; the newspaper reported that the changed American attitude was due to Len Jordan's removal from the IJC.) A day earlier, John Foster Dulles, the U.S. secretary of state, had sent a near identical letter to the chair of the American section of the IJC. Both letters are included in the IJC's Columbia River Docket 51R and are available online at http://www.ijc.org/en_/Dockets?docket=51.

39 Canada, Parliament, House of Commons, *Debates*, 24th Parl., 3rd Sess., 1 (1960): 257.

40 See the account of the treaty signing in H. Basil Robinson, *Diefenbaker's World: A Populist in Foreign Affairs* (Toronto: University of Toronto Press, 1989), 167; the quotation is from Lawrence Martin, *The Presidents and the Prime Ministers: Washington and Ottawa Face to Face: The Myth of Bilateral Bliss, 1867–1982* (Toronto: Doubleday Canada, 1982), 180. Cf. Diefenbaker's comments in the House of Commons on January 18, 1961: Canada, Parliament, House of Commons, *Debates*, 24th Parl., 4th Sess., 2 (1961): 1159.

41 For candid assessments of the troubled Diefenbaker-Kennedy relationship, see the insider's account by Basil Robinson (a Diefenbaker aide), in *Diefenbaker's World*, 165–69; as well as Knowlton Nash, *Kennedy and Diefenbaker: Fear and Loathing across the Undefended Border* (Toronto: McClelland & Stewart, 1990). Note, however, the useful revisionist assessment by Kevin J. Gloin, "Canada-U.S. Relations in the Diefenbaker Era: Another Look," in *The Diefenbaker Legacy: Canadian Politics, Law and Society since 1957*, ed. Donald C. Story and R. Bruce Shepard (Regina: Canada Plains Research Center, 1998), 1–14, and the similar analysis in Tammy Nemeth, "Consolidating the Continental Drift: American Influence on Diefenbaker's National Oil Policy," *Journal of the Canadian Historical*

42   *Association*, n.s., vol. 13 (2002): 191–215.

42   For the formation and deliberations of the Canada-BC Policy Liaison Committee, see Swainson, *Conflict over the Columbia*, 102–4; as well as the comments of one of the BC representatives, Hugh L. Keenleyside, *Memoirs of Hugh L. Keenleyside*, vol. 2, *On the Bridge of Time* (Toronto: McClelland & Stewart, 1982), 506–8, and Eileen Williston and Betty Keller, *Forests, Power, and Policy: The Legacy of Ray Williston* (Prince George, BC: Caitlin, 1997), 184–93.

43   Donald Fleming to W.A.C. Bennett, Ottawa, January 31, 1961, copy, MG 32 B11, Vol. 66, file Columbia Treaty – BC – Canada Negotiations & Finances – 1960–1961, E. Davie Fulton fonds, Library and Archives Canada, Ottawa (hereafter, LAC).

44   For American support for the treaty, see the comments in *Columbia River Treaty: Hearing Before the Comm. on Foreign Relations*, 87th Cong. (1961).

45   See, for example, Patrick Kyba, *Alvin: A Biography of the Honourable Alvin Hamilton, PC* (Regina: Canadian Plains Research Center, 1989), 132–34.

46   The tensions within the Diefenbaker cabinet are well described in Fleming's memoirs, *So Very Near: The Political Memoirs of the Hon. Donald M. Fleming*, vol. 2, *The Summit Years* (Toronto: McClelland & Stewart, 1985), esp. 259–75, 465–71.

47   W.A.C. Bennett, "The Power Development Story in British Columbia," typescript copy of speech, David Mitchell Fonds, F-56, Container 4, F-56-1-0-97, Chapter 9 – Speeches and Press Releases – C.R.T., 1961–1974, Simon Fraser University Archives, Burnaby, BC (hereafter, Mitchell Fonds). A copy of the riposte by Davie Fulton—a speech at the University of British Columbia six days later—survives in the W.A.C. Bennett Fonds, F-55, Container 58, F-55-37-0-18, Power Development (28-9) – Notes, charts, file notes, speech, statements, resolution, 1961–1962, SFU Archives (hereafter, Fulton speech, SFU Archives). In the House of Commons, an opposition MP asked Prime Minister Diefenbaker about Bennett's Prince George speech, which he said was circulating in printed form. According to the MP, the speech included "caustic criticisms on the part of Premier Bennett of certain aspects of the Columbia river treaty." Diefenbaker responded with a one-liner: "I do not get much time these days to read fiction." See Canada, Parliament, House of Commons, *Debates*, 24th Parl., 4th sess., 8 (1960–1961): 8715.

48   "Battle Growing on River Treaty," *New York Times*, December 1, 1961, 19. The paper reported that Fulton had "accused [Secretary of State] Udall of 'joining a propaganda campaign because he hopes for a decision that will be an enormous advantage to his country.'" Cf. the description of the speech in Fleming's memoirs, *So Very Near*, 273.

49   See "NDP Cheered by Fulton Decision, Sees Victory through Split Vote," *Globe*, December 1, 1962, 3; and "Mr. Fulton's Formidable Task," editorial, *Globe*, December 3, 1962, 6.

50 See "Debate Bid Fails," *Globe*, December 8, 1962, 2.

51 "Memorandum on Implications of Treaty Delay", a thirty-two-page typescript report dated January 11, 1963, and prepared by W.D. Kennedy, G.J.A Kidd, G.M. Mac-Nabb, and P.R. Purcell (emphasis in original). The memo opens with a summary, noting, "This report is an evaluation of a proposal made by the United States for a development of the three Columbia River Treaty projects of Duncan, Arrow and Mica." It is appended to a memo from R.G. Robertson (deputy minister of Northern Affairs and National Resources) to Donald Fleming (minister of justice), January 22, 1963, copy, E. Davie Fulton fonds, MG 32 B11, Vol. 38, 62-35-2, IJC Columbia River – Negotiations, LAC.

52 This was Paddy Sherman's "Columbia River Power Plan: A Special Report," a four-page supplement that appeared in *The Province* on January 24, 1963. It is difficult to believe that the article's appearance was not a staged event. For an intriguing description of the politics behind the piece, see Williston and Keller, *Forests, Power, and Policy*, 200-1. In a speech at Simon Fraser University ten years after the event, Ray Williston recalled that Sherman was critical of Larratt Higgins's article on the Columbia River Treaty—"The Columbia River Treaty: A Critical View," *International Journal* 16, no. 4 (1961): 399-404—but had found it difficult to respond. "Mr. Sherman explained his predicament to me and I responded by turning over the relevant files on the Columbia negotiations. This opened the door to further information from national and American sources, which occupied his complete attention for some months. The resulting published article was the best analysis on the subject that had been written until that time, and it came from British Columbia not Eastern Canada. It was subsequently printed as a separate section and many thousand copies were distributed by all those closely associated with the joint river development—nationally, internationally and provincially. It did much to bring sanity to some of the arguments then propounded based upon speculation and misinformation." Williston typescript, March 1974, 26-27, copy, Mitchell Fonds.

53 Fleming, *So Very Near*, 574-75.

54 See the account of the Hyannis Port meeting in Lester B. Pearson, *Mike: The Memoirs of the Right Honourable Lester Bowles Pearson*, vol. 3, *1957-1968*, ed. John A. Munro and Alex. I. Inglis (Toronto: University of Toronto Press, 1975), 111-12; John English, *The Life of Lester Pearson*, vol. 2, *Worldly Years, 1949-1972* (Toronto: Lester & Orpen Dennys, 1992), 270; and Charles Ritchie, *Storm Signals: More Undiplomatic Diaries, 1962-1971* (Toronto: Macmillan of Canada, 1983), 48-49. It was perhaps illustrative of the new and warmer relationship between Canada and the United States that Pearson appeared on the cover of *Time* at this point. See "Canada: A New Leader," *Time*, April 19, 1963.

55 For an excellent review of the events leading up to the announcement, see John Hilliker and Donald

Barry, *Canada's Department of External Affairs*, vol. 2, *Coming of Age, 1946–1968* (Montreal: McGill-Queen's University Press, 1995), 267–71. For contemporary coverage, see the useful review "Accord Eases Columbia Impasse," *Globe*, July 13, 1963, 9. Two days earlier, on July 11, 1963, the newspaper had published a series of stories on the new agreement, including "Columba Pact Hinges on Terms Offered by U.S.," "Fulton Says Treaty Is Far from Reality," "Premier Bennett Lauds Columbia River Deal," and "Washington Anxious for Early Discussions" (all on p. 3). The accord between British Columbia and the federal government is now online: "Canada-BC Agreement," July 8, 1963, http://blog.gov.bc.ca/columbiarivertreaty/files/2012/04/Can-BC-Agreement-July-8-1963.pdf.

56 See the account in Martin's memoirs, *A Very Public Life*, vol. 2, *So Many Worlds* (Toronto: Deneau, 1985), 390–92. As Hilliker and Barry point out, the federal government used the device of a protocol to avoid having to reopen the treaty. *Canada's Department of External Affairs*, 268.

57 On the relationship of the Pacific intertie and the treaty, see Binus, "Bonneville Power Administration," esp. chap. 6, "The Columbia River Treaty and the Canadian Entitlement." More generally, see Douglas Norwood, "Administrative Challenge and Response: The Role of the Bonneville Power Administration in the West Coast Intertie Decision" (BA thesis, Reed College, 1966); Alan Evan Schenker, *The West Coast Intertie* (Occasional Paper No. 4, Institute of Governmental Affairs, University of California, Davis, 1964); Luce and Kaseberg, "Bonneville Power"; Michael C. Blumm, "The Northwest's Hydroelectric Heritage," in *Northwest Lands, Northwest Peoples: Readings in Environmental History*, ed. Dale D. Goble and Paul W. Hirt (Seattle: University of Washington Press, 1999), 229–63; and Paul Hirt, *The Wired Northwest: The History of Electric Power, 1870s–1970s* (Lawrence: University Press of Kansas, 2012).

58 Charles Luce, BPA administrator from 1961 to1965, recalled a phone call that he received from Bennett: "At one point, Premier Bennett called me . . . , and he said, 'We are ready to start the construction of Duncan Dam,' that was the first of the three dams. 'Immediately, if you'll pay 5 mills for the downstream benefits on that dam.' And I said, 'Well, have you the approval of the national government in Canada, Premier Bennett?' 'No!' he said. 'I don't have it. I don't need it. Water runs downhill doesn't it?' So he said, 'If I build that dam, you're going to get the benefits, there's nothing Ottawa can do about that.' So I said, 'Well, I'll, I don't think our State Department will agree to that kind of an agreement, Premier Bennett, but I will check it out and I'll call you tomorrow.' So I called up Ivan White and our Minister to Canada and we talked to the general counsel to the State Department. Of course they were aghast that we would think of our Federal Government making a deal with a Provincial Government over the objection of the National Government of Canada. I knew they would be and they should be. So

I had to call Bennett the next day and tell him that I had conferred with our State Department and we were unable to do this. We had to have the concurrence of the National Government of Canada. He was furious. He said, 'The Treaty's dead! Treaty's dead. Don't ever talk to me again about the Treaty. I'll never talk to you again about the Treaty!' And he hung up. It was kind of a bad moment." Charles F. Luce, interview by Gene Tollefson, September 7, 1984, transcript, item no. 191, Columbia River Treaty Digital Library, 24–25, http://crtlibrary.cbt.org/items/show/191.

59 For a description and analysis of this important commission, see Stephen Azzi, *Walter Gordon and the Rise of Canadian Nationalism* (Montreal: McGill-Queen's University Press, 1999), 34–65; and Walter Gordon, *A Political Memoir* (Toronto: McClelland & Stewart, 1977), 59–70. As Azzi notes, "Before the Gordon Commission [i.e., the 1957 Royal Commission on Canada's Economic Prospects], Canadian economists did not consider foreign investment a proper topic for debate. For them it went without saying that governments should not limit the free flow of capital across national borders. The Gordon Report was seminal, triggering considerable political and academic discussion of the subject. The report gave Gordon's concerns over foreign investment an air of legitimacy" (p. 57).

60 Dust jacket of Aitken, *American Capital*.

61 The report was A.D.P. Heeney and Livingston T. Merchant's *Canada and the United States: Principles for Partnership* (Ottawa: R. Duhamel, Queen's Printer, 1965). The study (dated June 28, 1965) arose from a meeting between U.S. President Johnson and Prime Minister Pearson in January 1964, where they had "discussed at some length the practicability and desirability of working out acceptable principles which would make it easier to avoid divergencies in economic and other policies of interest to each other." (Joint communiqué, January 22, 1964, quoted in Heeney and Merchant, *Canada and the United States*, Annex B, 1.) On the report's reception, see Greg Donaghy, *Tolerant Allies: Canada and the United States, 1963–1968* (Montreal: McGill-Queen's University Press, 2002), 32, 44, 132; Azzi, *Walter Gordon*, 127–28; Hugh L. Keenleyside, *Memoirs of Hugh L. Keenleyside*, vol. 1, *Hammer the Golden Day* (Toronto: McClelland & Stewart, 1981), 500–2; and the wry memories of the Canadian coauthor, in Arnold Heeney, *The Things That Are Caesar's: Memoirs of a Canadian Public Servant*, ed. Brian D. Heeney (Toronto: University of Toronto Press, 1972), 190–94. Contemporary Canadian views of the United States are well described in Azzi, *Walter Gordon*, 125–39; cf. Al Purdy, ed., *The New Romans: Candid Canadian Opinions of the U.S.* (Edmonton: M. G. Hurtig, 1968), and the public reflections of two prominent journalists, James Reston and Bruce Hutchison, "What's Happening to U.S.-Canada Relations?" *Reader's Digest*, July 1966, 27–32.

62 One of the best sources of the many papers, articles, and cyclostyled typescripts that represent

the public mood against the treaty is the James G. Ripley Fonds, held the University of Victoria Archives; the collection fills a number of archival boxes. Public opinion is also briefly noted in Benjamin Isitt, *Militant Minority: British Columbia Workers and the Rise of a New Left, 1948–1972* (Toronto: University of Toronto Press, 2011), esp. 36–40, 119.

63 On the impact of the flooding of the Arrow Lakes, see James Wood Wilson, *People in the Way: The Human Aspects of the Columbia River Project* (Toronto: University of Toronto Press, 1973); J. W. Wilson and Maureen Conn, "On Uprooting and Rerooting: Reflections on the Columbia River Project," *BC Studies*, no. 58 (1983): 40–54; Tina Loo, "People in the Way: Modernity, Environment, and Society on Arrow Lakes," *BC Studies*, no. 142–143 (Summer/Autumn 2004): 161–96; and Joy Parr, *Sensing Changes: Technologies, Environments, and the Everyday, 1953–2003* (Vancouver: UBC Press, 2010), 103–35. See also the materials available on the website Arrow Lakes, accessed January 22, 2014, http://megaprojects.uwo.ca/ArrowLakes.

64 See Susan Toller and Peter N. Nemetz, "Assessing the Impact of Hydro Development: A Case Study of the Columbia River Basin in British Columbia," *BC Studies*, no. 114 (Summer 1997): 5–30.

65 See George L. Cook, "Aural History on the Classroom: The Columbia River Treaty Lecture Series," *Sound Heritage* 3, no. 3 (1974): 31.

66 See Hugh L. Keenleyside Fonds, MG 31, E 102, Box 12, Files 13 & 14, LAC. Both men were very sensitive to any criticisms of the treaty. Keenleyside's paper include draft chapters for a book on the treaty that he planned to write, as well as his swift replies to various public criticisms of the treaty. For Williston's concern with the way in which the treaty was remembered, see Williston and Keller, *Forests, Power, and Policy*, 220–22.

67 I am referring to the treaty itself. The *consequences* of the treaty, particularly the flooding of the Arrow Lakes, continue to attract scholarly interest.

68 See, for example, the proceedings of the Boundary Waters Treaty Centennial Symposium, reprinted in the *Wayne Law Review* 54, no. 4 (2008).

69 This is described in Michael Laitta, "Canada-U.S. Transboundary Hydrographic Data Harmonization Efforts Gain Momentum" (unpublished manuscript, October 11, 2010), PDF, http://www.ijc.org/rel/boards/watershed/Canada-US_Hydro_Harmonization_e.pdf. Because Laitta is a GIS coordinator and physical scientist with the IJC (both the Canadian and U.S. sections), his views are presumably indicative of the IJC's views. Cf. Craig Schiffries, "Broadening Canada–United States Cooperation on Transboundary Geoscience Issues," Paper No. 268-10 (paper presented at the annual meeting of the Geological Society of America, Minneapolis, October 9–12, 2011); the abstract is available at https://gsa.confex.com/gsa/2011AM/finalprogram/abstract_198168.htm.

70 See Alvin Hamilton's speech on the national development program, in Canada, Parliament,

House of Commons, *Debates*, 24th Parl., 2d Sess., 5 (July 10, 1959): 5796–5800. Note also the comments of both Diefenbaker and Hamilton, quoted in Robert Duffy, "Minding Your Business," *Globe*, September 10, 1959, 6.

71 See the reference in Canada, Parliament, House of Commons, *Debates*, 24th Parl., 5th Sess., 2 (March 19, 1962): 1923; Karl Froschauer, *White Gold: Hydroelectric Power in Canada* (Vancouver: UBC Press, 1999), esp. 212–15; and Swainson, *Conflict over the Columbia*, 209–10. Note also the argument in Nemeth, "Consolidating the Continental Drift." Ironically, the Pacific Intertie carrying BC's power entitlement to southern California was viewed by Americans as a step in establishing just such a national grid in their country; see Blumm, "Northwest's Hydroelectric Heritage," 275.

72 See, for example, Jorge Niosi, *Canadian Capitalism* (Toronto: James Lorimer, 1981), 100; H.V. Nelles, *The Politics of Development: Forests, Mines and Hydro-Electric Power in Ontario, 1849–1941* (Toronto: Macmillan of Canada, 1974), 248–49; John Richards and Larry Pratt, *Prairie Capitalism: Power and Influence in the New West* (Toronto: McClelland & Stewart, 1979); James L. Kenny and Andrew Secord, "Public Power for Industry: A Re-Examination of the New Brunswick Case, 1940–1960," *Acadiensis* 30, no. 2 (2001): 84–108; and James L. Kenny and Andrew Secord, "Engineering Modernity: Hydroelectric Development in New Brunswick, 1945–1970," *Acadiensis* 39, no. 1 (2010): 3–26. For a more general discussion, see Tieleman, "Political Economy."

73 For a carefully researched account of the downstream impact of the Bennett Dam on the Athabasca Chipewyan First Nation, see Indian Claims Commission, *Athabasca Chipewyan First Nation Inquiry: W.A.C. Bennett Dam and Damage to Indian Reserve 201* (Ottawa: ICC, 1998). The Indian Claims Commission concluded that "Canada had breached its statutory and fiduciary obligations towards the Athabasca Chipewyan First Nation by failing to take reasonable steps to prevent, to mitigate, or to seek compensation for an unjustified infringement on its treaty right and for environmental damages to IR 201 caused by the construction and operation of the W.A.C. Bennett Dam" (109–10). The commission's report also illustrates the disdain with which British Columbia responded to any criticisms of the Peace River project; see esp. 40–43, 97–98. On the local impact of the Bennett Dam and the Williston Reservoir, see Daniel Sims, "Tse Keh Nay-European Relations and Ethnicity, 1790s–2009" (MA thesis, University of Alberta, 2010), 130–34. BC Hydro is currently refusing to include any downstream impacts in its environmental assessment of its latest project on the Peace River; see Bob Weber, "Alberta Aboriginals Oppose BC Hydro's Dam Project, Say It Needs More Study," *Vancouver Sun*, March 3, 2013.

74 This is not a retrospective analysis: two significant players in the debates around BC hydro development made similar points at the time. For example, in September 1961, Davie Fulton argued in a

speech that "it is axiomatic [that] if we dispose of our cheapest source of power south of the border [by selling the Columbia's downstream benefits] we will have to consume more expensive power at home.... The higher cost of power means a higher cost of production. It means an impaired competitive position. It is a hindrance to the industrial expansion that I have referred to, and that is so necessary to our future prosperity. It also means an obstacle in the way of the diversification of our economy and of job security." Fulton speech, SFU Archives. For a similar analysis, see A.E. Dal Grauer, "The Export of Electricity from Canada," in *Canadian Issues: Essays in Honour of Henry F. Angus*, ed. R.M. Clark (Toronto: University of Toronto Press, 1961), 283. Grauer headed BC Electric, the private utility nationalized by W.A.C. Bennett.

PART THREE

*Challenging the Border:
Ecological Agents of Change*

Openings

Border Ecologies in Boundary Waters

JAMES W. FELDMAN

Borders mean different things in different places. Along the line that divides the United States from Mexico, the border brings to mind armed patrols, tunnels and fences, illegal immigration, and one of the thorniest modern political issues. In the Quetico-Superior country—a 199-mile/320-kilometre stretch between the state of Minnesota and the province of Ontario, the border means something else entirely: old-growth forests, world-class fishing, and the northern lights; voyageurs and portages rather than coyotes and maquiladoras. While there are three formal border crossings and customs stations along the line that divides the Boundary Waters Canoe Area Wilderness (also known as the BWCA, a unit of the United States Forest Service) in Minnesota from Quetico Provincial Park in Ontario, in most places one could simply walk—or paddle—across the border. This region of pristine lakes and boreal forests contains a hydrological boundary as well as an international one: the Laurentian Divide. Water north of the divide flows into the Arctic Ocean; water to the south flows to the Atlantic. At one point, the international border and the hydrological border overlap: the Height-of-Land portage, where modern-day canoe travellers carry their gear eighty rods (1,320 feet/402 metres) between North and South Lakes, straddling the border as they go. The occasional small metal obelisk marks the location of the international border, while a weather-beaten sign denotes the hydrological one.

There is not, however, much of an ecological border here. The BWCA includes 1,086,953 acres, while the Quetico contains 1,180,000 acres. The two parks together create one of the largest protected areas in the eastern half of North America. Both parks rest on top of the basalts and granites of the Canadian Shield—some of the oldest exposed rock formations in the world, created in the heart of the Earth 2.7 billion years ago. The rocky shorelines and sharp cliffs created by the ancient bedrock frame a landscape of dense boreal forest and deep, cold lakes. The northern boreal forests, containing a community of pine, fir, aspen, maple, and spruce, provide a home for a rich diversity of wildlife. Both parks include some of the most significant remnant stands of old growth in the Great Lakes Basin. The BWCA provided the last shelter in the continental United States for grey wolves, although that population has now recovered and spread to other Great Lakes states. The water quality along the border is so high that many wilderness visitors to the BWCA and Quetico take their drinking water straight from the lakes, without boiling or filtering—a rarity in North America and a sign of the ecological health of the region.

Elemental ecological forces such as wind, fire, and water pay no heed to the international border, of course. Neither do more anthropogenic (though still ecological) agents such as mercury or invasive species. And yet the way that Canadians and Americans manage these ecological forces must acknowledge the border. One contiguous ecosystem in two countries: the perfect place to consider how ecological agents blur the lines on the map and how the lines on the map often shape the environment—creating unique border ecologies in the process. The two chapters in this section reveal these complicated dynamics and border ecologies.

While the Quetico and the Boundary Waters together protect over two million acres of a remarkably healthy and wild ecosystem, the human construct of the border still makes a significant difference. Patterns of visitor use and impact in the two parks reveal the ecological and social impact of the border. Over a quarter million people visit the BWCA each year, making it the most heavily visited wilderness area in the United States. To manage the large number of visitors, regulations require that campers stay in designated campsites, each one findable on a map and equipped with a fire grate and a primitive fibreglass latrine. Evidence of past use at these sites is often quite extensive—log seating areas around the fire grate, clearly defined tent pads, limited supplies of firewood, occasional trash in the fire pits. Across the border, however, the Quetico receives one-tenth of the annual visitation of the Boundary Waters. Wilderness travellers find their own spots to spend the night and may camp anywhere they choose. Signs of visitor use are still present—the same places still get used—but the impact of this use is far lighter than that south of the border.

The heavier use in the Boundary Waters has both social and ecological consequences. In short, the two places simply *feel* different. Activists, scholars, and wilderness travellers have long struggled to define the "wilderness experience": an alchemy of isolation, natural beauty, antimodernity, and ecological health. The BWCA is simply more crowded. A 2012 study of visitor use patterns found that travellers encountered an average of 8.6 other groups per day, up from 4.1 and 4.2 in 1969 and 1991, respectively. Trail crews maintain the portages—the trails between lakes—regularly in the BWCA; portages in the Quetico are notoriously overgrown, hard to find, and harder to cross. Most visitors perceive crowding as a serious social threat to wilderness values. The ecological impacts of high visitor use in wilderness areas include vegetation trampling, the creation of pathways for invasive species, and wildlife disturbance, among other issues. In the BWCA, scholars have demonstrated a clear link between portage travel and the spread of invasive species. Species of concern include plants (such as purple loosestrife, oxeye daisy, and hawkweed) and animals (such as earthworms and gypsy moths). Visitors carry seeds and insects in their footwear and equipment, and the trampling along trails alters soil characteristics and damages native species, creating the conditions for exotic species to gain a foothold in a region otherwise known for its ecological health. The worms and insects, in particular, have the capacity to move beyond the portage trails and dramatically alter forest composition.[1]

The differences between the BWCA and the Quetico derive from modern management decisions, but also from different histories of use and industry. For nearly 150 years, the Boundary Waters area has been more accessible and more influenced by industrial development. Rich deposits of iron drew Euro-American settlers to northeastern Minnesota as early as the 1870s. The town of Ely, Minnesota—the closest town to the BWCA—grew into a rough-and-tumble mining town in the early twentieth century. Intensive logging began in the area in the 1880s, as well, and continued through the mid-twentieth century. The creation of Superior National Forest brought federal administration to the area. The U.S. Forest Service designated parts of the forest as a roadless area in 1926—among the earliest American steps toward wilderness management and a recognition of the region's growing recreational appeal. Although the Quetico had a similar history of logging, it is much farther away from urban population centres and has never had the same kind of recreational or industrial pressures. The first road into the Quetico region was not built until 1954. The differential patterns of visitor use on opposite sides of the border today have a deep historical precedent.[2]

In other ways, the human construct of the international border barely matters. Consider, for example, the "Boundary Waters–Canadian Derecho" of 1999—also called the "Boundary Waters Blowdown." On July 4, a ferociously powerful windstorm gathered over the North American Great Plains and began moving east. The term "derecho," derived from the Spanish word for straight, indicates straight-line winds as opposed to rotational ones. When the storm reached the boundary waters, winds blasting at over one hundred miles per hour ripped through both the BWCA and the Quetico, flattening trees over 500,000 acres in Minnesota and 288,000 acres in Ontario—an area more than five times greater than that affected by the eruption of Mount St. Helens in 1980. The derecho knocked down tens of millions of trees across both sides of the border, with some areas losing virtually every single tree. Bluffs and high areas were particularly hard hit; the more wind-resistant stands along the shores of the region's larger lakes fared slightly better. The derecho paid no attention to the international border. Indeed, after leaving canoe country, the storm proceeded through Ontario and Quebec before turning south toward Maine and northern New England.[3]

The forest fires that followed the blowdown disregarded the border, as well. The dead and drying trees in the area altered fire behaviour and fire management planning. Fire suppression throughout the 1900s elevated fuel loads on the forest floor; the trees felled by the blowdown added to the problem, elevating the risk of particularly hot fires that could potentially damage the region's thin topsoil and retard forest regeneration. For the first time ever in designated wilderness areas, American authorities conducted prescribed burns to help mitigate the risk of major conflagrations. Fires of historic proportions have burned on both sides of the border in the years since the 1999 derecho. The two largest fires in the region since 1918 both burned in the blowdown area: the Ham Lake Fire of 2007, which straddled the border and burned 76,000 acres, and the Pagami Creek Fire of 2011, which burned over 100,000 acres inside the BWCA.[4]

Management response to the fires in the blowdown, however, has had to acknowledge the border. Management authorities in Minnesota and Ontario use a series of compacts and international agreements to coordinate fire management. The Great Lakes Forest Fire Compact includes the fire management agencies of Wisconsin, Michigan, Minnesota, Ontario, and Manitoba. The compact allows the agencies to coordinate planning, share personnel and equipment, and respond effectively to cross-border fires. Other agreements detail procedures for border crossings during fire emergencies and the management of air space over the border. A separate border agreement between Minnesota, Ontario, and several American federal agencies creates a "common border"—an area ten miles on either side of the border—in which air and ground resources can be shared. The necessities of fire management make the border into an instrument of cooperation rather than division. Following an ecological lead, fire management authorities acknowledge the border by blurring it.[5]

All of these issues—border ecologies, invasive species, blowdowns, fire management—take on new meaning in light of the threats and challenges posed by climate change. The Quetico-Superior country lies close to another border: the boundary between the conifer-dominated boreal biome to the north and the deciduous forest biome to the south. Scholars forecasting the ecological impact of climate change have speculated that plant communities will shift radically in response to changing rainfall and temperature patterns. This might be particularly true for the Quetico-Superior region, where, some scholars have noted, the vegetation "is particularly sensitive to climate change, with little inertia."[6] This might mean a shift to a grassland/savannah ecosystem or temperate hardwood forest and an end to the ecological conditions that currently define the region. Climate change raises all sorts of complicated questions about causality, turning upside down long-held notions of just what kinds of ecological change are "natural" and which are anthropogenic. Might the 1999 derecho, for example, have had its origins in new weather patterns influenced by rising levels of carbon dioxide in the atmosphere? Border ecologies—changing ecosystems and changing social systems embedded within each other, all buffeted by a changing climate—provide the context for the two chapters in this section.

The environmental historian Joseph Taylor powerfully explores these contested border ecologies in his chapter, "Lines That Don't Divide: Telling Tales about Animals, Chemicals, and People in the Salish Sea." He traces the emergence of a new biocultural region—the Salish Sea—located in the coastal networks and ecosystems between British Columbia and Washington. Chemicals flowing into the water on both sides of the border have altered natural and human communities, in the process creating a place with new social and ecological characteristics. The tendency of mercury, PCBs, and other persistent organic pollutants to bioaccumulate has reshaped the bodies of both fish and human residents of the region. Cultural practices and social divides have pushed the hazards associated with these pollutants toward some groups and away from others, in ways that often follow preexisting sociopolitical lines. Taylor reveals the "contingent significance of borders"—the borders between countries, between social groups, and between humans and nature.

In "Resiliency and Collapse: Lake Trout, Sea Lamprey, and Fisheries Management in Lake Superior," the environmental historian Nancy Langston explores the complexities of a single case study in border ecology: the collapse and recovery of the Lake Superior lake trout fishery. For years, fisheries managers have blamed the invasive sea lamprey for the collapse of the fishery. The lamprey made an easy target; the voracious and invasive parasite travelled up the St. Lawrence River, latched onto the sides of juvenile and adult trout, and sucked out their insides. And yet, Langston shows, the story was never this simple. Lake trout proved remarkably resilient for nearly 150 years, weathering "multiple stressors at multiple scales": changing land-use patterns (deforestation and agricultural development); intensifying pressure from a commercial fishery that grew more mechanized and market-based; paper mills that treated Lake Superior as a dumping ground for industrial byproducts. Determining the cause of the lake trout collapse means reconciling all of these factors, none of which remained constant. The border confounded many of these variables as well, precluding an effective management response. Regulations on fishing and chemical dumping varied from state to state and country to country; so did the intensity of logging and land-use change. It is the special task of environmental historians, Langston suggests, to piece together these constantly changing variables into a plausible narrative, one that explains why trout "were resilient for so long—until suddenly they weren't."

The environmental historian Paul Sutter recently challenged the field to explore more deeply the implications and origins of what he labels "hybridity": the recognition of the complex interconnections between nature and culture that shape the material world. The exploration of this concept has come to define the modern field of environmental history. Borders of all kinds—be they ecological, political, social, international—provide perfect places to study the past and future of hybrid landscapes. If, as Sutter suggests, "all environments are hybrid," then border environments are especially so.[7] Both Taylor and Langston add to our understanding of hybridity along the border—Taylor by documenting the creation of a new and hybrid space from several different pasts and environments, and Langston by exploring the many different social and ecological causes necessary to understand a single episode of the environmental past. Taylor and Langston together demonstrate that the most consistent variable in border ecologies is change itself. Ecosystems shift and move in response to both natural and anthropocentric forces; the human systems built upon and embedded within those ecosystems struggle to catch up. The borders themselves serve as agents of division in some times and places, and agents of cooperation in others. In all cases, the *meaning* of the border—and of border ecologies—constantly evolves.

Notes

1   Robert G. Dvorak et al., *The Boundary Waters Canoe Area Wilderness: Examining Changes in Use, Users, and Management Challenges*, Research Paper No. RMRS-RP-91 (Fort Collins, CO: U.S. Dept. of Agriculture, Forest Service, Rocky Mountain Research Station, 2012), 9; "Threats to Wilderness from Overuse," *Wilderness.net*, University of Montana, accessed September 15, 2014, http://www.wilderness.net/nwps/threatsOveruse; Sara Jo M. Dickens, Fritz Gerhardt, and Sharon K. Collinge, "Recreational Portage Trails as Corridors Facilitating Non-Native Plant Invasions of the Boundary Waters Canoe Area Wilderness (USA)," *Conservation Biology* 19, no. 5 (2005): 1653–57; Lee E. Frelich and Peter B. Reich, "Wilderness Conservation in an Era of Global Warming and Invasive Species: A Case Study from Minnesota's Boundary Waters Canoe Area Wilderness," *Natural Areas Journal* 29, no. 4 (2009): 385–93.

2   Benjamin Heber Johnson, "Conservation, Subsistence, and Class at the Birth of Superior National Forest," *Environmental History* 4, no. 1 (1999): 80–99; Gerald Killan, *Protected Places: A History of Ontario's Provincial Parks System* (Toronto: Dundurn / Ontario Ministry of

Natural Resources, 1993); R. Newell Searle, *Saving Quetico-Superior: A Land Set Apart* (St. Paul: Minnesota Historical Society Press, 1977).

3   Christine Mlot, "The Perfect Windstorm Study: What Happens when Millions of Trees Fall Down in a Forest Wilderness?" *BioScience* 53, no. 7 (2003): 624–29; "July 4–5, 1999 Derecho: The Boundary Waters–Canadian Derecho," accessed April 4, 2016, http://www.spc.noaa.gov/misc/AbtDerechos/casepages/jul4-51999page.htm.

4   Bryan Hansel, "Fire Management in the Boundary Waters Canoe Area Wilderness after the Pagami Creek Fire," *Paddling Light*, September 19, 2011, http://www.paddlinglight.com/articles/fire-management-in-the-boundary-waters-canoe-area-wilderness-the-pagami-creek-fire.

5   The Great Lakes Forest Fire Compact website can be found at http://www.glffc.com. See also Minnesota Incident Command System, "Northeastern Minnesota Aviation In-Briefing," January 15, 2010, http://mnics.org/wpress/wp-content/uploads/2012/04/NE-Minnesota-Aviation-Inbriefing-1-15-10.pdf.

6   Frelich and Reich, "Wilderness Conservation," 387.

7   Paul S. Sutter, "The World with Us: The State of American Environmental History," *Journal of American History* 100, no. 1 (2013): 96.

Lines That Don't Divide: Telling Tales about Animals, Chemicals, and People in the Salish Sea

Joseph E. Taylor III

> Chucho. Bird flying south: you think he sees that line? Rattlesnake, javelin—whatever you got—halfway across that line they don't start thinking different. So why should a man?
>
> —*Lone Star* (1996)

We border our worlds to establish order—my side of the room, your side of the backseat, our province, your country—but boundary making is never a simple exercise. Among the many brilliant things about John Sayles's film *Lone Star* is its deft exposure of the psychic and material porosity of the lines we draw. Chucho's speech reminds us that nature has its own geographies, from the dust and mould that spread relentlessly from my bunkmate's side of the dorm to the exotic species that vex environmental managers around the world. Nature reveals the limits of our spatial projects. In fact, the more we try to keep each other at bay, the more nature draws us together. Conservative Montana farmers built fences to demarcate their private property, but rolling tumbleweeds forced them to establish socialistic "weed districts" and coerce collective responses to keep their fields clean. Similarly, every nation subjects immigrants to health examinations to keep out the sick, but the mutability of pathogens also compels every nation to collaborate in a global disease-tracking system. We try to separate yours from mine to keep out that which is unwanted, but the only constant is transgression, from the 1832 cholera epidemic that swept the globe to the Fukushima-Daiichi-radiated bluefin tuna that arrived off California less than a year after the 2011 Tōhoku tsunami. Neither our national borders nor our cultural containers succeed very well at containing nature's dynamism.[1]

The globalized economy exposes daily the problematic nature of modern borders. Planes and ships carry cargo from every corner of the planet—everything from Afghani-raised poppies to Zimbabwean-mined platinum—to a world of eager consumers. Most of this is intended freight, but there are always stowaways ranging from migrant labourers to insects and pathogens, that are less welcome yet ubiquitous. Our insatiable appetites have so accelerated species transfers that North America now hosts a remarkably cosmopolitan ecology. The tales we tell about such invasions are telling. When we discuss starlings and kudzu, we tend to dwell on human agency, even if only to illustrate the limits of customs agents. Nature is a tag-along companion, the undocumented alien slipping in off-manifest in bilges, bodies, and holds. Just in 2012, Pacific Northwesterners learned about infectious salmon anemia spreading from farmed to wild salmon, whooping cough spreading from British Columbia to Washington and Oregon, and debris from tsunami-plagued Japan washing onto North American beaches from Alaska to California. Nature matters in these tales, but it resembles Dr. Frankenstein's monster: a horrifyingly unnatural beast unleashed by human caprice.[2]

Although this plot can unnerve, it is familiar and reliable, even comfortable, because the moral of the story is always that somebody behaved badly. But how do we narrate when nature takes the lead, when humans are merely supporting players and the most disturbing monsters are largely a consequence of natural processes? Hollywood offers a few such tales. In the movie *Contagion*, for example, pathogenic mutations unleash a super-virulent influenza epidemic that rapidly outpaces humans to devastate the world. The camera dwells on individual experiences, but biological processes drive this viral plot. Life history, bioaccumulation, and migration similarly frame movies such as *Andromeda Strain*, *Minamata*, and *World War Z*. Like the Frankensteinian narrative, these nature-propelled dramas illustrate the contingent significance of borders. Social spaces matter, but their meanings shift when nature crosses a line. In the case of *Contagion* and *World War Z*, human borders not only fail to keep citizens safe; they actually stymie the state's ability to comprehend natural threats. In such cases the only rational form of boundary making is individual quarantine. Characters literally wall themselves off from the rest of humanity, yet the underlying, almost too-subtle lesson is that isolation is impossible.[3]

This applies equally to the lines we draw between ourselves and nature. Although in the late nineteenth century the germ theory of disease led medical professionals to reimagine human bodies as separate ecosystems, the hermetic body never fully displaced the older view of bodily health as entwined with its environments. Twentieth-century researchers such as Macfarlane Burnet and Rene Dubos drew links between parasites, disease, and ecology, while environmental advocates such as Rachel Carson, Lois Gibbs, and Sandra Steingraber highlighted the linkages between chemicals, morbidity, and extinction. Clusters of rare cancers, birth defects, and chronic diseases kept epidemiologists focused on the role of place in human health. Horrors such as HIV and Ebola made most of the world more conscious of how zoonosis has shaped human history. Every major epidemic from Justinian's Plague to smallpox, measles, anthrax, yellow fever, the Spanish flu, and West Nile virus began when a pathogen jumped from an animal to us. The demarcations between humans, other species, and the environment seem less and less clear. One particularly instructive way to trace this blurred reality is via the ecology of chemicals along the northwestern edge of North America.[4]

The waterscape abutting southwestern British Columbia and northwestern Washington State was once known as the Puget Sound, Strait of Juan de Fuca, or Strait of Georgia (Figure 1). Now it is called the Salish Sea, a vast inland sea studded with rocky islands, complex currents, charismatic fauna, spectacular scenery, and very large cities. In most ways the Salish Sea is a seamless ecology teeming with life, yet as Emma S. Norman and Alice Cohen illustrate elsewhere in this volume, it has always lapped up against a complicated social geography. Native peoples dominated the region for millennia. Most groups spoke dialects of the Salish language, and all relied primarily on marine and riverine resources, especially the Pacific

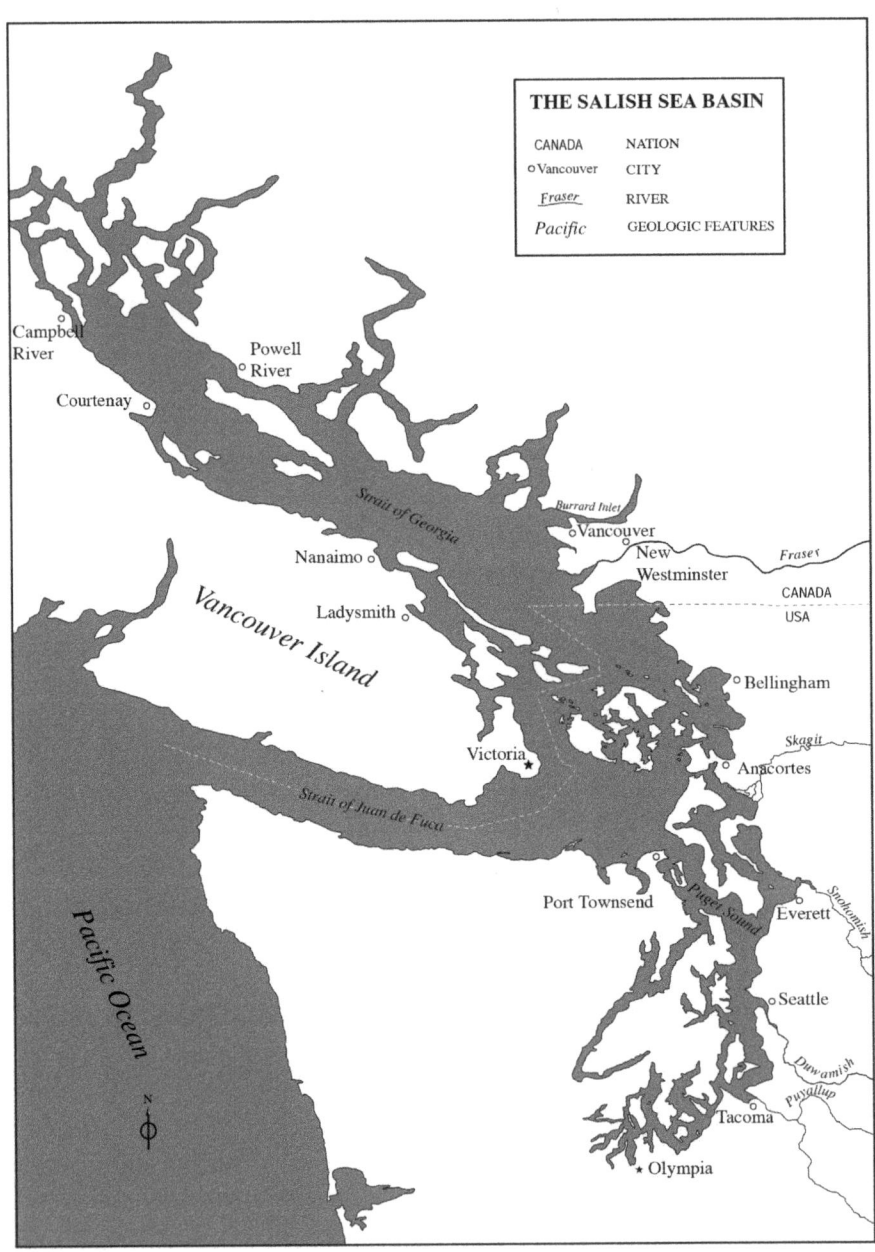

7.1 Salish Sea basin. The "Salish Sea" is the official geographical term now applied to a waterscape whose individual components are also called the Strait of Georgia, Strait of Juan de Fuca, and Puget Sound. Map by author.

salmon (*Oncorhynchus* spp.) and whales that plied these waters. Residents interacted both peacefully, via marriage and trade, and violently, through war and slave raiding, but sovereignty rarely reached beyond the village. Europeans overlaid but did not erase this fractured world. Even during the hegemony of the Hudson's Bay Company in the 1820s and 1830s, or after Great Britain and the United States formally divided the continent at the 49th parallel in 1846, Aboriginal seasonal movements continued to bare the porosity of corporate and state space. No single sovereign has ever ruled the Salish Sea, and British Columbia's ongoing land claims process with First Nations groups in the province reminds us that the modern state has not yet perfected its title to the region.[5]

This social dynamism depended heavily upon a setting of ecological continuity, but food chains became ever less reliable over the nineteenth and twentieth centuries. The Salish Sea had never been a pristine wilderness. Indigenous peoples harvested vast amounts of nature for millennia, but with little change to the sea's ecology or chemistry. Nineteenth-century farmers, fishers, loggers, and miners accelerated the rate of extraction, especially by denuding forests, silting spawning beds, and blocking streams. Lumber mills, tanneries, and coal mines dumped their wastes into rivers and bays in a giant circle from Port Townsend to Olympia, Seattle, New Westminster, Powell River, Campbell River, Courtenay, Ladysmith, and Victoria. Sawdust leachates altered water chemistry and, in large depositions, absorbed all the suspended oxygen, while tannins toxified the water. Still, resettlement's ecological impact on the sea was slight until the end of the century, when industrialization and urbanization transformed the Salish Sea ecosystem in ways similar to what Nancy Langston describes for Lake Superior in the next chapter. In the 1880s, railroads solidified the line between water and land by filling marshes, tidal flats, and river banks with rock and dirt. Towns expanded the hardscape with ports, levees, and pavement. Population growth and industrial development substantially deepened the ecological impact. Every urban centre poured raw sewage into the sea. Petroleum facilities on Burrard Inlet in 1908 and in Seattle in 1911 disposed wastes similarly, as did ships, shipyards, and steel mills. By 1930 the Salish Sea had suffered significant habitat loss and diminished oxygen content. The main contributors then intensified with World War II and the Cold War.[6]

The distinguishing ecological theme of the twentieth century was not simply the Salish Sea's increasingly polluted state but the changing nature of the things flushed into it. Petroleum- and electrical-based energy used an array of new chemicals that refineries routinely dumped into the sea, including benzene, toluene, and xylene. The widespread practice of burning domestic and industrial wastes released mercury into the air. Pulp and paper mills poured chlorine and heavy metals into the water. Electrical transformers leaked PCB-laden coolants in the Puyallup, Duwamish, Snohomish, and Fraser Rivers and Burrard Inlet. From the 1930s to the 1970s all these chemicals—plus PCDDs, PCDFs, PVCs, and an array of organochlorines such as DDT and 2,4-D—entered the ecosystem in ever increasing amounts. A key period in the watershed was the early 1970s, when federal, state, and provincial regulatory agencies began to rein in pollution. Halting the production and distribution of toxins was a critical turning point, but the chemicals were not easily erased. All would continue to seep into and remain in the sea for decades. The sediment became a kind of safety deposit box of horrors. Moreover, even as the production and release of some compounds abated, new flame-retardant PBDEs, introduced during the 1970s as part of consumer safety legislation, entered the sea in ever increasing amounts through the air and water. Researchers also discovered a much vaster category of unregulated "nonpoint source pollution" as chemicals washed into the sea from urban streets, suburban yards, and rural farms. Most chemicals had structures and modes of action similar to dioxin—a particularly awful carcinogen—and their resilience to decay led all to be dubbed "persistent organic pollutants."[7]

To this point the narrative resembles the Frankenstein plot. In our heedless pursuit of progress, humans have unleashed new, sometimes frightening, forms of nature, fouling nests and wreaking unintended consequences. The plot is so familiar—especially because of those 1950s sci-fi flicks featuring ants and blobs—that we can ignore the details and still accurately predict the outcome: giant women, toxic avengers, Ninja Turtles, and the residents of Hinkley, California, whom Erin Brockovich rescued. We focus on the human victims, but some of the things that were flushed down the toilet—birth control pills, steroids, and other artificial hormones with endocrine-disrupting properties—mutated the sea itself. Biologists have begun to detect broad changes in water chemistry. During winter holidays the sea around sewer outfalls tastes more like vanilla and cinnamon, and the entire Pacific is more caffeinated these days. Salmon farms transmit epizootics and heavy metals to wild fish. Similar to the effect that Langston describes for trifluoromethyl-4-nitrophenol on larval lampreys in Lake Superior, the endocrine-disrupting properties of PCBs and mercury may have changed reproductive rates and sex ratios in bottom fish in heavily industrialized areas such as the Duwamish River and Hylebos Waterway. Make no mistake: there be monsters here, but this narrative is more complex and devastating than *Godzilla* redux.[8]

What makes the Salish Sea's chemical history so disturbing is that its environmental processes were utterly natural. Ecosystems are the sum of acts of production and consumption. Sunlight is the foundation of nutrient flows, and food chains are how they cycle. This is life, pure and simple, but the effect on the sea was anything but simple or pure. When chlorine, mercury, PCBs, and PBDEs settled into sediments, microphytes and algae broke down and absorbed these chemicals. This began many cycles of uptake. Anaerobic organisms in the sediment transformed mercury into methylmercury, a more toxic form of the element easier for other organisms to absorb. Those microorganisms were in turn consumed by plankton floating in the current, which were eaten by small fish and shellfish. At each step predators became prey. Smaller-bodied species fed larger, higher-trophic species such as bottom fish, maturing salmon, and marine mammals, while decomposers recycled nutrients and persistent organic pollutants at every level of the ecosystem. Most of the pollutants had anthropogenic origins, but their journey through the Salish Sea was utterly natural, as was the tendency for larger-bodied, longer-lived species to metabolize them—called "bioaccumulation" or "biomagnification"—in ever greater concentrations than smaller-bodied, shorter-lived species. The same process that coloured the flesh of salmon by consuming carotene-laden krill and shrimp, and made longer-lived, fattier chinooks (*O. tshawytscha*) and sockeyes (*O. nerka*) redder than shorter-lived, leaner pinks (*O. gorbuscha*) and chums (*O. keta*), also turned these high-trophic predators into toxic-waste sites.[9]

By the early 2000s, wildlife biologists had a fairly clear picture of what bioaccumulation was doing at the top of the Salish Sea food chains. It was not a pretty sight. Adult chinook bore significant loads of PCBs and PBDEs back to spawning grounds and hatcheries, and persistent organic pollutants accumulated in the blubber and hair of Steller sea lions and harbour seals at even higher levels. Organochlorines were linked to cancer rates in California sea lions in British Columbia. Resident killer whales "exceeded the health-effects threshold for PCBs in blubber and, most notably, the four juvenile whales exceeded the threshold by factors of 2-3.6." The impact on juvenile orcas was particularly devastating. Lactating orcas were managing to lower their toxic levels by transferring pollutants to their calves through maternal milk. Although researchers focused on those apex species most likely to harbour pollutants in high concentrations, they knew this was a systemic problem that affected every link in the sea's many food chains. And just as the ecosystem did not stop at the 49th parallel, neither did it stop at the water's edge. Biologists traced additional chemical pathways to surf scoters grazing in the nearshore environs of the Salish Sea, to grizzly bears eating adult salmon and excreting the nutrients and pollutants across the forest, and to American dippers feeding on the spawned-out carcasses of salmon in the upper Fraser River basin.[10]

Humans were ultimately linked to both ends of these food chains. Salmon eaters were made aware of their connectedness to the sea through a pair of scientific studies in 2004 that documented high concentrations of PCBs and PBDEs in farmed salmon. As in other tales of bioaccumulation, this was about toxins naturally concentrating as they moved up the trophic ladder. The researchers noted that farmed salmon, because they were fed processed bottom fish, functionally ate at a higher trophic level than wild salmon, which preyed on smaller-bodied fish. From an ecological perspective, there was little surprise in finding that farmed-salmon flesh contained higher concentrations of PCBs and PBDEs than did that of wild salmon, but there *was* a surprise: the single highest PBDE score came from a wild salmon (Figure 2). The data point seemed anomalous until researchers learned that it came from a large-bodied, long-lived chinook whose subpopulation matures in the Salish Sea; unlike most wild salmon, which spend the ocean part of their lives far out in the Pacific, these chinooks remain locavores and pay a price.[11]

The research on PCBs and PBDEs also illustrates how humans inhabit the highest trophic level in the Salish Sea's persistent organic pollutant ecosystem. Every human bioaccumulates, but we do not all consume toxins equally. Although most Salish Sea residents eat salmon, they do not all eat the same species of salmon. Wealthy residents consume fresh sockeye and chinook shipped from the nonindustrialized, far less toxic Skeena,

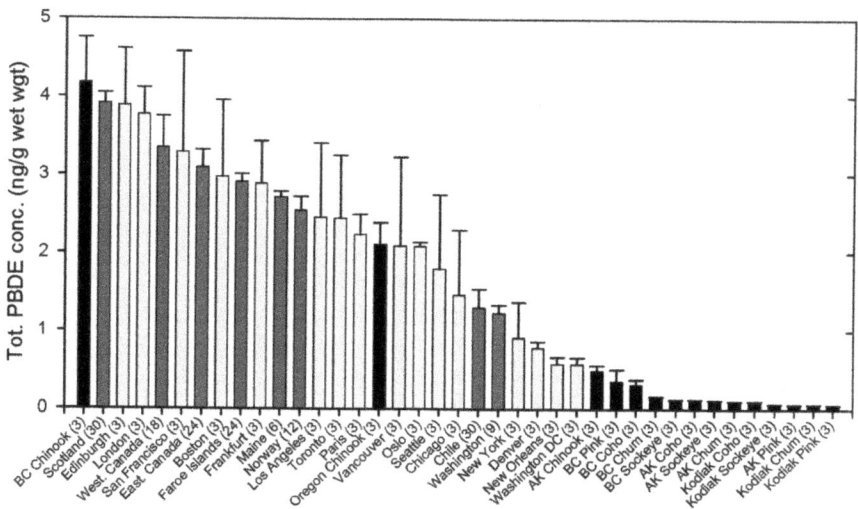

7.2 PBDEs in salmon. In 2004, researchers published studies on the bioaccumulation rates of persistent organic pollutants in farmed and wild salmon. The above graph illustrates PBDE accumulation, with wild salmon (black bars) mostly scoring at the low end. The higher uptake values among wholesale- and supermarket-supplied farmed salmon (grey and white bars respectively) was unsurprising, but the two exceptions involving Pacific Northwest runs, especially the BC chinook at the far left-hand edge of the graph, underscored the polluted state of Northwest waters. Reproduced with permission of Ronald A. Hites and American Chemical Society.

Copper, and Bristol Bay watersheds. Middling Northwesterners tend to dine on coho and chinook caught by local trollers and anglers or on Atlantic and steelhead salmon farmed in Washington and British Columbia. The poor eat pink and chum canned in northern British Columbia and western Alaska or bottom fish and crab harvested from urban piers. Thus, the middle class and poor most often consume local nature, and the poor eat more local fish per capita than any other segment of society. This is not a good thing. Bioaccumulation operates the same way in humans as it does in birds, fish, pinnipeds, and cetaceans. Toxins accrete in adipose tissues, especially the buttocks and breasts, and females can pass concentrated doses of these chemicals to nursing infants. Mammalian babies, it turns out, are the apex consumers of the Salish Sea's toxic ecology. The biological mechanisms that led nursing juvenile orcas to have above-average levels of toxins are the same ones that place poor kids in Seattle—whose mothers consume high amounts of locally caught fish—at a higher risk for toxic contamination and cognitive delays. In this respect, the Salish Sea differs little from other heavily industrialized environments such as Lake Superior, New York's East River, Baden-Württemberg in Germany, and Zhejiang in China, but at this point even places like Arctic Canada suffer from persistent organic pollutants.[12]

Because toxic ecologies exist pretty much everywhere, so do their environmental and social consequences. The intellectual and geopolitical borders that run through the Salish Sea offer a rare opportunity to consider the physical and cultural obstacles that thwart our ability to think ecologically. The sea that captures modern imaginations is decidedly not the world that Aboriginal peoples inhabited two centuries ago, yet its timeless beauty and bounty are why people continue to invoke regional identities that ignore the 49th parallel. Although the imperialistic ambitions of the Hudson's Bay Company and American jingoists lost favour, environmentalists and entrepreneurs suggested transnational spaces that were, each in its own way, as imperialistic and blinkered. In 1975, Ernest Callenbach's *Ecotopia* included the Salish Sea in an imagined nation that would encompass the entire northern Pacific coast. Underlying his fantasy, and repeated even more expansively in Joel Garreau's *The Nine Nations of North America* (1981) and Colin Woodard's *American Nations* (2011), is a belief that local nature nurtures unique environmental sensitivity. The Salish Sea's history of persistent organic pollutants complicates such claims, but it has not stopped Washington and British Columbia entrepreneurs from asserting their own kindredness with nature and each other in the "Cascadia" campaign that claims the Pacific Northwest is a natural bioregion and economy that is artificially divided by two nation states. In the words of a Canadian booster, Cascadia "is a spectacular array of natural and built environments, with wilderness coexisting in relative harmony with sophisticated urban centres."[13]

The coinage of "Salish Sea" is thus the latest in a long genealogy of regionalisms. First proposed in the late 1980s by Bert Webber, a Canadian-born marine biologist who spent his professional career at Western Washington University, "Salish Sea" slowly grew more popular among activists, artists, bureaucrats, and scientists. By early 2010, state, provincial, and federal geographical naming boards had approved the term. Like previous ideas, "Salish Sea" conflates nature and culture too tidily. In honouring the Salishan-speaking people who had long resided around the edges of the sea, Webber memorialized the dominant language but homogenized the region's fractured political and linguistic geography, which included many independent groups, ten distinct dialects, and three Wakashan-speaking peoples (Kwakwaka'wakw, Nuu-chah-nulth, and Makah) who were effectively defined out of the modern "Salish Sea." Webber hoped his neologism might even erase memory of the old Georgia Strait, Puget Sound, and Strait of Juan de Fuca. His aim was "to restore the damaged waters by raising awareness that this is one shared ecosystem spanning the border between Canada and the United States." This was probably the most radical element of Webber's agenda, and a marked departure from previous coinages, both because it lacked an entrepreneurial edge and because it gained official sanction. Nevertheless, some reactions to the new name revealed that the most formidable obstacles to ecosystemic management are not the geopolitical lines on maps but the boundaries inside people's heads. One Canadian academic readily lumped "Salish Sea" together with "Cascadia" as another act of American "cultural imperialism," ignoring both Webber's Canadian nativity and the BC business community's support of the Cascadia campaign. The critic bristled, "It's just another one of the American efforts to erase the border. . . . It's a silly idea. We have beautiful [geographical] names." One is tempted to add, "and really ugly sediment chemistry," but as historian Carl Abbott observes, the international border has indeed grown less porous over the course of the twentieth century.[14]

The "Salish Sea" is thus less a resurrection of ancient geography than a thoroughly modern construct, yet the sea's environmental past is the single most important reason for embracing the new label, provided, of course, that the messiness of the past informs residents' understanding of the present ecosystem. This is not a given. Environmentalists who care about this waterscape, for example, like to wax poetic about the beauty of the sea and its magnificent breaching whales and salmon runs. These are charismatic environmental emblems, mythic both in their place in regional culture and in their historical emptiness. They capture the imagination, but they are rather timeless in a bad way. Only by moving past the superficiality of this imagery can residents grasp the ecosystemic implications. They must drill down to the blubber and fat, linger on the ickiness of their chemical compositions, to see how biology and chemistry link sea to land and fish to mammals and birds in historically contingent ways. Only then will residents develop the sort of holistic vision of humans *and* nature necessary to comprehend the true extent of the Salish Sea's persistent organic pollutant ecoystem. Historically grounded perspectives of the Salish Sea are imperative. Some local environmentalists promote locavorism—the ideal of eating locally to minimize the carbon footprint of consumption—but they seem unaware that the urban poor have long consumed local nature, and that this has not been good for them. Persistent organic pollutants no longer affect just the poor, however. Toxic fish are actually a remarkably democratic problem. Research has detected growing amounts of heavy metals in salmon that spawn in remote Alaska lakes. Thus, even well-educated consumers who avoid toxins by frequenting upscale stores and restaurants unwittingly eat tainted fish. DNA testing has also revealed that many vendors mislabel fish products, and the environmental labelling programs of the Marine Stewardship Council, Blue Ocean Institute, and Monterey Bay Aquarium are less than fully reliable.[15]

Such shortcomings may be a good thing. If fewer Salish Sea residents regard upscale consumption as an ecological refuge, perhaps more of them will work to make the sea an ecology that they, or at least their children and grandchildren, can consume without fear. Right now the sea is studded with signs along urban shores warning residents *not* to consume locally (see Figure 3). The signs offer several key lessons. First, usually written in multiple languages to inform the sea's many immigrants, the signs underscore the socioeconomy of locavorism. It is ultimately the poor and marginalized who most regularly consume the sea. Second, the signs remind us of the devastating effects of locavorism. Dangers range from immediate poisoning to delayed cancers to inherited birth defects. The poor and marginalized run a higher risk of suffering these fates, but society as a whole pays in the form of higher costs for medical, educational, and social services. Third, the signs reveal an uneven geography of concern. Even though the Georgia Strait's history of persistent organic pollutants mirrors that of the Puget Sound, and even though poor immigrant and First Nations fishers rely heavily on those polluted waters, the British Columbia government has been slower to erect warning signs. Finally, the signs reveal the limits of conceptualizing environmental and social problems. The public and media lean on predictable metaphors. They liken environmental monsters

7.3 Warning sign, 2015. The chemical legacy of 150 years of industrialization emerges in signs alerting residents not to eat fish from the Salish Sea. The above warning, posted at a popular park on the lower Duwamish River, is given in nine languages: English, Spanish, Korean, Chinese, Vietnamese, Russian, Laotian, Cambodian, and Somali. There is a marked difference between the United States and Canada in the frequency of these warnings. Photo by Matthew W. Klingle.

7 / Lines That Don't Divide

to Frankenstein, and victims to H.G. Wells's Morlocks, but the biological and ecological processes that cycle persistent organic pollutants through the Salish Sea and back to us are more subtle and complex than the monster and mutant tales can convey.[16]

The Salish Sea's toxic ecosystem reveals how easily and thoroughly nature transgresses governmental and cultural borders. Geopolitically, an increasing number of governments claim the sea as if it can be parsed into American, Canadian, and tribal space, while corporations and environmental groups regularly cross international boundaries to shape environmental policies. Norman and Cohen argue in chapter 2 that this fragmentation opens possibilities for a broader array of voices to shape environmental management, but those voices are not all equal. Moreover, adding more will not necessarily make management more responsive. The sea is a transnational space. Its sovereignty, though, is still exercised through territoriality—and governments, all governments, jealously guard their powers. The Salish Sea is thus, as always, a seamless ecology deeply fractured by an ever growing array of social and political geographies that might actually make regulatory coordination more difficult. The nature of this place also poses challenges to its intellectual boundaries. Environmental scientists, even when they seek "an integrated analysis of the marine social-ecological system," still speak of "natural and human drivers" as though these can be teased apart. The persistent organic pollutant ecology of salmon, seals, and people plays havoc with such distinctions. The United States and Canada, Nature and Culture; the Salish Sea merges our comfortable antonyms in a world of hybrids that cannot and ought not be segregated. Heavy metals and chemicals course through orca and human bodies via the same natural processes. To separate the natural from the cultural in apex predators, or any other species, does violence to the tangle of social and ecological systems that link species and countries. This is a messy world, one requiring messy explanations. Its human residents, and indeed all humans, will do better by nature and themselves to acknowledge the limits of the lines they draw. Intellectual and political borders get in the way of understanding. As Chucho says in *Lone Star*, no other animal thinks differently when it crosses our lines. Neither do persistent organic pollutants. Why should we?[17]

Notes

1. I would like to thank Mark Fiege, Lynne Heasley, Matt Klingle, Nancy Langston, Dan Macfarlane, and Louis Pubols for their advice and encouragement with this chapter.

    Lone Star, directed by John Sayles (West Hollywood: Castle Rock Entertainment, Rio Dulce Productions, 1996); Mark Fiege, "The Weedy West: Mobile Nature, Boundaries, and Common Space in the Montana Landscape," *Western Historical Quarterly* 36, no. 1 (2005): 22–47; World Health Organization, *Bugs, Drugs and Smoke: Stories from Public Health* (Geneva: WHO, 2011), 119–38; Charles E. Rosenberg, *The Cholera Years: The United States in 1832, 1849, and 1866* (Chicago: University of Chicago Press, 1987); Daniel J. Madigan, Zofia Baumann, and Nicholas S. Fisher, "Pacific Bluefin Tuna Transport Fukushima-Derived Radionuclides from Japan to California," *PNAS* 109, no. 24 (2012): 9483–86.

2. Alfred W. Crosby Jr., *Ecological Imperialism: The Biological Expansion of Europe, 900–1900* (New York: Cambridge University Press, 1986); Harriet Ritvo, "Going Forth and Multiplying: Animal Acclimatization and Invasion," *Environmental History* 17, no. 2 (2012): 404–14; Derek H. Alderman and Donna G'Segner Alderman, "Kudzu: A Tale of Two Vines," *Southern Cultures* 7, no. 3 (2001): 49–64; Brian Comon, *Tooth and Nail: The Story of the Rabbit in Australia*, rev. ed. (Melbourne: Text Publishing, 2010); Richard Tucker, *Insatiable Appetite: The United States and the Ecological Degradation of the Tropical World* (Berkeley: University of California Press, 2000); William Yardley, "Canada Holds Hearings on Suspected Virus in Salmon," *New York Times*, December 16, 2011; Pamela Fayerman, "BC Health Officials Aren't Following Washington State's Lead on Whooping Cough," *Vancouver Sun*, May 15, 2012; Lori Tobias, "Tsunami-Loosened Dock on Oregon Coast Raises Concerns about Future Debris, Foreign Organisms, What to Do with It," *Portland Oregonian*, June 7, 2012; T.F. Sutherland and C.D. Levings, "Quantifying Non-Indigenous Species in Accumulated Ballast Slurry Residuals (Swish) Arriving at Vancouver, British Columbia," *Progress in Oceanography* 115 (August 2013): 211–18.

3. Jules M. Blais et al., "Biologically Mediated Transport of Contaminants to Aquatic Systems," *Environmental Science & Technology* 41, no. 4 (2007): 1075–84; *Contagion*, directed by Steven Soderbergh (Burbank: Warner Brothers, 2011); Michael Crichton, *Andromeda Strain* (New York: Knopf, 1969); *Minamata*, directed by Noriaki Tsuchimoto (Japan: Higashi Productions, 1971); Max Brooks, *World War Z: An Oral History of the Zombie War* (New York: Crown, 2006).

4. Warwick Anderson, "Natural Histories of Infectious Disease: Ecological Vision in Twentieth-Century Biomedical

Science," *Osiris* 19 (2004): 39–61; Nancy Langston, *Toxic Bodies: Hormone Disruptors and the Legacy of DES* (New Haven: Yale University Press, 2010); Linda Nash, *Inescapable Ecologies: A History of Environment, Disease, and Knowledge* (Berkeley: University of California Press, 2007); Conevery Valençius, *The Health of the Countryside: How American Settlers Understood Themselves and Their Lands* (New York: Basic Books, 2002); Rachel Carson, *Silent Spring* (Boston: Houghton Mifflin, 1962); Lois Marie Gibbs, *Love Canal* (Albany: State University of New York Press, 1982); Sandra Steingraber, *Living Downstream: An Ecologist's Personal Investigation of Cancer and the Environment* (Boston: Addison-Wesley, 1997); Robert D. Bullard, *Dumping in Dixie: Race, Class, and Environmental Quality* (Boulder: Westview, 1990); Barbara L. Allen, *Uneasy Alchemy: Citizens and Experts in Louisiana's Chemical Corridor Dispute, 1945–1980* (Cambridge, MA: MIT Press, 2003); David Quammen, *Spillover: Animal Infections and the Next Human Pandemic* (New York: W.W. Norton, 2012).

5   Richard Mackie, *Trading beyond the Mountains: The British Fur Trade on the Pacific, 1793–1843* (Vancouver: UBC Press, 1997); R. Cole Harris and Eric Leinberger, *Making Native Space: Colonialism, Resistance, and Reserves in British Columbia* (Vancouver: UBC Press, 2002); Alexandra Harmon, "Lines in Sand: Shifting Boundaries between Indians and Non-Indians in the Puget Sound Region," *Western Historical Quarterly* 26, no. 4 (1995): 428–53; John Lutz, "Work, Sex, and Death on the Great Thoroughfare: Annual Migrations of 'Canadian Indians,'" in *Parallel Destinies: Canadians, Americans, and the Western Border*, ed. John Findlay and Ken Coates (Seattle: University of Washington Press, 2002), 80–103; Paige Raibmon, *Authentic Indians: Episodes of Encounter from the Late-Nineteenth Century Northwest Coast* (Durham: Duke University Press, 2005), 74–134; Jennifer Seltz, "Epidemics, Indians, and Border-Making in the Nineteenth-Century Pacific Northwest," in *Bridging National Borders in North America: Transnational and Comparative Histories*, ed. Benjamin Johnson and Andrew Graybill (Durham: Duke University Press, 2010), 91–115; Lissa Wadewitz, *The Nature of Borders: Salmon, Boundaries, and Bandits on the Salish Sea* (Seattle: University of Washington Press, 2012); Keith Carlson, ed., *A Stó:lo-Coast Salish Historical Atlas* (Vancouver: Douglas & McIntyre, 2001); Coll Thrush, *Native Seattle: Histories from the Crossing-Over Place* (Seattle: University of Washington Press, 2007); Alexandra Harmon, ed., *The Power of Promises: Rethinking Indian Treaties in the Pacific Northwest* (Seattle: University of Washington Press, 2008).

6   On precontact fishing, see Patricia Berringer, "Northwest Coast Traditional Salmon Fisheries: Systems of Resource Utilization" (MA thesis, University of British Columbia, 1982); and Joseph

E. Taylor III, *Making Salmon: An Environmental History of the Northwest Fisheries Crisis* (Seattle: University of Washington Press, 1999), 13-38. On nineteenth-century environmental change, see Robert Bunting, *The Pacific Raincoast: Environment and Culture in an American Eden, 1778-1900* (Lawrence: University Press of Kansas, 1997); Thomas R. Cox, *The Lumberman's Frontier: Three Centuries of Land Use, Society, and Change in America's Forests* (Corvallis: Oregon State University Press, 2010), 266-330; Michael Kennedy, "Fraser River Placer Mining Landscapes," *BC Studies*, no. 160 (Winter 2008/2009): 35-66; Richard A. Rajala, *Clearcutting the Pacific Rain Forest: Production, Science, and Regulation* (Vancouver: UBC Press, 1998); and "A Tannery Has Been Established," *La Conner Puget Sound Mail*, December 16, 1882, 3. On twentieth-century urbanization and industrialization, see Margaret W. Andrews, "Sanitary Conveniences and the Retreat of the Frontier: Vancouver, 1886-1926," *BC Studies*, no. 87 (Autumn 1990): 3-22; Norman H. Clark, *Mill Town* (Seattle: University of Washington Press, 1970); Matthew W. Klingle, "Frontier Ghosts along the Urban Pacific Slope," in *Frontier Cities: Encounters at the Crossroads of Empire*, ed. Jay Gitlin, Barbara Berglund, and Adam Arenson (Philadelphia: University of Pennsylvania Press, 2013), 121-45; Matthew D. Evenden, *Fish versus Power: An Environmental History of the Fraser River* (New York: Cambridge University Press, 2004); Charles M. Gates, "A Historical Sketch of the Economic Development of Washington since Statehood," *Pacific Northwest Quarterly* 39, no. 3 (1948): 214-32; Howard A. Hanson, "More Land for Industry: The Story of Flood Control in the Green River Valley," *Pacific Northwest Quarterly* 48, no. 1 (1957): 1-7; Arn Keeling, "Sink or Swim: Water Pollution and Environmental Politics in Vancouver, 1889-1975," *BC Studies*, no. 142-143 (Summer/Autumn 2004): 69-101; Matthew Klingle, *Emerald City: An Environmental History of Seattle* (New Haven: Yale University Press, 2007), 1-118; W.K. Lamb, "Building Submarines for Russia in Burrard Inlet," *BC Studies*, no. 71 (Autumn 1986): 3-26; Norbert MacDonald, "A Critical Growth Cycle for Vancouver, 1900-1914," *BC Studies*, no. 17 (Spring 1973): 26-42; and William J. Williams, "Accommodating American Shipyard Workers, 1917-1918: The Pacific Coast and the Federal Government's First Public Housing and Transit Programs," *Pacific Northwest Quarterly* 84, no. 2 (1993): 51-59. On hardening borders, see Bruce Miller, "The 'Really Real' Border and the Divided Salish Community," *BC Studies*, no. 112 (Winter 1996/1997): 63-79; and Carl Abbott, "That Long Western Border: Canada, the United States, and a Century of Economic Change," in *Parallel Destinies: Canadians, Americans, and the Western Border*, ed. John Findlay and Ken Coates (Seattle: University of Washington Press, 2002), 203-18.

7   A quick elaboration of terms: PCBs = polychlorinated biphenyls; PCDD = polychlorinated dibenzodioxins; PCDF = polychlorinated dibenzofurans; PVCs = polyvinyl chlorides; DDT = dichlorodiphenyltrichloroethane; 2,4-D = 2,4-Dichlorophenoxyacetic acid; PBDEs = polybrominated diphenyl ethers. For general overviews, see Gerald Markowitz and David Rosner, *Deceit and Denial: The Deadly Politics of Industrial Pollution* (Berkeley: University of California Press, 2002), 139–94; Joe Thornton, *Pandora's Poison: Chlorine, Health, and a New Environmental Strategy* (Cambridge, MA: MIT Press, 2000)1–199; Shinsuke Tanabe, "PBDEs, An Emerging Group of Persistent Pollutants," *Marine Pollution Bulletin* 49, no. 5–6 (2004): 369–70; Yasunobu Aoki, "Polychlorinated Biphenyls, Polychlorinated Dibenzo-*p*-dioxins, and Polychlorinated Dibenzofurans as Endocrine Disrupters—What We Have Learned from Yusho Disease," *Environmental Research* 86, no. 1 (2001): 2–11; Ronald A. Hites, "Dioxins: An Overview and History," *Environmental Science & Technology* 45, no. 1 (2011): 16–20; and P. Agamuthu, "Mercury—The Real Story," *Waste Management and Research* 31, no. 3 (2013): 233–34. For studies on the Salish Sea, see Federal Water Pollution Control Administration, *Pollution Effects of Pulp and Paper Mill Wastes in Puget Sound: A Report on Studies Conducted by the Washington State Enforcement Project* (Portland: U.S. Dept. of Interior, 1967); D.E. Konasewich et al., *Effects, Pathways, Processes, and Transformation of Puget Sound Contaminants of Concern*, NOAA Technical Memorandum OMPA-20 (Boulder: U.S. Dept. of Commerce, 1982); S.L. Walker et al., "Canadian Environmental Effects Monitoring: Experiences with Pulp and Paper and Metal Mining Regulatory Programs," *Environmental Monitoring and Assessment* 88 (2003): 311–26; Peter S. Ross et al., "Large and Growing Environmental Reservoirs of Deca-BDE Present an Emerging Health Risk for Fish and Marine Mammals," *Marine Pollution Bulletin* 58, no. 1 (2011): 7–10; and John E. Elliott, Laurie K. Wilson, and Bryan Wakeford, "Polybrominated Diphenyl Ether Trends in Eggs of Marine and Freshwater Birds from British Columbia, Canada, 1979–2002," *Environmental Science & Technology* 39, no. 15 (2005): 5584–91. On halting efforts to address pollution, see Leon Kolankiewicz, "Compliance with Pollution Control Permits in the Lower Fraser Valley, 1967–1981," *BC Studies*, no. 72 (Winter 1986/1987): 28–48; and Klingle, *Emerald City*, 154–264.

8   On taste, see Robert McClure, "The Sound Is Flavored by the Holidays," *Seattle Post-Intelligencer*, December 25, 2006; Zoe Rodriguez del Rey, Elise F. Granek, and Steve Sylvester, "Occurrence and Concentration of Caffeine in Oregon Coastal Waters," *Marine Pollution Bulletin* 64, no. 7 (2012): 1417–24; James P. Meador et al., "Contiminants of Emerging Concern in a Large Temperate Estuary,"

Environmental Pollution 213 (2016): 254–267. On salmon farms, see A.D. McIntyre, "Environmental Interactions of Aquaculture," *Fisheries Research* 62, no. 3 (2003): 235; A.M.H. Debruyn et al., "Ecosystemic Effects of Salmon Farming Increase Mercury Contamination in Wild Fish," *Environmental Science & Technology* 40, no. 11 (2006): 3489–93. On sex ratios and reproduction, see Tracy K. Collier et al., "A Comprehensive Assessment of the Impacts of Contaminants on Fish from an Urban Waterway," *Marine Environmental Research* 46 (July 1998), 243–47; Lyndal L. Johnson et al., "Contaminant Effects on Ovarian Development in English Sole (*Parophrys vetulus*) from Puget Sound, Washington," *Canadian Journal of Fisheries and Aquatic Science* 45, no. 12 (1988): 2133–46; Holly Pyhtila, "Pink Water: Plastics, Pesticides, and Pills Are Contaminating Our Drinking Supply," *Earth Island Journal*, Autumn 2008, http://www.earthisland.org/journal/index.php/eij/article/pink_water; Anders Goksøyr, "Endocrine Disruptors in the Marine Environment: Mechanisms of Toxicity and Their Influence on Reproductive Processes in Fish," *Journal of Toxicology and Environmental Health, Part A* 69, no. 1–2 (2006): 175–84; Peter Thomas and Md. S. Raham, "Extensive Reproduction Disruption, Ovarian Masculinization and Aromatase Suppression in Atlantic Croaker in the Northern Gulf of Mexico Hypoxic Zone," *Proceedings of the Royal Society B* 279, no. 1726 (2012): 28–38; and Karen A. Kidd et al., "Collapse of a Fish Population after Exposure to a Synthetic Hormone," *PNAS* 104, no. 21 (2007): 8897–901.

9   Heloise Frouin et al., "Partitioning and Bioaccumulation of PCBs and PBDEs in Marine Plankton from the Strait of Georgia, British Columbia, Canada," *Progress in Oceanography* 115, no. 1 (2013): 65–75; James E. West, Sandra M. O'Neill, and Gina M. Ylitalo, "Spatial Extent, Magnitude, and Patterns of Persistent Organochlorine Pollutants in Pacific Herring (*Clupea pallasi*) Populations in the Puget Sound (USA) and Strait of Georgia (Canada)," *Science of the Total Environment* 394, no. 2–3 (2008): 369–78; S.C. Johannessen et al., "Joined by Geochemistry, Divided by History: PCBs and PBDEs in Strait of Georgia Sediments," *Marine Environmental Research* 66 (Supplement 2008): S112–S120; Paul B.C. Grant et al., "Environmental Fractionation of PCBs and PBDEs during Particle Transport as Recorded by Sediments in Coastal Waters," *Environmental Toxicology and Chemistry* 30, no. 7 (2011): 1522–32; S.C. Johannssesen et al., "Water Column Organic Carbon in a Pacific Marginal Sea (Strait of Georgia, Canada)," *Marine Environmental Research* 66 (Supplement 2008): S49–S61.

10 For "exceeded" see Margaret M. Krahn et al., "Effects of Age, Sex, and Reproductive Status on Persistent Organic Pollutant Concentrations in 'Southern Resident' Killer Whales," *Marine Pollution Bulletin* 58, no. 10 (2009): 1527; see also Brett

Walker, *Toxic Archipelago: A History of Industrial Disease in Japan* (Seattle: University of Washington Press, 2010), xvii–xviii. On salmon, see Brian R. Missildine et al., "Polychlorinated Biphenyl Concentrations in Adult Chinook Salmon (*Oncorhynchus tshawytscha*) Returning to Coastal and Puget Sound Hatcheries of Washington State," *Environmental Science & Technology* 39, no. 18 (2005): 6944–51; D. Stone, "Polybrominated Diphenyl Ethers and Polychlorinated Biphenyls in Different Tissue Types from Chinook Salmon (*Oncorhynchus tshawytscha*)," *Bulletin of Environmental Contamination and Toxicology* 76, no. 1 (2006): 148–54; Barry C. Kelly et al., "Tissue Residue Concentrations of Organohalogens and Trace Elements in Adult Pacific Salmon Returning to the Fraser River, British Columbia, Canada," *Environmental Toxicology and Chemistry* 30, no. 2 (2011): 367–76. On marine mammals, see Juan José Alava et al., "PBDE Flame Retardants and PCBs in Migrating Stellar Sea Lions (*Eumetopias jubatus*) in the Strait of Georgia, British Columbia, Canada," *Chemosphere* 88, no. 7 (2012): 855–64; and Donna L. Cullon, Steven J. Jeffries, and Peter S. Ross, "Persistent Organic Pollutants in the Diet of Harbor Seals (*Phoca vitulina*) Inhabiting Puget Sound, Washington (USA), and the Strait of Georgia, British Columbia (Canada): A Food Basket Approach," *Environmental Toxicology and Chemistry* 24, no. 10 (2005): 2562–72. A recent study suggests that levels have begun to fall: Peter S. Ross et al., "Declining Concentrations of PCBs, PBDEs, PCDEs, and PCNs in Harbor Seals (*Phoca vitulina*) from the Salish Sea," *Progress in Oceanography* 115, no. 1 (2013): 160–70. For toxification beyond the water, see Rachel D. Field and John D. Reynolds, "Sea to Sky: Impacts of Residual Salmon-Derived Nutrients on Estuarine Breeding Bird Communities," *Proceedings of the Royal Society B* 278, no. 1721 (2011): 3081–88; Jennie R. Christensen et al., "Persistent Organic Pollutants in British Columbia Grizzly Bears: Consequence of Divergent Diets," *Environmental Science & Technology* 39, no. 18 (2005): 6952–60; Christy A. Morrissey et al., "American Dippers Indicate Contaminant Biotransport by Pacific Salmon," *Environmental Science & Technology* 46, no. 2 (2012): 1153–62; L.K. Wilson et al., "Properties of Blood, Porphyrins, and Exposure to Legacy and Emerging Persistent Organic Pollutants in Surf Scoters (*Melanitta perspicillata*) Overwintering on the South Coast of British Columbia, Canada," *Archives of Environmental Contamination and Toxicology* 59, no. 2 (2010): 322–33.

11   For studies of salmon and toxic chemicals, see Ronald A. Hites et al., "Global Assessment of Organic Contaminants in Farmed Salmon," *Science* 303 (9 January 2004), 226–29; Ronald A. Hites et al., "Global Assessment of Polybrominated Diphenyl Ethers in Farmed and Wild Salmon," *Environmental Science & Technology* 38, no. 19 (2004): 4945–49; and Daniel L. Carlson and Ronald A.

Hites, "Polychlorinated Biphenyls in Salmon and Salmon Feed: Global Differences and Bioaccumulation," *Environmental Science & Technology* 39, no. 19 (2005): 7389–95. On trophic levels, see A. Ardura et al., "Forensic DNA Analysis Reveals Use of High Trophic Level Marine Fish in Commercial Aquaculture Fish Meals," *Fisheries Research* 115–116 (2012): 115–20.

12   On fish consumption, see Anna Schmidt, "An Evaluation of Fish Consumption and Environmental Concern in Low Income and Food Insecure Populations in Seattle" (MS thesis, University of Washington, 2011); Maureen O'Hagan, "Washington State Casts Line for Residents' Fish-Consumption Rate," *Seattle Times*, July 9, 2012; and Joseph E. Taylor III, "The Food of Kings: The Social and Cultural Geography of Salmon Consumption" (paper presented at the Gulf of Georgia Cannery National Historical Site, Steveston, BC, April 23, 2006). On consumption of farmed salmon, see Tracy Hampton, "Farmed, Wild Salmon Pollutants Probed," *JAMA* 291, no. 8 (2004): 929–30; and Jeffery A. Foran et al., "Quantitative Analysis of the Benefits and Risks of Consuming Farmed and Wild Salmon," *Journal of Nutrition* 135, no. 11 (2005): 2639–43. On toxic fish, breast feeding, and cognitive development, see R.Y. Wang and L.L. Needham, "Environmental Chemicals: From the Environment to Food, to Breast Milk, to the Infant," *Journal of Toxicology and Environmental Health, Part B* 10, no. 8 (2007): 597–609; Josef G. Thundiyil, Gina M. Solomon, and Mark D. Miller, "Transgenerational Exposures: Persistent Chemical Pollutants in the Environment and Breast Milk," *Pediatric Clinics of North America* 54, no. 1 (2007): 81–101; and Edward Groth III, "Re: Maternal Fish Intake during Pregnancy, Blood Mercury Levels, and Child Cognition at Age 3 Years in a U.S. Cohort," *American Journal of Epidemiology* 168, no. 2 (2008): 168. For similarly toxified environments elsewhere, see Laura Anne Bienenfeld, Anne L. Golden, and Elizabeth J. Garland, "Consumption of Fish from Polluted Waters by WIC Participants in East Harlem," *Journal of Urban Health* 80, no. 2 (2003): 349–58; Pamela Valera et al., "'Trying to Eat Healthy': A Photovoice Study of Women's Access to Healthy Food in New York City," *Affilia* 24, no. 3 (2009): 304–6; Bernhard Link et al., "Biomonitoring of Persistent Organochlorine Pesticides, PCDD/PCDFs and Dioxin-Like PCBs in Blood of Children from South West Germany (Baden-Wuerttemberg) from 1993 to 2003," *Chemosphere* 58, no. 9 (2005): 1193; Gaofeng Zhao et al., "Biotransfer of Persistent Organic Pollutants from a Large Site in China Used for the Disassembly of Electronic and Electrical Waste," *Environmental Geochemistry and Health* 28, no. 4 (2006): 341–51; and J. Van Oostdam et al., "Human Health Implications of Environmental Contaminants in Arctic Canada: A Review," *Science of the Total Environment* 351–352 (2005): 165–246.

13 Quoted in Matthew Sparke, "Excavating the Future in Cascadia: Geoeconomics and the Imagined Geographies of a Cross-Border Region," *BC Studies*, no. 127 (Autumn 2000): 17. See also John Findlay, "A Fishy Proposition: Regional Identity in the Pacific Northwest," in *Many Wests: Place, Culture, and Regional Identity*, ed. David M. Wrobel and Michael R. Steiner (Lawrence: University Press of Kansas, 1997), 37–70; Abbott, "Long Western Border"; Ernest Callenbach, *Ecotopia: The Notebooks and Reports of William Weston* (Berkeley: Banyan Tree, 1975); Joel Garreau, *The Nine Nations of North America* (Boston: Houghton Mifflin, 1981); Colin Woodard, *American Nations: A History of the Eleven Rival Regional Cultures of North America* (New York: Viking, 2011); and Signe Marie Cold-Ravnkilde, Jaidev Singh, and Robert G. Lee, "Cascadia: The (Re)Construction of a Bi-National Space and Its Residents," *Journal of Borderlands Studies* 19, no. 1 (2004): 59–77. On toxic narratives elsewhere, see Scott C. Doney, "The Growing Human Footprint on Coastal and Open-Ocean Biogeochemisty," *Science* 328, no. 5985 (2010): 1512–16; David S. Page et al., "Polycyclic Aromatic Hydrocarbon Sources Related to Biomarker Levels in Fish from Prince William Sound and the Gulf of Alaska," *Environmental Science & Technology* 38, no. 19 (2004): 4928–36; T.G. Knowles, D. Farrington, and S.C. Kestin, "Mercury in UK Imported Fish and Shellfish and UK-Farmed Fish and Their Products," *Food Additives and Contaminants* 20, no. 9 (2003): 813–18; Goksøyr, "Endocrine Disruptors"; Diana Mitsova et al., "Variability in Road Runoff Pollution by Polycyclic Aromatic Hydrocarbons (PAHs) in the Urbanized Area Adjacent to Biscayne Bay, Florida," *Journal of Environmental Protection* 2, no. 10 (2011): 1317–30; Shinsuke Tanabe et al., "PCDDs, PCDFs, and Coplanar PCBs in Albatross from the North Pacific and Southern Pacific Oceans: Levels, Patterns, and Toxicological Implications," *Environmental Science & Technology* 38, no. 2 (2004): 403–13; E.M. Krummel et al., "Delivery of Pollutants by Spawning Salmon," *Nature* 425, no. 6955 (2003): 255–56; Jules M. Blais et al., "Arctic Seabirds Transport Marine-Derived Contaminants," *Science* 309, no. 5733 (2005): 445; W.L. Lockhart et al., "A History of Total Mercury in Edible Muscle of Fish from Lakes in Northern Canada," *Science of the Total Environment* 352–352 (2005): 427–63; J. Ruelas-Inzunza, J. Hernández-Osuna, and F. Páez-Osuna, "Total and Organic Mercury in Ten Fish Species for Human Consumption from the Mexican Pacific," *Bulletin of Environmental Contamination and Toxicology* 86, no. 6 (2011): 679–83; Dorothea F.K. Rawn et al., "PCB, PCDD and PCDF Residues in Fin and Non-Fin Fish Products from the Canadian Retail Market 2002," *Science of the Total Environment* 359, no. 1-3 (2006): 101–10.

14 For "restore," "imperialism," "erase," and "silly," see Warren

Cornwall, "'Salish Sea' Proposed Name for Waters Washington, BC Share," *Seattle Times*, March 14, 2009; Carlito Pablo, "Washington State Adopts 'Salish Sea' Name for Body of Water Including Strait of Georgia," *Strait.com*, October 30, 2009, http://www.straight.com/article-268225/washington-state-adopts-salish-sea-name-body-water-including-strait-georgia; and Michael Fellman, "Sleeping with the Elephant: Reflections on an American-Canadian on Americanization and Anti-Americanism in Canada," in *Parallel Destinies: Canadians, Americans, and the Western Border*, ed. John Findlay and Ken Coates (Seattle: University of Washington Press, 2002), 274–94. Historian Carl Abbott argued that, if anything, "the national border actually divided the Northwest more thoroughly at the end of the twentieth century than it did at the beginning." Abbott, "Long Western Border," 203.

15 On localvorism, see Gary Paul Nabhan, *Coming Home to Eat: The Pleasures and Politics of Local Food* (New York: W.W. Norton, 2001). On Alaska, see Matthew R. Baker et al., "Bioaccumulation and Transport of Contaminants: Migrating Sockeye Salmon as Vectors of Mercury," *Environmental Science & Technology* 43, no. 23 (2009): 8840–46. On mislabelled fish, see Erica Cline, "Marketplace Substitution of Atlantic Salmon for Pacific Salmon in Washington State Detected by DNA Barcoding," *Food Research International* 45, no. 1 (2012): 388–93; Sheryl A. Tittlemier et al., "Polybrominated Diphenyl Ethers in Retail Fish and Shellfish Samples Purchased from Canadian Markets," *Journal of Agricultural and Food Chemistry* 52, no. 25 (2004): 7740–45; and F. Sun et al., "A Preliminary Assessment of Consumer's Exposure to Pesticide Residues in Fisheries Products," *Chemosphere* 62, no. 4 (2006): 674–80. On labelling, see Peter B. Marko, Holly A. Nance, and Kimberly D. Guynn, "Genetic Detection of Mislabeled Fish from a Certified Sustainable Fishery," *Current Biology* 21, no. 16 (2011): R621–22; Erik Stokstad, "Seafood Eco-Label Grapples with Challenge of Proving Its Impact," *Science* 334, no. 6057 (2011): 746; and Peter B. Marko et al., "Mislabeling of a Depleted Reef Fish," *Nature* 430, no. 6997 (2004): 309–10.

16 On local consumers and effects, see Douglas C. Harris, *Landing Native Fisheries: Indian Reserves and Fishing Rights in British Columbia, 1849–1925* (Vancouver: UBC Press, 2008), 2–4, 106–26; Klingle, *Emerald City*, 249–80; and Thrush, *Native Seattle*, 193–207.

17 For "integrated analysis" and "natural and human drivers," see R. Ian Perry and Diane Masson, "An Integrated Analysis of the Marine Social-Ecological System of the Strait of Georgia, Canada, Over the Past Four Decades, and Development of a Regime Shift Index," *Progress in Oceanography* 115 (2013): 26. On the 49th parallel, see Wadewitz, *The Nature of Borders*. On sovereignty, see Allan K. McDougall and Lisa Philips Valentine, "Sovereign

Survival: Borders as Issues," *Journal of Borderlands Studies* 19, no. 1 (2004): 23–35; Patrick J. Smith, "Transborder Cascadia: Opportunities and Obstacles," *Journal of Borderlands Studies* 19, no. 1 (2004): 99–21; Donald K. Alper, "Emerging Collaborative Frameworks for Environmental Governance in the Georgia Basin-Puget Sound Ecosystem," *Journal of Borderlands Studies* 19, no. 1 (2004): 79–98; Emma S. Norman, "Cultural Politics and Transboundary Resource Governance in the Salish Sea," *Water Alternatives* 5, no. 1 (2012): 138–60; and Joseph E. Taylor III, "Boundary Terminology," *Environmental History* 13, no 3 (2008): 454–81. For recent discussions of hybridity, see Linda Nash, "Furthering the Environmental Turn," *Journal of American History* 100, no. 1 (2013): 131–35.

Resiliency and Collapse: Lake Trout, Sea Lamprey, and Fisheries Management in Lake Superior

NANCY LANGSTON

> Just as quick as they began to clear the country up the fish began to disappear.
>
> —John Barret Van Vlack, Georgian Bay fisher, 1894[1]

Lake trout (*Salvelinus namaycush*)—voracious predators at the top of Great Lakes food chains—sustained a tribal and commercial fishery in Lake Superior for centuries. Even after other fish populations crashed under commercial fishing pressure, pollution, and habitat loss, lake trout appeared surprisingly resilient. But in the mid-twentieth century, their populations fell off the edge of a cliff (see Figure 1). In 1944, the commercial catch of lake trout in Wisconsin alone totalled more than six million pounds; a decade later, only a few fish were caught, and by 1956, lake trout had vanished from most of the Great Lakes. Having been top predators, the loss of lake trout had rippling effects. Populations of rough fish such as alewives and smelt exploded when their predators vanished, and zooplankton

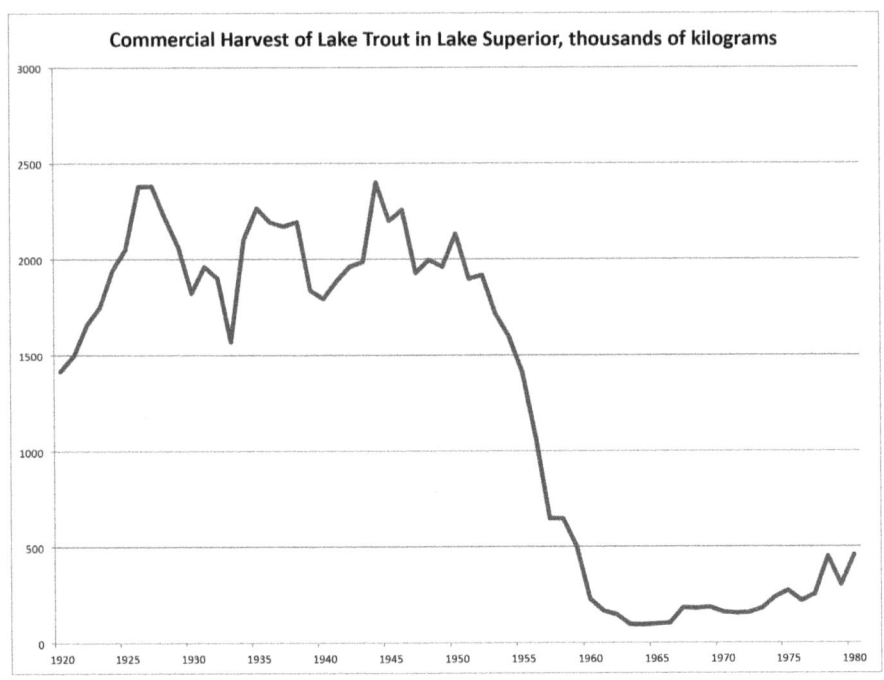

8.1 Lean lake trout harvests, 1920–1980. Data courtesy of R.E. Hecky et al., Global Great Lakes.

populations dropped sharply.[2] When commercial and tribal fisheries shut down, leaving local economies with little to support them, the social effects were devastating.

Why did lake trout crash so suddenly? For decades, fisheries biologists have placed most of the blame on the sea lamprey (*Petromyzon marinus*), which the U.S. Geological Survey calls "a marine invader from the Atlantic Ocean" that "quickly devastated the fish communities of the Great Lakes."[3] The historical narrative offered by fisheries biologists is that sea lamprey invaded the upper Great Lakes after modifications to the Welland Canal allowed marine organisms to make their way upstream past Niagara Falls. Sea lampreys sucked the fluids from lake trout, soon devastating their populations. Eventually, chemists and fisheries biologists managed to restore lake trout with the help of TFM, a synthetic chemical that kills developing lampreys without hurting too many young lake trout.[4]

This story has satisfied many folks, perhaps because it essentially takes the blame off people. Yes, people did modify the Welland Canal in this story and open the Pandora's box of invasive species. But they did not intend to do this, and anyway, scientists saved the day. The problem is that the evidence supporting this story is equivocal at best. Sea lampreys did indeed parasitize a lot of lake trout, but it is not clear that the sea lamprey really were non-native invaders that snuck into the upper Great Lakes and then wiped out their hosts. Nor is it clear that lake trout would have been fine if only the sea lamprey had not shown up. Intensive harvests, toxic chemicals, and loss of habitat had already stressed fish populations in the Great Lakes before the lamprey invaded. Most frustrating for the sea lamprey hypothesis, controlling sea lamprey populations has failed to restore breeding populations of lake trout in most of the Great Lakes. This chapter argues that while sea lamprey were an important factor in the collapse of lake trout populations, focusing on them alone ignores the larger context of ecological change and restoration in the Great Lakes.

Lake Trout

Lake trout, a huge freshwater char, were once present in enormous populations within the Great Lakes. Slow growing, they typically become sexually mature at seven to ten years of age, making their populations vulnerable to overfishing. In the Lake Superior basin, biologists identify two different subspecies of lake trout—the lean lake trout and the siscowet lake trout—and two additional varieties (humpers and hybrids). Both varieties are fond of eating other fish, particularly whitefish. This puts them near the top of the food chain in Lake Superior, making them vulnerable to chemical bioaccumulation. Toxic chemicals found at very low levels in water become concentrated by orders of magnitude as they make their way up food chains.

Historically, siscowet lake trout made up most of the lake trout biomass in Lake Superior. Siscowet prefer very cold, very deep water; they live their entire lives in waters colder than 4°C, and as adults, they spend much of their lives at depths greater than 150 metres. Their fat content is extremely high—from 30 percent to 90 percent by weight—which means they are well adapted for the coldest depths of Lake Superior.[5] Lean lake trout have much lower fat content than the siscowet and tend to be smaller, live shorter lives, and spawn in shallower waters.

Early records note that, like whitefish and coaster brook trout, lean lake trout and siscowet could spawn in rivers (siscowet also spawned on offshore reefs). Unlike coaster brook trout, whose populations declined after logging and dam-building reduced their access to good stream spawning habitat, lake trout populations were resilient enough to adapt to the loss of tributary spawning habitat.[6] Lean lake trout spawned in shallow, nearshore habitat less than thirty metres deep, preferring spawning reefs that were washed clean of sediments by flowing lake currents. Both lean and siscowet subspecies returned to spawn at the place where they were born.

Lake Superior Overview

Lake Superior lies at the head of the Great Lakes Basin, which contains about 21 percent of all the fresh surface water on the planet (Figure 2). Water from the Great Lakes provided power, transportation, and a convenient sewer for late-nineteenth-century industrialization.[7] While few of those factories or cities were located in the Lake Superior portion of the basin, the effects of local pollution discharges were intensified by the fact that in Lake Superior, only about 0.5 percent of the lake's water turns over each year. A drop of water that enters Lake Superior takes, on average, 191 years to leave the lake.[8]

Lake Superior is a big, deep lake. Its surface area is the largest of any freshwater lake in the world: 82,103 square kilometres—which, *Wikipedia* helpfully tells us, is approximately the size of South Carolina. At its deepest, the lake is 406 metres deep with an average depth of 147 metres. For comparison, Lake Erie, the shallowest Great Lake, averages only 19 metres deep.[9] Lake Superior is big enough to swallow all the other Great Lakes, with room left over for three additional Lake Eries. Put another way, there is enough water in Lake Superior to cover all of North and South America in a foot of water. The Canadian Shield's thin soils and high resistance of rocks to weathering helps Lake Superior to remain clear, biologically unproductive, and slow to accumulate sediments.[10]

Lake Superior is also very cold, with an average annual temperature of 4°C (39°F). Cold waters shape its ecology in profound ways. Like a few

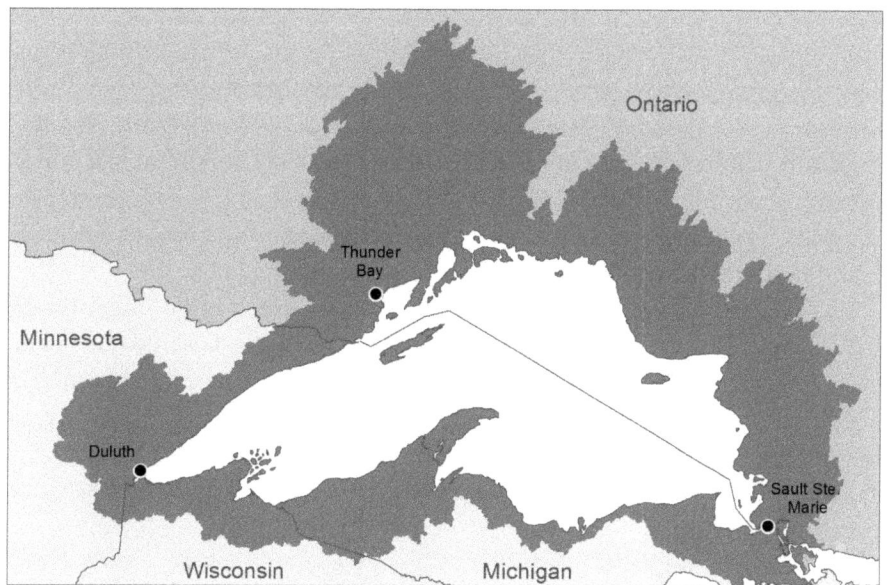

8.2 Lake Superior basin. Map by Jason Glatz.

other cold, deep lakes, Lake Superior is ultra-oligotrophic, meaning that it is quite low in productivity (i.e., aquatic plant and algae production) and high in dissolved oxygen. In the summer, surface temperatures rise while temperatures below 200 metres remain at 4°C, and this variation in temperature stratifies the lake into three distinct layers: the epilimnion (the uppermost, warmest layer); the metalimnion or thermocline (the middle layer, which may change depth during the day); and the hypolimnion (the deepest, coldest layer). Twice each year the water column reaches a uniform temperature from top to bottom and the waters mix.[11]

In most lakes, fish rarely use the hypolimnion, because when organic matter decays, oxygen gets depleted down in the deepest layers of the lakes. However, in large, oligotrophic, stratified lakes such as Lake Superior, low nutrient levels mean that populations of algae (and the animals that feed on them) remain low, so the water remains clear and dissolved oxygen levels remain high all the way down to the bottom. Lake Superior's coldness and lack of productivity means that siscowet lake trout, which need substantial concentrations of oxygen, can thrive in the hypolimnion, so deep that fishermen find it hard to reach them, giving the fish a measure of resiliency even when fishing pressures are quite high. But the particular ecological conditions that make Lake Superior excellent habitat for lake trout—cold, clear, and clean—also make it vulnerable to tipping over thresholds of sudden environmental change, such as a warming climate. If conditions warm, lake levels decrease, or nutrient levels increase, the hypolimnion may become depleted of oxygen, depriving cold-water fish of necessary habitat. Lake trout fisheries are therefore sensitive to anything that increases temperature or inputs of organic matter.[12]

Considering its enormous surface area, the lake's watershed is relatively small, which has historically helped minimize the contaminants that wash off the land into the water. But fewer sources of contaminants from the watershed have not always meant better water quality for fish, for two main reasons. First, the long retention time of Lake Superior means that a drop of water (and an associated contaminant) that enters the lake may remain there, on average, for nearly two centuries.[13] Second, the cold temperatures of the lake and the structure of the lake bed mean that once contaminants enter Lake Superior, they may stick around near the shore for a long time, where fish can easily encounter them. In the spring, the nearshore waters of Lake Superior heat up more quickly than the deeper offshore waters. Because warm water is less dense than cold water, a thermal bar forms at the convergence of the nearshore water and the colder, denser, offshore water. This early-season concentration of nutrients promotes primary production in the nearshore area, accelerating the establishment of warm, eutrophic conditions along the shoreline. The thermal bar also acts as a barrier, concentrating floating debris, warm water discharges, and pollutants within the nearshore area.[14]

Because of Lake Superior's geographic position on the Canadian Shield, lake depths sharply increase quite close to shorelines. This means that shallow, nearshore habitat (which is required by lean lake trout) is rare on the lake. Unlike Lake Erie, for example, where most of the lake is shallow, warm, and productive, only 20 percent of Lake Superior's area consists of nearshore open water habitat (technically defined as areas where the water is less than 80 metres deep). In the nearshore, waves and current scour sediment from the substrate, maintaining good spawning and nursery habitat for many fish species while also providing excellent habitat for many aquatic invertebrates.[15] The relatively small area of nearshore habitat in Lake Superior means that fish that spawn in the nearshore habitat—such as lean lake trout—are particularly vulnerable to toxics held close to shore by the thermal bar in spring.

Why does all this biophysical detail matter? While fishermen often paid close attention to the physical details that helped them catch fish, regulators and planners in the basin often ignored biophysical complexity. In the late nineteenth and early twentieth century, towns such as Port Arthur (now Thunder Bay) were not oblivious to the potential problems of urban development and pulp mill pollution in the lake. They knew that their drinking water usually came from the lake, and they also knew that the commercial fishing industry might collapse if pulp mill waste killed too many spawning fish. Early pollution discussions, however, tended to assume that the lake was one homogenous body of water. If you dumped a few gallons of toxics near the shoreline, surely that would quickly be diluted by the vast quantity of water in the lake.[16]

Yet Lake Superior's enormous size, which made planners hope that dilution might be the solution to pollution, actually worked against them. Lake Superior is large enough and cold enough that when thermal bars form, they hold pollution close to the nearshore; it concentrates there and makes its way into sediments or into the water column and, from there, eventually into the bodies of large predatorial fish—and of those who eat them. Fish also refuse to distribute themselves uniformly throughout the lake. They experience the lake as a complex set of interconnected ecosystems. During certain periods of spawning and fry development, they take refuge in the same places where pollution gets concentrated. Pulp mills and towns tried to manage pollution as simply and cheaply as possible, but their models did not account for the complexity of nearshore habitats, limnological conditions, bumpy shore bottoms, shoals that catch currents carrying sediments, or fish with minds of their own.

Watershed Changes

Changes to Lake Superior watersheds began long before industrialization intensified in the late nineteenth century. After the glaciers retreated, forests developed along the shores of the lake. These forests were neither stable nor uniform; they ebbed and flowed with fires, insect outbreaks, windstorms, and human pressures. Between twenty-five and ten thousand years ago, the Wisconsin glaciation shaped the physical geography of soils that still serve as a key template for today's forests. When the glaciers retreated, cold lingered, and forests were slow to move in. About seven thousand years ago, as the climate warmed, people, pines, and hardwoods migrated into the region. Three thousand years ago, the climate cooled again and precipitation increased, leading to rippling changes in basin forests; hemlock invaded pine stands on rich, loamy soils in the southern portion of the watershed, while pines, aspen, and birch persisted on sandier soils and a boreal forest covered the northern shore.

As people came, they changed the watershed. Changes on the land had significant impacts on aquatic habitat, especially in the nearshore environments where lean lake trout spent most of their lives. While quantifying these land-use effects on fish populations is difficult, if not impossible, it is important to recognize that they were key stressors in fish changes.

Mining was one of the key ways that people—both Indigenous and of European ancestry—made a living along the shores of Lake Superior. Copper ore–refining processes required huge amounts of water for the stamping mills. Water was returned to the lake contaminated with particles of copper-bearing tailings that filled bays, harbours, and inland lakes. By 1882, stamp mills were dumping about 500,000 tons of stamp sands into local waterways each year. The Keweenaw Peninsula near Hancock and Houghton was soon deforested to fuel the copper smelters and remained bare for three-quarters of a century.[17]

Iron mining changed fish habitat as well. In the mid-1840s, the first of the iron ranges in the Great Lakes drainage basin came into production near Marquette, Michigan. Iron tailings were often less toxic than copper tailings, but the refining process added significant quantities of mercury to the watershed, soon becoming an important source of mercury in the lake. Some iron mines were vast open pits, while others were deep shaft mines; both led to significant changes in fish habitats. Miners sliced off forests and the soils that sustained them to create the open pit mines, leading to increased runoff and siltation in tributary streams. Deep shaft mining pumped groundwater to keep the mines dry, lowering the water table and creating silt-filled runoff. Timber shored up shaft tunnels in deep mines, while the smelting furnaces demanded timber. By 1903, for example, the iron furnaces of the Upper Peninsula consumed thirty acres of hardwood forest a day, every day of the year.[18] Mining-related runoff led to increased siltation that covered spawning beds, raised water temperatures, and changed river flows.

Loggers on the American shores of Lake Superior between 1890 and 1910 created new disturbances, the scale of which dwarfed that of earlier ones. By 1898, the federal forester Filbert Roth estimated that only 13 percent of the white pine was still standing. Roth wrote that deforestation had made "decided changes in drainage and soil moisture," diminishing the flow of larger rivers. Swamps had dried up, while hardwood thickets replaced wetland forests.[19] Log drives scraped streambeds clean, spring dams destroyed riparian habitat, and dams for logging blocked the passage of fish upstream for spawning. Sawmills dumped vast quantities of sawdust and wood scrap into nearshore estuaries and rivers. The sawdust floated on the surface and then became waterlogged and sank, clogging harbours, covering spawning and feeding grounds for fish, and filling in the critical nearshore estuarine habitat. Large quantities of sawdust on the shallow bottoms could consume enough oxygen to kill fish.[20]

As forests fell, farms briefly replaced them. The geologist Faith Fitzpatrick's research suggests that, along the clay plain of Wisconsin's south shore, erosion from farming dwarfed the contribution from logging. Nutrients bound to sediments moved off the farmland into the estuaries and streams, lowering levels of the oxygen critical to fish reproduction and adulthood. Clear bottoms became smothered with silt, which harmed spawning of cold-water fisheries (and later offered a perfect habitat for developing sea lampreys).[21] Many contemporary observers were concerned that stream flow seemed to change after logging and farming, with floods and erosion becoming more common, as well as late summer drought.[22]

On the Canadian shore, except for isolated logging of white pine along the north shore for shipbuilding, and near Thunder Bay for paper-industry development, relatively little logging took place until World War I.[23] After the war, the Canadian government encouraged industry partnerships to develop towns around enormous pulp mills on the shores of Lake Superior. Government and industry partnership infused funds into the region to develop the tremendous fibre resources of the boreal forests, particularly the long, thin fibres of black spruce. The Anglo population in northern Ontario soared, drawn by company-built towns with inexpensive housing and good jobs in the mills.

Pulp mill development depended on abundant sources of cheap water. Water was critical for transportation, pulp processing, and power to run the mills. Entire rivers were diverted from one watershed to another, in part to provide hydropower for the pulp industry (see chapter 4 in this volume). Above all, water was essential for disposal of toxic effluents. As early as 1894, contemporary observers expressed concern about pulp mill pollution, noting that the Alpena Sulphite Fiber Company produced acid waste that drained directly into the local river; according to Casper Alpern, a local fish dealer, that waste was "poison to the fish."[24] Yet to planners, as mentioned earlier, Lake Superior seemed like a reasonable place to dump toxic wastes from the mills. Dilution is the solution to pollution, experts reasoned. Their models predicted that Lake Superior could handle the effluents from pulp production, including high levels of mercury, PCBs, and phenolic acids from the natural plant chemicals, which were unnaturally concentrated in pulp processing.[25] Moreover, while urban planners worried about human health and drinking water, they believed that bacterial diseases were most significant. It seemed much cheaper to filter and treat bacterially contaminated waste for human use with chlorine (which harmed fish) and hope that the natural waters would dilute most pollution.[26]

For a generation, pulp and paper towns boomed along the Canadian shore. Marathon, Terrace Bay, and Thunder Bay all relied on an industry made possible by the perception that pulp and paper production made the best use of boreal forests, that logging increased water yield from forests, that lake water was best devoted to industrial development, and that pollution would be so diluted by the abundance of water in Lake Superior that it could not harm fisheries or human health.

Fishing

People had begun fishing in the Lake Superior basin as soon as the glaciers had retreated.[27] By 3000 to 2000 BCE, Indigenous peoples had adapted a broad range of fishing technologies to the conditions they found in the Great Lakes, using spears, gaffs, hooks and lines, and weirs in Lake Superior. In the lower Great Lakes, they had begun using nets about 2,500 BP, but in Lake Superior, net fishing did not begin for at least another two thousand years (sometime between 300 and 200 BP).[28] Well into the twentieth century, these core technologies remained at the heart of the fishery: what changed, however, were the new national and global markets that drove expansion of harvests.

From the 1600s to the 1800s, French exploration, the fur trade, and wars created market pressures that led to intense extraction first of beaver and then of fish.[29] When beavers were removed from much of the watershed, stream patterns changed, wetlands eroded, and nearshore fish habitat diminished.[30] The fur trade created new markets for fisheries, with the American Fur Company establishing a commercial fishing industry on Lake Superior in the 1830s. The goal was not to feed the traders themselves, but to replace corporate income that had diminished as the beaver were depleted. In 1837, the company shipped two thousand barrels of combined lake trout and whitefish; in 1838, four thousand barrels were shipped, and in 1839, five thousand were shipped. For comparison, this means a peak harvest of about one million pounds—which is a lot of fish. In fact, it is slightly less than a sixth of the highest yield between 1941 and 1950 of lake trout and whitefish combined, an average yield of 5.8 million pounds.[31]

How many lake trout did Lake Superior support before the advent of land-use change and commercial fishing? And when did those populations change? It is impossible to state with certainty the pre-nineteenth-century fishing populations of lake trout in Lake Superior. Descriptive archival records stress their abundance—but people exaggerate, particularly when they are writing home about the natural wealth they have stumbled upon. While these anecdotal records can suggest presence or absence and also give a sense of abundance or rarity, they cannot help us identify or quantify the specific declines that followed specific land-use changes.

Fishing catch records provide quantitative data about change over time, but they too have problems.[32] Fish hauls reflect effort and technology, not just the number of fish swimming in the lake. The catch data show relatively low catches of lake trout and whitefish between 1872 and 1893, which tells us less about the populations of fish than about the size of the fishing industry. Catch per unit effort is a more useful measure, because it adjusts for the number of fishermen and the efficiency of their gear, but it still offers only an estimate of the fish that swim under the surface. Fishermen, like travellers, may lie about catches for reasons of their own. Nevertheless, we can use available data to get a sense of changes in fishing effort and production over time and, from that, a proxy estimate of changes in fish populations.[33]

In Lake Superior, 4.4 million pounds of lake trout were caught in 1885; this amount had risen to 5.8 million pounds by 1899.[34] In 1880, $1.5 million was invested in Great Lakes fishing, while a decade later, $5.9 million was invested. But the ratio between capital invested and returned plummeted, suggesting that fish populations were being depleted. In 1880, for every dollar of capital invested, the harvest yielded $1.23; by 1890, the return had dropped to $0.46.[35] The key point from these records is that, while we do not know much about the pre-commercial fishing populations of lake trout in Lake Superior, we do know that well before sea lamprey were noticed in Lake Superior, intensive fishing combined with habitat loss and pollution had already led to a drop in lake trout populations.

Does this matter? As Ray Hilborn and Ulrike Hilborn argue in *Overfishing*, population declines are an unavoidable function of fisheries.[36] But lower populations can still be sustainable over a long time, provided that harvests are not greater than recruitment (i.e., the number of young fish that make it to a certain age, usually the age at which a fish can be harvested). So, were lean and siscowet lake trout populations sustainable under the fishing pressures they experienced? They might have been, had additional ecological stressors—invading lamprey, habitat loss, sedimentation, toxic pollution—not also come into play as factors. But unpredictable ecological stressors are always part of complex systems. Historically, fisheries managers have tried to calculate the maximum sustainable yield, or the highest possible rate of fishing that a population can withstand. But, as modern fisheries biologists are increasingly arguing, under fluctuating environmental conditions and multiple stressors, it is risky to maximize fish harvests. What seems to work when environmental conditions are stable can make populations vulnerable to collapse when a new stressor (such as lamprey) enters the picture.[37]

As fishing pressures, habitat loss, and pollution increased throughout the Great Lakes, people noted the collapse of one fish population after another. By the 1870s, native fish communities in much of Michigan, for example, were in sharp decline, from a combination of overharvest, pollution, dams, and habitat destruction. Unable to implement harvest regulations, the state responded by creating hatcheries, hoping that culturing and stocking large numbers of fry (young fish) would solve the larger ecological problems. For reasons that historian Joseph Taylor enumerates in *Making Salmon*, this did not work. Margaret Bogue's study, *Fishing the Great Lakes*, explores in great detail the political responses to overfishing in the Great Lakes. Bogue shows how wholesale fish dealers such as A. Booth and Company quickly monopolized the industry. Fishermen squeezed by declining harvests and predatory pricing used ever more intense technologies to catch ever declining fish. Governments tended to blame the fishermen for dwindling fish populations, while fishermen tended to blame habitat destruction. When governments did try to respond to clear signs that fish populations were collapsing, their measures were ineffective because jurisdictions were fragmented across two nations, several tribes, three states, and one province.

Sea Lamprey

When the sea lamprey came, the lake trout went away. Or at least that is what the data on Wisconsin and Michigan commercial trout fishing suggest. But of course the story is more complicated.

Sea lampreys attach to lake trout near their hearts and suck their bodily fluids. Adult siscowet, which can survive parasitism at higher rates than can the lean lake trout, may have gaping, oozing wounds from numerous lampreys.

Where did these lamprey come from? Sea lamprey had been recorded in Lake Ontario by the 1830s. Many biologists believe that sea lamprey found in Lake Ontario represent relict populations from the last Pleistocene glaciation. Analysis of mitochondrial DNA supports the hypothesis that sea lamprey are native to Lake Ontario.[38] However, it was not until the 1890s that sea lamprey in that lake threatened commercial fish populations.[39] In 1894, investigators reported that lamprey were often found on Lake Ontario whitefish—and that these were not native freshwater lamprey typically found in creeks. Waldman and colleagues argue that sea lamprey populations in Lake Ontario may have remained rare because of cold temperatures and lack of good habitat for ammocoetes, that is, silty bottoms. Deforestation, industrial development, and pollution that followed the opening of the Welland Canal led to warming water temperatures and silty streams: favourable conditions for sea lamprey populations to expand.[40]

Niagara Falls had once blocked the movements of fish from Lake Ontario into Lake Erie and from there into the upper Great Lakes. When modifications to the Welland Canal were completed in 1919, ocean fish (including sea lamprey) could more easily migrate up into the upper Great Lakes when searching for new tributary streams for spawning. Over the next twenty-five years, sea lamprey moved into Lake Superior, using its many tributary streams for spawning and juvenile habitat.[41] When sea lamprey began to devastate Lake Superior lake trout, the Welland Canal was a convenient target for blame.[42]

Yet this story is too simple. Decades before the 1919 Welland Canal modifications that allowed free passage of oceanic fish into the upper Great Lakes, biologists were already noticing that some lamprey were not only present but also already attacking fish. Yet lamprey populations remained low. For example, the biologist Samuel Wilmot noted in 1893 that lamprey in Lake Huron and Georgian Bay were attacking whitefish and other fish. In 1915—still four years before the canal modifications—the zoologist B.A. Bensley described two different species of lamprey in Georgian Bay: one freshwater species, long known as native to the upper Great Lakes, and another new species similar to what is now known as the sea lamprey. Bensley called this new species the "lake lamprey" and described it as a "dwarfed fresh water representative of the marine lamprey."[43] These records suggest that the Welland Canal modifications alone do not explain why sea lamprey suddenly became a problem.

Sea lamprey populations quickly exploded in Lake Superior—not just because the Welland Canal allowed their passage, but because habitat changes due to logging, farming, and mining created favourable habitat. To understand this, we need to understand a little bit about sea lamprey development and a little bit about habitat changes in the watershed. Sea lamprey require three distinct but interconnected habitats. Spawning adults need clear brooks with fast water and sand or gravel bottoms. These brooks must be connected by free-flowing streams to larval habitat, which typically consist of slow-moving water in medium to large streams, where the larvae spend up to six years buried in soft silt and sediments. During development, they require silty conditions—conditions that were once fairly rare in most Lake Superior tributaries, but that became much more prevalent after deforestation and farming caused massive erosion.[44]

Increased water temperatures caused in part by deforestation also led to increased lamprey hatching and growth rates.[45]

Lamprey, in other words, cannot mature in cold, clear waters, but they thrive in slow, sediment-laden streams—habitats that were once rare in the Lake Superior watershed. But a century of logging, mining, and farming had turned many of the lake's once clear and cold tributaries into silty, warmer, shallower streams, making them excellent lamprey habitat. Lamprey triggered a sudden threshold change. Like the proverbial straw that broke the camel's back, they were not the sole cause of lake trout crashes, but they were the final stressor that pushed the populations over the edge of a cliff.[46]

Lake Trout Recovery

Serious attempts to control sea lamprey began in 1950, with the installation of mechanical barriers that blocked spawning runs. Electrical barriers across 132 Great Lakes tributaries had been installed by 1960. However, these barrier control measures were not perfect, and enough sea lamprey snuck through them to continue hammering the lake trout.

In 1958, a chemical lampricide (and potent endocrine disruptor) named 3-trifluoromethyl-4-nitrophenol (TFM) was developed that killed larval lamprey in streams without killing adult trout. That is, at the concentrations needed to kill lamprey, TFM did not kill lake trout, but the chemical did kill many stream invertebrates that were essential for maintaining the health of fish populations. In an attempt to control lamprey ammocoetes without devastating macroinvertebrates, fisheries biologists developed treatment protocols that called for tributary streams to be poisoned every three to five years, giving the invertebrates some time to recover before the lamprey recovered.

In the 1970s, sea lamprey populations in treated areas were found to be severely skewed in sex ratio, with few males. In the 1990s, researchers discovered that TFM was an estrogen agonist that affected male lamprey development. Few studies have been done on its hormonal effects on other species, so we simply do not know how treatment of tributary streams might or might not be contributing to the continued decline of the endangered coaster trout and other fish that require tributary habitat. There is no question but that chemical control was necessary for lake trout recovery. Yet chemical control alone was not sufficient. A combination of hatcheries, barriers, habitat restoration, toxic-waste reductions, and fishing restrictions were important factors in the recovery.[47]

Even with coordinated recovery efforts focusing on sea lamprey control, breeding populations of lake trout have not been restored to any of the Great Lakes other than Lake Superior. Contamination from out-of-basin sources may partly explain this failure to breed. Recent research has established a connection between dioxin levels, larvae mortality, and lake trout decline in Lake Ontario. Dioxins are byproducts of industrial processes; they typically form during the burning of chlorine-containing waste products or during herbicide production.[48]

Lake trout are extremely sensitive to early-life-stage mortality associated with dioxin exposure.[49] At 30 parts per trillion (ppt), dioxin will begin to kill some lake trout larvae. At 100 ppt, no lake trout larvae survive. Measurable levels of dioxins first showed up in Lake Ontario in the 1930s, and between 1950 and 1975, levels were above 100 ppt. This meant 100 percent mortality of larvae. Only hatchery fish could survive in the lake, and they did not survive for long.[50] In Lake Superior, dioxin levels never reached those found in Lake Ontario, which may be part of the reason why breeding lake trout populations did manage to survive.[51]

Dioxins are not the only contaminants that affect lake trout. In the early 1980s, biologists discovered that Lake Superior lake trout were contaminated with high levels of the detritus of industrial civilization, including PCBs, DDT and its metabolites, toxaphene, and dioxins. Pollution had not been diluted into the deep lake, but instead had become concentrated in the fish that people were eating. Grassroots fury at governments and corporations eventually led to a set of regulatory reforms that banned or strictly limited persistent organic pollutants, and a gratifyingly rapid response was seen in the levels of contaminants measured in fish tissue. Those contamination levels, however, soon levelled off well above zero, even decades after bans were instituted. For example, phenolic compounds from resins, dyes, pulp mills, and petrochemical plants continue to be ubiquitous pollutants in lakes and rivers (TFM, the lampricide, is a phenolic compound as well). Fish exposed to phenols may show changes in thyroid and sex hormones, leading to growth and sexual maturation problems as well as immune system changes. But no studies have yet assessed the impacts these common pollutants may have had on entire populations.[52]

Because siscowet have such high fat levels, they tend to accumulate higher levels of many toxic compounds than other fish, and these compounds can suppress growth and reproduction of individual fish. Ironically, the toxic chemicals also suppressed commercial fishing, which may have given the siscowet additional respite from human pressures. In Wisconsin, siscowet thrived in the St. Louis River estuary (near Duluth and Superior) where, from the 1910s on, pulp mills and oil refineries released wastes that accumulated in siscowet fat and gave the fish a bad taste. Freed from fishing pressure, these populations thrived even in the face of sea lamprey invasions, when the lean lake trout that were being heavily fished collapsed. Similarly, decades later, in the 1980s, Canada banned the sale of siscowet when they were found to be high in PCBs.[53] Even with continued sea lamprey predation, siscowet stocks began to recover while those of the lean lake trout continued to decline, suggesting that fishing had been a significant factor in the population crash.

Siscowet lake trout were the fish upon which the first commercial fishery in Lake Superior was built. Yet they survived environmental change better than the other varieties, for reasons that are not yet entirely clear.[54] Their use of the greatest depths in Lake Superior made them less vulnerable to harvest pressures. Additionally, they rarely spawn in the nearshore habitats, so they are less affected by habitat loss and pollution during their most vulnerable life stages. When they do survive lamprey parasitism, siscowet and lean lake trout have different responses (called sub-lethal responses): siscowet mount an immune response, which drains their lipid reserves but allows them to combat parasitism; lean lake trout are more likely to show an overt stress response. Siscowet show higher lamprey wounding rates than do leans, possibly because leans are more likely to die from parasitism; siscowet are more likely to survive, yet with reduced fecundity and growth.[55]

Climate Change and Lake Superior

Climate change is adding an additional set of stressors to Lake Superior's ecosystems. Since 1980, Lake Superior's water temperatures have been warming at twice the rate of increases in air temperature. Ice cover is diminishing significantly; total ice cover on the lake has shrunk by about 20 percent over the past thirty-seven years.[56] Decreased ice cover affects lake trout habitat and reproduction. For example, many salmonids have higher reproductive success under ice cover, so reduced ice cover may be leading to changing fish populations. Decreased ice cover also leads to greater evaporation, which in turn lowers water levels.

Total precipitation in the Lake Superior basin may not change over the next century, but models predict that summers may be drier and hotter, while spring storms may intensify. By 2100, summer temperatures there may resemble current summer temperatures in central Kansas, 1,440 kilometres (896 miles) south. More intense early-season rains could increase runoff in the spring and lower water in the summer, while also increasing sediment and nutrient loads in tributaries and the nearshore environment.

What does this mean for lake trout? Not surprisingly, it could be bad news for the fish. Increased water temperatures and increased runoff in Lake Superior may tip the lake over from being an oligotrophic lake with abundant oxygen in the hypolimnion to becoming a more nutrient-rich lake. More nutrients might sound like a good thing for many fish, but this is not necessarily true for lake trout. Lake trout, as discussed above, have thrived in Lake Superior because the depths—the hypolimnion—remain rich in oxygen even in the hottest months of the summer. These depths offer lake trout critical refugia from predation and fishing pressure, and they are probably a significant element in lake trout's historic resiliency to environmental change. But if air temperatures continue to warm and water temperatures continue to increase at twice the rate of air temperatures, algal blooms are likely to increase and the lower levels of the lake will become depleted of oxygen, thus triggering a dramatic loss of habitat for lake trout.

While lake trout do not thrive in warming temperatures, sea lamprey do. When water temperatures warm, sea lamprey feed faster, develop into adults more quickly, and lay more eggs. Other invasive species, such as zebra mussels, also like the warming temperatures; further, they can move toxics that were bound to sediments back up into the water column and, from there, into fish.

Climate change and endocrine-disrupting chemicals may magnify each other's effects. Researchers in Australia found that sub-lethal concentrations of two pesticides can significantly reduce the tolerance of some freshwater fish to increasing water temperatures—a finding with disturbing implications for lake trout and other cold-water fish.[57]

Conclusion

Why does it matter to historians why one fish in one lake nearly vanished? Environmental history is filled with similar stories. The important thing about lake trout is that they were resilient for so long—until suddenly they were not. They managed to persist through deforestation and its associated siltation, through intensive commercial fishing harvests and unrestricted pollution. Moreover, people in the basin had plenty of warning that this last great fishery might collapse if fishing restrictions were not implemented and enforced. Lake Superior lies at the top of a Great Lakes Basin filled with examples of fisheries that had already collapsed in lakes that had become too polluted to support much aquatic life.

Yet, as Bogue shows, the political chaos of different jurisdictions meant that few effective actions were taken to regulate the catch, protect spawning habitat, or clean up the nearshore environment.[58] On the land, the chaos of local, state, federal, and provincial laws and policies may have benefitted forests, for it probably shaped an increased ecological diversity in the recovered forests. But in the water, that political fragmentation had very different effects, leading to a regulatory paralysis that thwarted effective action to prevent the collapse of the lake's fisheries.

Into this context swam the sea lamprey, an easy target for blame. But the lamprey never entirely explained the collapse of lake trout. First, the timing was off. Lamprey had been in Lake Ontario long before lake trout populations began to drop, and the lamprey arriving in Lake Erie initially had little effect on lake trout. Similarly, commercial fishing pressures alone do not explain the collapse, because other fish that crashed at the same time were not being commercially fished. For example, populations of four-horned sculpin and burbot also declined sharply, and they are generally not netted by commercial fishermen. Finally, efforts to remove sea lamprey and reduce overfishing did not lead to recovery of breeding populations, except in Lake Superior. Hatcheries still stock all the lake trout that swim in the other Great Lakes, where they are either quickly caught by fishermen or sucked dry by the sea lampreys that have escaped chemical control.

Why then have biologists and agencies placed so much emphasis on lamprey? Perhaps because it has proven to be much easier to coordinate lamprey control efforts across political boundaries than to coordinate regulations on fishing effort or gear. Sea lamprey were an easy scapegoat, but as Taylor argues, "there has also been an evolving awareness in fisheries management over the last half century of the dynamic relationship between fish and habitat, and the conception of relevant habitat has expanded to include much greater sensitivity to chemicals and whole watershed factors. The most obvious example of this evolving awareness is the increased concern for non-point-source pollution, something that simply was not in the lexicon before the 1980s or 1990s."[59]

One key lesson of this history is that, while terrestrial and aquatic ecosystems are interconnected in Lake Superior's watershed, their management is rarely integrated. Events within the basin helped to destroy the lake trout, but processes originating far outside the basin had perhaps even more of an impact. Yes, pulp mills dumped toxic waste over spawning grounds, but the pollutants that blew in from coal plants and industrial agriculture thousands of miles away may have had greater effects on fish. Local fishermen took too many fish, but market domination by A. Booth and Company continued excessive fishing harvests even after fish populations had begun to dwindle. Local towns never managed to control dumping, and slicing up the basin into multiple jurisdictions, each with different political priorities, made effective regulations elusive. Lake trout populations, resilient as they had been for decades, eventually crashed because of multiple stressors at multiple scales. Lamprey may have pushed the fish over the cliff, but land-use change, pollutants, and overfishing had already dragged them right to the edge.

Notes

1. Thanks to the Bad River Band of Lake Superior Tribe of Chippewa Indians and to my colleagues on the Lake Superior Binational Forum for their generous insights. Thanks also to Lynne Heasley and Daniel Macfarlane for fostering this project and to the other authors who participated in a stimulating workshop during the summer of 2012.

    Quoted in Margaret Bogue, *Fishing the Great Lakes: An Environmental History, 1783–1933* (Madison: University of Wisconsin Press, 2000), 128.

2. Harold M. Tyus, *Ecology and Conservation of Fishes* (Boca Raton, FL: CRC Press, 2011), 130–31.

3. "Sea Lamprey: A Great Lakes Invader Fact Sheet," U.S. Geological Survey, Great Lakes Science Center, January 2008.

4. B.R. Smith and J.J. Tibbles, "Sea Lamprey (*Petromyzon marinus*) in Lakes Huron, Michigan, and Superior: History of Invasion and Control, 1936–78," *Canadian Journal of Fisheries and Aquatic Sciences* 37, no. 11 (1980): 1780–801; Daniel W. Coble et al., "Lake Trout, Sea Lampreys, and Overfishing in the Upper Great Lakes: A Review and Reanalysis," *Transactions of the American Fisheries Society* 119, no. 6 (2011): 2; John W. Heinrich et al., "Sea Lamprey Abundance and Management in Lake Superior, 1957 to 1999," *Journal of Great Lakes Research* 29, no. S1 (2003): 6; Michael J. Hansen, "Lake Trout in the Great Lakes," in *Our Living Resources: A Report to the Nation on the Distribution, Abundance, and Health of U.S. Plants, Animals, and Ecosystems*, ed. Edward T. LaRoe et al. (Washington, DC: U.S. Dept. of the Interior, National Biological Service, 1995).

5. In Canada alone, lake trout used at least two hundred different spawning grounds, including twenty rivers that once had September runs of lake trout. Lake trout tend to return to the spawning grounds where they were born. Charles R. Bronte and Shawn P. Sitar, "Harvest and Relative Abundance of Siscowet Lake Trout in Michigan Waters of Lake Superior, 1929–1961," *Transactions of the American Fisheries Society* 137, no. 3 (2008): 916–26, doi:10.1577/T07-096.1.

6. Bogue, *Fishing the Great Lakes*, 154.

7. S.L. Schantz, "Editorial: Lakes in Crisis," *Environmental Health Perspectives* 113, no. 3 (2005): A148.

8. Scott Fields, "Great Lakes: Resource at Risk," *Environmental Health Perspectives* 113, no. 3 (2005): A164–73.

9. *Wikipedia*, s.v. "Lake Superior," accessed May 8, 2013, http://en.wikipedia.org/wiki/Lake_Superior; *Wikipedia*, s.v. "Lake Erie," accessed May 8, 2013, http://en.wikipedia.org/wiki/Lake_Erie.

10. Farrell M. Boyce, "Lake," in *Canadian Encyclopedia*, published December 14, 2006, accessed July 11, 2012, http://www.thecanadianencyclopedia.com/articles/lake.

11. Ibid.

12. "Trophic Status," Lake Access website, accessed July 11, 2012, http://www.lakeaccess.org/ecology/lakeecologyprim15.html.

13. "Lake Superior," Minnesota Sea Grant website, accessed July 11,

2012, http://www.seagrant.umn.edu/superior/overview.

14   Thomas A. Edsall and Murray N. Charlton, "Nearshore Waters of the Great Lakes" (background paper, State of the Lakes Ecosystem Conference 1996, December 1997), http://publications.gc.ca/collections/Collection/En40-11-35-1-1997E.pdf.

15   Lake Superior Binational Program, "The Aquatic Environment," chap. 6 in *Lake Superior Lakewide Management Plan 2006* (Washington, DC: U.S. Environmental Protection Agency, 2006).

16   See chapters 2 and 3 in Nancy Langston, *Sustaining Lake Superior* (New Haven: Yale University Press, in press).

17   Larry D. Lankton and Charles K. Hyde, *Old Reliable: An Illustrated History of the Quincy Mining Company* (Hancock, MI: Quincy Mine Hoist Association, 1982); Larry D. Lankton, *Cradle to Grave: Life, Work, and Death at the Lake Superior Copper Mines* (New York: Oxford University Press, 1991).

18   Harlan H. Hatcher, *A Century of Iron and Men* (Indianapolis: Bobbs-Merrill, 1950), 102.

19   Filbert Roth, *On the Forestry Conditions of Northern Wisconsin* (State of Wisconsin, 1898), 41–42.

20   Sawdust dumping attracted persistent critics, as Bogue discusses in *Fishing the Great Lakes*, 125ff. Samuel Wilmot, for example, in his 1890 study of fish-breeding operations, devoted twelve pages to the problems of sawdust pollution. Wilmot, *Report on Fish-Breeding Operations in the Dominion of Canada 1890* (Ottawa: F.A. Acland, 1891).

21   Faith A. Fitzpatrick et al., *Effects of Historical Land-Cover Changes on Flooding and Sedimentation, North Fish Creek, Wisconsin* (Washington, DC: U.S. Geological Survey, 1999).

22   See George Perkins Marsh, "Report Made under Authority of the Legislature of Vermont: On the Artificial Propagation of Fish" (Burlington VT: Free Press Print, 1857). George Whitney has a good discussion of the complex effects of deforestation on stream flow in *From Coastal Wilderness to Fruited Plain: A History of Environmental Change in Temperate North America, 1500 to the Present* (Cambridge: Cambridge University Press, 1996).

23   H.V. Nelles, *The Politics of Development: Forests, Mines and Hydro-Electric Power in Ontario, 1849–1941*, 2nd ed. (Montreal: McGill-Queens University Press, 2005); E.A. Forsey, "The Pulp and Paper Industry," *Canadian Journal of Economics and Political Science* 1, no. 3 (1935): 501–9; Daniel Douglas, *Northern Algoma: A People's History* (Toronto: Dundurn, 1996); Mark Kuhlberg, *In the Power of the Government: The Rise and Fall of Newsprint in Ontario, 1894–1932* (Toronto: University of Toronto Press, 2015).

24   Bogue, *Fishing the Great Lakes*, 127n23.

25   See Langston, *Sustaining Lake Superior*.

26   This was not unique to Lake Superior. Craig E. Colten and Peter N. Skinner, *The Road to Love Canal: Managing Industrial Waste before EPA* (Austin: University of Texas Press, 1996).

27 Charles E. Cleland, "Indians in a Changing Environment," in *The Great Lakes Forest: An Environmental and Social History* (Minneapolis: University of Minnesota Press, 1983), 83–95.

28 On tribal fishing, see Richard White, *The Middle Ground: Indians, Empires, and Republics in the Great Lakes Region, 1650–1815* (Cambridge: Cambridge University Press, 1991); and Bogue, *Fishing the Great Lakes*.

29 White, *Middle Ground*.

30 Bogue, *Fishing the Great Lakes*, 15; Nancy Langston, *Where Land and Water Meet: A Western Landscape Transformed* (Seattle: University of Washington Press, 2003); Robert J. Naiman, Jerry M. Melillo, and John E. Hobbie, "Ecosystem Alteration of Boreal Forest Streams by Beaver (*Castor canadensis*)," *Ecology* 67, no. 5 (1986): 1254–69; Robert J. Naiman, Carol A. Johnston, and James C. Kelley, "Alteration of North American Streams by Beaver," *BioScience* 38, no. 11 (1988): 753–62; Carol A. Johnston and Robert J. Naiman, "Browse Selection by Beaver: Effects on Riparian Forest Composition," *Canadian Journal of Forest Research* 20, no. 7 (1990): 1036–43.

31 Jerold F. Rahrer, *Great Lakes Fishery Commission Technical Report*, vol. 19, *Lake Superior: A Case History of the Lake and Its Fisheries* (Ann Arbor, MI: GLFC, 1973).

32 For an analysis, see Joseph E. Taylor III, "Knowing the Black Box: Methodological Challenges in Marine Environmental History," *Environmental History* 18, no. 1 (2013; published online November 14, 2012): 108.

33 Bogue, *Fishing the Great Lakes*, 155.

34 Ibid., 41.

35 Ibid., 57.

36 Ray Hilborn and Ulrike Hilborn, *Overfishing: What Everyone Needs to Know* (Oxford: Oxford University Press, 2012).

37 For a detailed analysis, see Carmel Finley, *All the Fish in the Sea: Maximum Sustainable Yield and the Failure of Fisheries Management* (Chicago: University of Chicago Press, 2011). For an analysis of similar failures for the Pacific salmon fisheries, see Joseph E. Taylor III, *Making Salmon: An Environmental History of the Northwest Fisheries Crisis* (Seattle: University of Washington Press, 1999).

38 John R. Waldman et al., "Mitochondrial DNA Analysis Indicates Sea Lampreys Are Indigenous to Lake Ontario," *Transactions of the American Fisheries Society* 133, no. 4 (2004): 950–60. Debate continues regarding genetic differences between the Atlantic and Lake Ontario populations.

39 Bogue, *Fishing the Great Lakes*, 163.

40 Waldman et al., "Mitochondrial DNA."

41 Ibid.

42 Bogue reports that "in 1921, a fisherman caught and brought into the Royal Ontario Museum in Toronto an 'eel,' the like of which he had never seen in Lake Erie. Biologists identified it as a sea lamprey like those found for many decades in Lake Ontario, where in the 1920s it was on the increase." *Fishing the Great Lakes*, 330.

43 Quoted in Ibid., 164.

44 Freshwater lamprey, which also parasitize big fish, are native to the upper Great Lakes, but they never seemed to do much damage to lake trout. Tyus, *Ecology and Conservation*.

45 John A. Holmes, "Sea Lamprey as an Early Responder to Climate Change in the Great Lakes Basin," *Transactions of the American Fisheries Society* 119, no. 2 (1990): 292–300.

46 Lack of natural predators is the usual reason given for the sea lamprey's population explosion, but it is unlikely to be the sole reason. Sea lamprey had lacked predators for centuries in Lake Ontario, yet their populations had not expanded until after Anglo settlement. By 1893, Samuel Wilmot had noted changing proportions of fish species throughout the Great Lakes, suggesting an "upset in natural balance" because of disturbance of predator prey relationships. He warned that, "once weakened by heavy fishing, commercial species could be destroyed by their natural enemies and parasites." Quoted in Bogue, *Fishing the Great Lakes*, 171.

47 Smith and Tibbles, "Sea Lamprey."

48 Philip M. Cook et al., "Effects of Aryl Hydrocarbon Receptor–Mediated Early Life Stage Toxicity on Lake Trout Populations in Lake Ontario during the 20th Century," *Environmental Science and Technology* 37, no. 17 (2003): 3864–77; Christopher Steiner, "Experts Reel In Clues to Lake Trout's Killer," *Chicago Tribune*, November 9, 2003, http://articles.chicagotribune.com/2003-11-09/news/0311090005_1_lake-trout-largest-freshwater-system-lake-michigan.

49 Cook et al., "Effects of Toxicity."

50 Ibid.

51 Steiner, "Experts Reel In Clues."

52 Linda M. Campbell et al., "Hydroxylated PCBs and Other Chlorinated Phenolic Compounds in Lake Trout (*Salvelinus namaycush*) Blood Plasma from the Great Lakes Region," *Environmental Science and Technology* 37, no. 9 (2003): 1720–5, doi:10.1021/es026225m.

53 Wayne R. MacCallum and James H. Selgeby, "Lake Superior Revisited 1984," *Canadian Journal of Fisheries and Aquatic Sciences* 44, no. S2 (1987): S23–S36.

54 Bronte and Sitar, "Harvest and Relative Abundance," 916.

55 Cheryl Murphy et al., "Estimating the Sublethal Effects of Lamprey Parasitism on Lipid Allocation, Reproduction and Population Dynamics of Lake Trout" (research completion report, Sea Lamprey Research Program, Great Lakes Fishery Commission, January 2013), http://www.glfc.org/research/reports/Murphy_2013.htm.

56 Jay Austin and Steve Colman, "A Century of Temperature Variability in Lake Superior," *Limnology and Oceanography* 53, no. 6 (2008): 2724–30.

57 M. Jake Vander Zanden and Joseph B. Rasmussen, "A Trophic Position Model of Pelagic Food Webs: Impact on Contaminant Bioaccumulation in Lake Trout," *Ecological Monographs* 66, no. 4 (1996): 451–77.

58 Bogue, *Fishing the Great Lakes*.

59 Joseph E. Taylor III, email communication with the author, August 22, 2012.

PART FOUR

Reflections in the Water

Openings

The Lakes at Night

Jerry Dennis

Late one night, standing on the deck of a two-masted schooner sailing across the top of Lake Huron, I had an encounter with history. The *Malabar* was a replica of schooners that had worked the lakes by the thousands in the nineteenth century. That was part of the history I sensed. Another part of it was personal history, memories brought vividly to mind while seeing new places—or old places in new ways. That night it was possible to imagine that the Great Lakes had not changed in hundreds, maybe thousands, of years. I saw what the First Peoples must have seen: the lake calmed to mirror flatness, the stars as bright on the water as they were in the sky, water extending in every direction to the horizon. I sensed the wash of time and an old longing rose in me: to engage more fully with the world, to get beneath the surface, to try to understand a place I cared deeply about.

The Great Lakes have always been a powerful presence in my family. As a young man, my mother's father worked as a lifesaver at the U.S. Life Saving Station on South Manitou Island, in northern Lake Michigan. Later, he raised his family a short walk from the lake in Leelanau County, the "little finger" of Michigan's mitten, and told his children stories of shipwrecks and storms. He died a few months before I was born, but I grew up hearing his stories from my mother as we walked the beaches or fished the lake or climbed the dunes at Empire and Sleeping Bear. As a family we made regular excursions north, across the Mackinac Bridge connecting

Lakes Michigan and Huron, across the Upper Peninsula to the wildest lake of all, Lake Superior. Every summer we went farther north yet, across the border into Ontario at Sault Ste. Marie, and into the bush to fish rivers and lakes in country that in those days was still wilderness. On the way home we would stop along the rocky, wave-battered shore of Superior to fish for coaster brook trout and pick wild blueberries.

But even after a lifetime on the lakes, I didn't truly understand them until that journey from Michigan to Maine on the schooner *Malabar*. Our trip up the northern quarter of Lake Michigan and across the lengths of Huron, Erie, and Ontario was not a casual tour, but a job. I was one of five crewmen who had been assigned to deliver the schooner to its new owner in Bar Harbor, and I went along not as a writer but as a volunteer deckhand. As such, I hauled sails, sweated lines, pumped the bilge, secured dock lines, and piloted the yawl boat to nudge the *Malabar* into its dockages. I took my turn cooking and washing dishes; repairing toilets and motors; helping to dismantle the rigging and step the masts for the Erie Canal, and then to raise the mast and re-rig in Albany before we descended the Hudson River to the Atlantic. I stood watch at all hours of the day and night, in all weather, on fresh water, brackish, and salt, and took the helm during the worst storm I have ever experienced.

During all those weeks, I never lost sight of the lakes themselves. They wouldn't allow it. The Great Lakes are like five beautiful and charismatic sisters: willful, tempestuous, frequently charming, ultimately unfathomable. I had set out to know them, but it was an impossible task. Knowing a small place is hard enough—you can spend a lifetime getting to know a woodland pond or a patch of woods. The Great Lakes are beyond our capabilities. They're too big, too varied; they sprawl across too large a swath of the continent.

For centuries the Great Lakes were the main trade route to the interior of North America. For that reason, and because they are surrounded by lands flush with resources, they were central in transforming the United States and Canada into industrial and economic giants. Yet the lakes remain among the least appreciated of North America's major geographic features. No longer am I surprised to meet people who don't know that the lakes are too large to see across or that they contain most of the surface fresh water on the continent. I am constantly surprised, however, by the number of people I meet who assume that the water is there to be ransacked.

Maybe the lakes are too great for their own good. If they were contained entirely within a single province or state, they would be easier to defend. Instead, they overlap two provinces, eight states, and more than two hundred tribal governments and thus are constantly snarled in legislative complexities that make them vulnerable. And because they contain such an enormous volume of water—nearly a fifth of all the liquid fresh water on the surface of the Earth—many assume that they're inexhaustible. With that much water, the thinking goes, there should be plenty for everyone.

That could possibly be true if the lakes were merely storage containers. But they are vital ecosystems supporting complex communities of animals and plants—some of them found no place else, all of them dependent upon a consistent supply of clean water. Some of those communities are human: about forty million of us live around the lakes, drawing our drinking water from them, bathing in them, fishing from them, boating upon them. Many of our cities sacrificed their environmental health to build the United States and Canada and have since been abandoned for their troubles. Go to Gary or East Chicago or Hamilton to see what the steel mills and petroleum distilleries have wrought. The best hopes for those and dozens of other cities are the lakes themselves. Once they were highways for shipping and dumping grounds for waste, but the current renaissance of waterfronts in Toronto, Milwaukee, Duluth, Cleveland, Erie, Buffalo, and many other cities makes it clear that we've entered a new stage in our relationship. The Great Lakes are no longer merely useful. They have become determinants and indicators of the quality of our lives.

I thought of many of these things that night on the *Malabar*. I thought also of the borders we were crossing. National borders lay north, south, and east of us; anyone who travels on or around the lakes must negotiate customs and security checkpoints at many places between the two countries. But those borders are porous. Fish and wildlife don't recognize them. Neither do the storms that sweep the lakes or the winter ice that clogs the shipping channels. Earlier in the night we had passed over a pair of oil pipes on the bottom of the Straits of Mackinac that for sixty years have transported a constant flow of petroleum from Canada, across Michigan, and back to Canada at Sarnia. Those pipes are the subject of much concern because they are old and insufficiently inspected and barely regulated; many of us worry that they will rupture, pumping millions of gallons of crude oil into the lakes and creating a catastrophe on both sides of the border.

I was on that journey in part to observe and document the hazards of petroleum transport and other environmental concerns. Already I had spent years talking to people and observing the consequences of our misuse of the Great Lakes: invasive species, chemical and petroleum spills, faulty municipal sewage plants, agricultural runoff of fertilizers and pesticides, degraded shorelines—the list was long and getting longer. And I was starting to lose heart.

But those hours of night watch on the *Malabar* gave me a break from worry. Alone, surrounded by starlight, with the water spread out to the horizon, it was possible to imagine that we had never introduced zebra mussels into the water or pumped crude oil through it in deteriorating pipes. I wasn't sticking my head in the sand—just the opposite. I was opening my eyes and seeing more clearly than I ever had the beauty and singularity that make the lakes a natural wonder of the world and a place worth defending at all costs. The history of the Great Lakes and my personal history were joined for just a moment—and I was lucky to be transformed by the encounter while the lakes remained unchanged.

The chapters that follow are very different from those that make up the rest of this volume. The title of the section, "Reflections in the Water," suggests the introspective and meditative tone of many of the pieces as well as their subject. That water figures so prominently is notable not only because the political border dividing the United States and Canada is such a waterlogged one, but because water is so often a central and transformative element for those who grow up near it. It is a theme that runs through Western literature from *The Odyssey* to *Huckleberry Finn* to *Life of Pi*. I suspect it is a prominent theme as well in the personal histories of many of the people who devote themselves to environmental studies and the natural sciences.

The contributors to this section are a varied and well-travelled group. All, in one way or another, have committed a significant portion of their careers to studying aspects of the border between Canada and the United States. But their studies have not been limited to analytic research. They have been to the places they study; have waded in and gotten muddy; have hiked, sailed, canoed, kayaked, bicycled, and fished there. I would argue that those immersive activities have carried them deeper into their subjects than scholastic work alone could take them.

Such personal and immersive connections with the land are central to the long tradition of nature writing, a genre that the essayist Edward Hoagland defined as "biology with love."[1] Writers and thinkers as varied as Montaigne, Gilbert White, Darwin, Thoreau, Rachel Carson, Aldo Leopold, Annie Dillard, Barry Lopez, and E.O. Wilson have demonstrated that writing creatively about a place makes that place immediate to readers. A narrative that includes a deeply felt personal connection draws the reader even closer. Done well, such writing engages us, stimulating our imaginations to see, hear, scent, and feel the place as vividly as if we had actually been there. The same process is at work in fiction when a character "comes alive" for the reader. Precise and evocative language and carefully chosen images inspire emotional responses that many readers find more convincing than even the most carefully crafted dialectic treatments.

It should surprise no one that writing about experiencing a place is markedly different than writing about the place from a purely academic or scientific point of view. It's personal, and it should be. There's room for personal pronouns and the active voice. There's room also for humour, metaphor, and imagination. In my own experience—being a writer trained in literary arts, and having earned my living for many years writing about personal encounters in nature for a popular audience—those techniques are completely natural. They're the tools I reach for reflexively. So it always interests me to work with scholars who have been trained to eliminate the personal and imaginative from their work. It is equally interesting to see how eager many of them are to break those strictures and make their writing more vivid, lively, and interesting. I'm confident that those qualities are appreciated by readers of every kind.

What follows are the reflections of seven very different writers remembering the very different waters that have wound through their lives. The results are as diverse and interesting as the border country itself.

Note

1 *Tigers & Ice: Reflections on Nature and Life* (New York: Lyons, 2000).

Finding Our Place

~ *Crossings*
Jeremy Mouat

~ *Meditations on Ice*
Colin A.M. Duncan and Andrew Marcille

~ *Bordering on Significance?*
Daniel Macfarlane

~ *To Market, to Market*
Joseph E. Taylor III

~ *Leading Waters*
Noah D. Hall

~ *On Frames, Perspectives, and Vanishing Points*
Lynne Heasley

~ *Headwaters of Hope*
Dave Dempsey

Crossings

Jeremy Mouat

One of Alberta's most well-known features is the tar sands outside of Fort McMurray. The controversial resource boom fuelled by the tar sands is not the first to have made outside investors rich. An earlier boom began in the late eighteenth century, when beaver pelts from the region went to distant markets. Anticipating the title of this book, that earlier boom was all about border flows—about the flow of water either side of a continental divide.

For a number of years I lived in Athabasca, Alberta, bordering the river of the same name. The river swings north at the town, flowing up to Fort McMurray and beyond from its source in the Rockies. At Fort McMurray, the Clearwater River joins the Athabasca, coming west from Saskatchewan. The Clearwater was the vital artery that enabled that earlier resource boom.

The river forms part of an Arctic drainage system, a fact that helps to explain its significance. When in 1670 the British king signed a Royal Charter for the Hudson's Bay Company, he gave the company monopoly trading rights over the lands that drained into Hudson Bay. Once traders entered the Arctic Ocean watershed—once they had crossed that continental divide and reached the Clearwater—the company's exclusive rights no longer applied.

Fur traders and voyageurs crossing the divide between the Hudson Bay drainage system and the Arctic system did so via a famous portage: the Methye Portage. It had the same sort of status for voyageurs as the equator did for sailors: newbie voyageurs went from being *mangeurs de lard* (pork eaters) to *hommes du nord* (men of the north) after crossing it. This new status likely reflected the gruelling work involved: the portage was twenty kilometres in length, over which the voyageurs packed loads of more than eighty kilograms. Of course, once I had moved to Athabasca, I wanted to get to the portage and become a man of the north myself.

The Methye Portage is in northwestern Saskatchewan, pretty much due east of Fort McMurray. It begins—if you're approaching from the eastern side—on the northwest side of Lac La Loche, well past the nearest road. To get to it, you either paddle across the lake or fly in.

Although it took a dozen years, a colleague and I organized a trip early this century over the Methye. We were both historians with little backcountry experience so we recruited two other friends—a psychologist and a philosopher—as both had done a lot of wilderness canoeing. (It was a group that sounds like the beginning of a bad joke: "What do you get when a . . . .") With backing from a TV production company, we drove up to Fort McMurray with two canoes, left the truck there, and flew over to Lac La Loche with the canoes strapped onto the pontoons. The TV crew filmed us as we each lugged about fifty-five kilograms over the portage. They left once we'd reached the Clearwater River. We slipped the canoes into the river and headed west. We got to Fort McMurray a few days later, relaxed by the days in the wilderness and the beauty of the river. Our calm did not last long, however; we came out of the bush on September 11, 2001.

Western Canada is home to a series of continental divides, although only one is marked: the one that forms the southern half of the border between Alberta and British Columbia. These days you can cross watersheds without even noticing them. Once I drove from Athabasca down to Montana to attend a conference and later realized that I'd crossed three watersheds along the way, from my home overlooking the Athabasca River flowing up to the Arctic, across the North Saskatchewan River flowing east to Hudson Bay, and then to the Upper Missouri River, which flows south to the Gulf of Mexico. The trip was easily done in a day but you have to pay close attention to figure out where the water changes flow.

Like the changing flow of water, history is illusive in the western Canadian landscape. It's difficult to see the marks that the past has left on the land. We don't have the cobblestones and castles of Europe. And those marks that we do see—the straight lines of the surveyors that signify so many borders in western North America—seem so commonplace and so obvious that we don't question them. We need to pay more attention to the border flows and the history that is hidden from view.

Meditations on Ice

Colin A.M. Duncan and Andrew Marcille

Historians and other ordinary people tend to think of lakes and rivers as liquid. But in central North America, where the Great Lakes–St. Lawrence River Valley is located, most bodies of water are substantially icebound for several months each year. In this well-watered zone, sailing iceboats were long used (in winter) as the best way to transport people and goods to and from islands and across wide, slow parts of rivers.

Iceboats are fast, often frighteningly so, and quite unencumbered with any braking mechanism. Rather than lolling about, attended by liveried servants, iceyachters experience many forms of discomfort when getting ready for their sport, untying frozen knots and assembling fiddly bits of deeply chilled equipment without gloves. When sailing, they commonly feel wind-chill effects around −50 degrees Celsius, often with wet feet. Any ease comes only after the boats are put away for the night.

It is precisely because iceboats are very fast that they were, however counterintuitively, the safest and most comfortable way to move people across large frozen expanses. The huge area over which an iceboat spreads its weight makes it possible to sail safely on ice too thin for skating or walking—a point freshly proved each year by keen racers. To this day, iceboats retain with ease the speed records for craft not reliant on motors. Though iceboat skates are very heavy, the friction between them and a slightly bumpy hard ice surface is risibly small. But perhaps the most astonishing thing about iceboats is not their top speeds, but their rates of acceleration. That said, global defrosting may explain why the top speed record dates from the first half of the last century. It is difficult now, perhaps impossible, to find good ice of sufficient extent to allow the buildup to speeds around two hundred miles per hour. What eventually restricts the speed of an iceboat is generally its own aerodynamic drag. But we have been skating away from the serious purpose of transportation. It suffices to say that pretty well any iceboat promised vastly shorter travel time than any alternative until the mid-twentieth century. Anybody seated riverside on an express train going

9.1 Iceboating at the very starting point of the St. Lawrence River, 2014. Courtesy of John Curtis.

along the Hudson River when an iceboat challenged the steam engine's driver to an impromptu race could see the speed of solid-water sailing.

The big, heavy iceboats of yore also built up formidable momentum if sailed much distance. Though there is little chance that the captains and crew found their work to be drudgery, they did face one tough task. Not quite as bad as it sounds (as one of the authors, who has experienced this, can attest), it entailed slipping overboard in heavy clothing and then dragging at the end of a rope to help bring the boat to a standstill at voyage's end. Iceboats are creatures of motion: if the wind is strong and the ice surface good, stopping one is far harder than setting it moving. Indeed, and rather amusingly, on a quiet day an iceboat with sail up can be induced to come on command, but only in response to impatience; the sailor stamping his or her feet on the ice can be enough to break the surface tension that was actually keeping the boat fixed. Once the craft is stopped, a kind of pointed metal device can—and should—be activated to serve as a sort of "parking brake." The qualifier and scare quotes are serious. If the wind is gusty, changing strength and direction violently, it can cause a pivoted device to become disengaged. Iceboats left untended with sail up and no brake set are notoriously apt to wander off. They have been known to sail aimlessly for miles, going both upwind and down as the forces of lift and drag jostle each other with nobody in charge. It is an inconvenience if this truancy occurs near open water, but luckily, despite the mass of the skates, the buoyant wood of an uncrewed iceboat prevents its sinking even if it does run out of ice. Though the speeds attained by an empty iceboat are not very high, chasing one in heavy clothing is a mug's game. Having a large number of helpful people spread out on the ice makes it easier to catch a runaway iceboat, but generally, one has to wait until it just happens to stop.

Of necessity, some time was spent every year determining when the ice was "strong" enough to support the craft. While the dangers of ice breakage seem obvious when the ice first grows at the start of any season, they are subtler at its end, as eventually even very thick ice loses its integrity. Indeed, the safest surface is new, clear ice whose thickness can be instantly discerned by looking at the edge of a crack. Changing its elasticity markedly with temperature, thinnish ice is safer on warmer days, other things being equal. Strong currents disturbingly can and do erode ice from below—a dastardly deed when the ice is opaque, which sadly it usually becomes. Near the shore, too, ice can be unsafe. Dark objects absorb immense amounts of heat from sunlight: piers and large rocks can create patches of open water even on cold days. Iceboat skates, thin as they are, absorb so much heat that if left on the ice for even a few minutes of blazing sun, they will drop down into the ice surface. With refreezing at dusk, the boat may become trapped. Prudent iceboaters prop their idle boats up by arranging lumps of wood beneath the skates, which also reduces the chance of an unmanned journey. Even with no sail up, an iceboat on a good surface can move very fast if the wind is strong.

Some physicists and engineers tell us they like to dream of a frictionless world. Iceboaters seem to live the reality—but in fact the noise made by metal moving over ice is considerable. Iceboats roar much like trains when going fast, giving everyone not on board a decent chance of keeping clear even with their ears muffled against the cold. Not surprisingly, many people have been frightened by iceboats. But the primary enemy of the iceboat itself is deep snow. Even the friction of thin, wet snow can "ground" the craft. The speed of iceboats means that whiteouts from fog or falling snow tell everyone to go home. As ice grows laterally as well as vertically, dangerous pressure deformations develop in restricted places such as harbours and rivers, much complicating navigation. These big cracks often relocate overnight. Iceboaters along the edges of the Great Lakes face one occasional source of huge frustration, most commonly at the start of the season. Massive wave systems generated by gales damage nearshore ice sheets that are not yet very thick, rendering the surface (in the worst cases) a jumbled mass protruding at as many angles as there are fragments. Only a huge thaw plus refreezing can clear that obstacle, with help from heavy snowfall to "fair" the surface. Usually, eventually, a large, moist, warm air mass from the Gulf of Mexico comes to the rescue of the Great Lakes–St. Lawrence iceboaters.

Although they, like farmers, watch the weather keenly and know its quirks inside out, iceboaters everywhere have no better luck than anybody else at ordering weather à la carte. Most major planned competitions have to be relocated overnight by hundreds of miles. Even the Iron Curtain never prevented ice yacht racers from pursuing clear ice across Europe. The large prewar iceboats that could carry many people and boxes and bags and dogs had skates so large they could cope with a wider range of surface imperfections than can a contemporary vessel, built light to be nimble enough for the many sudden direction changes involved in course racing in a fleet. Let us hope that global warming trends do not proceed so far as to render the trivial joy of iceboating a thing of the past.

Bordering on Significance?

Daniel Macfarlane

I was *almost* born in eastern Ontario, an area abundant in water. Instead I ended up growing up in a place that some might consider the inverse: Saskatchewan. It is not as if the Canadian prairies are completely bereft of water, particularly in the northern half, but whenever we went to visit family in Ontario, as we frequently did, I was intrigued by the waters of the St. Lawrence, the locks of the Rideau and Trent Canals, the Great Lakes, and Niagara Falls.

I started writing this piece in Kingston, on Lake Ontario, continued it along the St. Lawrence River, added to it in Canada's capital along its eponymous waterway, and revised it in parts of Michigan astride various Great Lakes. All this moving about, with my family in tow, gives one some perspective on the ways that borders matter, and the ways that they don't. Water flowing naturally doesn't respect human-made boundaries, but in the case of the Niagara and St. Lawrence projects (see chapter 4 in this volume), borders clearly matter. The border has a deep impact on how nations perceive their water and nature. As problematic as it is to generalize about societal views of the environment, crossing borders—province to province, state to state, country to country—has left me with the impression that both similarities and differences exist in these views when it comes to northern North America.

The picture of old Highway 2 running into the St. Lawrence shows another kind of border: a line between past and present, between memory and history. It appears to show a border between built and natural environment. But that is a false distinction—not only here, but probably everywhere. Roads lead somewhere, just like "progress." But where does this road lead? Where does "progress" on the scale of the St. Lawrence Seaway and Power Project lead?

Other questions about the artificial/natural divide—or lack thereof—can be asked of waters that form the border between Canada and the United States. They are both natural systems and political/cultural/social constructions. Rivers and lakes are bioregions unto themselves, but water

9.2 Old Highway 2. Photo by Daniel Macfarlane.

also divides land; thus, from the perspectives of those carving out political boundaries, bodies of water naturally make good boundaries. While the waters of the Great Lakes–St. Lawrence basin serve as convenient and "natural" (or intuitive) borders in a certain sense, the divided political jurisdictions that result make policy actions concerning these waters more fragmented and difficult.

Such dichotomies, or contradictions, certainly apply to Niagara Falls. Consider the pictures of Terrapin Point (Figure 9.3, 9.4). This used to be part of the waterfall until it was "reclaimed," for two reasons: to mask the scenic impact of water diversions for hydroelectric production by shrinking the Horseshoe Falls, and to give tourists a better view.

In the course of discovering the historical manipulation of Niagara Falls, I went through a sort of progression of emotions: first dismay, then despair, then disillusionment. But somehow, over time, I returned to my childhood fascination with Niagara. I saw through the manipulations and reordering. I once again saw water going over rock, H_2O over granite, the largest freshwater system in the world plunging over a magnificent cliff.

9.3 Terrapin Point. Photo by Daniel Macfarlane.

9.4 Artificial edge of Horseshoe Falls. Photo by Daniel Macfarlane.

9 / *Bordering on Significance?* *281*

9.5 Maple leaf in water. Photo by Daniel Macfarlane.

I've watched theses waterscapes from many perspectives, and I've photographed them from many angles. I've watched the St. Lawrence while standing on the remains of long submerged towns, up to my waist in water. I've watched from a dock, from a power dam, from a plane, from a freighter. I've watched Niagara from Terrapin Point and Table Rock; I've watched from on high in a hotel room and from below peering out of a cave, from the *Maid of the Mist* and from a jet boat. The hotel is obviously part of the built environment—but, really, so is Terrapin Point.

At Terrapin Point, I'm literally on the border. Does crossing the border change the view? What baggage do I bring that influences my perspective? We go back to where I started this: where I am from. Does being a Canadian—or a western Canadian, a central Canadian, a Michigander, or a central North American—have a perceptible impact on how I conceive of these border waters, or how I view the other side? Does the fact that I now live in the United States alter this view? Does my transnational, environmental historian outlook alter my perspective more than my nationality? Does framing through a camera lens change my gaze in profound ways?

At the very least, it is clear that the border doesn't just shape countries physically; it shapes ideas and perspectives metaphorically. They shape me. Does the border change the river or the waterfall? I think it does. But they also change the nature of the border—pun intended.

To Market, to Market

Joseph E. Taylor III

I like to believe that my consumer choices are rational decisions, but somewhere deep down inside I know that they are more like prayers. This is partly because of my work on the Salish Sea, which I can gaze upon from my university office, but my doubts have been honed by my relationship to another inland sea: the San Francisco Bay. I have been immersed in salt water since childhood, but my most instructive interactions have happened recently in a Berkeley fish market. The staff recall an era when buyers and sellers knew each other as neighbours. Their open banter conveys information about the fate of local fish and fishing seasons, and their cases confirm the quality they tout. When my turn comes, a mutual interrogation begins:

"How can I help you?"
"The rockfish looks good, but I have a couple questions."
"Fire away."
"Where was it caught, and is it fresh or fresh frozen?"
"It came out of Bodega. It's probably fresh."

I favour this shop because they handle fish well *and* they openly acknowledge what they do not know. I want to make informed decisions, and nothing irritates me like a seller blowing smoke.

I may be a historian, but I also know fish. Every boyhood summer, my brothers and I feasted on salmon, rockfish, ling cod, crabs, mussels, and clams. We harvested with glee the land and waters around Pacific City, Oregon. We immersed ourselves in the intimate details of nature until our great aunt learned that the Forest Service sprayed the hills with dichlorophenoxyacetic acid and tricholorophenoxyacetic acid, better known as 2,4-D and 2,4,5-T. Unlike Vegas, what happened in the forest did not stay there. Herbicides washed into streams, estuaries, and the sea. The following year we stopped picking marionberries, huckleberries, and blackberries for the same reason, and ever since, I have reflexively thought about the ecology of what I eat.

I also fished commercially. In fact, but for one very bad fishing season and a careening drunk driver, I might have captained a boat in the Bering

Sea. At least, that was my vector until the mid-1980s. Thus I have a peculiar understanding of fish, markets, and sellers. I killed and sold more than my fair share of fish; I know how fishers and merchants handle fish and the truth; and I am fascinated by how persistent organic pollutants (POPs) move through food webs. My knowledge and pickiness probably make me a fish monger's nightmare customer.

Learning that the rockfish was offloaded in Bodega, short for Bodega Bay, raises red flags. Bodega Bay is a lovely town in western Sonoma County. The port is modest, the fishing boats small. The seller is surely correct that the rockfish wasn't flash frozen, because that requires larger ships, but Bodega is hours from Berkeley. Best case scenario: the rockfish was caught yesterday afternoon, so it's been on ice at least twenty-four hours. Most fish flesh needs a day to set, but after three days—which is likely, having come out of Bodega—the flesh will get rubbery. Ironically, Salish Sea markets rely on larger, more distant fleets, so the flesh quality of the flash-frozen fish they sell is more consistent.

More concerning is my suspicion that, because the Bodega fleet is small, captains work the San Francisco Bay plume. The bay is scenic but riddled with Superfund sites. Its waters, sediments, flora, and fauna are laced with 150 years of industrial and military wastes. As with the Salish Sea, locavorism is a marker of poverty and a menu of POPs, heavy metals, and other Very Bad Things. And like forest herbicides, pollutants in the bay flow through the Golden Gate and out onto the fishing grounds of boats from Bodega Bay. One perverse appeal of my Berkeley fish market is that it helps me avoid eating too locally. By contrast I know little about the provenience of fish sold in British Columbia, and the average fish counter, staffed by apathetic attendants and labelled in disingenuous ways, is an ecological black box.

With the rockfish eliminated, I shift my interrogation to a higher-priced choice: "I see the salmon is certified. Do you know which port it came from in Alaska?"

"Port? No, but it's from Bristol."

"Bristol" is Bristol Bay in western Alaska. Local salmon runs are mind-bogglingly large and well managed. These emblems of wild nature mature in the Bering Sea and Alaska gyre and spawn far from industrialization, but they are hardly pure. The mining conglomerate Rio Tinto is proposing a potentially devastating mine near Lake Iliamna, worrying environmentalists about future pollution, but the fish that spawn in Iliamna and the other lakes and streams of Bristol Bay are already compromised. The problem is mercury. While each salmon bioaccumulates only tiny quantities of the heavy metal during its ocean sojourns, collectively the salmon deposit huge amounts in the sediments of lakes where they spawn and die by the millions each year. This mercury is biotransported from the same seas that also nurture salmon from as far away as the Lena, Amur, Fraser, and Columbia Rivers. And like those other watersheds, Bristol Bay's streams and lakes are *natural* toxic dumps, produced by global ecological chains. I favour markets that help me obtain fish from beyond the Salish Sea and San Francisco Bay, but no place stands outside the POP ecosystem.

Certification labels capture none of this complexity. The buying guides of the Blue Ocean Institute, Marine Stewardship Council, and Monterey Bay Aquarium tell us important things about species and stocks, but their information is coarse-grained and their guides are as much about luring consumers as educating them. Moreover, none of these organizations do quality control well. This I learned the hard way. When our daughter was conceived, her mom and I learned to think of wombs as ecosystems, and when our baby was diagnosed with autism and digestive disorders, we learned to patrol what went into her body. We discovered that consumer guides are less useful than medical journals for understanding how POPs bioaccumulate in adipose tissues, cross the placental barrier, and pass to infants through breast milk. We also learned that research published in chemistry and biology journals is far more useful for understanding the nature of the nature we consume than anything gleaned from a pocket guide or phone app.

All this runs through my head as I ponder the sockeye fillet in the display case. "Nothing is perfect," I tell myself. Then I tell the counterperson, "I'll take the salmon." We do the deal, but even this relatively transparent fish market feels a bit like a postindustrial wilderness. Every fish counter contains nature that is simultaneously from nowhere and everywhere, and no consumer has sufficient knowledge. Even my decades of experience on the water and in libraries feels inadequate to parse all the questions that inhere in fish bodies. Even my purchases are acts of faith that transcend empirical evidence. No label or counterperson can tell us all that we need to know when we head to the market.

Leading Waters

NOAH D. HALL

I was born in the Catskill Mountains of upstate New York, a beautiful watershed that was cleared out and reshaped to serve New York City with drinking water. Now it is pristine and protected, and the flooded towns at the bottoms of the reservoirs are history. The landscape has been healed with new forests that provide critical habitat and refuge for urban humans, my family included.

We soon moved just a short distance to the neighbouring Hudson River watershed. My childhood home had a nearby lake—really more of a pond by adult standards, but with plenty of water and shoreline for a small boy to explore and escape in. I swam, lay in the sun, and enjoyed my own thoughts. Adult vacations should be so simple.

I roam. The small lake soon gave way to states, countries, and continents. I moved west, first to Michigan, then Minnesota—Colorado was cool but didn't have much water. Along the way I fell in love with Lake Superior. And it brought me back to Michigan.

For many years I lived a short walk through neighbours' woods to the Huron River, a lovely, peaceful, and sustaining presence. The trails along the river were my daily bread. It is beautiful in all seasons, a perfect Michigan river.

I now live on an island in the Detroit River. It's a powerful body of water and the soul of the Great Lakes. Most nights I sleep on my boat and feel the headwater energy of Superior, Michigan, and Huron flow around me. Canada is south and Lake Erie is downstream. It's an intersection of waters, countries, and commerce, but often I have the place to myself.

I always love the water where I live, and never know where that will be. My favourite home is the beaches and forested shorelines of Vancouver, where the Fraser River meets the Pacific Ocean. Reaching the West Coast, starting from the East Coast, built in Detroit on the way—feels like destiny manifested. It may be a false hope, as with the water cycle, there is no end or final destination. It just comes back around and around. Nature is never finished. Enjoy the ride.

On Frames, Perspectives, and Vanishing Points

Lynne Heasley

When past, present, and future intersect so visually—so unexpectedly and mysteriously—as they did in this astonishing scene on the Escanaba River, you can't help but reflect on the histories that might explain such a place. Here are juxtaposed two companion stories from the same spot on the riverbank. The first, a romantic ruin, succumbing to nature's time—a sublime refuge where trees are powerful over concrete and the divine appears luminous through the clouds of a passing storm. The second, three bridges in human time: a rare lattice truss bridge still carrying iron to Great Lakes steel mills, an abandoned concrete highway, and finally, barely visible in iron shadows, pilings from a long-ago wooden frontier road. Story upon story reconciled for a moment in the layers of a place.

No one viewing the images would imagine the humble scenes outside the frame. To my left, a family fishes off the riverbank. Overhead, my teenage son, Jake, scrambles where train trestle meets land. With each lunge, he looses a small avalanche of stones and taconite iron pellets. My husband, Phillip, stands next to me pointing, and pointing again, to make sure I see the details. The old pilings under the bridge are phenomenal.

And there's Lowell. Lowell circles us. Lowell talks. Lowell brings us a big leaf. Do we know what a buckeye tree is? Yes, I grew up in Ohio, the Buckeye State. Lowell says how unusual it is to have a buckeye tree this far north. Lowell marvels at how much time I spend "to take one picture." Lowell asks Phillip if it's hard to wait so long for one picture. Lowell queries me about my lens, my tripod, the places we've been. Lowell talks.

I get klutzy and frazzled when I can't concentrate. My tripod height is wrong; my graduated neutral density filter isn't level with the horizon; my remote shutter release won't release. Why won't it release? How in the world does our friend Conrad, a landscape painter, paint while people talk to him? How does he paint while I talk to him? I am clearly monophasic—one thing at a time, thank you. In my mind I call Lowell "Lull." The wind

9.6 "American Ruins 1," Escanaba, Michigan, 2011. Concrete remnants of the long-abandoned Bay Shore Road bridge (old U.S. Highway 41 over the Escanaba River). Photo by Lynne Heasley.

9.7 "American Ruins 2," Escanaba, Michigan, 2011. On the left runs the Canadian National Railway bridge over the Escanaba River, one of only two historical lattice truss bridges in Michigan. The company removed and replaced the bridge in 2015. On the right, ruins of the Bay Shore Road bridge jut into the river. Delta County and the U.S. Army Corps of Engineers demolished this bridge in 2015. Photo by Lynne Heasley.

blows the clouds through the scene. They're starting to break. We'll lose this light in minutes. Lowell. Is. Irritating.

But here's the catch: It was Lowell who pointed the way. Lowell, the retiree. Lowell, on his bicycle. Lowell, who saw us driving aimlessly through his remote Escanaba neighbourhood. He pulled beside us and asked if we were lost. No, we were just scouting the Escanaba River. We were looking for industrial history, for maritime history, for hidden waterscapes. (Our son's face at "hidden waterscapes": mute humour perfected.)

"Oh." Lowell paused. Then: "Have you found the fishing spot yet?"

Research, writing, art: capturing data or sentences or scenes sometimes means solitary episodes, blocking out other people. Likewise, no person appears within the frame of these photographs; the visual and intellectual perspectives lead elsewhere. But outside the frame are expanding ripples of "we": a visiting family (us) and their intelligent local guide (Lowell), other families and their fish, and so on, through the relationships that make up a place on the river and a river running into a great lake. Here at the fishing spot is Great Lakes history boiled to an essence. Its stories are our stories, too.

Headwaters of Hope

Dave Dempsey

Growing up in southeast Michigan in the 1960s, I experienced a permeable water border. My parents occasionally chose recreation destinations on the Canadian side of the Detroit River, one day including Point Pelee National Park, jutting into an unexpectedly algae-choked Lake Erie. At age nine, I wasn't thinking about borders that day, but I think I absorbed the notion of a lake bigger than anyone—including nations—in trouble. It wasn't an American or Canadian lake. It was a shared lake.

Even when we didn't cross the boundary, Canada was in our sights. Inexpensive entertainment for a young family subsisting on an assistant professor's salary was watching freighters pass up and down the Detroit River against the backdrop of downtown Windsor, Ontario. You couldn't gaze at those vessels without sensing the role water played in connecting, rather than dividing, nations.

That base in southeast Michigan was also part of a binational cultural ecosystem. At a time when television shaped the world view of many children, I spent countless hours watching Canadian programming. I watched hockey, of course, but also shows aimed at kids. I didn't differentiate these shows from those on American television. I grew up thinking Canadians were friends, people much like us; they just had a few quaint differences like saying "zed" instead of "zee." The border wasn't a technicality, exactly, but it wasn't a fearsome wall—or a moat.

Professionally, the value of those early lessons has persisted. Perhaps the differences between Americans and Canadians are more numerous and subtle than a nine-year-old child can discern, but mutual respect and cooperation spanning the border are real. The water that shapes the border also shapes a shared ethic of water stewardship.

More than water flows along and across the Canada-U.S. border. So does human capital. It is a profound resource and, unlike water, inexhaustible. It is the headwaters of hope for a future of wisely guarded and sustainably used water.

Afterword

Keeping Up the Flow

GRAEME WYNN

My first, perhaps unfathomable, reaction to *Border Flows* was to think of the authors of this diverse set of essays as *mearcstapas*. The term comes from Old English; its most well-known occurrence is probably in *Beowulf*, where it is used to characterize Grendel, the foremost, fearsome antagonist of the hero of that eponymous epic poem. Literally translated as "mark-stepper" (or one who walks borders or boundaries—i.e., "marks"), the word conjures up, for Oxford English scholar John Carey, "a whole way of thinking about territory, and the need to keep safe within it, and what horrors lie beyond it, that no modern word can represent."[1] So, it seemed to me, the essays gathered here provoked new modes of thinking about the extended, discontinuous (and surprisingly fluid) territory marked by the border between Canada and the United States of America. They also pointed, in various ways, to anxieties about security and coexistence, and included more-than-passing reference to once unimagined or blissfully remote, but now all-too-threatening, horrors (such as synthetic chemicals and sea lamprey). But then I recoiled. Grendel, after all, was a monstrous giant shrouded in darkness. Great though their stature may be/come, our authors belie such an association by throwing new light on old questions and taken-for-granted topics.

Boundaries, borders, and borderlands have long been a focus of scholarly interest. Historians, political scientists, sociologists, economists, anthropologists, and others have all had their analytical ways with them.

According to the rather formal language of the *Dictionary of Human Geography*, boundaries are at once both geographical markers and geographical makers of "regulative authority in social relations"; borders are a particular form of boundary associated with the rise of the modern nation-state; and the term "borderlands" connotes the geographical regions surrounding international borders. Further, we are told, "there has been a recent explosion of articles and edited volumes on border-region development that are increasingly attuned to the ways in which such regions make manifest diverse political geographies of reterritorialization." All of which is to say, these brief exegeses continue, that "borderlands provide usefully prismatic lenses on to the changing geography of power in the context of globalization."[2] Looking at these distinctions slightly differently, we might rest content with the view that borders are primarily barriers, or lines of separation and division, whereas borderlands are areas of "exchange, interaction, and integration . . . in which hyphenated identities are allowed to exist and encouraged to flourish."[3]

Yet the world is neither quite as simple nor quite as static as such phrases imply. In Africa, borders drawn through preexisting tribal territories by colonial powers are being re-envisaged to lessen the divisions they created.[4] In a somewhat different vein, leaders of the European Union have recently sought ways to transform the external borders of the EU "from areas of demarcation and division to areas of exchange and interaction" as they wrestle with the challenge of fixing "final frontiers, while preventing future EU borders from becoming hard exclusionary boundaries." Thus, the European Neighbourhood and Partnership Instrument (ENPI) aims both "to promote border security and develop cross-border contacts and cooperation between the enlarged EU and its neighbours."[5]

So too the Canadian-American border ill fits the clean abstractions of dictionary definitions. Since the twentieth century, at least, its location as a line on a map has been settled (except for the still-disputed question about the limits and extent of Canadian sovereignty in high Arctic waters [the Northwest Passage], and a small handful of minor differences such as those over Machias Seal Island—occupied by a Canadian lighthouse but claimed by the United States—and neighbouring North Rock; the Exclusive Economic Zone at the Pacific entrance to the Strait of Juan de Fuca; and Dixon Entrance, regarded by Canada as part of its territorial waters but subject to a middle-water line claim by the United States).

Almost nine thousand kilometres in length, this Can-Am line was touted, for decades, as the longest undefended border in the world. Indeed, a 2005 volume written by John Bukowczyk, Nora Faires, David Smith, and Randy Widdis announced in its title the existence of a "permeable border" and treated the Great Lakes Basin between 1650 and 1990 as a transnational region.[6] A decade after the book's publication, however, such assertions have been rendered questionable by the events of September 11, 2001—and the subsequently heightened concern of U.S. officials about "homeland security"—which reduced both the porosity of the border and the postnational optimism that seized the minds of some North Americans a quarter century ago.

Against this backdrop, the doubled meaning of the title *Border Flows* gains both clarity and significance. This book is a self-declared environmental history of water along the border between Canada and the United States, but it is also an exploration of transboundary flows—flows of people, ideas, animals, objects, and power (in both political and energetic senses)—across the borderland. As Heasley and Macfarlane point out, the borderline between Canada and the United States is remarkably fluid—in the sense that a considerable part of it is drawn on water rather than land, and because it is crossed, ignored, transcended, and contested in a variety of ways that defy its conceptualization as an immutable object. By focusing their concerns upon the watery sections of this boundary, contributors to this volume enhance and add nuance to our understanding of considerable parts of the North American continent, even as they broaden the compass of environmental historical scholarship.

The international boundary at the heart of this book is, of course, a jurisdictional tangle. Eight Canadian provinces and territories and thirteen American states share the line. Well over 2,000 kilometres of Alaska, Ontario, and British Columbia abut foreign country; Michigan and Yukon count about 1,200 kilometres in this category; Maine, Minnesota, and Montana face Canada for 800 to 1,000 kilometres; and Quebec shares approximately 800 kilometres of its perimeter with the United States. At the other end of the scale, New Hampshire, Idaho, and Pennsylvania are each involved with their northern neighbour for less than 100 kilometres. These simple metrics suggest a certain complexity, but at one level they are straightforward and mean only that different legal systems prevail across space. So highway speed limits may vary north and south of the international boundary. So American teenagers anxious to celebrate their birthdays with a beer can do so legally at age eighteen in Alberta, Manitoba, and Quebec but need to wait another year to slake their thirst if they cross into Saskatchewan or Ontario, and two more after that if they remain stateside. And woe betide the twenty-year-old British Columbian in a Washington State campground who unthinkingly opens an ale at the end of the day, as he might do at home. Such things are clear, and humans adapt to them more or less easily.

Things get much more complicated when nonhuman nature is introduced into the picture. As several chapters in this collection show, birds, deer, wolves, fish, wind, and fire don't read boundary markers and are not, for the most part, subject to legal restraint. But human interactions with "wild nature" are often governed by laws (those governing hunting seasons, permitting logging or mining, or restricting the catch if contaminant levels exceed certain thresholds, for example), and competing sovereignties and the strongly defended rights of provinces/states have often conspired against unified, consistent management of the nonhuman. History tells us that boundaries are often-contested human constructs, nature reminds us that human efforts to organize and manage the world are constrained, and *Border Flows* assists variously in identifying the challenges that result, in understanding our human capacities to respond to them, and in recognizing those particular conjunctures of circumstances that enable divides (between jurisdictions, interests, humans, and nonhumans) to be bridged in ways that sustain rather than destroy Earth's productivity and potential.

The essays in this book do much to sharpen appreciation and deepen understanding of core themes identified in the introduction: "binational conflict and cooperation; water governance and control of natural resources; ecological impacts on economy and politics (and vice versa); multiple identities; a sense of place." Measured against earlier efforts to essay the border—or parts thereof—these contributions stand out in many ways. Sensitive to the give-and-take of politics and the tensions between national autonomy and shared interests, this volume is as bright day to the dark night of mid-twentieth-century portrayals of Canada as a quaint and trivial American frontier in a string of movies characterized as "Northerns." In this genre, argues Richard Baker, "the line separating Canada from the U.S. fades beneath the furtive skulk of stealthy criminals and the frantic passing of galloping cowboys."[7] Attentive to ecological questions, these essays carry discussion of the border into realms untilled by works such as the aforementioned *Permeable Border* that emphasize the twinned themes of nation building and capital formation. With case studies ranged along the Canada-U.S. line (including its Arctic reaches), *Border Flows* has a broader, inherently more comparative, spatial scope than John Riley's *The Once and Future Great Lakes Country*, which offers a detailed history of the environment and environmental change in that area through five hundred years.[8] Although there are inevitably some points of substantive overlap between these two volumes—between Langston's chapter "Resiliency and Collapse" and Riley's "Invasives" (nicely subtitled "The Unintended Consequences of the Uninvited"), for example—most of the essays in *Border Flows* draw upon the perspectives of political ecology and consistently espouse a more critical analytical approach than is offered in Riley's pages. And if Riley's recollections of his own roles as resident and conservation worker in Ontario add an important sense of place to his account, this effect is achieved in multiple ways in the reflections that constitute the fourth section of *Border Flows*.

Reading, and learning, from *Border Flows* in the drought-afflicted western North American summer of 2015, when every forest fire seems to be attributed to climate change and people grumble about not being allowed to wash their sport-utility vehicles, I am inclined to ask, along with Swarthmore professor and environmental activist Giovanna Di Chiro, whether "our environmental imaginations [are] robust or capacious enough to grasp an understanding of the 'close to home' issues affecting daily life (i.e. the 'local scale' comprising our neighbourhoods, families, children) while conceiving of the 'global scale' concerns of the earth and its systems and processes (including big issues like global warming and climate change, problems that can seem overly abstract, distant, and perhaps too big to comprehend)."[9] After years of being encouraged to think globally and act locally, many people still find it difficult to think and act across the range of scales, or to develop the sort of scale-crossing environmental consciousness upon which effective responses to the environmental challenges that now confront us must depend.

This, I think, is why the sort of thoughtful, intelligent, tightly focused, border-straddling, scale-shifting analysis on display in these pages is both helpful and hopeful in pointing a way forward. Although the chapters in this volume focus, legitimately and usefully, on various aspects of border flows, climate change runs through them as a subtext, precisely because it stands to influence so many of the specific themes discussed in this book—including, as James W. Feldman summarizes them, "border ecologies, invasive species, blowdowns, [and] fire management." The editors raise the spectre of climate change in their introductory discussion of abundance and scarcity and when they discern an emergent Pan-American narrative of water shortages. Other chapters include allusions to the possible implications of northward-moving biomes, melting polar ice caps, and the pipelines that carry oil from Canadian wells (and "fields") to American refineries (and automobiles). All, importantly, are anchored in specific times and places, deal with particular thematic concerns, and range collectively across scales. Together they constitute, to borrow a luminous phrase from Lynne Heasley's luminous reflection, "story upon story reconciled for a moment in the layers of a place." Ignore for the moment that that place—the border—is attenuated, diverse, and fluid (and thus rather unplace-like), and savour the accomplishment of this collection: taken as a whole (and especially if we attend to "the humble scenes outside the frame," as Heasley encourages us to do), these essays lead us to think anew about our place in the world.

Borders generally set things apart. In days of old, parishioners used to beat the bounds of *their* ecclesiastical domain. Today, we divide *our* property from both public space and the private holdings of neighbours with picket fences, hedges, or walls. We describe those who cross borders to enter our territory as "come-from-aways," "foreigners," or "aliens" depending upon the importance attached to the boundary they transgress. Nine thousand kilometres of international boundary separate *my* Canadian home from American space. But half the contributors to this book would reverse that assertion. Still, we rarely think of the border between Canada and the United States as a fence or a wall. The international boundary is a line (or more accurately a number of lines) on a map, made material along parts of its length by border-crossing posts, linear clearcuts in the forest, motion-detection sensors, and the like, but impossible to see on the lakes and unmarked and invisible in many remote areas. A library and opera house, a tavern, and several homes straddle the border between Quebec and neighbouring states. Half a dozen airports—legacies of a diplomatic manoeuvre to facilitate the transfer of military aircraft under the Lend-Lease Program early in World War II—also stand astride the line.

This boundary is more complicated, and fluid, than mere semantics might suggest. The Peace Arch border crossing in British Columbia bears two inscriptions: on the American side, "Children of a common mother"; on the Canadian, "Brethren dwelling together in unity." The saccharin sentiments seem dated, but at base they imply that the Earth, north and south, is part of the family home, and they remind us that we share responsibility for its stewardship.

So, in their various ways, do many of the chapters in this volume, by detailing the negotiations, treaties, disputes, resolutions, and compromises that have addressed the selfsame challenge of figuring out how Americans and Canadians might live together, and mutually beneficially, in and across the liminal space of the international boundary. Perhaps we need to recalibrate our sense of borders as dividers. Changing scale can help in this. Let us, in conclusion, narrow our gaze to think not (at least directly) of nine thousand kilometres of international borderline, but of another form of boundary: the stone walls that marked the perimeter of many a New England farm in decades gone by. And let us follow the inspired lead, in this, of legal/environmental scholar Eric Freyfogle, by summoning that great American poet and chronicler of everyday experience, Robert Frost, as our guide.[10]

Frost's "Mending Wall" is "a narrative poem about boundaries and walls in nature, culture, and the human mind."[11] It tells of the spring ritual when two farmers meet at their shared boundary, at an hour previously agreed upon, each to walk his side of the wall and repair, in tandem, the ravages of time, nature, and other humans. Its most well-known line, the only utterance of the dour member of the toiling pair, is now a mantra repeated almost unthinkingly: "Good fences make good neighbors." But the second farmer thinks more than this. Musing about the gaps that appear in the wall each spring, some so wide that "even two can pass abreast," though "No one has seen them made or heard them made," he wonders at their cause and more fundamentally about the very purpose of the wall itself. "Walls make sense when there are cows," he says, but these neighbouring farms have no stock. "He is all pine and I am apple orchard. / My apple trees will never get across / And eat the cones under his pines." Hunters have no use for walls, and pull stone from stone to "have the rabbit out of hiding, / To please the yelping dogs." Would it not be sensible, the narrator wonders, to know what needed to be walled in or out, and to whom the building of a wall "was like to give offense," before erecting (or maintaining) one. Clearly, the springtime ritual of picking up and re-emplacing the fallen stones suggests that there is "Something . . . that doesn't love a wall, / That wants it down"; the likeliest of culprits in the mind of the narrator is nature, which "sends the frozen-ground-swell under it, / And spills the upper boulders in the sun." But, equally, the annual continuation of the rebuilding ritual suggests a very human need for boundaries and the importance of custom and cooperation in maintaining them.

This wonderfully insightful and provocative poem raises enduring questions about living on the land, boundary making, and territoriality. For Freyfogle it forces us to think "about why we like walls so much and how they reflect and shape who we are."[12] Frost's vignette of a quotidian event in backcountry New England resonates with tension—between accepting tradition and questioning it; between individual and community; between freedom and solidarity; between the human need for boundaries and the unboundedness of nature. But these oppositional pairings are not the proprietary possessions of the poet or the region. Switch scale and registers once more, from orchard edge to international boundary and from "Mending Wall" to *Border Flows*, and find their echoes in the pages of the latter. We have heard the "good fences make good neighbors" adage invoked several times in reference to the Canadian-American boundary over the years, but the contributors to this volume are the antithesis of Frost's dour farmer who owns those words and "moves in darkness as it seems to me, / Not of woods only and the shade of trees." They lead us to think again, and more deeply, about the lines that divide, the things that bring us together, and the nature that we residents of Canada and the United States share as North Americans. I was indeed mistaken about Grendel. The contributors to this collection are less *mearcstapas* than *tidfaran*, or [border-crossing] travellers whose time has come.

Notes

1. John Carey, *The Unexpected Professor: An Oxford Life in Books* (London: Faber & Faber, 2014), 103.

2. *The Dictionary of Human Geography*, 5th ed., ed. Derek Gregory et al. (Chichester, UK: Wiley Blackwell, 2009), s.vv. "border," "borderlands," "boundary," by Matthew Sparke.

3. Michele Comelli, Ettore Greco, and Nathalie Tocci, "From Boundary to Borderland: Transforming the Meaning of Borders through the European Neighbourhood Policy," *European Foreign Affairs Review* 12, no. 2 (2007): 204.

4. K. Bennafla, "Les frontières africaines: Nouvelles significations, nouveaux enjeux," *Bulletin de l'association de géographes français* 79, no. 2 (2002): 134–46.

5. Comelli, Greco, and Tocci, "From Boundary to Borderland," 208.

6. John J. Bukowczyk et al., *Permeable Border: The Great Lakes Basin as Transnational Region, 1650-1990* (Pittsburgh: University of Pittsburgh Press, 2005).

7. Richard G. Baker, "'Nothing But Hill and Hollow': The Canadian Border as American Frontier in the Hollywood Northern," *Comparative American Studies* 13, no. 1–2 (2015): 114.

8. John Riley, *The Once and Future Great Lakes Country: An Ecological History* (Montreal: McGill-Queen's University Press, 2013).

9. Giovanna Di Chiro, "Climate Justice Now! Imagining Grassroots Ecocosmopolitanism," in *American Studies, Ecocriticism, and Citizenship: Thinking and Acting in the Local and Global Commons*, ed. Joni Adamson and Kimberly N. Ruffin (New York: Routledge, 2013), 206.

10. Eric T. Freyfogle, "Bounded People, Boundless Lands," in *Stewardship across Boundaries*, ed. Richard L. Knight and Peter B. Landres (Washington, DC: Island, 1998), 15–38; Eric T. Freyfogle, *Bounded People, Boundless Lands: Envisioning a New Land Ethic* (Washington, DC: Island, 1998), 3–6.

11. Freyfogle, "Bounded People, Boundless Lands," 15. See Robert Frost, "Mending Wall," in *The Poetry of Robert Frost*, ed. Edward Connery Lathem (New York: Holt, Rinehart & Winston, 1969), 33–34.

12. Freyfogle, "Bounded People, Boundless Lands," 17.

Further Reading

I. Archival Collections

Bennett, W.A.C., Fonds. F-55. Simon Fraser University Archives, Burnaby, BC.

Bragdon, John S., Records. Staff Files: St. Lawrence Seaway. Dwight D. Eisenhower Presidential Library and Archives, Abilene, KS.

State Department Central Files. RG 59. National Archives and Records Administration (NARA) II, College Park, MD.

Fulton, E. Davie, Fonds. Library and Archives Canada, Ottawa.

International Joint Commission. Dockets 51R, 55R, 64R, 68A. Accessed August 17, 2016. http://www.ijc.org/en_/Dockets.

Keenleyside, Hugh L., Fonds. Library and Archives Canada, Ottawa.

Mitchell, David, Fonds. F-56. Simon Fraser University Archives, Burnaby, BC.

Records of the Department of External Affairs. Series 1268-A-40, Government of Canada, RG 25. Library and Archives Canada, Ottawa.

St. Lawrence Power Project Series. Hydro-Electric Power Commission of Ontario (HEPCO) Archives, Toronto.

II. Printed Primary Sources and Government Documents

Am. Iron & Steel Inst. v. EPA, 115 F.3d 979, 1001 (D.C. Cir. 1996).

Arctic Environmental Protection Strategy, June 14, 1991. Rovaniemi, Finland.

Boundary Waters Treaty. United States–Great Britain (for Canada). January 11, 1909. Temp. State Dept. No. 548, 36 Stat. 2448.

Canada. Department of External Affairs. *The Columbia River Treaty and Protocol: A Presentation*. Ottawa: Queen's Printer, 1964.

Canada. Parliament. House of Commons. *Debates*, 22nd/24th/26th Parl. (1954–1963).

Canadian Territorial Sea and Fishing Zones Act, S.C. 1964, c. 22.

Cavell, Janice, ed. *Documents on Canadian External Relations, 1960*. Vol. 27. Ottawa: Foreign Affairs and International Trade Canada, 2007.

Council of Great Lakes Governors. *The Great Lakes Charter Annex: A Supplementary Agreement to the Great Lakes Charter*. June 18, 2001. http://www.cglslgp.org/media/1369/greatlakescharterannex.pdf.

Council of Great Lakes Governors. *The Great Lakes Charter: Principles for the Management of Great Lakes Water Resources*. February 11, 1985. http://www.greatlakes.org/Document.Doc?id=148.

Delaware River Basin Compact, 75 Stat. 688 (1961).

Grannemann, N.G. (2000). *The Importance of Ground Water in the Great Lakes Region*. U.S. Geological Survey Water Resources Investigations Report No. 00-4008. Washington, DC: U.S. Geological Survey.

Great Lakes Basin Compact. Pub. L. No. 90-419, 82 Stat. 414 (1968).

Great Lakes–St. Lawrence River Basin Sustainable Water Resources Agreement. December 13, 2005. http://www.glslcompactcouncil.org/Docs/Agreements/Great%20Lakes-St%20Lawrence%20River%20Basin%20Sustainable%20Water%20Resources%20Agreement.pdf.

Great Lakes–St. Lawrence River Basin Water Resources Compact. December 13, 2005. http://www.glslcompactcouncil.org/Docs/Agreements/Great%20Lakes-St%20Lawrence%20River%20Basin%20Water%20Resources%20Compact.pdf.

Great Lakes Water Quality Agreement. Canada–United States. April 15, 1972. 23 U.S.T. 301; amended November 22, 1978, 30 U.S.T. 1383; amended November 18, 1987, T.I.A.S. No. 11551.

International Joint Commission. *The IJC and the 21st Century*. Washington and Ottawa: International Joint Commission, 1997.

International Joint Commission. *Ninth Biennial Report on Great Lakes Water Quality: Perspective and Orientation*. Washington and Ottawa: International Joint Commission, 1998.

International Joint Commission. *Pollution of Lake Erie, Lake Ontario and the International Section of the St. Lawrence River*. Washington and Ottawa: International Joint Commission, 1964.

International Joint Commission. *Protection of the Waters of the Great Lakes: Final Report to the Governments of Canada and the United States*. Washington and Ottawa: International Joint Commission, 2000.

Kansas v. Colorado, 206 U.S. 46 (1907).

New Jersey v. New York, 283 U.S. 336 (1931).

Susquehanna River Basin Compact, 84 Stat. 1509 (1970).

United States Army Corps of Engineers. *Six-State High Plains Ogallala Aquifer Regional Resources Study: Summary Report*. Washington, DC: U.S. Army Corps of Engineers, Southwestern Division, 1982.

United States Coast Guard. *U.S. Coast Guard Polar Operations: Report to Congress*. Washington, DC: U.S. Coast Guard, 2008.

United States Congress. *Estimate of Cost of Examinations, Etc., of Streams Where Power Development Appears Feasible*. 69th Cong., 1st Sess., House Document 308. Statement of Dwight F. Davis, secretary of war and chairman of Federal Power Commission, April 12, 1926.

United States. Department of State. *Foreign Relations of the United States, 1958–1960, Western European Integration and Security, Canada*. Vol. 7, part 1. Edited by Ronald D. Landa, James E. Miller, David S. Patterson, and Charles S. Sampson. Washington, DC: Government Printing Office, 1993.

United States. Department of State. *Foreign Relations of the United States, 1969-1976*. Vol. E-1, *Documents on Global Issues, 19691972*. Edited by Susan K. Holly and William B. McAllister. Washington, DC: Government Printing Office, 2005.

Water Resources Development Act, Pub. L. No. 99-662, § 1109, 100 Stat. 4082 (1986). Codified as amended at 42 U.S.C. § 1962d-20.

Water Resources Development Act, Pub. L. No. 106-541, § 504, 114 Stat. 2572 (2000). Codified as amended at 42 U.S.C. § 1962d-20(b)(2).

Wisconsin v. Illinois, 278 U.S. 367 (1929).

Wisconsin v. Illinois, 281 U.S. 179 (1930).

Wisconsin v. Illinois, 281 U.S. 696 (1930).

Wisconsin v. Illinois, 289 U.S. 395 (1933).

Wisconsin v. Illinois, 388 U.S. 426 (1967).

Wisconsin v. Illinois, 449 U.S. 48 (1980).

III. Secondary Sources

Agnew, J.C. "No Borders, No Nations: Making Greece in Macedonia." *Annals of the Association of American Geographers* 97, no. 2 (2007): 398–422.

Agnew, J.C. "The Territorial Trap: The Geographical Assumptions of International Relations Theory." *Review of International Political Economy* 1, no. 1 (1994): 53–80.

Aitken, Hugh G.J. *American Capital and Canadian Resources.* Cambridge, MA: Harvard University Press, 1961.

Alexander, Jeff. *Pandora's Locks: The Opening of the Great Lakes–St. Lawrence Seaway.* East Lansing: Michigan State University Press, 2009.

Annin, Peter. *The Great Lakes Water Wars.* Washington, DC: Island, 2006.

Armstrong, Christopher, H.V. Nelles, and Matthew Evenden. *The River Returns: An Environmental History of the Bow.* Montreal: McGill-Queen's University Press, 2009.

Arnold, Samantha. "Nelvana of the North, Traditional Knowledge, and the Northern Dimension of Canadian Foreign Policy." *Canadian Foreign Policy Journal* 14, no. 2 (2008); published online 14 March 2011: 95–107.

Azzi, Stephen. *Walter Gordon and the Rise of Canadian Nationalism.* Montreal: McGill-Queen's University Press, 1999.

Bakker, Karen, ed. *Eau Canada: The Future of Canada's Water.* Vancouver: UBC Press, 2006.

Beck, R.E. *Waters and Water Rights.* Newark, NJ: LexisNexis, 2006.

Becker, William H. *From the Atlantic to the Great Lakes: A History of the U.S. Army Corps of Engineers and the St. Lawrence Seaway.* Washington, DC: U.S. Army Corps of Engineers, 1984.

Behiels, Michael, and Reginald Stuart, eds. *Transnationalism: Canada–United States History into the Twenty-First Century.* Montreal: McGill-Queen's University Press, 2010.

Belfield, Robert. "Technology Transfer and Turbulence: The Evolution of an International Energy Complex at Niagara Falls, 1896–1906." *HSTC Bulletin: Journal of the History of Canadian Science, Technology and Medicine* 5, no. 2(18) (1981): 69–98.

Berton, Pierre. *Niagara: A History of the Falls*. Albany: State University of New York Press, 1992.

Billington, David P., and Donald C. Jackson. *Big Dams of the New Deal Era: A Confluence of Engineering and Politics*. Norman: University of Oklahoma Press, 2006.

Blomquist, William, and Edella Schlager. "Political Pitfalls of Integrated Watershed Management." *Society and Natural Resources* 18, no. 2 (2005): 101–17.

Bloomfield, L.M., and Gerald F. Fitzgerald, *Boundary Waters Problems of Canada and the United States: The International Joint Commission, 1912–1958*. Toronto: Carswell, 1958.

Bocking, Stephen. "Fishing the Inland Seas: Great Lakes Research, Fisheries Management, and Environmental Policy in Ontario." *Environmental History* 2, no. 1 (1997): 52–73.

Bogue, Margaret Beattie. *Fishing the Great Lakes: An Environmental History, 1783–1933*. Madison: University of Wisconsin Press, 2000.

Borre, L., D.R. Barker, and L.E. Duker. "Institutional Arrangements for Managing the Great Lakes of the World: Results of a Workshop on Implementing the Watershed Approach." *Lakes and Reservoirs: Research and Management* 6, no. 3 (2001): 199–209.

Botts, Lee, and Paul Muldoon. *Evolution of the Great Lakes Water Quality Agreements*. East Lansing: Michigan State University Press, 2005.

Bourassa, Robert. *Power from the North*. Toronto: Prentice-Hall, 1985.

Boyer, Marcel. *L'exportation d'eau douce pour le développement de l'or bleu québécois*. Montreal: Les Cahiers de recherche de l'Institut économique de Montréal, 2008. http://www.iedm.org/files/cahier0808_fr.pdf.

Bratspies, Rebecca M., and Russell A. Miller, eds. *Transboundary Harm in International Law: Lessons from the* Trail Smelter *Arbitration*. Cambridge: Cambridge University Press, 2006.

Bukowczyk, John J., Nora Faires, David Smith, and Randy Widdis. *Permeable Border: The Great Lakes Basin as Transnational Region, 1650–1990*. Pittsburgh: University of Pittsburgh Press, 2005.

Bunting, Robert. *The Pacific Raincoast: Environment and Culture in an American Eden, 1778–1900*. Lawrence: University Press of Kansas, 1997.

Byers, Michael, and Suzanne Lalonde. "Who Controls the Northwest Passage?" *Vanderbilt Journal of Transnational Law* 42, no. 2 (2009): 1161–70.

Cain, Louis P. "Unfouling the Public's Nest: Chicago's Sanitary Diversion of Lake Michigan Water." *Technology and Culture* 15, no. 4 (1974): 594–613.

Cavell, Janice. "'A Little More Latitude': Explorers, Politicians and Canadian Arctic Policy during the Laurier Era." *Polar Record* 47, no. 243 (2011): 289–309.

Cavell, Janice. "The True Northwest Passage: Explorers in Anglo-Canadian Nationalist Narratives." *The Northern Review*, no. 32 (2010): 5–34.

Chacko, Chirakaikaran Joseph. *The International Joint Commission between the United States of America and the Dominion of Canada*. New York: AMS Press, 1968.

Chevrier, Lionel. *The St. Lawrence Seaway*. Toronto: Macmillan, 1959.

Chiarappa, Michael, and Kristing M. Szylvian. *Fish for All: An Oral History of Multiple Claims and Divided Sentiment on Lake Michigan*. Lansing: Michigan State University Press, 2003.

Clamen, Murray, and Daniel Macfarlane. "The International Joint Commission, Water Levels, and Transboundary Governance in the Great Lakes." *Review of Policy Research* 32, no. 1 (2015): 40–59.

Clark-Jones, Melissa. *A Staple State: Canadian Industrial Resources in Cold War*. Toronto: University of Toronto Press, 1987.

Coates, Ken, and John Findlay, eds. *Parallel Destinies: Canadian-American Relations West of the Rockies*. Seattle: University of Washington Press, 2002.

Coen, Russ. *Breaking Ice for Arctic Oil: The Epic Voyage of the SS* Manhattan *through the Northwest Passage*. Fairbanks: University of Alaska Press, 2012.

Cohen, Alice. "Rescaling Environmental Governance: Watersheds as Boundary Objects at the Intersection of Science, Neoliberalism, and Participation." *Environment and Planning A* 44, no. 9 (2012): 2207–24.

Cohen, Alice, and Seanna Davidson. "The Watershed Approach: Challenges, Antecedents, and the Transition from Technical Tool to Governance Unit." *Water Alternatives* 4, no. 1 (2011): 521–34.

Cold-Ravnkilde, Signe Marie, Jaidev Singh, and Robert G. Lee, "Cascadia: The (Re)Construction of a Bi-National Space and Its Residents," *Journal of Borderlands Studies* 19, no. 1 (2004): 59–77.

Conca, Ken. *Governing Water: Contentious Transnational Politics and Global Institution Building*. Cambridge, MA: MIT Press, 2006.

Conway, Kyle, and Timothy Pasch, eds. *Beyond the Border: Tensions across the 49th Parallel in the Great Plains and Prairies*. Montreal: McGill-Queen's University Press, 2013.

Cosens, Barbara. *The Columbia River Treaty Revisited: Transboundary River Governance in the Face of Uncertainty*. Corvallis: Oregon State University Press, 2012.

Cox, Thomas R. *The Lumberman's Frontier: Three Centuries of Land Use, Society, and Change in America's Forests*. Corvallis: Oregon State University Press, 2010.

Creighton, Donald. *The Empire of the St. Lawrence*. Toronto: Macmillan of Canada, 1956.

Crosby, Alfred W., Jr. *Ecological Imperialism: The Biological Expansion of Europe, 900–1900*. New York: Cambridge University Press, 1986.

Day, J.C., and Frank Quinn. "Water Diversion and Export: Learning from the Canadian Experience." Department of Geography Publication Series No. 36, University of Waterloo, 1992.

Delaney, Jason M., and Michael Whitby. "'The Very Image of a Man of the Arctic': Commodore O.C.S. Robertson." *Canadian Naval Review* 4, no. 4 (2009): 25–29.

Dellapenna, J.W. "Interstate Struggles over Rivers: The Southeastern States and the Struggle over the 'Hooch.'" *NYU Environmental Law Journal* 12 (2005): 828–900.

Dempsey, Dave. *Great Lakes for Sale: From Whitecaps to Bottlecaps*. Ann Arbor: University of Michigan Press, 2008.

Dempsey, Dave. *On the Brink: The Great Lakes in the 21st Century*. East Lansing: Michigan State University Press, 2004.

Denison, M. *The People's Power: The History of Ontario Hydro*. Toronto: McClelland & Stewart, 1960.

Dennis, Jerry. *The Windward Shore: A Winter on the Great Lakes*. Ann Arbor: University of Michigan Press, 2012.

Dietrich, William. *Northwest Passage: The Great Columbia River*. New York: Simon & Schuster, 1995.

Donaghy, Greg. *Tolerant Allies: Canada and the United States, 1963–1968*. Montreal: McGill-Queen's University Press, 2002.

Douglas, Daniel. *Northern Algoma: A People's History*. Toronto: Dundurn, 1996.

Dreisziger, Nandor Alexandre Fred. "The International Joint Commission of the United States and Canada, 1895–1920: A Study in Canadian-American Relations" PhD diss., University of Toronto, 1974.

Dubinsky, Karen. *The Second Greatest Disappointment: Honeymooners, Heterosexuality, and the Tourist Industry at Niagara Falls*. Toronto: Between the Lines, 1999.

English, John. *The Life of Lester Pearson*. Vol. 2, *Worldly Years, 1949–1972*. Toronto: Lester & Orpen Dennys, 1992.

Evans, Sterling, ed. *The Borderlands of the American and Canadian Wests: Essays on Regional History of the Forty-Ninth Parallel*. Lincoln: University of Nebraska Press, 2006.

Evans, Sterling. *Bound in Twine: The History and Ecology of the Henequen-Wheat Complex for Mexico and the American and Canadian Plains, 1880–1950*. College Station: Texas A&M Press, 2007.

Evenden, Matthew. *Allied Power: Mobilizing Hydro-Electricity during Canada's Second World War*. Toronto: University of Toronto Press, 2015.

Evenden, Matthew. *Fish versus Power: An Environmental History of the Fraser River*. New York: Cambridge University Press, 2007.

Evenden, Matthew. "Mobilizing Rivers: Hydro-Electricity, the State, and World War II in Canada." *Annals of the Association of American Geographers* 99, no. 5 (2009): 845–55.

Evenden, Matthew, and Graeme Wynn. "Fifty-Four, Forty, or Fight? Writing within and across Boundaries in North American Environmental History." In *Nature's End: History and the Environment*, edited by Sverker Sörlin and Paul Warde, 215–46. New York: Palgrave Macmillan, 2009.

Eyre, Kenneth C. "Forty Years of Military Activity in the Canadian North, 1947–1987." *Arctic* 40, no. 4 (1987): 292–99.

Feldman, James W., and Lynne Heasley. "Re-centering North American Environmental History." *Environmental History* 12, no. 4 (2007): 951–58

Ficken, Robert E. *Rufus Woods, the Columbia River, and the Building of Modern Washington*. Pullman: Washington State University Press, 1995.

Finley, Carmel. *All the Fish in the Sea: Maximum Sustainable Yield and the Failure of Fisheries Management*. Chicago: University of Chicago Press, 2011.

Flader, Susan. *The Great Lakes Forest: An Environmental and Social History*. Minneapolis: University of Minnesota Press, 1983.

Fleming, Donald. *So Very Near: The Political Memoirs of the Hon. Donald M. Fleming*. Vol. 2, *The Summit Years*. Toronto: McClelland & Stewart, 1985.

Fletcher, Thomas H. *From Love Canal to Environmental Justice: The Politics of Hazardous Waste on the Canada-U.S. Border*. Peterborough, ON: Broadview, 2003.

Forest, Benjamin, and Patrick Forest. "Engineering the North American Waterscape: The High Modernist Mapping of Continental Water Transfer Projects." *Political Geography* 31, no. 3 (2012): 167–83.

Forest, Patrick, and Frank Quinn. "Quebec's Northern Waters: Export Opportunity or Illusion?" Munk School Briefings No. 16, Munk School of Global Affairs, University of Toronto, 2011.

Froschauer, Karl. *White Gold: Hydroelectric Power in Canada*. Vancouver: UBC Press, 1999.

Gibbs, Lois Marie. *Love Canal*. Albany: State University of New York Press, 1982.

Gingras, Pierre. *L'eau du Nord: Un projet réaliste, durable et rentable pour exploiter l'or bleu du Québec*. Montreal: Marcel Broquet, 2010.

Gordon, Walter. *Walter Gordon: A Political Memoir*. Toronto: McClelland & Stewart, 1977.

Grant, Shelagh. *Sovereignty or Security: Government Policy in the Canadian North, 1936–1950*. Vancouver: UBC Press, 1988.

Griffin, C.B. "Watershed Councils: An Emerging Form of Public Participation in Natural Resource Management." *Journal of the American Water Resources Association* 35, no. 3 (1999): 505–18.

Griffiths, Franklin, ed. *Politics of the Northwest Passage*. Montreal: McGill-Queen's University Press, 1987.

Hall, Noah D. "Toward a New Horizontal Federalism: Interstate Water Management in the Great Lakes Basin." *University of Colorado Law Review* 77 (2006): 405–56.

Hall, Noah D. "Transboundary Pollution: Harmonizing International and Domestic Law." *University of Michigan Journal of Law Reform*, 40 (2007): 681–746.

Harden, Blaine. *A River Lost: The Life and Death of the Columbia*. New York: W.W. Norton, 1996.

Harmon, Alexandra. "Lines in Sand: Shifting Boundaries between Indians and Non-Indians in the Puget Sound Region." *Western Historical Quarterly* 26, no. 4 (1995): 428–53.

Harmon, Alexandra, ed. *The Power of Promises: Rethinking Indian Treaties in the Pacific Northwest*. Seattle: University of Washington Press, 2008.

Harris, Douglas C. *Landing Native Fisheries: Indian Reserves and Fishing Rights in British Columbia, 1849-1925*. Vancouver: UBC Press, 2008.

Harris, Douglas C. *Making Native Space: Colonialism, Resistance, and Reserves in British Columbia*. Vancouver: UBC Press, 2004.

Hartig, John H. *Burning Rivers: Revival of Four Urban-Industrial Rivers that Caught On Fire*. Burlington, ON: Ecovision World Monograph Series, 2010.

Head, Ivan, and Pierre Trudeau. *The Canadian Way: Shaping Canada's Foreign Policy, 1968-1984*. Toronto: McClelland & Stewart, 1995.

Heeney, A.D.P., and Livingston T. Merchant. *Canada and the United States: Principles for Partnership*. Ottawa: R. Duhamel, Queen's Printer, 1965.

Heeney, Arnold. *The Things That Are Caesar's: Memoirs of a Canadian Public Servant*. Edited by Brian D. Heeney. Toronto: University of Toronto Press, 1972.

Higgins, Larratt. "The Columbia River Treaty: A Critical View." *International Journal* 16, no. 4 (1961): 399-404.

High, Steven C. *Industrial Sunset: The Making of North America's Rustbelt, 1969-1984*. Toronto: University of Toronto Press, 2003.

Hilborn, Ray, and Ulrike Hilborn. *Overfishing: What Everyone Needs to Know*. Toronto: Oxford University Press, 2012.

Hilliker, John, and Donald Barry. *Canada's Department of External Affairs*. Vol. 2, *Coming of Age, 1946-1968*. Montreal: McGill-Queen's University Press, 1995.

Hills, Theo L. *The St. Lawrence Seaway*. London: Methuen, 1959.

Hirt, Paul. *The Wired Northwest: The History of Electric Power, 1870s-1970s*. Lawrence: University Press of Kansas, 2012.

Hughes, Thomas P. *Networks of Power: Electrification in Western Society, 1880-1930*. Baltimore: Johns Hopkins University Press, 1983.

Innis, Harold A. *The Fur Trade in Canada: An Introduction to Canadian Economic History*. Toronto: University of Toronto Press, 1930.

Irwin, William. *The New Niagara: Tourism, Technology, and the Landscape of Niagara Falls*. University Park: Pennsylvania State University Press, 1996.

Jackson, John N. *The Welland Canals and Their Communities: Engineering, Industrial, and Urban Transformation*. Toronto: University of Toronto Press, 1997.

Jackson, John N., with John Burtniak and Gregory P. Stein. *The Mighty Niagara: One River—Two Frontiers*. Amherst, NY: Prometheus, 2003.

Jenish, D'arcy. *St. Lawrence Seaway: Fifty Years and Counting.* Manotick, ON: Penumbra, 2009.

Johnson, Benjamin, and Andrew Graybill, eds. *Bridging National Borders in North America: Transnational and Comparative Histories.* Durham: Duke University Press, 2010.

Jordan, F.J.E. "Great Lakes Pollution: A Framework for Action." *Ottawa Law Review* 5 (1971): 65–83.

Keeling, Arn. "Sink or Swim: Water Pollution and Environmental Politics in Vancouver, 1889-1975." *BC Studies*, no. 142-143 (Summer/Autumn 2004): 69–101.

Keenleyside, Hugh L. *Memoirs of Hugh L. Keenleyside.* Vol. 2, *On the Bridge of Time.* Toronto: McClelland & Stewart, 1982,

Kehoe, Terence. *Cleaning Up the Great Lakes: From Cooperation to Confrontation.* Dekalb: Northern Illinois University Press, 1997.

Kennedy, Michael. "Fraser River Placer Mining Landscapes," *BC Studies*, no. 160 (Winter 2008/2009): 35–66.

Killan, Gerald. *Protected Places: A History of Ontario's Provincial Parks System.* Toronto: Dundurn / Ontario Ministry of Natural Resources, 1993.

Kirkey, Christopher. "The Arctic Waters Pollution Prevention Initiatives: Canada's Response to an American Challenge." *International Journal of Canadian Studies*, no. 13 (Spring 1996): 41–59.

Klingle, Matthew. *Emerald City: An Environmental History of Seattle.* New Haven: Yale University Press, 2007.

Knight, D.B. "Identity and Territory: Geographical Perspectives on Nationalism and Regionalism." *Annals of the Association of American Geographers* 72, no. 4 (1982): 514–31.

Kolankiewicz, Leon. "Compliance with Pollution Control Permits in the Lower Fraser Valley, 1967-1981." *BC Studies*, no. 72 (Winter 1986/1987): 28–48.

Konrad, Victor K., and Heather Nicol. *Beyond Walls: Re-inventing the Canada-United States Borderlands.* New York: Ashgate, 2008.

Lang, William L., and Robert C. Carriker, eds. *Great River of the West: Essays on the Columbia River.* Seattle: University of Washington Press, 1999.

Langston, Nancy. *Toxic Bodies: Hormone Disruptors and the Legacy of DES.* New Haven: Yale University Press, 2010.

Langston, Nancy. *Where Land and Water Meet: A Western Landscape Transformed.* Seattle: University of Washington Press, 2003.

Lankton, L.D. *Cradle to Grave: Life, Work, and Death at the Lake Superior Copper Mines*. New York: Oxford University Press, 1991.

Lasserre, Frédéric. "Les projets de transferts massifs d'eau en Amérique du nord." *VertigO – la revue électronique en sciences de l'environnement*, special issue 2 (September 2005). DOI:10.4000/vertigo.1929.

Lasserre, Frédéric. "Managing Water Diversion from Canada to the United States: An Old Idea Born Again?" *International Journal* 62, no. 1 (Winter 2006/2007): 81–92.

Lasserre, Frédéric, ed. *Transferts massifs d'eau: Outils de développement ou instrument de pouvoir?* Quebec City: Presses de l'Université du Québec, 2005.

Lemarquand, D.G. "Preconditions to Cooperation in Canada–United States Boundary Waters." *Natural Resources Journal* 26, no. 2 (1986): 221–42.

Loo, Tina. "Disturbing the Peace: Environmental Change and the Scales of Justice on a Northern River." *Environmental History* 12, no. 4 (2007): 895–919.

Loo, Tina, with Meg Stanley. "An Environmental History of Progress: Damming the Peace and Columbia Rivers." *Canadian Historical Review* 92, no. 3 (2011): 399–427.

Mabee, Carleton. *The Seaway Story*. New York: Macmillan, 1961.

MacDonald, Brian, ed. *Requirements for Canada's Arctic*. Ottawa: Conference of Defence Associations Institute, 2007.

Macfarlane, Daniel. "'Caught between Two Fires': St. Lawrence Seaway and Power Project, Canadian-American Relations, and Linkage." *International Journal* 67, no. 2 (2012): 465–82.

Macfarlane, Daniel. "'A Completely Man-Made and Artificial Cataract': The Transnational Manipulation of Niagara Falls." *Environmental History* 18, no. 4 (2013): 759–84.

Macfarlane, Daniel. "Creating a Cataract: The Transnational Manipulation of Niagara Falls to the 1950s." In *Urban Explorations: Environmental Histories of the Toronto Region*, edited by Colin Coates, Stephen Bocking, Ken Cruikshank, and Anders Sandberg, 251–67. Hamilton, ON: L.R. Wilson Institute for Canadian Studies / McMaster University, 2013.

Macfarlane, Daniel. *Negotiating a River: Canada, the U.S., and the Creation of the St. Lawrence Seaway*. Vancouver: UBC Press, 2014.

Mackie, Richard. *Trading beyond the Mountains: The British Fur Trade on the Pacific, 1793-1843*. Vancouver: UBC Press, 1997.

Martin, Lawrence. *The Presidents and the Prime Ministers: Washington and Ottawa Face to Face: The Myth of Bilateral Bliss, 1867–1982*. Toronto: Doubleday Canada, 1982.

Martin, Paul. *A Very Public Life*. Vol. 2, *So Many Worlds*. Toronto: Deneau, 1985.

Martin-Nielsen, Janet. "South over the Wires: Hydro-Electricity Exports from Canada," *Water History* 1 (2009): 109–29.

Massell, David. "'As Though There Was No Boundary': The Shipshaw Project and Continental Integration." *American Review of Canadian Studies* 34, no. 2 (2004): 187–222.

Massell, David. *Quebec Hydropolitics: The Peribonka Concessions of the Second World War*. Montreal: McGill-Queen's University Press, 2011.

McCaffrey, Stephen C. "The Harmon Doctrine One Hundred Years Later: Buried, Not Praised." *Natural Resources Journal* 36, no. 3 (1996): 549–90.

McCaffrey, Stephen C. *The Law of International Watercourses: Non-Navigational Uses*. Oxford: Oxford University Press, 2001.

McDorman, Ted. *Salt Water Neighbors: International Ocean Law Relations between the United States and Canada*. New York: Oxford University Press, 2009.

McGreevy, Patrick. *Imagining Niagara: The Meaning and Making of Niagara Falls*. Amherst: University of Massachusetts Press, 1994.

McGreevy, Patrick. *The Wall of Mirrors: Nationalism and Perceptions of the Border at Niagara Falls*. Orono: Canadian-American Centre, University of Maine, 1991.

McKinsey, Elizabeth R. *Niagara Falls: Icon of the American Sublime*. New York: Cambridge University Press, 1985.

McNeill, J.R., and Corinna R. Unger. *Environmental Histories of the Cold War*. Cambridge: Cambridge University Press, 2010.

Miller, Bruce. "The 'Really Real' Border and the Divided Salish Community." *BC Studies*, no. 112 (Winter 1996/1997): 63–67.

Mitchell, David. *W.A.C. Bennett and the Rise of British Columbia*. Vancouver: Douglas & McIntyre, 1983.

Molle, François. "River-Basin Planning and Management: The Social Life of a Concept." *Geoforum* 40, no. 3 (2009): 484–94.

Mouat, Jeremy. *The Business of Power: Hydro-Electricity in South Eastern British Columbia 1897–1997*. Victoria: Sono Nis, 1997.

Nash, Knowlton. *Kennedy and Diefenbaker: Fear and Loathing across the Undefended Border*. Toronto: McClelland & Stewart, 1990.

Nash, Linda. "Furthering the Environmental Turn." *Journal of American History* 100, no. 1 (2013): 131–35.

Nash, Linda. *Inescapable Ecologies: A History of Environment, Disease, and Knowledge.* Berkeley: University of California Press, 2007.

Neering, R. *The Pig War: The Last Canada-U.S. Border Conflict.* Surrey, BC: Heritage House, 2011.

Nelles, H.V. *The Politics of Development: Forests, Mines and Hydro-Electric Power in Ontario, 1849–1941.* 2nd ed. Montreal: McGill-Queen's University Press, 2005.

Nemeth, Tammy. "Consolidating the Continental Drift: American Influence on Diefenbaker's National Oil Policy." *Journal of the Canadian Historical Association* 13, no. 1 (2002): 191–215.

Netherton, Alexander. "The Political Economy of Canadian Hydro-Electricity: Between Old 'Provincial Hydros' and Neoliberal Regional Energy Regimes." *Canadian Political Science Review* 1, no. 1 (2007): 107–24.

Newman, David, and Anssi Paasi. "Fences and Neighbours in the Postmodern World: Boundary Narratives in Political Geography." *Progress in Human Geography* 22, no. 2 (1998): 186–207.

Norman, Emma S. "Cultural Politics and Transboundary Resource Governance in the Salish Sea." *Water Alternatives* 5, no. 1 (2012): 138–60.

Norman, Emma S. *Governing Transboundary Waters: Canada, the United States and Indigenous Communities.* London: Routledge, 2015.

Norman, Emma S., and Karen Bakker. "Transgressing Scales: Water Governance across the Canada-U.S. Border." *Annals of the Association of American Geographers* 99, no. 1 (2009): 99–117.

Norman, Emma S., Alice Cohen, and Karen Bakker, eds. *Water without Borders? Canada, the United States, and Shared Waters.* Toronto: University of Toronto Press, 2013.

Norwood, Gus. *Columbia River Power for the People: A History of the Policies of the Bonneville Power Administration.* Portland, OR: Bonneville Power Administration, 1980.

Nye, David E. *Electrifying America: Social Meanings of a New Technology, 1880–1940.* Cambridge, MA: MIT Press, 1990.

Paasi, Anssi. "Region and Place: Regional Identity in Question." *Progress in Human Geography* 27, no. 4 (2003): 475–85.

Parham, Claire. *The St. Lawrence Seaway and Power Project: An Oral History of the Greatest Construction Show on Earth*. Syracuse, NY: Syracuse University Press, 2009.

Parr, Joy. *Sensing Changes: Technologies, Environments, and the Everyday, 1953–2003*. Vancouver: UBC Press, 2009.

Passfield, Robert W. "Construction of the St. Lawrence Seaway." *Canal History and Technology Proceedings* 22 (2003): 1–55.

Pearson, Lester B. *Mike: The Memoirs of the Right Honourable Lester Bowles Pearson*. Vol. 3, *1957–1968*. Edited by John A. Munro and Alex I. Inglis. Toronto: University of Toronto Press, 1975.

Pennanen, Gary. "Battle of the Titans: Mitchell Hepburn, Mackenzie King, Franklin Roosevelt, and the St. Lawrence Seaway." *Ontario History* 89, no. 1 (1997): 1–21.

Pisani, Donald. *To Reclaim a Divided West: Water, Law, and Public Policy, 1848–1902*. Albuquerque: University of New Mexico Press, 1992.

Popescu, Gabriel. *Bordering and Ordering the Twenty-First Century: Understanding Borders*. Lanham, MD: Rowman & Littlefield, 2012.

Quinn, Frank. "Water Diversion, Export, and Canada-U.S. Relations: A Brief History." Munk Centre for International Studies (MCIS) Briefings No. 8, Program on Water Issues, MCIS, University of Toronto, 2007.

Raibmon, Paige. *Authentic Indians: Episodes of Encounter from the Late-Nineteenth Century Northwest Coast*. Durham: Duke University Press, 2005.

Rajala, Richard A. *Clearcutting the Pacific Rain Forest: Production, Science, and Regulation*. Vancouver: UBC Press, 1998.

Reisner, Marc. *Cadillac Desert: The American West and Its Disappearing Water*. New York: Penguin, 1993.

Revie, Linda L. *The Niagara Companion: Explorers, Artists, and Writers at the Falls, from Discovery through the Twentieth Century*. Waterloo, ON: Wilfrid Laurier University Press, 2003.

Riley, John. *The Once and Future Great Lakes: An Ecological History*. Montreal: McGill-Queen's University Press, 2013.

Ritvo, Harriet. "Going Forth and Multiplying: Animal Acclimatization and Invasion." *Environmental History* 17, no. 2 (2012): 404–14.

Robinson, H. Basil. *Diefenbaker's World: A Populist in Foreign Affairs*. Toronto: University of Toronto Press, 1989.

Rutley, Rosemary. *Voices from the Lost Villages*. Ingleside, ON: Old Crone, 1998.

Sabatier, P. A., W. Focht, M. Lubell, Z. Trachtenberg, A. Vedlitz, and M. Matlock. *Swimming Upstream: Collaborative Approaches to Watershed Management.* Cambridge, MA: MIT Press, 2005.

Savelle, M. *The Diplomatic History of the Canadian Boundary, 1759–1763.* New Haven: Yale University Press, 1940.

Savenije, Hubert H.G., and Pieter van der Zaag. "Conceptual Framework for the Management of Shared River Basins; with Special Reference to the Sadc and Eu." *Water Policy* 2, no. 1 (2000): 9–45.

Scott, James C. *Seeing like a State: How Certain Schemes to Improve the Human Condition Have Failed.* New Haven: Yale University Press, 1998.

Searle, R. Newell. *Saving Quetico-Superior: A Land Set Apart.* St. Paul: Minnesota Historical Society Press, 1977.

Sherman, Paddy. *Bennett.* Toronto: McClelland & Stewart, 1966.

Sheriff, Carol. *The Artificial River: The Erie Canal and the Paradox of Progress, 1817–1862.* New York: Hill & Wang, 1996.

Shields, Anne-Marie. *Lost Villages, Found Communities: A Pictorial History of the St. Lawrence Seaway.* Cornwall, ON: Astro, 2004.

Slocombe, D.S. "Implementing Ecosystem-Based Management." *BioScience* 43, no. 9 (1993): 612–22.

Sparke, Matthew. "Excavating the Future in Cascadia: Geoeconomics and the Imagined Geographies of a Cross-Border Region." *BC Studies*, no. 127 (Autumn 2000): 5–44.

Spencer, Robert, John Kirton, and Kim Richard Nossal, eds. *The International Joint Commission: Seventy Years On.* Toronto: Centre for International Studies, University of Toronto, 1981.

Spieler, Cliff, and Tom Hewitt. *Niagara Power: From Joncaire to Moses.* Lewiston, NY: Niagara Power, 1959.

Stagg, Ronald. *The Golden Dream: A History of the St. Lawrence Seaway at Fifty.* Toronto: Dundurn, 2010.

Steinberg, Theodore. "'That World's Fair Feeling': Control of Water in 20th Century America." *Technology and Culture* 34, no. 2 (1993): 401–9.

Steingraber, Sandra. *Living Downstream: An Ecologist's Personal Investigation of Cancer and the Environment.* Boston: Addison-Wesley, 1997.

Strand, Ginger. *Inventing Niagara: Beauty, Power, and Lies.* Toronto: Simon & Schuster, 2008.

Stunden Bower, Shannon. *Wet Prairie: People, Land, and Water in Agricultural Manitoba*. Vancouver: UBC Press, 2011.

Sutter, Paul S. "The World with Us: The State of American Environmental History," *Journal of American History* 100, no. 1 (2013): 94–119.

Swainson, Neil A. *Conflict over the Columbia: The Canadian Background to an Historic Treaty*. Montreal: McGill-Queen's University Press, 1979.

Taylor, Joseph E., III. "Boundary Terminology." *Environmental History* 13, no. 3 (2008): 454–81.

Taylor, Joseph E., III. *Making Salmon: An Environmental History of the Northwest Fisheries Crisis*. Seattle: University of Washington Press, 1999.

Thom, Brian. "The Anathema of Aggregation: Towards 21st-Century Self-Government in the Coast Salish World." *Anthropologica* 52, no. 1 (2010): 33–48.

Thrush, Coll. *Native Seattle: Histories from the Crossing-Over Place*. Seattle: University of Washington Press, 2007.

Toller, Susan, and Peter N. Nemetz. "Assessing the Impact of Hydro Development: A Case Study of the Columbia River Basin in British Columbia." *BC Studies*, no. 114 (Summer 1997): 5–30.

Tucker, Richard. *Insatiable Appetite: The United States and the Ecological Degradation of the Tropical World*. Berkeley: University of California Press, 2000.

Van Huizen, Philip. "Building a Green Dam: Environmental Modernism and the Canadian-American Libby Dam Project." *Pacific Historical Review* 79, no. 3 (2010): 418–53.

Van Huizen, Philip. "Flooding the Border: Development, Politics and the Environmental Controversy in the Canada-U.S. Skagit Valley." PhD diss., University of British Columbia, 2013.

Vouri, Mike. *The Pig War*. Charleston, SC: Arcadia, 2008.

Wadewitz, Lissa. *The Nature of Borders: Salmon, Boundaries, and Bandits on the Salish Sea*. Seattle: University of Washington Press, 2012.

Warner, Jeroen. *Multi-Stakeholder Platforms for Integrated Water Management*. Cornwall, UK: Ashgate, 2007.

Warner, J., P. Wester, and A. Bolding. "Going with the Flow: River Basins as the Natural Units for Water Management?" *Water Policy*, 2nd ser., 10 (2008): 121–38.

Wedley, John R. "Infrastructure and Resources: Governments and their Promotion of Northern Development in British Columbia, 1945-1975." PhD diss., University of Western Ontario, 1986.

Weller, Phil. *Fresh Water Seas: Saving the Great Lakes*. Toronto: Between the Lines, 1990.

White, Richard. *Land Use, Environment, and Social Change: The Shaping of Island County, Washington*. Seattle: University of Washington Press, 1980.

White, Richard. *The Middle Ground: Indians, Empires, and Republics in the Great Lakes Region, 1650-1815*. Cambridge: Cambridge University Press, 1991.

White, Richard. *The Organic Machine: The Remaking of the Columbia River*. New York: Hill & Wang, 1995.

Whitney, George. *From Coastal Wilderness to Fruited Plain: A History of Environmental Change in Temperate North America, 1500 to the Present*. Cambridge: Cambridge University Press, 1996.

Wilkinson. C. *Messages from Frank's Landing: A Story of Salmon Treaties and the Indian Way*. Seattle: University of Washington Press, 2000.

Williston, Eileen, and Betty Keller. *Forests, Power, and Policy: The Legacy of Ray Williston*. Prince George, BC: Caitlin, 1997.

Willoughby, William R. *The St. Lawrence Waterway: A Study in Politics and Diplomacy*. Madison: University of Wisconsin Press, 1961.

Wilson, James Wood. *People in the Way: The Human Aspects of the Columbia River Project*. Toronto: University of Toronto Press, 1973.

Woodward, J. "International Pollution Control: The United States and Canada—The International Joint Commission." *New York Law School Journal of International and Comparative Law* 9 (1988), 325-44.

Worster, Donald. *Rivers of Empire: Water, Aridity, and the Growth of the American West*. New York: Oxford University Press, 1992.

Wynn, Graeme. *Canada and the Arctic North America: An Environmental History*. Santa Barbara, CA: ABC-CLIO, 2007.

Contributors

ANDREA CHARRON holds a PhD from the Royal Military College of Canada (Department of War Studies). She obtained a master's degree in international relations from Webster University, Leiden, Netherlands; a Master of Public Administration from Dalhousie University; and a Bachelor of Science (Honours) from Queen's University. Dr. Charron worked for various federal departments, including the Privy Council Office in the Security and Intelligence Secretariat. She is now assistant professor in Political Studies and deputy director of the Centre for Defence and Security Studies at the University of Manitoba. Dr. Charron has written extensively on the Arctic.

ALICE COHEN is an assistant professor cross-appointed between the departments of Earth & Environmental Science and Environmental & Sustainability Studies at Acadia University in Wolfville, Nova Scotia. Prior to her time at Acadia, Dr. Cohen held a SSHRC postdoc at the Graduate School of Geography at Clark University in Worcester, Massachusetts. Dr. Cohen's research relates to water policy and governance; specifically, her work examines the relationships between water and boundaries of all kinds—political, physical, and social. This work has led her to study groundwater governance on the Gulf and San Juan Islands, watershed governance in Canada, Canada-U.S. transboundary waters, and most recently the role(s) of uncertainty in water governance. She lives on the border between geography, politics, and ecology.

DAVE DEMPSEY is a policy advisor on Great Lakes issues for the International Joint Commission and author of two books about the Great Lakes.

JERRY DENNIS is the author of many books, including *The Living Great Lakes: Searching for the Heart of the Inland Seas* (2003). He lives near the shore of Lake Michigan in northern Michigan.

COLIN A.M. DUNCAN taught British and environmental history at Queen's University and McGill University. He is the author of *The Centrality of Agriculture: Between Humankind and the Rest of Nature* (1996). He hopes to soon publish *The Great Disconnect: How the Eclipse of Human Provisioning by Particular Projects Eventuated in Global Defrosting (ca. 100,000 BC–the present)*.

MATTHEW EVENDEN is a professor of geography at the University of British Columbia whose research focuses on the environmental history of rivers and water. Several of his publications deal with transboundary waters and environments, including his first book, *Fish versus Power: An Environmental History of the Fraser River* (2004), and his latest book, *Allied Power: Mobilizing Hydro-Electricity during Canada's Second World War* (2015).

JAMES W. FELDMAN is the director of the Environmental Studies program and an associate professor of environmental studies and history at the University of Wisconsin Oshkosh. He is the author of *A Storied Wilderness: Rewinding the Apostle Islands* (2011) and *Nuclear Reactions: Documenting American Encounters with Nuclear Energy* (2017). His research interests include American environmental history, wilderness, and the history and sustainability of radioactive waste management. He is also an avid paddler who makes an annual pilgrimage to the Boundary Waters.

NOAH D. HALL is a law professor at Wayne State University Law School in Detroit, Michigan, specializing in environmental and water law. He has coauthored two leading casebooks in these fields, *Environmental Law and Policy: Nature, Law, and Society* (2010) and *Modern Water Law: Private Property, Public Rights, and Environmental Protection* (2013). Professor

Hall graduated from the University of Michigan Law School and the University of Michigan School of Natural Resources and Environment, concentrating in environmental policy. He previously served as the founding executive director of the Great Lakes Environmental Law Center and has extensive litigation experience and numerous published decisions in state and federal courts. Most recently, he was appointed Special Assistant Attorney General for the State of Michigan for the Flint water crisis.

LYNNE HEASLEY is an associate professor in the Department of History and the Institute of the Environment and Sustainability at Western Michigan University. She is the author of *A Thousand Pieces of Paradise: Landscape and Property in the Kickapoo Valley* (2005), which examined how evolving property rights debates intersected with ecological transformation in the Upper Midwest. Today Heasley is part of a growing community of scholars, policymakers, writers, artists, and activists concerned with the past, present, and future of the vast but vulnerable Great Lakes–St. Lawrence system of inland seas. She is currently writing *The Paradox of Abundance*, a book of creative nonfiction and historical essays on the Great Lakes.

NANCY LANGSTON is professor of environmental history in the Department of Social Sciences and the Great Lakes Research Center at Michigan Technological University. After serving for eighteen years on the faculty at the University of Wisconsin, she spent a year as the King's Professor of Environmental Science at Umeå University in Sweden. Past-president of the American Society for Environmental History and past editor of *Environmental History*, she is the recipient of fellowships from the National Science Foundation, the Marshall Foundation, the American Council of Learned Societies, and the American Philosophical Society. She is leading an NSF-funded project on mining, toxics, and watershed change in the Lake Superior basin and finishing her fourth book, *Sustaining Lake Superior*.

FRÉDÉRIC LASSERRE is a professor in the geography department at Laval University and the director of the Conseil québécois d'études géopolitiques (CQEG). He has published widely on the geopolitics of water in North America and around the globe.

DANIEL MACFARLANE is an assistant professor in the Institute of the Environment and Sustainability at Western Michigan University. He has previously held Fulbright, Banting, and SSHRC fellowships. Dr. Macfarlane's research and teaching focus on the historical and policy dimensions of Canadian-American borders waters, particularly in the Great Lakes–St. Lawrence basin. He is the author of *Negotiating a River: Canada, the U.S., and the Creation of the St. Lawrence Seaway* (2014) and is currently working on projects exploring the twentieth-century manipulation of Niagara Falls for beauty and power, as well as the history of the International Joint Commission.

ANDREW MARCILLE came to environmental history through intellectual history and an eclectic variety of fieldwork. Graduate studies took him first to the University of Western Ontario for an MA in history and now to the Memorial University of Newfoundland for an interdisciplinary PhD on the history of geology, but he remains an incorrigible Queen's alumnus, at home in Kingston and closely tied to Lake Ontario.

JEREMY MOUAT is professor of history and chair of the Department of Social Sciences at the University of Alberta – Augustana Campus. He is the author of three books, is coeditor of another, and has also published numerous articles in scholarly journals in Canada, the United States, New Zealand, and Australia. His major research and teaching interests are in western Canadian history, Canadian-American history, mining history, and the history of technology.

EMMA S. NORMAN is the chair of the Native Environmental Science department at Northwest Indian College in Bellingham, Washington, where she has been on the faculty since 2001. Her scholarship and teaching engages in issues related to transboundary water governance, environmental and social justice, and Indigenous environmental activism. Her book *Governing Transboundary Waters: Canada, the United States and Indigenous Communities* (2015) was awarded the Julian Minghi prize for best book in the field of political geography in 2015. Prior to entering academia, she served as a U.S. Peace Corps volunteer in Malawi, where she worked as an environmental educator with the Department of Parks and Wildlife (1995–1997).

PETER STARR graduated magna cum laude in 2013 from the University of Michigan Law School. He clerked for the Honorable Ed Carnes of the United States Court of Appeal for the Eleventh Circuit from 2013 to 2014 and is currently an associate at the New York office of Davis Polk & Wardwell LLP.

JOSEPH E. TAYLOR III teaches history and geography at Simon Fraser University. He has written widely about fisheries, outdoor recreation, gentrification, and conservation, including the award-winning *Making Salmon: An Environmental History of the Northwest Fisheries Crisis* (1999) and *Pilgrims of the Vertical: Yosemite Rock Climbers and Nature at Risk* (2010), plus more than twenty articles in history, geography, and science journals and anthologies. Taylor is currently building a website with Stanford University's Spatial History Project to map federal payments to western American counties since 1906, and he is writing three books: an update of his salmon research, titled *Five-Dimensional Salmon: Thinking Contingently about the Past and Future of Environmental Problems*; a biography of the author of the Taylor Grazing Act, titled *Voice of the West: Colorado's Ed Taylor and the Rise of Modern America*; and an untitled history of Progressive conservation examining the motives and actions of Congress from 1891 to 1939.

GRAEME WYNN is professor of geography at the University of British Columbia, president-elect of the American Society for Environmental History, and a former Brenda and David McLean Professor of Canadian Studies at UBC.

Index

A

Aberdeen, Lord (George Hamilton-Gordon, 4th Earl of Aberdeen), 70
Aboriginal Peoples and cultures, 101, 104n8, 202n73, 219, 224. *See also* First Nations; Indigenous Peoples and cultures; Inuit Peoples an cultures
Alaska, 90, 92, 95, 101, 104n10, 108n49, 153, 216, 223, 226, 285–87, 301
Alberta, 190, 273, 274, 302
Aral Sea, 9
Arctic Cooperation Agreement (1988), 99
Arctic Council, 100–101, 103, 108n53
Arctic Environmental Protection Strategy, 100
Arctic Waters Pollution Prevention Act (1970), 96–98
arid zones, 5, 21n10
Army Corps of Engineers, U.S., 3, 48, 129, 172, 173, 175 fig. 6.1, 176, 293 fig. 9.7
Asian carp, 25n45, 47–48

B

Bay of Fundy, 11
Bennett, W.A.C., 119, 170–71, 178–80, 182–87, 190, 197n47, 199n58

blue green algae, *see* cyanobacteria
Boldt, George, 75
Boundary Waters Treaty of 1909, 11, 12, 13, 40–41, 47, 48, 57, 59, 116, 125, 126, 171, 177, 189
Bourassa, Premier, 118, 121n17, 151, 153, 154–5, 156, 158, 164n3
British Columbia, 119, 153, 217, 274, 286, 301–2, Chapter 6 *passim*, Chapter 7 *passim*

C

California, 176, 187, 216, 285–87
Chicago, 18, 45–8, 129, 130, 267
Cities (relations to the Great Lakes), 267
Clark, Joe, 98
Climate change, 31, 35, 62, 117, 211, 255–57, 303, 304
Clinton, Bill, 108n49
Cold War, 13, 87–88, 92, 124, 132, 138, 144, 145, 174, 193n22, 278, 219
Colorado Compact of 1922, 5
Colorado Doctrine, 5
Colorado River, 5, 7, 10, 22n16, 44, 115
Columbia River, 11, 119, 287
Columbia River Treaty (1961), 119

333

Compact Commissions (empowered to regulate amongst states), 44
Congress (U.S.), 44–45, 48, 55, 56, 58–59
Constitution (U.S.), 58–59
Convention of 1818, 70
cyanobacteria, 31, 36n5

D

Diefenbaker, John, 170–2, 180, 182, 184–85, 189, 192n14, 197n47
diversion (conflicts and/or rules regarding), 46–48, 52, 53–54, 55, 60, 115, 117, 118–19, 124–26, 129–31, 135, 137, 144, 146n3, 146n7, 151–53, 155, 161, 163, 164n7, 165n11, 177, 182, 193n27, 193n28, 248
Drain Commissioner, Michigan, 8, 22n23
Dust Bowl, 6

E

Eisenhower, Dwight, 132, 171, 180, 182, 192n14
enforcement problems, 49, 51, 57–58, 60, 91. *See also* sovereignty
Environment Canada, 49, 77
Environmental Protection Agency, 49, 77
equitable apportionment, doctrine of, 43

F

First Nations, 13, 66, 82, 190, 202n73, 219, 226. *See also* Aboriginal Peoples and cultures; Indigenous Peoples and cultures
Flint, Michigan, 8. *See also* Drain Commissioner, Michigan.
Frank, Billy (Jr.), 71 fig. 2.4, 72, 74–75
Free Trade Agreement (1988), 117
GRAND, *See* Great Re-cycling and Northern Development Canal
Great Lakes Charter (1985), 31, 32, 51, 53. *See also* Great Lakes Charter Agreement Annex
Great Lakes Charter Agreement Annex (2001), 53–54, 56

Great Lakes Basin Compact (1968, U.S. interstate), 45, 59
Great Lakes Agreement and/or Compact. *See* following entry
Great Lakes-St. Lawrence River Basin Water Resources Compact (effective 2008) and companion Great Lakes-St. Lawrence River Basin Sustainable Water Resources Agreement (binational), 4, 9, 10, 11, 13, 32, 35, 53, 56–61
Great Lakes Fishery Commission (est. 1955), 32
Great Lakes Water Quality Agreement (est. 1978), 33, 49–51, 145
Great Re-cycling and Northern Development Canal, 4, 118, 151, 154–55, 160, 164n3
grid (electrical), 187, 189, 193n21, 202n71
Ground water, 55, 79, 161, 246
Gulf of Mexico, 274, 278

H

Hepburn, Mitch, 129
High Modernism, 16, 17, 136–38
Hudson Bay, 4, 7, 273

I

Idaho, 301
IJC, *See* International Joint Commission
Illinois, 46
Indian Affairs (U.S.), 75
Indiana, 56
Indigenous Peoples and cultures, 14, 17, 34, 66, 69, 72–76, 77, 82, 87, 88, 89, 90, 100–101, 103, 104n8, 108n49, 171, 201n73, 202n73, 217, 219, 224, 246, 248. *See also* Aboriginal Peoples and cultures; First Nations; Indian Affairs (U.S.); Inuit Peoples and Cultures
integrity (as a broad goal beyond ecology), 47
International Boundary Commission, 70

International Conference on Water and the Environment (and Dublin Statement on Water and Sustainable Development of 1992), 78
International Joint Commission, 11, 12, 13, 40, 49, 50–52, 79–80, 81, 85n27, 116, 125, 131, 135, 170, 176, 177, 180, 189, 196n38, 201n69
International Waterways Commission (est. 1903), 115–16
interstate compacts (as a type of law), 44
Inuit Circumpolar Council, 101, 103, 108n50
Inuit Peoples and culture, 89, 90, 94, 101, 102, 103, 104n7, 104n8, 108n50. *See also* Inuit Circumpolar Council

J

James Bay, 4, 151, 161, 164n2, *See also* Great Re-cycling and Northern Development Canal.
Johnson, Lyndon Baines, 186, 187, 200n61

K

Kansas, 256
Kansas v. Colorado (1907), 43
Kennedy, John F., 182, 185
Kierans, Tom, 4

L

Lake Champlain-Richelieu River basin, 31
Lake Erie, 46, 295
Lake Huron, 3, 7, 33, 46
Lake Michigan, 7, 46, 114
Lake Ontario, 46
Lake of the Woods, 70
Lake Superior, 4, 289
Lake Winnipeg, 31, 36n6
lake trout, 31, 258n5

M

Maine, 301
Manitoba, 101, 153, 211, 302

McNaughton, A.G.L., 170, 177, 195n30
media (biases in attention of), 35
Medicine Creek Treaty (1854), 75
Mexico, 115, 207
Michigan, 8, 32, 48, 56, 211, 265–56, 267, 279, 289, 295, 301. *See also* Drain Commissioner, Michigan.
Minnesota, 48, 70, 207, 211, 289, 301
Mississippi River, 22n16, 46, 48
Missouri, 46
Montana, 177, 186, 215, 274, 301
Montreal, 134

N

Native American Peoples and cultures. *See* Indigenous Peoples and cultures. *See also* Aboriginal Peoples and Cultures; First Nations
navigation (distinct early purpose for waterways), 40, 46, 47, 49, 113, 115, 124, 125, 130, 172. Of the Northwest Passage, Chapter 3 *passim*
New Hampshire, 301
New York State, 70, 124, 131–32, 144, 289
Newfoundland, 153
North American Free Trade Agreement (1994), 117
Northwest Boundary Survey (1857–1861), 71
Northwest Indian Fisheries Commission, 75
Northwest Passage, 300, Chapter 3 *passim*
nuclear power, 154. *See also* radioactive waste
nuisance law, 45

O

Obama, Barack, 48
Ogallala Aquifer, 3, 7, 117
Ohio, 48, 291
Ontario, 4, 45, 124, 131–32, 144, 207, 211, 279, 301–2, 303
Oregon, 216, 285

Oregon Treaty of 1846, 70–71
Ottawa River, 161

P

Palliser, John, 5
Paradox of Abundance, 2–3, 7–10
PCBs (polychlorinated biphenyls and related chemicals), 30, 94, 212, 231n7, Chapter 7 *passim*, Chapter 8 *passim*
Peace River, 179–80, 183–84
Pearson, Lester B., 92, 106n29, 185, 186–87, 198n54
Pennsylvania, 48, 301
Policy implementation (messy history of), 35
Polk, James K., 70
Powell, John Wesley, 5, 78
prior appropriation right, 5, 6
public trust doctrine, 10

Q

Quebec, 4, 45, 70, 301–2

R

radioactive waste, 33
Reclamation Act (1902), 114
Red River-Lake Winnipeg basin, 31
riparian rights, 5
Roosevelt, F.D.R., 129, 193n22

S

Salish Sea, 11, 76–77, 285–87, Chapter 2 *passim*
Saskatchewan, 190, 273, 279, 302
Seward, William H., 90
Sporhase v. Nebraska, 3, 4
St. Laurent, Louis, 91, 104n13, 131–32, 142, 170
St. Lawrence River, 11, 13, 14
St. Lawrence Seaway and Power Project, 13, 24n40, 131–34
sea lamprey, 32, 261n42, 262n44, 262n46

sovereignty (as fact and/or issue, including intranationally), 30, 31, 32, 33, 35, 40–41, 43–45, 57, 76, 78, 89, 93, 95–99, 103n5, 104n10, 106n29, 107n34, 143–44, 149n32, 150n35, 158, 183, 189, 191n5, 199n56, 200n59, 202n74, 219, 228, 300, 302
storage of water on mass scale, 173, 174, 175–76, 177, 178–79, 187, 191n9, 193n19, 196n38
Supreme Court, U.S., 3, 10, 43, 45–47, 48

T

Taft, William Howard, 47
Trudeau, Justin, 156
Trudeau, Pierre, 49, 96, 106n29
Truman, 131, 132

U

United Nations, 41
United Nations Convention on the Law of the Sea, 94, 98, 99
U.S.-Canada Convention on Great Lakes Fisheries (1955), 31
U.S. Geological Survey, 77

V

Vermont, 70

W

Washington (State of), 216, 217
water quality improvement and restoration, 54, 58
Water Resources Development Act (1986), 55, 56
Welland Canal (est. 1829), 14, 125, 240–41, 251–52
Wisconsin, 48, 211, 247
Wisconsin v. Illinois, 45, 48
withdrawals (limits on), 52, 53–54, 57–58, 60, 117, 167n43

www.ingramcontent.com/pod-product-compliance
Lightning Source LLC
Chambersburg PA
CBHW061253230426
43665CB00027B/2931